THE BIG SCORE

THE BIG SCORE

The Billion-Dollar Story of Silicon Valley

MICHAEL S. MALONE

Doubleday & Company, Inc.
Garden City, New York
1985

Library of Congress Cataloging in Publication Data

Malone, Michael S. (Michael Shawn), 1954–
  The big score.

  Includes index.
  1. Microelectronics industry—California—Santa Clara
County. I. Title.
HD9696.A3U5668 1985   338.4′76213817′0979473 82-46038
ISBN 0-385-18351-8

". . . cities are a second body for the human mind, a second organism, more rational, permanent and decorative than the animal organism of flesh and bone: a work of natural yet moral art, where the soul sets up her trophies of action and instruments of pleasure."—Santayana, *The Last Puritan*

"Moving from almost any other industry to the semiconductor industry is like going from a convent to a brothel."—Charles Missler, chairman of Western Digital Corp.

For Carol

ACKNOWLEDGMENT

As Silicon Valley has grown in importance, so has it increased in news coverage. Most of the nation's leading newspapers have reporters assigned to the high-technology beat. Further, at least one hundred (the number seems to grow daily) trade magazines use the products of Silicon Valley as their central focus. In preparing this book, and in my years of work in the Valley prior to that, nearly all of these publications have served as sources—and I am grateful to them and their hardworking writers.

By necessity, then, this acknowledgment can cover only the key sources for *The Big Score.* Central were my own articles on Silicon Valley, first for the San Jose *Mercury-News,* and later for the New York *Times,* the Boston *Globe* and the Dallas *Morning News.* At the *Mercury-News,* I'd like to thank Jim Mitchell and Jack Sirard for making me into a newspaperman, and my investigative reporting partners Susan Yoachum (chemical leaks) and Peter Carey (drugs, sweatshops, precious metals, espionage), the two best and hardest working reporters I know, both of whom made me look far better than I really am. At the New York *Times* I'd like to thank John Lee for giving me the chance. Also Paul Franson, PR guru and walking Silicon Valley encyclopedia, for his technical checks; J. Peter Nelson, Ross Snyder, and John Kane for the apprenticeship.

Sources for the early history of the Valley include *Electronics in the West: The First Fifty Years* by Jane Morgan, the excellent young people's book that has been the only text on the subject for twenty years. Also Christie Barrie's unpublished paper of 1963. I also greatly thank Dirk Hanson, whose highly informative *The New Alchemists* (1982) is my most distinguished predecessor.

Most newspaper and magazine references I have tried to include in the text. However, some sources deserve additional note. *Fortune* and *Business Week* continue to do a superb job in covering the Valley, and I am particularly grateful for the incisive writing of Jack Wilson at the latter. The individuals who have followed me at the San Jose *Mercury-News*, Bruce Entin, Evelyn Richards and David Sylvester, in the face of daily deadlines, have somehow managed to make their paper the pre-eminent source of information about Silicon Valley. At the Los Angeles Times, Katherine Harris remains the best in this tiny, but remarkable, business of covering high tech. Among the trade magazines, *Datamation* and *Electronics* are still the class acts, while *Infoworld* and Don Hoeffler's *Microelectronics News* are still champs at dishing the dirt.

I'd also like to thank the Valley leaders who were willing to devote so much time to an investigative reporter who'd done so much hurt to them in the past. That took considerable courage. The same is true for those anonymous people who've come forward over the years to tell me the *real* story of the Valley. I thank them for their trust.

Finally, I am grateful to all of the friends, family and acquaintances who got me through this project with ideas, anecdotes and moral support. They know who they are. I hope someday I can do the same for them.

CONTENTS

THE BIG SCORE

INTRODUCTION

For two decades, the Sunnyvale Historical Society had lived on a dream: to build a shiny new museum commemorating the city's century and a half of history. The need for such a facility seemed obvious. After all, Sunnyvale's history was now crushed into a closet-sized room in a scarcely used recreation center on a forgotten back street of town. The room was jammed to the ceiling with paintings and curios yet displayed less than a tenth of the important objects in the city's collection—the rest stored around town in the garages and dens of society members.

Even when the little museum was first opened in 1960, when Sunnyvale was still a burg of thirty thousand people living in a few housing developments in the midst of endless orchards, the facility was recognized as inadequate. Twenty years later, the crowding at the museum was absurd. In those two decades Sunnyvale had become a crossroads for the world's engineering genius, a Lourdes for the scientists of the Electronics Revolution, a Virginia City for entrepreneurs itching to mine the mother lode of tiny silicon chips. The sleepy bedroom community had grown into a horizontal metropolis, the center of "Silicon Valley," Sunnyvale's 110,000 citizens squeezed into every slip of land within a matrix of freeways.

The orchards had been bulldozed, plowed and zoned for industrial park and minimum-easement housing developments. Each morning, thousands of Sunnyvale citizens, and many thousands of other people from neighboring communities, crawled their way from their cheek-to-jowl homes and high-density "theme" apartment complexes to the tilt-up, smoked-glass and prestressed-concrete temples of high technology on the city's east side. During the day, when the Bauhaus cathedrals hummed with life; when, in rooms cleaner than an operating theater, slivers of silicon were etched with the landscape of intelligence and stuffed into computers, calculators, disk drives and video games, Sunnyvale became the capital of the New Technological Society. At night, the pattern reversed with the setting sun, the tidal surge of humanity poured back out of the manicured industrial parks toward the infinite lights of home.

The cycle of ebb and flood could not be ignored by the members of the Sunnyvale Historical Society. Few of these graying children of the city's agrarian past had ever seen the inside of an electronics plant. But the technological revolution had not overlooked them. They wore the newest digital watches, they balanced their checkbooks on pocket calculators, a few had even bought shiny new personal computers. They had also seen the orchards bulldozed, watched as the value of their homes skyrocketed, been trapped in overheated rush-hour gridlock and sadly stood by as Sunnyvale's quaint old downtown was razed for a climatically controlled shopping mall. They watched Porsches and Mercedeses and other nouveau riche totems flash by on freeways and shook their heads as the newly raised walls of million-dollar mansions scarred the once flawlessly verdant Coast Hills.

But though these disquieting sights disturbed the historical society members, it also gave them hope.

The museum.

What better time, they reasoned, could there be for the new museum? A big museum. A million-dollar museum to match the city's new wealth and importance. A repository of Sunnyvale's past glories to educate the first citizens of the Digital Age.

With the city council's blessing, the society mounted a campaign to build a museum in the likeness of the home of Sunnyvale's pioneering landowner, Martin Murphy, Jr. To pay lip service to professionalism, the society hired a fund-raising consulting firm to poll the citizenry for their opinions.

The Sunnyvale Historical Society was shocked by the results. It seemed that most of the people of Sunnyvale didn't give half a damn that Martin Murphy and his family were among the first American settlers to cross the Sierra, or that they were among the rescuers of the Donner party, or that, before it was covered with the Silicon Valley veneer of cement and asphalt, Santa Clara County boasted some of the richest farmland in the world. For the vast majority of Sunnyvale's population, the great local historical question was not why Martin Murphy left Missouri in 1847 for California, but why Dr. Robert Noyce left Fairchild in 1968 to found Intel.

The historical society members sadly concluded that for decades they had carefully preserved a past about which no one cared . . .

The man drinks two martinis to calm himself down before he talks, but even then his conversation is confused and fragmentary.

The Martini Man has called this meeting with two local business reporters to say that the reality of Silicon Valley business has almost nothing to do with the reams of press releases about new products and financial results. The true story of Silicon Valley, he says, is not one of technological breakthroughs or overnight tycoons, but of unbridled ambition, of the dream of vast riches that people will do anything to realize.

Anything? The Martini Man smiles mysteriously, takes another drink and steers the conversation in a new direction.

The Martini Man says he recently lost his wife. She had come out with him to the Silicon Valley gold rush, grown sick of the life and her husband's endless workweeks and gone home. But the Martini Man had stayed. You see, he says, they offer you so much money to stay that you can never find enough reasons to quit—not even when your wife has left you and you are drinking too much and are living far above your means.

But the irony of it all, says the Martini Man, is that the big money is just an illusion, because the cost of living in the style of a winner—the two-hundred-thousand-dollar home, the clothes, the girlfriends, the Porsche—eats it all up and more. And then, as the debts mount, you can't leave. And if you get to owing too much you have to resort to stronger measures—like stealing.

Some people steal the obvious stuff, like gold or chips, he says. But there are a million other scams for getting rich in Silicon Valley, from executives forming dummy companies overseas down to salesmen selling samples rather than returning them to the company.

And that's just the beginning, says the Martini Man. If you want to score big there is always industrial espionage. He claims to know a number of people who were hired by the top executives of one firm to take a job at a competitor and steal trade secrets. The first company gets the secrets, the spy gets two paychecks and the second company, its all-important technological edge lost, gets screwed. What companies do this sort of thing? My own for one, says Martini Man, and he names one of the largest semiconductor firms in Silicon Valley.

The Martini Man's motives are challenged. Why has he suddenly chosen to come forward?

The Martini Man takes another drink. Because I just got fired, he says. And even more than that, I'm sick of this valley. I can get a job here at another company, but I'm tired of all of the cheating and hypocrisy and bullshit and stress and I'm getting the hell out.

But the Martini Man is frightened about his decision to speak to the press. He admits to being afraid not only for his career but for his life. On the way out of the company he angrily told his boss that he was going to call the papers and expose all of the industry's ugly skeletons. Now he figures that the company will somehow stop him from talking.

Before he leaves, the Martini Man promises to contact industrial-spy friends to see if they'll be willing to talk about what they do. But weeks pass and he never calls. When he is finally located at his girlfriend's apartment, the Martini Man says that he has talked to his friends, but none are forthcoming. They are making too much money to blow a good thing.

The Martini Man adds that this will be the last conversation; the semiconductor company has hired him back at a sizable increase in salary and he is being transferred within the week to San Diego . . .

Four men in business suits sit around an upstairs table in a Menlo Park restaurant. The mood is one of careful secrecy and almost breathtaking exhilaration. The meeting has been convened to plot the creation of a new company. Among the four of them, there are two masters' degrees in business, a doctorate in computer sciences and a decade of experience as a corporate treasurer.

The product that the planned company will manufacture is a device to understand simple sentences spoken by a human voice and convert those words into the digital signals a computer can use. Although not a single product of this type has been built, much less sold, anywhere in the world, excited industry analysts have already begun calling this new "speech-recognition" business one of the fastest growing electronics industries of the 1980s. Some have pegged annual sales at the end of the decade at more than $1 billion.

These men have heard rumors that IBM is looking at the business, as are a number of Japanese firms. But the scientist at the table is one of the world's leading experts in computer semantics. He has assured them his newly designed algorithm, the basic equation of a speech-recognition computer program, is unmatched anywhere. His partners take the scientist's statement on faith; after all, they are businessmen, not engineers. If he says that he can build the thing, it's good enough for them.

After two hours of sober conversation about technology, capital formation and suggested personnel, one of the men leans forward and whispers very seriously, "I don't know about the rest of you, but what I want to get out of this is a shitload of money." The others burst into laughter. The unspoken has finally been voiced. Now the men know that they can trust each other's greed to build a company . . .

The twenty-year-old boy with long red hair sits back on a worn couch in a San Jose drug halfway house. He's there to cure his runaway abuse of amphetamines, booze and angel dust—habits and addictions he picked up working on the assembly lines of a half dozen Silicon Valley electronics companies.

At eighteen, fresh from four fruitless high school years, the red-haired boy had gone to work at the best place around for an unskilled worker to make money fast: Silicon Valley. Sure the work was boring enough to make your brains fall out, but a few months of it—particularly those new thirteen-hour-day three-day work weeks some firms were offering—and you could make the down payment on a Trans-Am.

His friends in the industry weren't kidding either, it really was robot work. Attaching wires to semiconductor chips the size of your fingernail, building subassemblies for products he'd never see, soldering chips to printed circuit boards according to the rote demands of a template.

There was only one way to get through that kind of bullshit—and that was to get stoned out of your skull. Everybody did it, says the red-haired boy. You could really tell after lunch: assembly workers chattering hysterically and working triple speed with a nose full of methamphetamine "crank," office workers buzzed on beer and joints. And sometimes the guys at the wafer aligners would get behind some acid or angel dust and just trip out looking through the microscope eyepieces.

No sweat. The trick, said the red-haired boy, was to time your drugs right. If you took speed too early you'd start crashing in the afternoon and be nodding off on the job. If you took it too late or too much you'd buzz all night. And if you mixed them, especially with heroin, you could end up like that lab girl who freaked out and attempted suicide by sticking her head in one of the nitric acid baths. That was bad news. But once you found a reliable source, learned your dosage and got into the habit of eating and sleeping on the stuff, it was just one long smooth groove. Weekends were a drag, usually because you'd crash and sleep through them. But think of that Trans-Am.

The red-haired boy sits back on the couch and lights a cigarette. He thinks for a minute then says he's decided that his mistake was in getting carried away. If I'd just stuck with the drugs I needed I would've been all right, he says.

The red-haired boy was working so fast on crank that his above-quota production came to the attention of his supervisor, who promoted him to quality control and testing. An easy job. Just sit and make sure the other guy did his job right. But it could also get slow too, and the speed could be a pain in the ass. So the red-haired boy began drinking at lunch. He also started to occasionally do angel dust. That angel dust was insane stuff, the kid says. He remembers one day being so strung out that the parts—military devices—just seemed to shrink out of sight. So, what the hell, you can't inspect what you can't see. So, the red-haired kid passed them all.

The company gave him a raise and promoted him to supervisor.

But that's when things went lousy. The drugs, even more than booze, began to catch up with him. The red-haired kid began to lose weight; he couldn't sleep at night but couldn't stay awake during the day. The inevitable pink slip finally came.

Luckily, says the red-haired boy, it was one of those boom times in the Valley, when every company was looking to hire any warm body they could find. Within hours he had located another job for more pay. But the drugs were now out of hand. He was spending all of his salary and more just to stay high. That's when he took to stealing: calculators, equipment, anything. And the last score was the biggest of them all: he located and sold the blueprints to an cesium atomic clock—the timing device for nuclear weapons—to two men for a few hundred dollars.

The red-haired boy lights another cigarette. He says he doesn't remember much about the men—"I was pretty fucked up by then"—only that they said they were teachers and that they both had foreign accents . . .

"Silicon Valley" has become synonymous throughout the world with the Electronics Revolution, the accelerating rush of technological innovation forever changing human society. It has even begun to change human thought: from the continuous, "analog" view of nature that governed humanity for a million years, to the new discrete, "digital"-

views universe that offers the prospect of reducing all reality to a series of zeros and ones, plusses and minuses, ons and offs.

But the Silicon Valley that exists as the symbol of perpetual change has a real (sometimes painfully real) counterpart: a twenty-mile-long, two-mile-wide stretch of industrial parks at the base of the San Francisco peninsula. Here, in this small cluster of factories and offices, resides America's industrial, military, commercial and social hope for the rest of this century and beyond. From this coterie of a couple of thousand feverishly active firms will come America's weapons, economic strength, balanced trade and medical breakthroughs. From them will also come life-enhancing inventions on the order of calculators and personal computers the Valley has already given the world.

For one thing, the place enjoys remarkable growth. In little more than two decades, the electronics industry, for which Silicon Valley is the heartland, has become, as much as steel and automobiles, the bedrock manufacturing sector in American business—and only one of the three still rapidly growing. Silicon Valley alone has produced more than a dozen firms in the Fortune 500, with scores more poised to enter the list. Not only has the electronics industry in itself become the vanguard of America's struggle to maintain its competitiveness vis-à-vis the rest of the world, but its products, from microprocessors to computer-controlled robots, offer the hope of a renaissance to other more mature—even dying—domestic industries.

A second special characteristic of the Valley is its unprecedented creation of wealth. Every boom industry has tossed rich new titans on the scene. But never before Silicon Valley so many, so young and with such equality: thirty-year-old tycoons in T-shirts, making their first hundred million before they buy their first pinstripe suit; secretaries worth millions thanks to a few dollars spent on stock options; garage inventors suddenly finding themselves on lists of the world's richest men. Apple Computer alone produced more than a hundred paper millionaires when it went public. Silicon Valley is vast wealth, unbelievable wealth, too much wealth, raining down on uncultured engineers not much older than children. It is said that by day, Sunnyvale—a city with no building taller than four stories—has more millionaires per capita than any city its size in the world. The result is the overnight-wealth story played out scores of times every month.

And there are other, less obvious characteristics special to Silicon Valley: its pursuit of technology for technology's sake, even when it seems to have little to do with the realities of the marketplace; the

Valley's relative isolation for the decade before it exploded on the scene in the early 1970s; the symbiotic relationship between the Valley and a single great university, Stanford, each making the other an important world force; and the all but untouched landscape of the area before the birth of Silicon Valley, providing the tabula rasa that gave the area its rip-roaring business style.

There is one other quality special to Silicon Valley—the most important for the fate of the United States. Silicon Valley has been, and for the present still remains, the most advanced and efficient incubator of new companies ever known. Here, the numerous and fragile variables of innovation, capital and organization required for the birth of important new companies have been not only realized (as they have during brief intervals throughout history) but actually sustained (as they never have anywhere before). If it is a paradise, then Silicon Valley is most certainly first and foremost an entrepreneur's paradise, where the founding and operation of new companies has been turned into a science. In this very special location the chance of business failure—as much as 50 percent in some other industries and locations—is almost negligible. In Silicon Valley, at least for now, entrepreneurs of courage almost never lose.

But best of all there is the hope that perhaps, just perhaps, the resident genius of Silicon Valley will one day come up with a revolutionary new way of life that offers to all people open and healthy cities, clean and safe industries, the blessings of the latest in social services, quality education and an infinite opportunity for personal development—a world resembling the dream image many people already have of Silicon Valley.

Indeed, the Valley is more than just another business enclave. Rather, more than any industry in history, it is a self-contained, living entity.

Claiming life for a bunch of buildings might seem to be anthropomorphic, but only because the analogy has never been so apt. Silicon Valley, more than any past industrial community, from the sixteenth-century Hanseatic League to twentieth-century Detroit, fulfills many of the biological requirements to be considered "alive." It has defined boundaries, is self-perpetuating and reproducing and has predictable behavior—including the instinct for self-preservation. Even in the electronics industry there is a tendency to speak of "Silicon Valley" as though it were a sensate being.

Silicon Valley cannot be looked at piecemeal, but only, like a great metacreature, as a whole live being in all of its dimensions. Until now that has not occurred. Instead, in dozens of scholarly papers, scores of books and hundreds of magazine and newspaper articles, Silicon Valley has been seen as its products, as if one could understand an oyster only by its pearl. The result has been a brand-new industry dedicated to describing the wonderful Elysian landscape the Electronics Revolution will create for us. Every day, we are thrilled with word of the next magic box that Silicon Valley, the electronic sorcerer, has awarded to us, its apprentices. What is rarely said is that in Silicon Valley, where this "wonderful" future already has arrived, the much-vaunted Paradise often seems to have been painted by Bosch.

To capture the truth about Silicon Valley—and America's future—one must approach it from every angle, like a team of scientists gathering data on a new species. As behaviorists, we must look at its activities (technological innovation) and personality (the engineering mind made manifest). As anatomists, we must cut into the body industrial to study functions and interrelationships between the various organs, fluids and bones (the companies, employees, communities). As geneticists and cytologists we must catalog each cell type (executive, venture capitalist, engineer, assembly worker, drug dealer, research scientist, industrial spy, foreign agent, consultant) to study its function and its relation to the body as a whole.

If Silicon Valley is a sensate being of concrete and steel, silicon and human flesh, the question remains whether it is a good creature or evil, providential or parasitic, domesticated or predatory? Is Silicon Valley indeed, as the trade press and other boosters claim, a modern Paradise? Or is it instead Paradise Lost, a thin, glittering surface of obsidian above a burning inferno of toxic chemical leaks and espionage and drug abuse and worker exploitation? There may be no more important question the modern industrial work can ask—because Silicon Valley is the future. One day we will all live in Silicon Valley, a coast-to-coast industrial park of concrete tilt-up buildings and manicured-grass berms; and then even the most remote citizen will know the meaning this new electronic zeitgeist—intimately. Then there will be no turning back. Already there is a Silicon Gulch, a Silicon Mountain and Silicon Prairie. In time there will be a Silicon World.

*   *   *

To snare this creature called Silicon Valley alive is the goal of this book. In the wild, as it were. As past efforts have shown, a single form of narrative is not enough. Neither a chronological history nor a survey of the present business environment is enough—just as one cannot fully know an animal by focusing just upon its morphology or its behavior; one must study how they bear upon one another. Further, just as living things exist in time, are born, develop and die according to a life cycle, so too do communities, even those with the limitless adolescent exuberance of Silicon Valley.

The net will be woven from a number of different narrative threads. First there are the Valley's two histories, financial and technological, each propelling the other forward. There is also the sociological story of Silicon Valley, the growth of the cities and the effect of the boom town mentality on the citizenry. There are also key players: the entrepreneur-geniuses and venture capitalists who built the great firms and enjoyed heavenly rewards, the Martini Men middle managers weathering the purgatory of the present in hopes of a future Big Score, and the assembly workers caught in the hopelessly deep circles of economic boom and bust, skyrocketing living costs and drugs.

And finally, no study of Silicon Valley can be complete without a look at the most remarkable event in Valley life: the birth of a new company and its first faltering steps along the path cut by its huge and famous predecessors.

As Virgil led Dante through a strange and often terrifying land, so I propose to guide you through the starkly beautiful landscape of Silicon Valley. I am no poet, but rhyme and meter aren't the language of this silicon wilderness. And unlike the great Roman, I needn't stop at the edge of the Inferno. In Silicon Valley, heaven and hell sit at adjoining workbenches.

No dark wood or lion or she-wolf marks the entrance to Silicon Valley. Just a freeway exit. Simply signal and turn off.

But stay close . . .

1

The New Athens

Before there was Silicon Valley there was Santa Clara Valley.

And although in recent years these two entities have shared the same geographic area, they are as different as their names.

Traditionally, Santa Clara Valley extended along the bottom and west bank of the San Francisco Bay a few miles northward up the San Francisco Peninsula. It was a valley only in the sense that it was bounded to the west by the green Coastal Range mountains tossed up by the San Andreas Fault and in the south where the collision of these mountains with the brown Diablo Range of the East Bay pinched shut the southern terminus of the alluvial plain that formed the "valley's" floor.

The valley's other boundaries were far less precise. On the bay side, the land petered out into marshes, river channels and miles of thick slurry mudflats and shallow water. The northern limit of the valley was so indistinct that it required man to designate it. Traditionally it lies somewhere near a tall, now scraggly pine tree that explorer Captain Gaspar de Portolá, governor of the Californias, spotted near his encampment in November 1769 and noted in his diary as *palo alto*—"tall tree."

Santa Clara, Palo Alto, Los Altos, San Jose and other Valley city names reflect the Spanish citizenship of its first white visitors. All of these explorers seemed to agree that Santa Clara Valley was one of the *nicest* places on God's Green Earth. Perpetually moderated by the great heat sink–air conditioner of the bay, the valley's climate was exquisitely hospitable, rarely dipping below freezing, raining heavily for only a week or two each year and narrowly escaping that damnable cold fog that slipped in through the Golden Gate nearly every summer night.

As if that weren't enough, beneath that gentle sky, and formed by the flood plains of the Valley's many creeks as they meandered between mountains and bay, was some of the world's finest farming soil. Rich black dirt marbled by streaks of clay, it put to shame even the much-vaunted Salinas Valley farmland fifty miles to the south.

Unlike San Francisco to the north, Santa Clara Valley was not created by the 1849 gold rush, but rather by ranchers and farmers hoping to one day become gentlemen squires.

This new gentry quickly began to require the quality things of life for themselves and their children. That led to a growing retail business in San Jose. The children also needed an education. The Jesuits were the first, founding Santa Clara at the mission in 1851. San Jose State Normal School (now San Jose State University) was established in a high school room in San Francisco in 1862 and moved south in 1870. Finally, and most important for the birth of Silicon Valley, in 1885, mourning the death of their son, railroad robber baron Leland Stanford and his wife built Leland Stanford Jr. University on eighty thousand acres of prime farmland just a few hundred yards from the Palo Alto tree. Stanford University would in time become one of the world's great academic institutions, a monument to benevolence that would all but erase the memory of all those dead Chinese coolies buried along the path of the transcontinental railroad.

At the time of Stanford University's opening in 1891, the New York *Mail and Express* wrote with characteristic subtlety that "the need for another university in California is about as great as that of an asylum for decayed sea captains in Switzerland." It would not be the last time that the East Coast press would underestimate the valley's vitality.

By 1911, Stanford had an enrollment of more than 1,700. Even more telling, in light of the valley's subsequent history, the class included students from throughout the world, the largest contingent (twenty) from Japan.

Even before the founding of Stanford, Santa Clara Valley was experiencing its first contact with the electronics age. In the 1870s, ledger records show that Thomas Edison bought eighty-five thousand dollars' worth of mercury ore from the valley's New Almadén Mines for use in the production of his lamps (Quicksilver Valley, so to speak). In 1879, the Edison Electric Light Co. installed the first on-board incandescent light on the doomed arctic sailing ship *Jennette,* based in the port of San Francisco.

Interestingly, the now long abandoned New Almadén Mine also played a role in what appears to have been one of the first electronics experiments on the North American continent. In 1898 and 1899, Charles Herrold, experimenting with radio wave propagation in earth and air, set up a transmitter on the third floor of San Jose's Garden City bank and two receivers, one atop Mine Hill and the other 2,350 feet down the deepest shaft of the mine.

In 1899, a Marconi wireless installed in a lighthouse off the coast and underwritten by the San Francisco *Call* newspaper announced to San Francisco the arrival of the troopship *Sherman* back from the war in the Philippines. Not only was this the first transmission of news by radio, but the event charmed an entire generation of Bay Area boys with the prospect of radio. Within a decade, San Francisco and the peninsula were covered by amateur radio clubs—with the attendant fires, explosions and electrocutions.

At Stanford University, amateur radio became an obsession, not only among engineering students (particularly Cy Elwell and James Muller) but also among sons of faculty members (such as Roland Marx and Fred Terman).

Like many students of electricity for generations after him, Cy Elwell chose to remain in the vicinity of the Stanford campus after his graduation in 1906. He had good reason to stay. Stanford University was by now a world center in electronics. In addition, in 1906, the San Andreas Fault, which ran along the crest of the Coast Hills down the spine of the peninsula, made one of its periodic adjustments and flattened San Francisco. Frightened of future catastrophic quakes and fires, a number of heavy-equipment firms (such as Hendy Iron Works) and canneries moved south—and gave the valley its first real industrial base.

In 1908, Elwell was asked to help a small wireless radio company in San Francisco. The firm, the McCarty Wireless Telephone Company, had been founded in 1902 to take advantage of an invention by fourteen-year-old child prodigy Francis McCarty: the wireless telephone. Young McCarty had discovered how to transmit voice over wireless radio. But public indifference, a shortage of capital and McCarty's own tragic death in a horse cart accident in 1906 had left the firm limping along.

In autumn 1909, Elwell demonstrated his wireless telephone to prospective backers and members of the Stanford faculty, notably progressive school president David Starr Jordan. Jordan was so impressed that he put up five hundred dollars in venture capital, spurring the other professors as well as the businessmen to join in. Some of the professors also agreed to act as consultants—the beginning of another vitally important relationship between Stanford and Silicon Valley.

Elwell's firm, Poulsen Wireless Telephone and Telegraph, was founded in October 1909. Within two years it had become one of the largest electrical firms of its kind in the country. That year the firm's name was changed to the Federal Telegraph Co. (later Federal Electric, it moved to New Jersey in 1932 and is now part of ITT). Also in 1911, Elwell hired at Federal a pivotal figure in electronics: Lee De Forest.

De Forest, a brilliant, intense, messianic and difficult man (who grew more difficult as the years passed), was already a famous name in electronics. In 1906, he had invented the first vacuum tube, the three-electrode audion—the first of more than three hundred patents De Forest would earn in his lifetime.

The audion was extremely useful for detecting signals from wireless telegraphs, so De Forest set up a company in New York to exploit the expected demand. Unfortunately, it was De Forest himself who was exploited, by his company officers, and by 1911 he was broke. (The first of many won and lost fortunes De Forest would know in his eighty-eight years.)

Looking for work, De Forest came to San Francisco, where he contacted Elwell, an old acquaintance. Elwell enthusiastically offered him a job and De Forest moved to Palo Alto with his mother. He immediately set to work improving his audion. However, his past reared up and shattered the peace he thought he had found in the Valley. In March 1912, De Forest was arrested by federal marshals for stock fraud relating to his old New York firm. Only the quick coverage of ten thousand dollars' bail by Federal's board of directors kept De Forest out of jail for the year before trial.

In the interim, with the cloud of a possible prison sentence over his head, De Forest spent one of the most feverishly active periods of his life. He and his two assistants fiddled with the audion, trying to find a way to speed up the transmission of telegraph messages. In the process, they discovered something far more important. By rewiring the audion, De Forest and his team, to their amazement, found they could make the device work as an amplifier. Connecting the audion and the telephone transmitter to some headphones and then holding his "trusty Ingersoll" watch in front of the telephone, De Forest nearly deafened himself and his assistants with the watch's amplified ticks.

So the Electronics Age had begun in a converted home in downtown Palo Alto. A direct line of technological inheritance had begun that would continue through many generations of young scientists and seven decades and lead to the transistor, television, the integrated circuit and the computer.

Ever the marketing man, De Forest raced to New York to try to license his invention to the phone company. While waiting for a decision, De Forest went out to New Jersey and screamed a description of his invention into the ear of Thomas Edison. Edison, whose incandescent bulb was the basis for De Forest's audion, was impressed. De Forest was on a roll. He returned to Palo Alto at the end of 1912 with a tentative agreement from Bell Telephone, a charter membership in the Institute of Radio Engineers and a chorus girl as a new bride (years later he would marry a movie actress). De Forest also had another job offer, this time from New York investors interested in the possibility of talking motion pictures.

So, in May 1913, De Forest left Federal for New York. That same year, Elwell also left the firm to pursue financial opportunities in Europe. De Forest did return once, in 1915, to assist in a demonstration of wireless radio at San Francisco's Panama-Pacific World's Fair. His partner on the project was Dr. Charles Herrold, the man who had put the radio in the San Jose mineshaft nearly two decades before. In the interim, Herrold had continued his work with radio. In 1909, he had established, in San Jose's "FN" (now KCBS in San Francisco), America's first commercial radio station. His wife was the first disc jockey.

The First World War was good business for the infant electronics industry (as wars have been ever since). So was the sinking of the *Titanic* and the resulting Radio Law of 1913 requiring passenger ships to install radios and hire operators. Federal Telegraph grew quickly, hired many Stanford graduates and gave them the experience they needed to continue their research and eventually in some cases to start their own firms. For example, as early as 1910, a pair of Federal Telegraph engineers, Peter Jensen and E. S. Pridham, left to build loudspeakers. In 1917, their new firm became Magnavox.

Federal was having its own successes. In 1919 company engineer James Miller installed stations in Annapolis, Maryland, and Bordeaux, France, and conducted the first intercontinental radio transmission.

(Twenty years later, Miller would direct the wireless link between Roosevelt and Churchill.)

By the end of the First World War, radio had come into its own, jumping from the garages of a few inspired amateurs to the living room of the average person. It was the first of a growing number of electronic revolutions that would sweep across society. In retrospect, as the first, the radio revolution was a prototype for subsequent eras in consumer (and with some changes, industrial) electronics.

First there are the key inventors, known only to a few brilliant peers in the field, then experimentation and improvement at the hands of a cultlike group of hobbyists; the formation of a few small firms (often by hobbyists) to support the growing cult market; government contracts—usually military and usually during war—to ascertain the use of these products in weapons and related military hardware; rapid expansion by the established firms and the creation of new firms to tap into the government money; the development of industrial and consumer products (usually variations on the military designs) both to pioneer those vast markets and to fill in the troughs of cyclical government demand; the entry of large, established firms into the industry, as well as the explosive growth of a few well-managed pioneering firms; a shift from innovation to production; a retail war to annihilate all but a handful of winning firms with the lion's share of the market—consigning the rest, even the famous founding firms, to oblivion or a relative stasis hanging for dear life to a tiny, specialized submarket.

Meanwhile, in society at large, this electronics revolution undergoes a similar life cycle. About the time the hobbyist period becomes a short-lived craze, the press begins to notice it. First there are the bemused feature articles and occasional news stories (arrests for thievery or vandalism and so forth) that describe these strange young geniuses and their incomprehensible hobby. As the hobbyist cult grows—or at least grows more visible—the tone of the articles shifts from amusement to awe and then a little fear. What was the crazy antics of a small and distant group (then: eggheads, now: nerds) suddenly crops up in your own son's bedroom or at the home of that nice young man (or, more rarely, young woman) across the street. Next there is the fear, expressed in letters to the editor and advice columns and in quotes by distraught parents and educators, that the obsession of these children with this new black art (crystal radios/ham radios/transistor radios/sirens/locker "shockers"/calculators/computers) is hurting his schoolwork, paralyzing his social life before it even has a chance to begin and slowly taking over the child's mind—changing its very thought processes—forever. Psychologists first warn about the damage being done to the nation's youth, then later decide these fads weren't so destructive after all.

In the segment of the press that specializes in explaining technology to average people, an increasing number of articles appear discussing the new phenomenon. Few are sober and judicious on the subject, many (in retrospect) are embarrassingly utopian, proclaiming a New Eden heralded by the arrival of the radio/television/computer and declaring said invention to represent a turning point in the history of humanity.

The national press joins the general uproar last, when the revolution has reached critical mass, and its approval turns an underground movement almost overnight into a worldwide trend. The resulting chain reaction in market demand, combined with the ruthless competition going on in the industry at the same time, conspires to turn the arcane device of a few years before into a common household appliance or office tool. Comedians include it in their jokes. Pop books and records are written about it. It creates a short-lived genre of novels. The revolution is now over. Only time will tell who really won.

Meanwhile, in some laboratory or bedroom or garage, the next revolution has begun, and bright young hobbyists are laying plans and saving cash to get in on the action.

The national press plays another crucial role. It writes the history and declares the victors. It prepares for the received view that will wait in newspaper morgues and library microfilm spools for future generations. By the time the New York *Times* or *Newsweek* or *Time* sends its science and technology correspondent out to write the all-encompassing cover story, the revolution has settled into the mature struggle among giants for market share. Only the winners remain to tell the story—and they do so usually in a manner that is in part due to a very human tendency toward self-promotion as well as to the monomania that often arises in people who have become unimaginably wealthy at a young age.

Thus, when the big story finally arcs out over the Associated Press wire and earns an hour special on the CBS television network, graces a photo spread in *Life* or appears on the *Times* best-seller list, the key cofounder of a newly heralded firm who was squeezed out of his job in an office power play a few years back is reduced to a footnote or remains unlisted in the caption of a grainy black-and-white photograph of the company founders. The same fate also holds true for the pioneering firms that didn't survive until the date of formal public recognition, their often important contributions downgraded by the companies that drove them out of business—sometimes with better products and management, but just as often through price bombing, employee raiding and deep-pocketed parent firms.

People, too, conduct their own sort of historical editing when the time comes to step into the national limelight. The reputation for cruelty or womanizing or mendaciousness that an entrepreneur cultivated when he was first trying to make his mark in Silicon Valley is conveniently forgotten when the evening news calls for a profile. As this book is being written, Silicon Valley is watching with amusement as one young, vastly wealthy entrepreneur is carefully glossing over with the press the felonious behavior of which he was so proud five years before.

That individual is busy backfilling because he has been selected by the press to represent the latest electronic revolution. At least since Edison, perhaps even since Franklin, the public has come to expect the name of a single individual ("the inventor") to be inextricably and singularly tied to a landmark product or design or theory ("the invention"). Unfortunately, this simple correspondence was rarely the case with Edison, much less, in this age of large research laboratories, with an applied science like electronics. But someone must be named, the readers demand it. To the chilly world of digital logic, silicon and plastic must be added a human face. Almost anyone will do.

Unfortunately, the founders of a technological revolution are often such queer ducks or vicious bastards that they can't get along with *anybody*—and it is precisely those character flaws that made them strike off into the unknown and stake their fortunes and careers on the outcome.

Publicity people know that fact all too well. They also know that the proper traits for selection are more likely to be found in executives on the periphery of the revolution: presidents of second-tier firms, marketing vice-presidents, cofounders who were brought in from the business world to raise money. Talented performers assert themselves until they become key spokespersons. When the national press arrives it finds exactly what it's looking for—the "face" of the revolution.

Once the selection is complete it becomes self-fulfilling. After forty years of great men in Silicon Valley, *Time* finally decides to put Steven Jobs of Apple on its cover. Henceforth, Jobs, more than David Packard or Charles Sporck or Robert Noyce, comes to represent Silicon Valley for millions of people.

It all began with the radio era of the 1920. Then, after Edison, the most popularly accepted "face" to represent the new invention was Lee De Forest, who had the necessary credentials (though many improvements were made by others to his original triode), tainted biography and pathological arrogance for the job. His type would be seen over and over again in the electronics industry, reaching a peak in the late 1970s, when it must have seemed to outsiders that Silicon Valley was filled to the rim with crazy tycoons.

In January 1930, convinced by his own press clippings that he was indeed the father of radio, De Forest put on the philosopher's sackcloth and wrote a letter to the Chicago *Tribune:*

A FATHER MOURNS HIS CHILD

What have you gentlemen done with my child? He was conceived as a potent instrumentality for culture, fine music, the uplifting of America's mass intelligence. You have debased this child, you have sent him out in the streets . . . to collect money from all and sundry, for hubba hubba and audio jitterbug. You have made of him a laughing stock to the intelligence, surely a stench in the nostrils of the gods of the ionosphere; you have cut time into tiny parcels called spots (more rightly "stains") wherewith the occasional fine program is periodically smeared with impudent insistence to buy or try . . .

Some day the program director will attain the intelligent skill of the engineers who erected the towers and built the marvel which he now so ineptly uses.

Thus, De Forest completed the cycle, from abrasive young overachiever to grand old man, from greedy capitalist to high-culture saint. It has been a bracing example for his descendants, from William Shockley to Steven Wozniak—the latter, in keeping with the speeded up nature of the industry, only half the age of De Forest at the time of his apotheosis.

As De Forest was calling for Armageddon, the radio revolution was maturing into its Golden Age.

Throughout the 1920s, although other schools such as the University of California (Berkeley) had begun offering courses in radio, Stanford retained its preeminence in the new field of electrical engineering. Most of the reputation was due to the efforts of two men, Dr. Harris Ryan and Dr. Fredrick Terman.

An extremely popular professor of electrical engineering, Ryan had been a devoted supporter of the local radio hobbyist ever since the turn of the century. Cy Elwell was one of his students, as were many other electronics pioneers. Ryan himself had gained a considerable international reputation for his research in the transmission of high-voltage electric power.

By then, Ryan had become the dean of the rapidly growing electrical engineering department. He and his faculty and students were deeply immersed in the study of radio as well as research into improving the vacuum tube, the child of De Forest's triode.

In 1924, Dean Ryan established a "radio communications laboratory" in the attic of the electrical engineering building. He selected a graduate, Fred Terman, to run the lab.

Terman had long been a fixture in local campus radio groups. The son of a Stanford professor (who developed the Stanford-Binet IQ tests), Terman had grown up at the school. With Herbert Hoover's son he had even built an amateur radio station. Nevertheless, Terman took his undergraduate degree at Stanford in chemistry, convinced it was the queen of sciences.

Upon graduating in 1920, Terman went to work for the most interesting employer in town, Federal Telegraph. The experience seemed to have rekindled old passions, because when Terman left the firm a few months later he enrolled in the master's program in electrical engineering at Stanford. Then he was off to MIT to take a doctorate in the same field. When he returned to Stanford in 1924, Ryan offered him a job as a teacher. Soon after, Terman was put in charge of the new radio lab.

Studious, soft-spoken and forever self-effacing, Terman was not a great scientist. Rather, he was a great synthesizer of knowledge, and it was this quality that made him first a brilliant teacher and later a profound visionary. Terman seemed to have the ability to inspire in his students an almost religious belief in the power of electronics to change the world.

Terman also inspired intense loyalty among his students. During his tenure as head of the communications laboratory (1924–45) it was the focal point of the college careers of many bright young scientific minds on campus (much as the computer lab is to "hackers" now). Because of this, until the end of the Second World War and Terman's promotion to dean, the Stanford communications lab was the heart of technological innovation on the West Coast. By the time Terman moved on, the ties between Stanford and the surrounding electronics community were so strong that the university was all but guaranteed its present role of providing apprenticeship to each generation of high-tech leaders.

By the late 1920s Terman's lab was changing the face of Santa Clara Valley. The valley was still one vast orchard broken only here and there by tiny burgs of three or four streets that had grown up around the farmhouse of an old landowner. The only true cities in the valley existed at the southern end in a two-mile-stretch enclave between Santa Clara University and the agricultural banking center of San Jose and at the northern end of the valley around Stanford University.

But almost from the advent of Terman's lab this northern area began to change. Every year new little buildings appeared or existing structures gained new tenants; inevitably bright young Stanford grads with arcane equipment and equally incomprehensible ideas, young men Terman later described as "electronic nuts, those young men who show as much interest in vacuum tubes, transistors and computers as in girls."

It is a testament to the reputation of the Stanford electrical engineering department as well as to the quality of Terman's teaching that so many chose not to go home after graduation but to stay in the Bay Area and in close touch with the school. It became a common career path to graduate from Stanford, teach a little or go to work for Federal Telegraph and then in time strike off in one's own company nearby.

That's what Charles Litton did. A San Francisco boy who built his first ham radio at ten, Litton taught himself glass-blowing in order to make his own vacuum tubes. His reputation for tube-making became so great that when he graduated from Stanford in 1924 Litton decided to go into business for himself. In 1928, the tall thin twenty-three-year-old was hired by Federal Telegraph to direct the firm's vacuum tube department and take on the already mighty RCA.

Litton did so by sidestepping RCA's patents and by producing a tube of such quality that it landed the contract from a newly created firm called the International Telephone and Telegraph. In retrospect, Litton would say, "I was just a lucky kid." Others would say that he was a gifted designer who could do the impossible with metal and glass. No less a man than David Packard would say: "Charlie Litton was one of the really brilliant engineers." And one of its first millionaires.

In 1932, Federal Telegraph decided to move back East. Litton chose to stay. He started his own firm, Litton Engineering Laboratories, up the peninsula in Redwood City (it later moved to nearby San Carlos). There Litton did the same thing he had always done: improve techniques for the mass production of precision glass vacuum tubes.

The Second World War and the accompanying rise in radar brought considerable prosperity to the young electronics industry, and nowhere more than to Charlie Litton's glass shop: "I woke up one day, and out of a clear blue sky I suddenly found myself the sole owner of a million-and-a-half-dollar concern."

After the war, Litton Engineering became a corporation, Litton Industries, the leading source of glass-forming machinery in the United States, and, increasingly, a major manufacturer of military electronics systems. The glass tube business, the original company, was sold. By the 1960s, Litton Industries was a billion-dollar corporation. The "lucky" glass blower had done very well.

Though few had the huge success of Charlie Litton, Terman's lab in its two decades produced scores of bright electrical engineers destined to make their names and fortunes in electronics. By the time Federal moved, it wasn't greatly missed, because there were a number of new employers to step into the breach and hire fresh young Stanford grads. An infrastructure was being built in Palo Alto: a bipolar structure with Stanford at one end and the new electronics firms on the other. In an increasingly intricate symbiosis, Stanford provided the local industry with talented new scientists and theoretical research, and the industry gave Stanford money, faculty and a place nearby for graduates to serve their apprenticeships.

Extending the network still further, as the firms grew they needed increasing numbers of workers. And not just electrical engineers, but machinists and truck drivers and plant managers and production engineers. Factories had to be constructed, products blueprinted, prototyped, mass-produced and delivered. Books had to be kept, invoices prepared and payrolls met. It was all pretty small and primitive in the early thirties, but it was thriving—and that meant jobs, a very popular item in that period.

With improved automobiles and highways, combined with staggering national unemployment, all roads seemed to lead to California. Local town populations swelled with the influx. The day of Old California—agrarian, provincial, often backward—was finally, and irrevocably, coming to an end.

In the tiny but teeming electronics industry around Palo Alto a last ingredient was still missing: a major company, a world-class firm to balance the huge mass of Stanford University; one that would bring the little business community worldwide recognition. Most of all, the local electronics industry needed a firm large enough and rich enough and sophisticated enough to propel the rest of the infrastructure into place: the advertising agencies and publicity firms, personnel managers, schoolteachers, restaurateurs, accountants, distributors, retailers, car salesmen, office equipment stores, tax planners, real estate agents, component suppliers and subcontractors, and the whole warp and woof of specialists needed to create the complex tapestry of a self-contained industrial region.

By the mid-1930s, Terman had just the boys for the job: Bill Hewlett and Dave Packard.

PROFILE
The Aristocrats

WILLIAM HEWLETT and DAVID PACKARD

The world had its first real glimpse of David Packard (as well as a satisfying brush with the HP Way) in December 1968, when he was nominated by the Nixon administration as deputy secretary of Defense.

Packard's nomination was met with cheers by the business community, jeers by the press and Congress. Hewlett-Packard, it was noted, had a number of defense contracts—a potential conflict of interest. Furthermore, looking from the far bank of the Potomac, Packard with all his millions seemed a stereotype of the fat-cat capitalist, a big-money boy in the military-industrial complex. That HP had never built a weapon was irrelevant; after all, Packard also sat on the board of General Dynamics, which most certainly had. For that matter, Packard also was on the boards of Crocker Bank, National Airlines, U.S. Steel and Equitable Life and on the international advisory committee of Chase Manhattan Bank. An all-American tycoon if ever there was one.

The idea of putting this pinstripe plutocrat second in command of the Armed Forces brought visions to Congress of Carnegie, Fisk and Gould. In the Washington *Post,* Adam Yarnowinski wrote: "Men who have made a career in the defense industry are likely to be less sensitive to controlling the expansionist tendencies of the establishment."

At this point, no sensible person would have blamed Packard for withdrawing the nomination. After all, he could only look forward to a hostile Congress publicly picking through the detritus of his life. Packard also would have to give up a job at the firm he had built over three decades that paid him in salary and stock about $1 million a year. All for a job as a thirty-thousand-dollar-a-year civil servant—an amount less than a change in value of Packard's HP stock of less than a penny per share.

Worse, if Defense Department precedent held, Packard would have to sell his $300 million in stock—30 percent of HP's outstanding shares —on the open market. This sudden liquidation might not only sink Hewlett-Packard into financial chaos but also send shock waves through the American economy.

But Dave Packard forged on with the confirmation hearings. Financial gain obviously wasn't the reason, nor it seemed was self-aggrandizement (not for a *deputy* secretary's position), and at home Hewlett-Packard had a pressing business matter in its attempt to enter the computer market. What seemed to be Packard's motive for accepting the nomination (which Washingtonians found hard to believe) was simply that he felt that business leaders, instead of complaining about the federal government's incompetence or ignorance, should become involved, donating their considerable expertise in management and decision-making.

It was such a remarkably honorable reason that the Washington political world at first found it absurd. However, the doubt began to dissolve as glowing quotes about Packard began to pour in from famous Americans.

Said a contemporary biography: "[Senators who supported Packard] noted that a man of Packard's wealth had little to gain by favoritism and that his integrity was a better insurance for the country than the sale of his stock." So, in the most antimilitary, antiwealth, antibigbusiness era in American history, multimillionaire David Packard had become the second most powerful man in the military-industrial complex.

* * *

Neither Hewlett nor Packard would have stood out among the many talented students in Terman's lab. Both were born in middle America, both had professional fathers and both had journeyed out to California to Stanford. But so had many others. Neither was a great scientist, like De Forest before them or Shockley after, though Hewlett was probably as good an engineer as anyone in his class. In all, the two boys were good students, by all appearances destined to be good engineers at some large radio company. Certainly not much more, and unless something awful happened, probably not much less.

If their curricula vitae gave little clue to the future of the two young men, one glance at them walking around campus would have told even the most casual observer that there was something different about the pair. "Mutt and Jeff" would be the phrase that would pop into minds for the next half century. At six feet five, with a long forehead and nose, Packard had the proper (if slightly softened) George Washington look.

Hewlett, on the other hand, pudgy and barely reaching Packard's shoulder, looked like neither an engineer nor a tycoon; he was more like a high school social studies teacher who coaches junior varsity football on the side. (For the HP annual report photograph each year, the only way to get the two men in the same frame was to have Packard sit down, which still brought him almost head to head with Hewlett.)

Difference in appearance aside, what was obvious in both men was an unusual sensitivity to the feelings of others. That, in the end, would be the key.

Bill Hewlett and Dave Packard came from opposite ends of the American heartland (Packard: Pueblo, Colorado; Hewlett: Ann Arbor, Michigan) but the same end of the socioeconomic scale. Packard's father was a lawyer, Hewlett's a professor of medicine at the University of Michigan—hardly Ragged Dick beginnings.

When Hewlett was three, his father accepted a medical professorship at Stanford's medical school, then located in San Francisco, and moved the family out to the Coast. Professor Hewlett died when Bill was twelve. In retrospect Hewlett has said that perhaps if his father had lived he might have followed him into medicine.

About the time Hewlett entered high school, he became interested in radio. He built a crystal set and picked up transmissions from the growing number of Bay Area radio stations. But Hewlett never really became a ham nut, not like his buddy Ed Porter, who would serve HP as a vice-president for forty years. Porter had converted the entire attic of his parents' house into a ham station. "It was literally the most haywire thing you ever saw," recalls Hewlett, complete with bare wires carrying as much as 1000 volts—threatening at any moment to electrocute the two boys and set modern electronics back several decades.

Hewlett was more interested in the physics of electricity and radio wave propagation. For a physics class he built and demonstrated one of those arc-spitting Tesla coils so loved by movie Mad Scientists. He also built an electric furnace to make carbide for acetylene. "But I never really got into the radio side of it."

Hewlett's aptitude for physics did not translate into good scholarship.

Hewlett is rare among Silicon Valley leaders for having been a poor high school student:

> I didn't really have a very outstanding record in high school. I guess I was lazy or did things I liked and didn't do the things I should have done. I remember I put in an application to Stanford and the principal called my mother in and he asked, "Mrs. Hewlett, your son has applied to go to Stanford. There's nothing in his record that would justify recommending him. Do you know why he wants to go?" And she said, "Well, his father taught there." And he asked, "Was his father Albion Walter Hewlett?" And she said, "Yes." And he said, "He was the best student I ever had . . ."
>
> And on that basis I got recommended.

During Packard's youth in Pueblo, his father often hinted that he would like young David to follow him into law. "I never had any interest at all in doing that and no inclination. And likewise, my father had very little mechanical ability or technical interest."

But Packard's parents were supportive of his interests and his father in particular had great hopes that Dave would pursue athletics, an area in which his son seemed particularly gifted. Young David, on the other hand, though he lettered in football, track and basketball in high school, seemed to find sports more an entertaining sidelight.

(It is interesting to note that after a half century of partnership and friendship, both men seem to know little about each other's early years. For example, Hewlett had always been under the impression that Packard had gone to Stanford on an athletic scholarship. In reality, Packard's father, who had been struggling to keep his law practice alive in the teeth of the Depression, had fortuitously (at least for *his* family) been named referee in a bankruptcy case and had made enough money in fees to help his son pay the astronomical Stanford tuition of $114 per quarter.)

Despite his less than enthusiastic attitude about sports, Packard did go out for freshman football—as did Bill Hewlett. Though they met, no real friendship was formed. Hewlett was cut, Packard made the team. Packard also went out for track—broad jump, high jump, high hurdles, low hurdles, discus and shotput—and in the annual school "Little Big Meet," set a record for most total points. He proceeded to break the coach's heart by deciding not to continue with track: "I had concluded when I decided to come to Stanford that I was not going to concentrate on athletics."

It wasn't until their junior year that Hewlett and Packard became friends. The catalyst was Ed Porter, the exposed-wire ham radio nut. A common interest in the outdoors made the two fast friends and they went on numerous fishing, hiking and skiing trips together. (The two of them own a ten-thousand-acre ranch that stretches for miles along the crest of the Diablo Mountains that run south of Silicon Valley—the last great northern California rancho.)

The good times ended with graduation. Says Hewlett, " 'Thirty-four was not a banner year for being employed . . . I thought I wanted to go on and get some more graduate work because I heard about this guy Terman who had a pretty good course in radio engineering. So I stayed on . . .".

Packard had already taken Terman's graduate radio course in his senior year. In it he had met Barney Oliver (later HP vice-president of research), a young junior transfer from Cal Tech who had been allowed to take the course on condition he passed the first exam. Oliver earned the highest score in class not only on that exam but on every other one that year.

After graduating Phi Beta Kappa, Packard took a job for young engineering graduates at General Electric in Schenectady, New York, where he worked first on military two-way radios, then on vacuum tubes.

Hewlett spent a year in graduate school at Stanford, then went to Cambridge for a master's degree at MIT. During that year he often would catch the train ("that shake, rattle and roll operation") to visit Packard. Packard was living in a rented house with three other bachelors—including John Fluke, who would become an electronics tycoon —and an atticful of electronic equipment. Most of the junk came from GE's building 97, a repository of defective equipment available to employees at a nominal fee. This attic laboratory manned by the young tinkerers posed a threat to the entire neighborhood. Recalls Packard, "We had so much power in [one] transmitter that when you pressed the key, the lights in the whole house would light up, whether they were turned on or not."

Hewlett graduated from MIT in 1936 and found he had only one job offer, at Jensen Speaker in Chicago. However, Fred Terman, knowing of Hewlett's predicament, found a doctor who needed an electroencephalograph built and landed the contract for him.

Packard meanwhile got married. He had met his future wife, Lucille Salter, a San Francisco woman, at Stanford. They were married in Schenectady in April. By August, Terman had found a fellowship for Packard at Stanford and the newlyweds came home. The fellowship was for research on a theory for a new tube developed by one of the brilliant young Varian brothers in the Physics Department.

While Packard worked on tubes and Hewlett on brain monitors, they both took some more courses from Terman at Stanford. In 1927, Harold S. Black of Bell Labs in New York had developed a theory for a new characteristic called negative feedback and developed an amplifier that made use of this discovery. But the invention didn't stoke the imaginations of electrical engineers for nearly a decade, and only then after the theory had been explicated in a number of technical articles.

However, one scientist was excited by the negative feedback principle —Fred Terman—and in his inimitable manner he passed this excitement on to his students. Says Hewlett, "Fred was greatly intrigued with [negative feedback] and really fired up the class on everything that could be done with this thing."

"Fred Terman made a very great contribution then," adds Packard, "because that article by Black was fairly sophisticated and Fred had a great ability to simplify those equations and make them easy to work with. I remember he wrote an article about negative feedback in which he had some of those equations simplified so that even I could understand it . . ."

The moment Packard returned to Palo Alto, he and Hewlett had made plans to start a company—and Hewlett's growing expertise in negative feedback would be the key. Hewlett had found Packard and his new bride a house (and a place for himself nearby) with a garage large enough to serve as a shop. Packard quickly filled the place with the equipment he had brought back from Schenectady.

The two men scratched about for work. No project was too outrageous. Buddy Ed Porter, working on air conditioning contracts in Sacramento, hired Hewlett and Packard to build control equipment for his constructions. A local bowling alley contracted the young men to develop lane signalling equipment. T. I. Moseley, one of the industry's first promoter-entrepreneurs (he founded Dalmo-Victor), decided to go into the harmonica-manufacturing business after he concluded that Nazi Germany, the world's primary source of harmonicas, would soon stop supplying its predominantly Jewish American harmonica retailers.

Moseley hired Hewlett and Packard to design an automatic harmonica tuner.

Lick Observatory (whose silver domes still gleam atop the tallest mountain overlooking Santa Clara Valley) contracted with Hewlett and Packard for a synchronous motor drive for its large telescope. Moseley also wanted the two young engineers to design for him an electrical exercise machine that would do all the work for the exerciser—an idea now once again in vogue.

The contracts were still so far between that Hewlett and Packard didn't even bother to incorporate. Nevertheless, by the end of 1938 everything was in place: the garage was fully equipped, Packard had learned something about business from his Schenectady job as well as on the recent contracts and Hewlett was using negative feedback in the design of a new product called an audio oscillator. Nineteen thirty-nine would be the first landmark year in the history of Silicon Valley.

The year kicked off with the signing of a partnership agreement between the two men. Recalls Packard, "I don't remember exactly the nature of the partnership agreement, and our financing as I recall was rather informal. I remember that [Hewlett was] in a position to advance some money for some components and things and then Lu of course was working and provided support for me, but somehow we had enough money to keep going."

Both men had great hopes for Hewlett's new audio oscillator, a device to produce controllable and accurate electrical signals at a predetermined frequency.

These hopes were confirmed when Harold Buttner, ITT vice-president for research and development, came to look at the first HP product. Buttner pronounced it a winner and offered the two young men five hundred dollars for the foreign patent rights as well as help in getting a U.S. patent. With that deal, the new garage-headquartered firm nearly doubled its capital assets.

With an apparently viable product in their hands, Hewlett and Packard now had to make some serious marketing decisions. For example, how should they designate the product? They decided to call it the 300A in hopes of appearing established. Pricing was equally arbitrary. They concluded it should be about fifty dollars and settled on $54.40 because it reminded them of "54-40 or Fight!"

Packard: We found out that we really hadn't understood the economics very well and we raised the price again. And fortunately, I think we very quickly learned that we could raise the price [if] it was a good value and that was a lesson that was very important because it made it possible for us to finance the company as we went along.

(The model 300A was the first and probably the last underpriced HP product.)

With the help of a small advertisement in a budding new trade magazine called *Electronics,* orders began to flow into the struggling firm.

Hewlett and Packard gained the services of Norm Neely, an electronics distributor in Southern California. Neely was a superb marketing man. In search of sales, he'd even made himself part of the Radio Engineers Club, a local group of engineers from the radio, phonograph and motion picture industries. He invited Hewlett down to give a formal presentation on the HP 300A. Says Hewlett, "I remember going down to some meeting of this Engineers Club, or whatever it was called, and some guy got up and gave me a very flowery introduction . . . that he'd known me for years and 'Now I'd like to introduce my friend *Bill Packard!*' "

One of the attendees, an old friend of Neely, was Bud Hawkins, another Stanford grad and chief sound engineer at Walt Disney Studios. He was in the midst of preparing a sound track for the new movie *Fantasia* and trying to figure out how to meet Disney's plan to have (in the "Flight of the Bumblebee" sequence) the sound of a bee come out of the screen and fly around the theater and return.

Hawkins was impressed by the 300A and contracted HP to produce seven of them with some slight modifications—the 300B—at a price of $71.50 apiece.

By the end of 1939, HP had total sales of $5,369, with profits of $1,653 (typically HP: even the first year showed 25 percent profits), $500 in cash on hand and no liabilities. However, a sizable portion of these revenues were still coming from custom projects. It was Neely who convinced Hewlett and Packard that they should focus on their sole mass producible product, the audio oscillator, and begin refining it as well as developing a family of related products.

Business was looking so good that by the spring of 1940, Hewlett-Packard moved to a small building a few blocks away, which offered an office in the front and a workshop in the back. "I remember at the time thinking that was a pretty good-sized building by comparison to the garage," says Packard (the building is now the company paint shed).

Nevertheless, the setting was still pretty primitive. During the winter rains, water would flood down Page Mill Road and the two founders would have to take off their shoes and roll up their trousers and go out and lay sandbags in front of the door.

The painted panels for the new HP instruments were still baked in Lu Packard's oven. Finally, the combination of increased production and Lu's desire to get her kitchen back led Hewlett and Packard to construct their own oven. They used an old refrigerator unit for its insulating capabilities. Unfortunately, the insulation was flammable kapok and late one night it caught fire. Luckily, one of the lonely travelers along El Camino Real saw the flames and called the fire department.

Orders continued to pour in and Hewlett and Packard responded by adding production capacity and hiring employees. Unfortunately, some of the customers didn't pay and more than once, in the face of a dwindling bank balance, Harold Buttner of ITT came through with a check to help the young men meet their payroll.

Other, nonmarket forces were at work in the world. In the spring of 1941, Hewlett was called up by his Army reserve unit. In typical snafu fashion, he was assigned to aviation ordnance. A quick letter to the right person got him reassigned to the Army Signal Corps Laboratory. He returned to the company in September.

The company was still growing, adding parts of nearby buildings, as well as anecdotes for the historians. There was the day Hewlett started up a drill press with the chuck key still in it—sending it rocketing past Hewlett's head and through a nearby windowpane. Or, in trying to obtain some privacy and security from gawking passersby, the company decided to paint its big front windows black—only to have them absorb so much heat from the afternoon sun that they all cracked.

By the end of 1941 and Pearl Harbor, HP was a one-hundred-thousand-dollar-a-year company with seventeen employees.

The war brought two important changes. First, Hewlett was called up in February 1942 for the duration. In 1943, he stopped by HP on his way out to the Pacific to study Signal Corp equipment in action. Upon his return, he joined the new development division of the War Department's special staff, where he made a number of military and corporate contacts that would be of great use in the postwar years.

On V-J Day, Hewlett was in the Pacific on another equipment tour. He was then assigned to an intelligence team "to go into Japan before they could destroy technical evidence and try to find out what they'd been doing." This experience with Japanese culture would be important in the early 1960s; HP became one of the first American firms to operate a wholly owned subsidiary in Japan. During Christmas 1945, Hewlett returned to Palo Alto to find himself the vice-president of a multi-million-dollar company.

World War II was the first high-technology war, the first to see the pervasive use of electronics. As a maker of electronic instruments to test the performance of electronic systems, HP was in a perfect position to take advantage of the sudden boom in radio, radar, sonar and nautical and aviation instrumentation. HP oscillators and voltmeters were used on assembly lines for the production of proximity fuses. The firm's microwave products and oscilloscopes were used in a radar-jamming system.

The task of building the company up to meet this burst of demand fell upon Packard. Hiring was fast; sometimes the only qualification for employment was a manual-dexterity test of tightening down a bolt in less than a specified period of time. Packard faced other problems too. A representative from the renegotiations board accused HP of making too much profit. Packard protested that all the profits were being plowed back into production and he was only taking out a tiny salary for himself. Nevertheless, HP had to pay back a small amount, and throughout the rest of the war, on top of an ever present pressure to produce, Packard annually had to perform a fiscal song and dance before a renegotiation board.

It is interesting to speculate just how much Hewlett and Packard's bad experiences with the government during the Second World War led to their subsequent behavior regarding government contracts. In his position at Defense, Packard came out against the government bail-out of ailing Lockheed. A few years later, Hewlett, tired of dealing with government paperwork and red tape, stunned the business community by announcing that henceforth HP would no longer accept custom government contracts. If the United States Government wanted HP parts, it would have to buy them off the shelf, just like the corner electronics store.

And there might have been another reason for Hewlett's desire to end his firm's dependence upon the military. By the end of the Second World War, HP was a $2-million company, with two hundred employees. But the end of the war brought a slump in demand—and for the only time in its history, HP laid off employees. More than a hundred of them. The founders would have cut even further, but the two men felt that they needed at least eighty to prepare for any future turnaround.

Further, in that eighty, Bill and Dave believed they had a very strong team.

It was one of HP's most difficult periods. Says Packard, "It was a tough dip. But we kept going even so . . . I recall being very worried at that time about the future. So we designed [the newest HP building] so it would be a general-purpose building. I remember thinking if we can't keep the company together we can at least lease it out to a supermarket or something."

By 1950, the firm was back up to two hundred employees.

By the end of the 1940s, Hewlett and Packard had finished their apprenticeship as businessmen. They were now the chief executives of a multimillion-dollar corporation (the firm had gone public in 1957) with several hundred employees. They were good executives, too. In time, Hewlett and Packard would be called the finest managers in American business.

A corporate philosophy was being forged, arising out of a combination of the firm's large percentage of extremely well educated employees, the innovative nature of the industry, rapid growth, and most of all the personalities of Hewlett and Packard. Called "the HP Way" in the breathless style of personnel managers, it was indeed a new type of corporate culture, an institutional morality never seen before in a large firm.

The HP Way included an intense orientation toward employees ranging from the most complete employee benefits program anywhere available to an extraordinary trust in the individual's own motivation to work. HP offered almost perfect job security. The firm never again had a layoff. In the height of the 1974 crunch, when Silicon Valley was bleeding workers from almost every lobby, HP went to a four-day workweek. The lesson wasn't lost on other Silicon Valley firms: in 1982, during an even larger recession, those firms imitated the HP Way.

It was a perennial joke among HP employees that the only way to get fired from the company was to kill one's boss—and then the company would probably give you a second chance. Even incompetents and malcontents were not let go—a position incomprehensible to many outside observers. Rather, these individuals were asked to look for work elsewhere—but if they still chose not to go, a lower-level position was always found for them where they could do no harm.

There were little touches too. From the earliest days of the company, all HP employees with a year of service were eligible for profit sharing. Before the company grew too big, Hewlett and Packard would hand out the checks themselves at the company Christmas party. Even when employment reached the tens of thousands, Hewlett and Packard made a point of meeting everyone. Every department had free coffee and doughnuts in the morning (typically Californian, in the 1970s, fruit was added), beer busts were every Friday, the company cafeterias were the best in town, stock options were offered to everyone, scholarships were available for employees' children and a large park was acquired in the nearby Santa Cruz mountains for employee use. In a precedent-setting (though, looking back, some would say regrettable) move, HP stopped building offices, replacing them with shoulder-high dividers spread mazelike through vast rooms—the idea being equality of all employees from top executives all the way down to the newest clerks.

The HP corporate structure was also innovative. By the mid-fifties, Hewlett and Packard had split the firm into four divisions—audio, microwave, counters and oscilloscopes—each with its own marketing, research and manufacturing staffs, as well as profit responsibility. The company also had those functions at the corporate level, most notably R & D under their brilliant classmate Barney Oliver, which conducted the firm's advanced theoretical and applied research.

A number of support functions—sales, publicity, advertising, etc.—were handled by outside contractors. As HP grew, and in keeping with its attitude of growing from within and maintaining established relationships, most of these private businessmen were brought into the firm to direct the same operations.

Throughout the 1950s, HP grew an astounding 50 percent to 100 percent per year. Hewlett and Packard, who weren't sure they could manage a company with more than two hundred employees, found themselves with a payroll of fifteen hundred. Yet the firm was still running smoothly. Hewlett and Packard realized that there was something in the way they had organized the management of the company that had enabled HP to climb right past the traditional growth plateaus. Hewlett: "We had the idea that really, if our managers knew what were the objectives of the company that in a sense they would be better able to make good decisions throughout the company than either [Packard] or I would sitting with all our wisdom on top . . . this kind of the forerunner of what's popularly known as management by objective. We'd never heard of it, but that was kind of the undergirding factor . . ."

Adds Packard: ". . . I believe it's very important that if people have some part in making decisions that they're going to be involved with, they're going to be much more effective in implementing those decisions."

These corporate objectives, codified in the late fifties, were purposely nebulous so as not to restrict the increasingly precise "subobjectives" that developed from them down to each level of the corporate hierarchy. With a few changes, those objectives stand today:

1. *Profit:* To achieve sufficient profit to finance our company growth and to provide the resources we need to achieve our other corporate objectives.

2. *Customers:* To provide products and services of the highest quality and the greatest possible value to our customers, thereby gaining and holding their respect and loyalty.

3. *Fields of Interest:* To build on our strengths in the company's traditional fields of interest and to enter new fields only when it is consistent with the basic purpose of our business and when we can assure ourselves of making a needed and profitable contribution to the field.

4. *Growth:* To let our growth be limited only by our profits and our ability to develop and produce innovative products that satisfy real customer needs.

5. *Our People:* To help HP people share in the company's success which they make possible, to provide job security based on their performance, to insure them a safe and pleasant work environment, to recognize their individual achievements and help them gain a sense of satisfaction and accomplishment from their work.

6. *Management:* To foster initiative and creativity by allowing the individual great freedom of action in attaining well-defined objectives.

7. *Citizenship:* To honor our obligations to society by being an economic, intellectual and social asset to each nation and each community in which we operate.

Hand in hand with management by objective was a leadership style that in time was amusingly nicknamed "management by walking around" by HP employees. Management by objective (and for that matter, the HP Way) could not function with a hierarchy of intrusive managers. Management by walking around was important in what its adherents *weren't* doing: telling subordinates what to do, second-guessing them and breathing down their necks. Instead, management was *there;* keeping activities within the general objectives; offering advice when asked or even advocating for the employee against the company bureaucracy. Once or twice each year managers would meet with their employees for a performance review in which actual achievement was compared with the initial objectives.

In time, some if not all of these programs would be adopted by other Silicon Valley firms as they forever imitated HP in hopes of capturing some of its singular success. But few companies are courageous enough to step beyond the window dressing to the heart of the HP Way: a complete trust in and respect for every employee. Without that, the par courses and swimming pools and softball teams were just bread and circuses, an employee-relations tool that would be taken away as easily as it was given—as employees discovered to their dismay every time Silicon Valley fell into a recession.

What made Hewlett and Packard great managers was their appreciation of the fact that the quality of an employee's work was a direct function of the company's trust. For that reason, they were forever pushing authority and responsibility for decision-making as far down the corporate hierarchy as it would go, and managers were expected to do the same. Empire-building and self-aggrandizement were the only cardinal sins. The result of all this diligence was an intense feeling of family among HP employees. Attempts at unionization were quickly rebuffed, even though Hewlett announced he would help negotiate a solid contract if the employees wanted it. Researchers in the early 1970s, preparing a profile of the average HP employee, found him to be a strong family person, tending toward a long marriage, planning to stay with HP until retirement and active in church and community activities—the perfect opposite, the researchers found, of the typical Silicon Valley middle manager.

It is no wonder then that HP has had a perpetual waiting list of employment applicants. In 1983, syndicated columnist Milton Moskowitz would write: "If you work for Hewlett-Packard—and 67,000 people do—you could be excused these days for going around with a swelled head. This California electronics company has won so many accolades in recent years that it may now lay claim to the title, 'Best Company in America.' "

Moskowitz was inspired to write this comment after the January 1983 issue of *Fortune* magazine reported on a survey of six thousand executives who "were asked to rate companies on eight different factors, including financial soundness, quality of management, community responsibility and innovativeness. HP, Moskowitz noted, "ended up in a virtual dead-heat with IBM as the most admired company in the land."

A number of legends have arisen about Hewlett and Packard's management style. As years pass, more and more of them are apocryphal. But all are positive, even worshipful, investing the two men with superhuman integrity, managerial skills and wisdom. In light of what Silicon Valley was to become, even the true stories seem hard to believe. Moskowitz tells one: "The story goes that during World War II the company had an opportunity to land an important military contract. To do so, it would have to bring in 12 new employees. Co-founder William Hewlett reportedly asked the manager: 'With the contracts finished, will we have work for those 12 people?' The manager said, 'No.' Hewlett said, 'Don't take the contract.' "

Dr. Lester Hogan, former president of Fairchild and Motorola, has another "Bill and Dave" story:

> Jack N——— left Sylvania in 1956 with three other engineers and founded a company that was very successful. He left the company in 1960, subsequently sold the stock; don't know how much he made, but he made a few million. He went to Dave Packard in 1960 and convinced Dave that he [Packard] had to be in the semiconductor business; integrated circuits had just been introduced, but obviously they were going to get bigger and more complex and, be it ten years or twenty years away, eventually you would not be able to build a unique state-of-the-art piece of equipment unless you had people who could design and even build unique chips. That's because the chip finally becomes the whole thing: you just put a box with some buttons on it around the chip and that's it.

> Dave had enough foresight to recognize this. He was impressed with Jack and he made him president of a new venture called Hewlett-Packard Associates, in which Hewlett-Packard owned like 50 percent and Jack and the principals he was going to attract to the firm would also own roughly 50 percent. Hewlett-Packard had an option to buy 100 percent—the other 50 percent—five years later and the contract stated that the price would be based upon the sales of Hewlett-Packard Associates as well as the profits. It would also be based on the contributions that Hewlett-Packard Associates made to the rest of HP by building unique products that made the company's equipment substantially better than competitors'.

Now that last is the subjective part of the contract, so when you come to the day of establishing the price, it gets hazy.

So [five years later], on a Friday night, Dave Packard called in the principals and said, "I guess you fellows know Monday morning I can buy you out. I have an option to buy and I'm going to exercise that option. I want you fellows to go home over the weekend and figure out what you think a fair price is."

Well, they not only did that, they had a forty-page flip-chart presentation to justify the price. And the flip-chart presentation consisted of: "Here is the lowest possible price you can offer, which gives us no credit for contributions . . . Now what the highest is is this, if you were very generous and gave us all kinds of credit for all these immeasurable contributions. We feel though that this is a top-level price and we think that it is probably too greedy. We think that some place in between these two would be proper."

As with all things like this you end up with an average and say that's fair.

So they walked into Dave Packard's office on Monday morning with this forty-page flip-chart presentation and he saw that it was awful thick and he said, "Hey, what's this?" And they said, "This is our presentation." And Packard said, "What do you need a presentation for? I just need a price, you know?"

"Well, this is to justify the price."

"Ohhhhh, I see," said Packard. "But look, I don't want to have to listen to this whole presentation. How's this? let me make my offer, and if you don't like it, I'll listen."

Then he offered them 20 percent *above* their high-ball price!

To meet one of these gentlemen in his own milieu, the halls of HP, away from the hubbub of politicians or boardrooms or honorary-award ceremonies, was to apprehend how these two men could build the best company in America. A meeting with Bill Hewlett and Dave Packard often came at the end of one of the periodic, but unscheduled, breaks in the day in which the firm's top executives (as well as twenty-five thousand other employees in forty nations at that time) would stand around the coffeepot and trays of doughnuts and fruit and swap gossip or jokes or even discuss business matters. Hewlett's handshake was small and firm, Packard's huge and gentle.

Incredibly tall, and well over two hundred pounds, with silver hair, and the softened features of an old Stanford varsity football player, Packard even at sixty was a fairly monumental sight, the impact mitigated only slightly by startlingly friendly, hound-dog eyes. Packard's huge hand didn't grasp yours, it engulfed it, giving the disconcerting feeling that he had grabbed your entire forearm and with the first shake would all but lift you off the ground.

Packard's office (his and Hewlett's were among the few private offices in the company; even division general managers often had little more than cubicles), though large, had none of the gentility or opulence one expected from the office of a captain of industry. If anything, it was a little shabby—an old desk, couch, coffee table, some bookshelves. Any hint of power remained precisely that, just a few mementos here and there. The only ostentatious display was Packard's Defense Department flag, neatly folded and mounted underneath the glass top of the coffee table like some Midwesterner's loving display of the children's vacation photos. Without the flag, after a cursory glance a stranger might have guessed that this was the office of the president of a medium-sized appliance company in Des Moines or a textile manufacturer in Raleigh.

(One nervous young employee, meeting Packard for the first time, ingenuously complimented Packard on his "magnificent" office. Packard smiled, pointed to the cracked floor tile at their feet, saying, "Well, I don't know about that. Even the linoleum is starting to buckle. I was thinking about having it fixed, but"—he winked—"I figure I won't be around here much longer anyway.")

All the talk about vast wealth, as well as their great international reputation, was a perpetual source of irritation to Hewlett and Packard. Packard resented being listed among the three or four richest men in America. Once a reporter from *Time* arranged to fly out and interview Hewlett. Beforehand she was warned by a company PR man that while she could ask about anything, it would be best to not discuss Hewlett's wealth. At the interview, Hewlett was extremely gracious, helping the woman get her tape recorder to work. But when the first question was, inevitably, "Tell me, Mr. Hewlett, how does it feel to be one of the richest men in the country?" Hewlett smiled, clicked off the tape recorder, said, "Thank you very much," and escorted the poor reporter out.

Part of this Calvinist distaste for flaunted wealth was that, unlike all of the other Silicon Valley tycoons, Bill and Dave were the originals. Every entrepreneur after them would say, "I want to be as successful as Bill and Dave." As the trend setters, Hewlett and Packard were in the enviable position of never having to compete with Bill 'n' Dave. They were archetypes upon whom their own myth rested with feather weight. As Page Mill Road, the central artery of the Stanford Industrial Park, began to fill up with an increasing number of the Rolls-Royces, Mercedeses and Porsches of the nouveau riche, HP had to fight to get Packard to give up his old Olds Toronado. Hewlett played penny ante poker and set up races between himself and his top executives to see who could first assemble from pieces the newest company products. (Hewlett, the sleeves rolled up in his inevitable white shirt, would attack the assembly challenge with great relish, cajoling his fellow competitors and gleeful when he had beaten some youngster.)

But Hewlett and Packard weren't paragons. Hewlett could be irascible, particularly when a manager didn't have a ready and precise answer. Packard was notoriously cranky in the morning and smart executives stayed out of his warpath. Both were of the old school regarding women in the workplace. When they retired from line positions in 1981, HP did not have a female manager anywhere near executive row (neither did most of Silicon Valley).

By the 1970s, when Hewlett and Packard entered their sixties, there was a growing feeling the two men had lost some of their gutsy innovativeness. As former HPer John Couch recounted in early 1983 after he led his new employer, Apple, in the development of the Lisa computer, "If I had asked Bill Hewlett to spend $30 million and let me take thirty guys into the Santa Cruz mountains to design a similar product, Hewlett would have said, 'What are you smoking?' " Further, the two men's staunch political conservatism set them at odds with many in the younger generations of Valley entrepreneurs.

Defenders of Hewlett and Packard in their final working years can counter that the 1970s were among the most dynamic and successful in HP's history, most notably in the creation of a new $1-billion computer division and the introduction of the world's first programmable calculator—the genesis of the personal computer revolution. Time has also shown that Couch and Apple could have used a little more of Hewlett's prudence (ironically, HP employee Steven Wozniak sold his HP calculator to raise the money to start Apple in 1977).

A more realistic explanation of HP's faltering steps throughout the sixties and seventies was that the firm was having to grope its way through unknown territory. As the first billion-dollar modern high-tech firm, it had no maps, no trails to follow. Many outsiders even questioned whether the HP Way, which worked well with fifty employees, would still function with twenty thousand. After all, even an optimist had to admit that the HP Way was a very nice idea, but utterly impossible to realize in the real world of clashing egos, naked ambition, greed and lust.

By the sixties, HP was beginning to face the special problems of a large firm. The company's first large expansion, to Loveland, Colorado, created bitterness among townspeople that survives to this day. It seems that some of the lonely young bachelor engineers transferred from the high life of California got a little too friendly with some of the farm wives. The move of the calculator division to Oregon cost a number of employees not only before the move but months later, when the rain brought cabin fever to stranded wives and children.

Another ongoing personnel problem for HP was both a mixed blessing and an inevitable by-product of the HP Way. A warm, paternalistic company like HP can be positively unbearable to entrepreneurial personalities. Whether the lost creativity is compensated by the strength that arises from the HP spirit of cooperation can never really be known; but the sum of the sales of Tandem, Apple and other firms founded by ex-HPers would amount to nearly half of HP's sales (and growing).

Increased size also meant the need to target new and larger markets. HP's dedication to producing the premier product in a given market usually meant that product also bore a premium price tag. It was a standing rule in the industry that an HP product inevitably cost 30 percent more than its competition. Peerless quality is all well and good when your customers can afford the best—as most engineers could when paying with their employers' money. But when the customer universe begins to expand beyond engineers to the general public the industrial price-elasticity curves begin to snap.

That's what happened in the mid-seventies to HP's calculator business. HP's magnificent scientific and engineering calculators were the dream of every college student sitting in a laboratory. Kids scraped together the $500 to $700 they needed to buy one just for the prestige it brought among their peers. The HP-65 programmable calculator, the flagship of HP's fleet, became the most stolen item of equipment in labs around the country. A black market in HP calculators even developed.

Recognition of this fad came quickly for the members of HP's Advanced Products Group in Cupertino, as young and entrepreneurial as any new products group HP has ever known. Advertising and sales strategies quickly shifted to pursue this apparently enormous new market. But HP, with its usual insularity and aloofness, did not seem to recognize that by going after college kids it had moved from industrial to consumer sales.

Electronics giant Texas Instruments knew the score. Fresh from demolishing an entire sector of Silicon Valley in the low-end calculator wars of 1973–74, TI turned its guns on the high-end market and HP.

TI's strategy was simple. It built lower-quality imitations of the HP calculators and sold them at half the price. The impact upon HP's pocket calculator division (caught in the midst of a move to Oregon) was devastating. The irony was that students and engineers and scientists still, in their heart of hearts, wanted HP calculators; they still wanted the best, they still wanted calculators that, as HP's did, survived falling off the back of speeding motorcycles, being dropped into a bucket of molten lead and being buried in snow for a winter—but they could *afford* the Texas Instruments calculators. Sure the TI machines were kind of shoddy—but who cares? the market said, the TI calculators are *half* the price.

HP made other mistakes. It entered the minicomputer market late (1968) because it tardily recognized that the product could have scientific as well as business applications—thus losing an edge to IBM and Digital Equipment which HP has never recouped. When HP decided to enter the business minicomputer market (1970), again belatedly, it suffered the horrible embarrassment, given its reputation, of having to reintroduce its first product (the HP 3000) three times before it finally worked.

HP's most humiliating moment came in the mid-1970s with the debacle of the HP-01 wrist calculator. In this one product came together all of HP's weaknesses: its misunderstanding of the consumer market, its obsession with quality and its tendency to build products for the engineering challenge rather than for customers.

The HP-01 was a magnificent achievement. It was more than just a calculator and a watch combined, it was a "time calculator." The HP-01 was beautifully engineered and indestructible enough to put John Cameron Swayze to shame. It also cost $795 and was so massive that shirt cuffs had to be retailored to wear one. Not surprisingly, hardly anyone bought the HP-01.

HP not only survived these mistakes but prospered. There was a sense that while the company might never produce a market monster like Pong or Apple II, it also would never fail horribly, either. Simply, HP was the best. It would continue to grow year after year; solid, dependable and usually quite dull. HP would never have scandals or big layoffs or disastrous quarters—nor would it ever be particularly exciting. Just a quiet family down the street raising its kids right and keeping the lawn mowed.

Looking back, despite the doubts, it is amazing how close HP came to achieving the HP Way. Even in the 1960s and 1970s, as Silicon Valley was raging in the plain below, HP somehow remained an oasis of sanity and truth. "The Country Club" was a nickname used to describe the place. "Sanctuary" might have been more appropriate. In bad times and good, HP had a perpetual waiting list of job applicants. Some were tired Valley veterans looking for a safe haven to lick their wounds, a place where they could eat their morning doughnut and not worry about the next round of layoffs or the next corporate power play. Others were of personalities unsuited from the beginning for the high-rolling Valley life and simply biding time until they came "home" to HP.

It was a remarkable company Bill and Dave had built. Here, at the historical heart of supercharged, double-dealing, wildcatting, card-sharping Silicon Valley was a company of Little League coaches and den mothers, Mormons and Republicans. Even more extraordinary, this low-keyed, often self-effacing company continued year after year growing at a breathtaking pace—without the usual sideshow of table-pounding executives, trade secret thievery, employee-raiding and price-slashing. Inside the beautiful buildings and quiet offices, things were being accomplished—almost *ex nihilo* for all the visible work being done. Bill and Dave had found a key to greatness, and the rest of Silicon Valley looked on in awe.

* * *

As retirement time approached, it became apparent that Hewlett and Packard had foreseen the difficult transition and had been carefully grooming a young man up through the corporate ranks. John Young, forty-six, Stanford graduate and HP employee since 1958, was named executive vice-president and heir apparent in 1974. Handsome and highly intelligent, Young was one of those blessed individuals destined for great things who seem to move through life with an absolute conviction about their own infallibility. Young's confidence was so complete that with utter authority, soon after his promotion to executive V.P., he could sit in the corporate boardroom with his fellow vice-presidents, many twenty years his senior, and put each shoe in turn up against the side of the table and pull up his drooping socks. Young also seemed in the mold of his mentors when he informed Hewlett and Packard that HP would always be their company and his was just a temporary stewardship in their name.

But Young's flaw may be his very flawlessness. The NO TURKEYS sign in his office says much about his personality. Unlike Hewlett and Packard, Young, though he tries, will never be the guy next door—unless you live in Beverly Hills. He lacks Hewlett's commonness and Packard's gentleness. Dave Crockett, a former executive, recalls a visit by Hewlett and Packard in 1973 to the company's computer facility in Cupertino and a tour of the assembly line. The two founders were supposed to have visited the year before but had canceled. The employees, who had hand-painted signs and ties for the two men, had stored them away for a year in anticipation of the next visit. Hewlett and Packard, says Crockett, were visibly pleased with the gifts, warmly thanking the employees and hurriedly stripping off their ties to try the new ones on.

"Young doesn't have that kind of human touch," Crockett says. "But on the other hand," he adds, "Young is imposing, impressive, handsome, and presents an image of confidence to the company—and he's gotten smooth over the years in dealing with key clients. He just looks like what a president's supposed to look like."

As this is written, Bill Hewlett and Dave Packard continue to exert their influence on the company. In an important move in the mid-seventies, after a disastrous triple failure at getting the HP 3000 computer out the door, Hewlett decreed that henceforth HP would never again announce a new product until it was ready to be shipped—a stunning move in the face of Silicon Valley's growing habit of introducing new products sometimes even before they were off the drafting board.

After his first taste of politics in the late sixties, Packard continued to be active in that sphere. He earned the enmity of campus protesters everywhere when he suggested that fellow Stanford alumni should stop supporting the university if it was to become a home for radicalism and criminal behavior. A few years later, a bomb, placed by a local Stanford radical group, did minor damage at one of the HP lab buildings.

By 1977, and Young's accession to the presidency, Packard had become a Brahmin of the American business establishment. Six universities, including the University of California/Berkeley and Notre Dame, had awarded him honorary doctorates. He sat on the boards of Caterpillar Tractor, Standard Oil of California and Boeing (in 1981, keeping on the leading edge of technology, he joined the board of Genetech, a genetic engineering firm). He was also a trustee of the Herbert Hoover Foundation and the American Enterprise Institute, the conservative research institutions. His list of memberships include that nemesis of conspiracy nuts the Trilateral Commission, the Business Roundtable, the U.S.-U.S.S.R. Trade & Economic Council and the White House Science Council, and he is a director of the Wolf Trap Foundation. His membership in the Bohemian Club annually listed Packard's name with U.S. presidents and other world leaders (he was also listed as a member of the Reagan "kitchen cabinet"). His list of awards ran one and a half single-spaced pages, ranging from the local Boy Scout Good Scout award to a gold medal from the National Football Hall of Fame to the Grand Cross of Merit from the Republic of Germany. Packard has also spent millions helping his daughter build a world-class aquarium in Monterey.

Despite a relatively parochial career, Hewlett also gathered a distinguished list of awards and credentials, including honorary degrees from Berkeley, Yale and Notre Dame, among others, and seats on the boards of Chrysler and the Chase Manhattan Bank. Where Packard's activities were political, Hewlett's were in technology, and ironically, given his scholastic record, in education. He was a member of the National Academy of Sciences, a fellow of the American Academy of Arts and Sciences, a trustee of the RAND Corporation and (for eleven years) a trustee of Stanford University. In 1954, Hewlett was president of the Institute of Radio Engineers (now the Institute of Electrical and Electronic Engineers), only the second Westerner to attain that distinction—the first being Fredrick Terman.

The loyalty of Hewlett and Packard to Terman is one of the most moving episodes in the Silicon Valley story. Terman sat on the board of HP for more than forty years, always treated with the respect afforded an admired teacher by his two former students long after all of them had become gray old men. In the late seventies, Hewlett and Packard gave millions to Stanford for the construction of the modernist Fredrick Terman, Jr., building in the Department of Electrical Engineering. Terman, old and infirm, was on hand for the dedication and to hear the glowing speeches from his "boys." When he died in 1982, wire services carried obituaries around the world describing him as father of the electronics revolution. And the classroom building ensured that the old professor's contribution to engineering would continue to future generations.

When the time came Bill Hewlett and Dave Packard left with the same type of quiet dignity with which they had built the most admired firm in America. Riding the range at their ranch or speaking to respectful peers in halls of power, Hewlett and Packard surely know that from the creaky Palo Alto garage they have constructed not just a great company but a standard for quality, decency and professionalism against which every high-technology company must be measured.

Bill Hewlett and Dave Packard proved all the theories; they personified Fred Terman's dream. With irreproachable integrity and infinite belief in their employees—not two of the most common attributes of business leaders—they constructed one of the strongest firms in American business history—innovative but conservative, aggressive but principled. Even the Japanese respect and fear HP and for the most part have stayed out of its market, a fact more telling about Hewlett-Packard's reputation than perhaps any other.

The greatness of Silicon Valley is that its generations of executives took as their role models "Bill and Dave" and struggled—if only at first —to build their companies after the Hewlett-Packard model. And it can be said that the tragedy of Silicon Valley is that almost all of them failed in the attempt, to different degrees falling short of the ideal.

*   *   *

Terman had another dream, and Hewlett and Packard helped him fulfill it. It was a grand vision of an "industrial park"; more like the second word than the first, a vast campuslike setting where business, academic and government interests could come together in a synergistic vision of the future. It was called the Stanford Industrial Park and it covers fifty thousand acres beside the university. When it opened in 1956, one of its first residents was Hewlett-Packard Co., which still maintains its headquarters there. In 1960, when Charles de Gaulle visited California, he asked to see only two places: Disneyland and the Stanford Industrial Park.

Driving through the park, one can admire Terman's vision. It is all there, the smokeless factories of glass and steel nestled in green hills, magnificent homes tucked away in glens, horses grazing in meadows, ancient gnarled oak trees. It is indeed the New Athens, with each company an intellectual Academy, each president a Scientist-King.

But the vision goes no further. And Hewlett and Packard were not destined to be anything more than a remote and forbidding ideal for their successors. The year the Stanford Industrial Park opened, another Stanford graduate came home, a Nobel Prize telegram just a few months away. One need only climb the crest of the single line of hills that marks the southern rim of the park to see the legacy of this other man: the enormous, teeming, concrete mass of Silicon Valley. And the prodigal son, Dr. William Shockley, was to be its first resident.

2

Shockley and the Pirates

Hewlett-Packard wasn't the only electronics company founded in Santa Clara Valley during the 1930s. There was a second important scientific laboratory at Stanford besides Terman's. This one was in physics and was run by Dr. William Webster Hansen.

The star pupils in Hansen's class were two brothers, Sigurd and Russell Varian, children of immigrant parents who'd come over from Ireland in 1903. The Varian brothers were local boys; in fact, they went to grammar school across the street from the home of triode inventor Lee De Forest.

Neither boy was a particularly good student: Sigurd out of indifference, Russell because of a learning disability that kept him perpetually behind in reading and arithmetic. The Varians lived in a small frame house on a quiet Palo Alto back street.

More exactly, an occasionally *unquiet* back street. Mr. Varian was a frustrated poet and playwright who fed his family through odd jobs, such as working as a masseur. He was also an intellectual and a bit of a bohemian and the Varian house was perpetually filled with literati.

The wonder of the Varian brothers was that they could work together at all, so opposite were they in every way. Sigurd, the younger, was handsome, polished, energetic and equipped with a mind adept at working out the fine details of an idea. Russell was huge, with oversized features and spiky hair, so uncoordinated he was dangerous in a small room, a genius at coming up with a new idea, but natively incapable of following that idea through to its logical end. The success of the Varian brothers seems to be a rare case of two individuals so different they match.

In 1914, when Russ was sixteen and Sig thirteen, the Varian family moved to Halcyon, California, a tiny town almost halfway between San Francisco and Los Angeles in the dry coastal mountains. There, Mr. and Mrs. Varian opened a general store and post office. Both young men finished high school at about the same time; Russ by then was twenty-one and only graduated because he learned to memorize what he read during the first slow pass through each assignment.

At this point, the lives and careers of the two brothers diverged for more than a decade. Sigurd became enamored with the romance of the airplane. And he couldn't have picked a better time, as the federal government was all but giving away surplus (and usually deteriorating) World War I aircraft.

As Sigurd himself described it: "Every young fellow who had lain on his back in the tall grass dreaming of flying could now buy a real airplane still in its original crate, with glistening wings—and maybe dry-rotted spars. But who cared about dry rot? In fact, who knew what it was anyhow?"

Sig soon had his own plane. By mid-decade he was running his own flying school. It was a wild period, with Sig and his friends and students jury-rigging their biplanes to keep them in the air in the face of increasing spare-parts shortages. According to Sig Varian, unusual measures were often taken to get the patched-up heaps home—from pounding in nails for added weight on broken propellors to having someone straddle the engine on the flight home squirting flammable fluid into the carburetor.

"We smashed our planes all over the state of California," Sig recalled. "We cracked up in ditches, ran over harrows, flew through fences, and one unlucky pilot ran into a family of hogs. We found out a lot about farming, and the farmers found out a lot about flying—each to his own disgust."

After crashing into wheat fields, what more could a young aeronaut want than to crash into exotic locales? In 1929, Sig signed on with the new Pan American World Airways to fly its new Mexico-to-Central America route.

He stayed with Pan Am on this route for six years, occasionally landing several hundred miles short of the runway in some all but impenetrable jungle. Sig also married the daughter of a British consul in Mexico.

During this same period, brother Russell was cutting his own special path. Against all odds, he was accepted to Stanford in 1919. Russ promptly packed his backpack and hiked the 225 miles to Palo Alto. On his arrival he sent his folks a letter announcing that the trip had cost only ten cents.

By 1927, while his brother was still plowing fields in Halcyon, Russ had earned his master's degree in physics. He had also become fast friends with Bill Hansen, the physics lab director, a machinist's son who had a reputation for both brilliance and an antipathy for rules (he was famous for having passed a German final exam a few years before by memorizing the professor's exams for a number of previous years). Hansen and Russ Varian were as alike as the two brothers were different. The two tall roommates could often be seen striding around the campus in deep technical conversation.

Upon graduation, Russ Varian went to work for an oil company. A year later he joined another Bay Area electronics pioneer, Philo Farnsworth, in San Francisco and spent four years helping in the development of television.

In 1935, Russ Varian returned to Stanford to continue his research in physics. He was now thirty-seven. That year Sigurd returned from Mexico and the two brothers, with baby brother Eric, decided to fulfill a lifelong dream and set up a family laboratory.

The brothers had many ideas for projects, but in the end they settled upon Sigurd's obsession. As a pilot, flying over wild and often dangerous terrain, Sig had developed an understandably deep and abiding love for instrumentation and navigational aids. Later, as the horrors of the Spanish Civil War were explained to him by his consul father-in-law, Sig became haunted by the image of defenseless people under attack by planes shielded in darkness. What kind of technology would enable the people on the ground to fight back? He had written to Russ about his dream during the years they were apart.

With the new family laboratory under way, Russ decided to call on his old roommate, now a tough professor of physics, to see if he had any ideas.

In particular, Russ was interested in the latest developments on Hansen's electromagnetic resonator—named a "rhumbatron" by a graduate student, recalled Hansen, "because the current moved very little at the top and bottom and a great deal around the middle section." Russ thought the rhumbatron might be the key to Sig's device and he invited Hansen down to Halcyon.

The timing was perfect. Hansen was in the midst of taking flying lessons and could assimilate the ideas put forward by master pilot Sig Varian.

The three men agreed that the device Sig had in mind would sweep ultrashort light waves across the sky in an invisible beam, reflecting back an "echo" of any solid object. They also agreed that the vacuum tubes available to produce such high-frequency waves had inefficient power to do the job. Sig suggested that he and his brother go to Stanford and see if they could get university support for their project. Russ was "rather dubious," he would say later, but went along anyway.

Dr. Daniel Webster, head of the Physics Department, was, thankfully, also a flier. He had even built bomb sights in the Great War. Webster was impressed and went to plead the men's case before the university president, Dr. Raymond Wilbur. Despite the Depression, Wilbur agreed to make the Varian brothers research assistants, *without pay*, and gave them one hundred dollars in project expenses in exchange for a cut of whatever came out of the experiments. (The $2 million in royalties Stanford eventually earned from the project was more than an acceptable return on investment.)

These were truly starvation wages, and the project quickly burned up most of the brothers' savings. Russ saved on meals by foraging among the fruit trees on campus.

Helping to propel the research project along were a number of interested graduate students in electronics and physics, among them Bill Hewlett.

Russ Varian and Bill Hansen worked almost around the clock for several months on the theoretical side of the project, talking in their own arcane private language. Russ, as usual, with his "substitute for thinking," made the great inductive leaps of imagination, while Hansen filled in the gaps with coherent mathematics. According to one historian, Hansen had the habit of rocking his chair back and forth on its back legs when he was concentrating on a problem. As a result, he wore two hollows in the wood floor. In the midst of intense research one day, the legs crashed through.

At the beginning of March 1936, the design was complete and Russ and Hansen turned it over to Sig, who immediately went to work, building the prototype from spare parts in the lab, junked pieces from the local dump and low-priced parts from the only electronics retail store in town.

Sigurd's work soon became the subject of great interest around campus. Students and teachers dropped by to watch, among them Fred Terman, who later said, "Unlike his brother, who was rather clumsy with apparatus, Sigurd had unusual design and mechanical sense, and great skill with his hands." It was a craft honed in California barnyards and Central American jungles.

About three months into the construction, Sig was told to abandon the project. Russ and Hansen had come up with a better design—one using two of Hansen's rhumbatrons in a vacuum. Dr. Webster even had a hand in the design, suggesting that the rhumbatrons be shaped like doughnuts (that is, as toruses)—an idea for which he earned a lucrative patent.

Sig set out again. Meanwhile, in a cross-disciplinary manner rarely found in the electronics industry nowadays, Dr. Webster walked over to the university's Classics Department and asked Professor Herman Frankel to come up with a suitably profound name for the new device. Because, as it was explained to him, this new device would emit successive waves of energy, Frankel chose the Greek verb *klystron,* meaning to splash in waves. The Klystron tube it would be.

There was a certain irony here, for Professor Frankel was a German refugee from Nazi persecution, and the device he named, the key component in airborne radar, would play a decisive role in smashing his Third Reich persecutors.

On August 19, 1937, Sig had the prototype Klystron emitting enough microwaves to create some flashes on a detector screen. Two days later, the entire screen was covered by a matrix of flashes. Screaming, "It oscillates!" Sig dragged his partners and everybody else into the lab to see.

The brothers quickly realized that inventing a new electronic device wasn't enough. They also needed to sell it—and fast, because their savings were running out. A prospective customer they thought would be enthusiastic, the United States Navy, was not. However, Sperry Gyroscope in New York came out to see the Klystron and was impressed. An agreement was reached, with the Varian brothers earning a salary, Stanford receiving royalties and Professors Hansen and Webster working on perfecting the Klystron in their spare time.

On January 30, 1939, Stanford publicly announced the Klystron and the story was carried that day throughout the world alongside reports of Hitler's latest speech.

It wasn't until after Pearl Harbor and America's entry into the Second World War that U.S. scientists learned of Britain's research into radar. The British had achieved the same result through a different technology (also invented by an American, A. W. Hall, in 1921) called a magnetron.

Magnetron-equipped radar stations were the godsend Britain needed to gain an edge over the Luftwaffe during the Battle of Britain. However, though they emitted considerable power, they were also very heavy and operated in shortwave. They could not be mounted in aircraft—a fatal weakness when the German bombers shifted to night attacks and the RAF fighters couldn't find them. That's where the Varian Klystron tubes came in: they could be mounted in fighters to enable the pilot to find the enemy as well as the way home through darkness or inclement weather. After the Luftwaffe was stopped, the Varian Klystron was reconfigured for use in the Battle of the North Atlantic, spotting German U-boats as they surfaced at night.

Throughout the war Russ and Sig Varian worked at Sperry Gyroscope in New York. They were joined part time by Hansen, who also worked on war-related projects at MIT—a regimen that finally broke his health. Dr. Terman, the father of Silicon Valley, took leave from Stanford to direct the thousand-person Harvard Radio Research Laboratory. In his most celebrated project there, he helped design a machine to spit out thin slices of aluminum that when dropped like rain in huge quantities would jam German radar—in effect to destroy the effectiveness of the devices whose development he had watched with great interest back at Stanford's physics lab.

Up the peninsula in Redwood City, Charlie Litton shifted the production of his vacuum tube works to make magnetrons. As always, they were the best in the world.

After the war, Russ Varian returned to Stanford's Physics Department, where he helped Hansen and Dr. Felix Bloch research the magnetic properties of atomic nuclei (for which Bloch would receive the Nobel Prize). Russ still dreamed of creating a Varian Bros. company.

In 1948, up the peninsula in San Carlos, Varian Associates was founded. By the early 1950s, Varian was a powerhouse of the electronic instruments business, dominating the markets that weren't owned by Hewlett-Packard. And Sigurd and Russell were accumulating wealth to match Bill and Dave's.

As for Bill Hansen, he had another dream. Despite deteriorating health, he pursued the idea of using magnetron-Klystron technology as tools in the search for basic components of matter. E. O. Lawrence at Berkeley had built a cyclotron, which shot positively charged particles in circles. Hansen believed he had a better way: a *linear* accelerator, a straight tube, that fired negative particles into a target, splintering off subatomic particles. In 1947, he built a working twelve-foot model. But Hansen knew that while magnetrons worked very well in the smaller model, he would need a battery of Klystrons, one after another along the length of the accelerator, to get the type of particle speeds he was aiming for.

But Hansen was dying. By the beginning of 1949, he could only work on his project with the aid of a homemade oxygen mask. By March, he was dead at thirty-nine of "lung failure."

Nevertheless the linear accelerator project continued. Within weeks of Hansen's death, the Stanford research team tested a Klystron ten thousand times as powerful as the one in common use. For seventeen years this team continued to refine the Klystron and build increasingly sophisticated (and lengthy) accelerators. Finally, in 1966, the team, now under Dr. Wolfgang Panofsky, unveiled one of the wonders of the world, the two-mile-long Stanford Linear Accelerator (SLAC), with a perfectly true, ten-thousand-foot firing range for subatomic particles— "the world's largest microscope." Positioned every forty feet were immense Klystrons to give impetus to the tiny "bullets" until they approached the speed of light.

As historian Jane Morgan wrote: "What a rich heritage has been left by these 'three men and a tube'—a tousle-haired inventor, a chair-rocking genius, a daredevil pilot, and their rhumba-dancing electrons in a copper doughnut!"

The Varian brothers had a little more time than their old lab partner. By the mid-1950s, Varian Associates was a multimillion-dollar concern, the world's largest maker of Klystrons, employing more than a thousand people. In 1953, Varian Associates was the first firm to move into Fred Terman's Stanford Industrial Park, just down the hill from HP's future headquarters. It is touching to note, as one drives through the famous industrial center, that Varian's headquarters is located on Hansen Way.

Varian remains a leader in the manufacture of Klystrons, though now it has more important product lines in microwave devices and semiconductor manufacturing equipment. The invisible giant of the Valley, Varian quietly pulls in $900 million in revenues each year and employs fourteen thousand people.

But Sig and Russ Varian weren't around to enjoy their celebrity and enormous wealth. Russell died in 1959 on a cruise near Juneau, Alaska.

In 1961, fittingly, Sigurd was killed in the crash of a plane he was flying in Mexico.

Now, two decades later, in the alphabet soup of high-tech names that are the rage in Silicon Valley, "Varian" seems just another, and to the new generation of Valley residents, the name has lost its historic link with two of the Valley's most appealing characters.

* * *

By the late 1940s, as the Varian brothers were building their company, all of California had begun the great population boom that would deliver it, on the threshold of the 1970s, as the most populous, most unpredictable state in the Union.

The first wave had begun in the 1930s, as Dust Bowl refugees and others dispossessed by the Great Depression came West to pick their grapes of wrath—Mojave, Salinas and San Joaquin fruit—under the endless sun. Others, more prosperous, came in the last gasp of Manifest Destiny in search of freedom, land, health and the Big Score.

But most of this migration was to the southern half of the state, where oranges and Hollywood were irresistible magnets. In the L.A. basin, a sleepy, static old Mexican town quickly became the largest city on the Pacific Coast.

Northern California changed comparatively little during the 1930s. San Francisco, rebuilt after the quake, remained a healthy port, not yet surrendering itself to the lures of tourism. Local boy Joe DiMaggio was making a name for himself in pinstripes back East.

To the southbound traveler from San Francisco, Santa Clara Valley would have seemed little different from the turn of the century. The towns were a little bigger. Palo Alto showed the advantage of being a university town, while San Jose, with its strong central banking district, was turning into a healthy metropolis. An increasing number of retail stores were opening up along El Camino Real, extending in each direction from the little towns—and one could imagine one day, if the Valley continued its constant growth, these business districts merging. At Santa Clara University, the Jesuits still pounded knowledge into thick-skulled young men, and San Jose State was heading toward being one of the largest schools in the state. The Valley had even produced its own pair of movie stars, Los Gatos sisters Joan Fontaine and Olivia de Havilland.

The Valley remained so dominated by San Francisco to the north that as late as 1947 a picture book entitled *San Francisco Bay Cities* offered only three pictures of the peninsula: two of Stanford University and a third showing a pair of beautiful homes and captioned "Attractive homes on the hills of the Peninsula where many San Franciscans live."

But Santa Clara Valley had begun to change. On November 26, 1933, the year Hewlett and Packard were seniors at Stanford, the South Valley underwent its rite of passage, its last communal act and a smudge on the area's history. Brooke Hart, the teenage scion of a wealthy (department stores) family in San Jose, was kidnapped and held for ransom. The kidnappers were paid but tossed the young man, bound and tied, off the Dumbarton railroad bridge, which spanned the bay at Palo Alto. Unfortunately Brooke survived the fall, clinging, bleeding, on a barnacle-covered piling until he was drowned by the tide.

San Jose was outraged. When the kidnappers were arrested, there was a groundswell of anger that legal strictures wouldn't be enough, that a more traditional form of punishment was called for. That night, the same day Brooke Hart's body was discovered, a crowd of ten thousand gathered in the San Jose downtown area. Many were Santa Clara University students, the curfew rule relaxed that evening for the occasion. At eleven o'clock, the crowd fought its way past tear gas and police, stormed the police station, grabbed the two accused kidnappers, stripped them and lynched them in St. James Park.

It was the last great mob lynching in America. San Jose had finally gained national exposure. The public revulsion, government speeches, editorials and even movies that followed the event haunted the Valley for a decade.

The Second World War changed everything. For a few short years, San Francisco, rather than Los Angeles, was the hub of activity on the West Coast. For tens of thousands of GI's, sailors and air crews, San Francisco was the last good drunk, the Golden Gate the last glimpse of the United States before shipping out to action in the Pacific. The emotion of the moment, combined with "Baghdad by the Bay's" own expansive charm, left an indelible image in the minds of many of these veterans, many of them away from home for the first time. After the war, some of these vets, armed with the GI Bill, some back pay, good memories and often a family in tow, pulled onto the improved transcontinental highway system and came West. For the next twenty years, thanks to these newcomers and their Boom Babies, cities such as San Jose and Sunnyvale became the fastest-growing cities in the nation.

One by one the orchards began to fall and foundations were laid for the newest housing development or shopping center. The Bay Area's schools and universities were jammed with middle-aged and married vets, working hard on the educational basis of a professional career. For many of them, after years of living with the awesome machinery and weapons of war, there could be only one curriculum that mattered in the new postwar world: engineering.

And there were jobs waiting for these veterans. Santa Clara Valley's business profile had evolved. The canneries still predominated, but for them the handwriting was on the wall. As local fruit-producing areas dwindled under the onslaught of growing populations, increasing amounts of production were shipped in by railroad from outside the Valley. Even San Jose's big Food Machinery Corp. kept up its wartime business of making tanks and armored personnel carriers.

The war years had a particularly profound effect upon the local high-technology industry. Hewlett-Packard, of course, did very well on defense-related business. So did Charlie Litton's glass shop. Fred Terman came home from the war with his dream of the Stanford Industrial Park, the Varian brothers with the goal of starting their own company.

Other critical events took place. In 1940 in Mountain View, on land in the shadow of the huge and empty hangar that had once housed the doomed Macon dirigible, Moffett Naval Air Station leased property to the young National Advisory Committee for Aeronautics (NACA). This facility, Ames Research Center, with its giant wind tunnels and scores of theoretical scientists, would become, in the post-Sputnik years when NACA became NASA, the home of much of the world's astrophysical research as well as the control center for many of NASA's interplanetary probes.

Two Los Gatos boys, Allan and Malcolm Lockheed, who first received national attention in 1913 flying a homemade hydroplane on San Francisco Bay (the Valley's contribution to aviation is as remarkable as its contribution to electronics), had founded their own aviation company in Southern California in 1932. The war had turned Lockheed Aircraft Corp. into one of the largest firms west of the Mississippi. In 1954, the company, to keep abreast of the changing nature of the industry, and with one eye on the work being done by Von Braun and others at nearby Vandenberg Air Base, formed Lockheed Missile & Space Co., a rather presumptuous name at the time. Two years later, the firm was ready to move the subsidiary. A primary criterion for any prospective home of LMSC was a supportive environment for the continuing educational needs of engineers. Having the prospect of NASA-Ames Research Center next door also helped the decision. So in 1956, at least part of Lockheed Aircraft Corp. came home. The new subsidiary, in its immense headquarters facility by the bay in Sunnyvale, quickly became —and still remains—the Valley's largest employer. At last count, thirty thousand Valley residents worked for Lockheed.

With Lockheed Missile and Space Co., the Valley passed a milestone. The agrarian era was now at an end—a fact driven home every workday as a long line of commuters poured down Mathilda Avenue toward the Lockheed plant. Henceforth, Santa Clara Valley would be an industrial region, a center of technological innovation. Until 1970, when total employment of the local electronics industry (minus HP) finally surpassed it, and the firm permanently tarnished its image with a series of shattering and callous mass layoffs, Lockheed would be the most important industrial force in the South Bay.

The complex academic-industrial matrix of Stanford/Santa Clara U./San Jose State/HP/Ames and eventually Lockheed, combined with the winning climate and the calm California way of life, began to bring Santa Clara County to the attention of major national technology firms. By the mid-1950s, no responsible large company could contemplate opening a new off-site research facility without giving the Valley serious thought. So, throughout the 1950s, the giants of the tube era of electronics came to the South Bay. General Electric built its nuclear power plant division in San Jose. Westinghouse built heavy equipment for the Navy in a big redwood building along the tracks in Sunnyvale across from the Del Monte cannery. Just to the North in Mountain View, Sylvania Electric built a plant next door to what was then the sole nationally famous company in the area, the Ferry-Morse Seed Company, purveyors of colorful little vegetable seed packets found in every hardware store and five-and-dime in America. On the northern end of Mountain View, just up from Moffett Field and Ames, Ford Philco built a research plant.

But in terms of its ultimate impact on the area—at least in the quality of people it lost to the still unborn Silicon Valley—the most important new corporate arrival was IBM, which opened a research lab in downtown San Jose to design the first computer disk memory. After a few years this operation would move to the southern terminus of the Valley, almost in Gilroy, at the entrance to the infamous patch of Freeway 101 called "Blood Alley." The unpleasant moniker came from the fact that along this stretch of narrow highway, cars and trucks would drift across the undivided road and disintegrate in horrendous head-on collisions.

(Until the late seventies, when road improvements were forced by pressure from the Valley to expand, Blood Alley remained the choke point at the base of Silicon Valley and the expansive grounds of IBM was the physical and mental limit of Valley life.)

But the arrival of industry big-leaguers wasn't all that was occurring in Santa Clara Valley and up the peninsula during the 1950s. By the end of the decade, a fifteen-year-old firm located in San Carlos, ten miles north of Stanford, would become one of the brightest stars in American industry, burning with such incandescence that it soon had to flicker and die.

Ampex Corporation was founded in 1944 by a remarkable man named Alexander M. Poniatoff. At the time, Poniatoff was working as an engineer at T. I. Moseley's Dalmo Victor Co. Dalmo Victor had obtained a government contract to manufacture a new type of radar antenna for fighter aircraft. The firm quickly encountered an impediment to manufacturing: the device required a special motor and generator, neither of which had ever before been built. Poniatoff volunteered for the job and, with five other employees, formed a spin-off firm located among the dust and pipes and bare walls of the attic of the Dalmo Victor building in San Carlos (a former furniture warehouse). The name Ampex came from Poniatoff's initials, with an *ex* thrown in for excellence. Clever at the time, this unfortunately became the precedent for the endless numbers of *ex* firms that now dot the American business landscape.

Poniatoff was not of the common run of engineers. His powerful mind was matched by a steel will. In fact, he was a true hero. Born in Russia, he had seen service against the Germans as a navy pilot. Following Brest-Litovsk and the fall of Kerensky, Poniatoff fought as a White Russian Army pilot during the civil war.

In a courageous but poignant moment of his military career, Poniatoff flew his plane into Red-occupied territory to his home village of Aisha, where he dipped down into bullet range and waved a last farewell to his parents.

By the early twenties, the beaten White army was in full retreat and Poniatoff found himself huddled in a boxcar with fellow soldiers racing across Siberia in a storm at 30 degrees below zero. In the midst of this hell, to ward off the cold, one of the soldiers began to tell the others of the most wondrous place he had ever seen, where it never snowed and the land was at peace and the women were beautiful: San Francisco.

Shivering in the boxcar, Poniatoff vowed to one day make that city his home.

It took him seven years, during which he was trapped in Shanghai, unable to obtain a visa. What Poniatoff did have, however, was a degree in mechanical engineering and a little knowledge of German and English. He found a job, which fortuitously required a lot of electrical engineering. So, for the rest of the twenties, Poniatoff worked in the Orient, learning electronics and dreaming of San Francisco.

In 1929, when he finally made his way to California, Poniatoff was turned away at the dock as a Shanghai "deportee." But the young Russian was not about to be denied by some minor bureaucrat after all he had been through and he somehow convinced the Bureau of Immigration to let him stay.

But something even greater than the United States Government conspired to keep Poniatoff away from his beloved city: the Depression. San Francisco had no jobs to offer, and the disheartened Russian was forced to take a job at General Electric in Schenectady, New York. But a year later, he finally found a job in San Francisco, as an engineer at Pacific Gas and Electric Co. He stayed for a decade, joining Dalmo Victor just before the outbreak of the Second World War.

By war's end, the young Ampex was swamped in military orders and had already moved out of the attic to a new facility just down the street. But then came Japan's surrender and, as at Hewlett-Packard, a sudden collapse in business. Like many other contractors of the era, Ampex hovered on the brink of bankruptcy.

But receivership was nothing after Siberia. Said Poniatoff later, "After some sleepness nights of indecision, I resolved not to go out of business."

The firm needed a new product. Small motors just weren't going to do it: already employees were having to forgo paychecks. High-fidelity sound reproduction equipment—then in the form of record disks and wire recorders—was considered as a possible market thrust. The general manager at Ampex told Poniatoff that he knew just the guy who might help, Harold Lindsay back at Dalmo Victor.

Lindsay, it turned out, had become obsessed with sound recording after attending a speech given by Jack Mullin at the Institute of Radio Engineers in San Francisco in July 1946. In that speech, Mullin had described his work as a communications officer in France studying captured German electronics equipment. One of the most remarkable of these devices, said Mullin, recorded sound on rolls of metal-coated plastic tape. These "magnetophones," as they were called, had played an important role in the Third Reich's propaganda efforts as the basis of ersatz broadcasts purportedly being transmitted live from bombed-out cities. Ordered to destroy all but one of the captured machines (the survivor was to be sent home for analysis), Mullin had begged permission to save two. Permission was granted and the young soldier sent his devices home to San Francisco piece by piece.

Lindsay was entranced by Mullin's presentation and afterward struck up a friendship with him, promising to find a way to build an improved version of the magnetophone. Three months later, Lindsay was at Ampex and Mullin had been hired by the firm as consultant.

Despite the fact that many electronics experts invited in to study the magnetophone found it impractical, Poniatoff was adamant in his support of the project. Meanwhile, Lindsay nearly starved. Ampex paychecks were far between and he was forced to ride to work on a bike because he couldn't afford gas for his car. But slowly, with the help of Myron Stolaroff, a small-motors expert, the first modern tape recorder was developed.

Simultaneously, Mullin created a market for the product. Bing Crosby, who had a weekly show on ABC radio, had long required that his programs be prerecorded. Unfortunately, this could only be done by recording on a disk. This meant editing was impossible without considerable loss of fidelity by rerecording from disk to disk. The resulting distortion of sound was costing Crosby listeners and the sponsor began pressing him to go live.

Crosby's team heard of Mullin and invited him for a demonstration. They were so impressed they signed him on to record twenty-six shows for the 1947–48 season. All Mullin had to work with was the two Nazi magnetophones. "The pressure put on these two solitary magnetophones was tremendous, as it was on my nerves . . . I lived in constant fear of breakdown."

But the recorders worked. Crosby was pleased. After viewing the Ampex prototype, Crosby ordered twenty recorders at four thousand dollars apiece. This single order built Ampex—and for the next six months the team worked around the clock, living on Mrs. Lindsay's sandwiches, to meet the delivery date.

Poniatoff and Ampex introduced their tape recorder to the world with a technique future competitor Memorex would find effective thirty years later: hidden from the audience in two rooms were a tape recorder and an orchestra (less expensive to hire then than Ella Fitzgerald now) playing simultaneously. The operator, sitting with the audience, would switch back and forth between the tape and the orchestra's microphone and then invited members of the audience to pick which was live and which was Ampex. They couldn't, and the company became an overnight success.

In 1950, the next recording challenge was encountered: video. This time, Ampex was competing with its old mentor, Jack Mullin, who had joined the Bing Crosby Enterprises Laboratory. Mullin won the race, showing a primitive videotape recorder in 1951, but lost the business to Ampex, which, with the help of a young San Francisco scientist named Charles Ginzburg, introduced the first practical industrial videotape recorder in April 1956.

The hidden star in this research effort was a remarkable young genius named Ray Dolby. Dolby had joined Ampex as a summer employee at sixteen and had worked for the firm through his college career at Stanford. The video recorder was introduced when Dolby was nineteen and it is no coincidence that his name appears on more patents than any other researcher's. The development of the video recorder tracks almost precisely with Dolby's appearances at Ampex. When he was at school, or serving his hitch in Korea, the project all but shut down.

Unfortunately, this young man was at Cambridge on a Rhodes scholarship when the recorder was formally introduced and thus received little of the acclaim—an experience about which, acquaintances say, Dolby is still bitter. However, the young man did have his comeuppance. During his long subsequent stay in England, Dolby invented the Dolby Noise Reduction Circuit, a mainstay of all audio recording, and he triumphantly returned to San Francisco to open Dolby Labs as a famous and rich man.

Like no other electronics firm before it, Ampex in its early years was in tall cotton, owning two vast, seemingly unlimited markets. In the late 1950s and early 1960s, it was consistently among the fastest growing stocks on the New York Stock Exchange, creating huge fortunes for investors. Ampex was a star of the great market boom of the Kennedy years. Sales, less than $1 million in 1951, reached $120 million in 1963, $300 million in 1969. Employment growth also was spectacular: 100 in 1950 to more than 13,000 in 1969.

But by then, Ampex was beginning to come apart. Numerous cracks appeared almost at the same time and in many areas. Perhaps the most devastating breakup came at the top. Poniatoff was growing old. Unlike the rest of Silicon Valley's pioneers, he had been deep into middle age when he founded his firm. By 1955, when Poniatoff left the company presidency to become chairman, he was sixty-three. In 1968, when the troubles started, he was seventy-six—still the heart of the company, all but elbowed out of management.

Poniatoff's replacements on executive row had big plans for Ampex and, at the time, enough profits to realize them. Throughout the sixties Ampex was pushed and pulled in several directions at once. Organizationally the company was split into five all but independent operating groups (the *Wall Street Journal* ran a story entitled "The Five Little Ampex's and How They Grew") which were later recombined again into a centralized company—with the inevitable infighting among the once independent group managers. The company launched into consumer products, home cassette decks and such, hoping the Ampex name would overcome the low quality of the Japanese-made components. It did—for a while, after which the company took a bath. At about the same time, the company went after the consumer recording media market. Cassettes sold well, but the firm jumped into the four- and eight-track cartridge business just in time for that market to wither and die.

Not content with the hardware side of the consumer market, Ampex also decided to expand into "software"—that is, to hire artists and set up its own recording company. Two New York producers were paid $5 million in a contract that allowed them to do next to nothing if they so desired—which is about what they did.

All told, one year Ampex lost nearly $40 million in consumer audio. And that doesn't count Ampex's failed foray into consumer video. As might be expected, Ampex's home video recorder was superior to anything on the market, but it was also too big and expensive to compete with Japanese competitors for the consumer business.

The irony of this decade-long debacle was that, in essence, Ampex's consumer strategy was brilliant. In time, both consumer audio and video would explode into enormous markets. Unfortunately, Ampex, one of the finest technology companies ever created, was not the firm to pull it off. The company, according to an ex-employee, "Only knew how to do things well and costly." President William Roberts, who had come to Ampex from Bell & Howell in 1961, knew that a consumer market was on the verge of being born but could not turn the research-oriented corporation around in that direction. So Ampex not only failed in the consumer market but, even worse, the exorbitant cost of that foray drained research and development money that should have gone into improving the company's good products: professional audio and video, video mass memory and an early line of computers.

The only individual who might have halted this decline and turned the company back onto the right path was Poniatoff—but he had other interests, many of them rather odd. While Ampex burned, Poniatoff became an eccentric. Truly one of the last tsarists, Poniatoff had always been exceedingly formal and erudite—"A real eighteenth-century man," says a former employee. In the 1970s, he became a health nut. He ate only unprocessed foods, drank carrot juice and had one of the first air ionization systems installed in his office. He began backing medical groups studying longevity and the effect of color on behavior. He drove only white cars and took to wearing a baseball cap. Mrs. Poniatoff held her Horticultural Society meetings in the Ampex cafeteria.

Perhaps some of Poniatoff's theories worked, because he died in 1980 at age eighty-eight. However, they didn't do much for the Ampex.

The last straw came in the early 1970s when it was discovered that the company's books were improper: equipment leased to customers had been booked as sales. The resulting adjustments to annual revenues and profits the next year devastated the public's perception of the firm. The value of Ampex stock fell precipitously, and it has never really recovered. This in turn led to the ignominy of a stockholders' suit.

By the early 1980s Ampex was back where it belonged: selling top-quality professional recording equipment. Unfortunately, even there Ampex was no longer secure. Years of putting research on the back burner cost Ampex its technological edge. At broadcast trade shows, where every Ampex product announcement was once jammed with customers waving checks, now there were other exhibits, bearing Japanese names and displaying often superior equipment. In April 1983, just when Silicon Valley seemed to be coming out of its latest business slump, Ampex Corp. announced the layoff of 210 employees—representing nearly 10 percent of its 1980 workforce—citing dwindling overseas sales.

Ampex now stands as a still breathing, but almost inert, shell of its former self. Most of the talent that once filled its labs and offices has scattered, seeding much of the recording industry. Ampex's legacy to Silicon Valley has come in two unusual and unexpected forms. First, Ampex built the first modern high-technology publicity department and its veterans have subsequently played a key role in presenting Silicon Valley to the outside world, at one time or another creating the public image of Hewlett-Packard, Intel, Apple, National Semiconductor, Activision and the San Jose *Mercury-News.* The second Silicon Valley inheritance from Ampex came in the form of a lesson about doing business, a warning to research-oriented companies to resist the siren call of the consumer business.

Sadly, no one listened.

* * *

By the mid-1950s, it must have been apparent to everyone in American business that there was something going on in the San Francisco Bay Area. Not a revolution, but certainly a healthy aggregation of firms sharing a common interest in exploiting the new markets in electronics and solid state physics. Any electrical engineer with ambition ran his résumé around the Valley circuit in hope of a response.

Only one last factor was needed, and in 1955 he came home to Santa Clara Valley. Into the Valley's story now briefly enters Dr. William Shockley, coinventor of the transistor, Nobel Prize winner the next year, one of the most brilliant and difficult children of the twentieth century. The first citizen of Silicon Valley.

And its first outcast.

Shockley had recently left Bell Labs, where he had directed the team that invented the transistor. While at Bell, Shockley and his group had also perfected the point-contact transistor (which by 1955 IBM was looking at for use in computers) and the junction transistor, the precursor of the modern integrated-circuit chip. Now, tired of Bell gleaning the profits from *his* device, Shockley wanted a piece of the action. Santa Clara County, his boyhood home, seemed like the perfect place to build a transistor factory that could stay a technological jump ahead of the competition.

The electronics industry watched anxiously as Shockley opened Shockley Laboratories Inc. near El Camino Real in Mountain View. They knew that the man was just brilliant enough to do anything. It was like Sir Isaac Newton announcing he was going to build a mill of his own design in seventeenth-century England.

Shortly, Shockley announced that he was hiring—and the applications that poured into Mountain View represented the cream of electronics research. Shockley, justly renowned as a superb judge of talent, hired eight of the very best: Julius Blank, Victor Grinich, Eugene

Kleiner, Jean Hoerni, Jay Last, Gordon Moore, Robert Noyce and Sheldon Roberts. It was the greatest collection of electronics genius ever assembled—and all of them were under thirty, at the height of their powers. Hoerni, who had come from Cal Tech, held two Ph.D.s (Cambridge and the University of Geneva); Grinich was a researcher at Stanford Research Institute; Kleiner (the oldest at twenty-nine) was a manufacturing engineer at General Electric; Moore was from the Applied Physics Laboratory at Johns Hopkins University; Noyce, destined to be the most famous, was from Philco-Ford.

Wherever they had come from, Shockley Labs was a bit of a shock, with its bare walls, concrete floor and exposed roof beams. Shockley too was a surprise. The great scientist, whom all of these young men had revered at conferences and lectures, turned out to be the least desirable of bosses. Not only was the great scientist's concept of marketing both diffuse and wildly overambitious, but he was utterly devoid of management skills, even of the ability to relate to other human beings. "A genius, but a real prick," says one Valley executive who has known Shockley for many years.

In marketing, according to Gordon Moore (as quoted in *Circuit News)*, Shockley's original goal was to produce a five-cent transistor—a price barely achievable in 1980, much less 1955. Failing that, he focused the firm on original research. Said Hoerni, "It was evident that Shockley was expecting to invent another milestone product and exploit it commercially. And when he didn't succeed in doing so, he continued to expend everyone's time and effort on trying new things instead of working on improved transistor technology."

This scattershot approach all but kept Shockley Labs from bringing anything to market. In fact, during the next two years, the firm would only introduce one diode, a relatively simple device, and no transistors.

As a manager, Shockley took employee alienation to new heights. Recalls Noyce, "Shockley used to say that one in ten people are psychotic, so he had two psychotic people working for him. [For that reason, he made all of his employees take psychological tests.] He didn't have trust and faith in other individuals. So that left him at a very distinct disadvantage. If we'd come up with results in the lab, he would call his old friends at Bell Labs and ask if it was really true—which didn't do a lot for morale."

Add to this Shockley's tendency to talk to people contemptuously, as though they were children, the desire of these young men to get back on the firing line in transistor research and finally the same ambition affecting most modern Silicon Valley residents, and by 1957, seven of the young men were looking to bail out of Shockley Labs. According to Hoerni, it was sheer luck for the future of Silicon Valley that Shockley managed to antagonize all of the men simultaneously. "Most people become dissatisfied and choose to leave a place at their own pace. But we all decided to depart at the same time."

Unbeknown to Shockley, the seven men began to look for a way out. It wasn't easy, as all seven had decided to stick together. Says Noyce: "The first obvious thing to do was to go look for jobs in existing companies. But that didn't work because of the problem of hiring such a large group. One of the guys then wrote to an investment bank in New York, Hayden Stone. And Hayden Stone said, 'Well, just hold on, we'll get somebody to sponsor the group out here.' "

At the time, there was no real venture capital industry outside of a few places like Applied Research & Development in Boston and the Rockefeller Brothers in New York. And neither of them was interested. So Hayden Stone went searching for a corporate sponsorship. Finally, the twenty-third company it approached, Fairchild Camera and Instrument Corp. of New Jersey, said it would like to hear more. The young president of Fairchild, John Carter, had developed a taste for technology sitting on government boards during the war as well as at Corning Glass Works, where he had been the youngest vice-president in that company's history. Carter had been searching for a high-tech firm to acquire, and, in the most important decision of his business career, settled on the seven young men.

But Carter, in agreeing to finance the Santa Clara Valley operation as a separate venture, still had some doubts, the largest being the apparent lack of management skills among the seven. With big bucks hanging in the balance, the seven set out to recruit the only holdout at Shockley Labs, the only member of the original eight who seemed to exhibit characteristics of a budding leader. Bob Noyce.

It didn't take much effort. Noyce, Shockley's golden boy, was as disenchanted as the rest. The eight soon submitted their resignation en masse to a stunned, then enraged Bill Shockley. He called them traitors —and "the Traitorous Eight" is how they are known—and wouldn't speak to any of them for many years.

Shockley's dream had collapsed. The most famous electronics scientist in the world would never again be part of Silicon Valley. He had set out to surpass the great entrepreneurial scientists of the thirties and forties, the patricians like Hewlett and Packard. Although he exceeded them in brilliance, they were far his superior in the human qualities that made successful businessmen. Shockley Labs was sold to Clevite Laboratories in 1960, then to ITT in 1965, and closed down for good in 1968. (Its building is now a stereo store, selling equipment filled with the transistors Shockley invented but could not build.)

Without knowing it, Shockley had set a number of important forces into motion in his short stay in Silicon Valley. The powerful minds he had gathered would in a few years create the integrated circuit and change the world. One of the young men, Arthur Rock, who at Hayden Stone had participated in the search for a corporate investor, would in time come out to the Coast and become the world's preeminent venture capitalist, backer of Intel and Apple, his company the model for scores of other operations that would make up the vast multibillion-dollar venture capital industry. By moving back to Santa Clara Valley and bringing all that talent with him, Shockley put the last stone in place in the construction of Silicon Valley.

But if Shockley himself went on to other fields—and other controversies—his legacy still lives everywhere in Silicon Valley. A cynical mind might even say that he has had his revenge. For it is Shockley, not Hewlett and Packard, who is the prototypical Silicon Valley executive. It was Shockley who built a company solely as a moneymaking machine. It was Shockley who built his firm on the dry valley floor, not in the green hills of Palo Alto. And it was Shockley who ran his company with utter indifference to his employees' cares and needs.

So, it was all there at Shockley Labs: greed, genius, divided loyalty, ambition, tragedy and sudden destruction—recurring themes in Silicon Valley. It would be up to Fairchild now to turn these plot ingredients into the stuff of an epic.

PROFILE

St. Bob

ROBERT NOYCE

The canonization of Bob Noyce began long before *Esquire* magazine hired that chronicler of cultural icons Tom Wolfe to profile the Silicon Valley pioneer for the special "50 Who Made a Difference" issue of the magazine. Rather, it had begun two decades earlier, when Fairchild Semiconductor burst on the scene to become the hottest young company in America, and most of all, when Noyce kicked out the last shivering piling holding up the decaying structure of Fairchild by quitting to help found Intel, the new darling of American business.

But this process of promoting Noyce as the name attached to the semiconductor revolution didn't really occur until recent years, with the belated recognition that, by God, something really did happen out there in Silicon Valley. And then the promotional program began with the newest bigwigs on the block, like Bushnell and Jobs, and then worked its way back. In the seventies, Noyce's peers, like Sanders and Sporck, were accorded at least as much attention as their old boss, and now one of Noyce's partners, volcanic Andy Grove, is earning at least as much attention with his theories of "high-output management."

But perhaps Bob Noyce wants it that way; one suspects that another part of him thrills at every new burst of publicity and bristles when he is passed over for some glory he thinks he deserves. Because Dr. Robert N. Noyce is a man of contradictions. He is neither an individual suffering from deep scars, like Jerry Sanders, nor an unabashed pursuer of fame and glory like Grove. But, unlike partner Gordon Moore, Noyce is not content with relative obscurity. Rather, Noyce *loves* fame, only he is not sure if he should. He wants to be loved, yet knows that to be a successful businessman requires the periodic administration of suffering to others. He wants to be a good man, but has found that all but impossible with the twin bedevilments of Silicon Valley life and fabulous wealth.

Probably such duality can only be found in a minister's son, and from the Midwest to boot. Much has been made of the fact that so many of the pioneers of Silicon Valley came from Middle America. What is often forgotten is that when these men were born there wasn't a whole helluva lot west of the Rockies, and after the war, when there was, most of the settlers came from the Plains and not from the East Coast. Further, the roots of these Valley pioneers vary from windswept towns with little more than a general store and a church to the crowded life of big cities.

In reality, when commentators speak of the heartland roots of Silicon Valley's leaders, they are speaking specifically of Bob Noyce, because his childhood seems to capture the essential schizophrenia between wild ambition and sober engineering conservatism that is at the center not only of Noyce's career but of Silicon Valley itself.

Noyce was born in 1927 in southeastern Iowa in a tiny town called Denmark. He was the third of four boys, and his father was a preacher in the Congregational church (as were his two grandfathers). Like most small-town ministers, the senior Noyce was perpetually on the move to new congregations, his family in tow. When Bob Noyce was six weeks old, just old enough to travel, his family moved the length of the state, to the southwestern corner and the town of Atlantic.

Noyce lived in Atlantic until he was eight years old. "My earliest memory of that period was that it was Depression time. The church wouldn't pay Dad, so they paid him produce."

In 1935, the family moved across the state again, this time to the northeastern region and Decorah ("a standard Scandinavian/Norwegian Iowa town"). At age ten Noyce moved to Webster City, then, at twelve, to Rennow.

The young Noyce was imbued with the small-town attitude of independence and that, combined with natural curiosity, impelled him to learn how things work. Still, Noyce doesn't remember having a particular affinity for things mechanical; rather, his brushes with what might be called engineering simply grew out of the environment in which he lived. "It was just sort of the way life was. Dad always managed to have some sort of workshop in the basement. And it was the usual rural environment of harvesting in the summer and canning in the winter."

When he was twelve, Bob and his next older brother built themselves a hang glider—more like an oversized box kite really—which nearly got them killed. A year later came their first car. "We made our first 'kluge' [primitive] motorized vehicle from an old gasoline engine off a washing machine. Back in the days when rural electrification was just coming in there were a lot of gasoline-driven washing machines that were being dumped, and so they were cheap."

By this time, the Noyces had moved to the "metropolis" of Grinnell, a college town founded by another Congregational minister, Josiah Grinnell, in 1854 as his own version of a New Eden. Grinnell, a stiff, Republican and religious town leavened only slightly by college life, would become Bob Noyce's first—and perhaps only—real home, the place he would credit for his eventual success and on which he would rain some of the gild of that success in later years.

Being a Congregational center, Grinnell was home to much of that sect's bureaucracy for the state. Bob Noyce's father had proved himself an able preacher and was awarded the associate superintendency of the Iowa Conference of Congregational Churches, headquartered at Grinnell College. It wasn't a high-paying or influential position, but it finally afforded Bob and his brothers a measure of stability in their lives. Now they could weave themselves into the fabric of the community, become Boy Scouts and develop their reputations in organized sports, attend dances, meet girls and lead their lives free from the ever present fear of having to pack up and leave everything they thought mattered.

Young Noyce went through junior high school, graduating at the top of his high school class. It was in his final years in high school, he recalls, "that I began to feel that maybe I had little bit more than average ability . . . My last year I took college courses, specifically in physics, just simply because I was relatively bored with the stuff that was going on in high school."

He also worked during those years detasseling corn and hoeing beans, delivered newspapers and special-delivery letters.

When the Noyces decided to move to Illinois, Bob chose to stay behind and attend Grinnell, primarily because he had developed a good relationship with the head of the Physics Department and decided that this was where he wanted to go to school.

Remarkably, there was almost no better place in the country for Bob Noyce to have been at that time. His physics professor, Grant Gale, had been in contact with John Bardeen (a childhood friend of Gale's wife) and had obtained from him two of the first transistors, which he studied with his students, including Bob Noyce. This was in 1948.

In the competitive Noyce family, doing well in school wasn't enough to stand out among overachieving older siblings. But Bob found a unique distinction by being the only brother to letter in a varsity sport in college—a fact of which he still seems more proud than any grades. The letter was in swimming; Noyce won the state diving championship, and it remains a hobby he still indulges with snorkeling and scuba diving (the Intel insurance underwriters hold their breath every time Noyce holds his).

College was pretty much of a skate for Bob, despite a double major in physics and mathematics. Just how easy is exemplified by the fact that he was presented the Brown Derby Award as the student who got the best grades with the least effort. Noyce filled in his free time with oboe-playing and acting, appearing as the lead in a local radio soap opera. But in retrospect, the critical education during the Grinnell years came not from the classrooms but the community itself: "I think a small town has some significant advantages, particularly in that you can see a one-to-one relationship between work and success."

But there was a darker, intolerant and repressive side to small-town life, and in his senior year Robert Noyce ran smack into it. The occasion was a dorm party and the organizers, some of them veterans, had decided to reproduce a South Seas luau, probably the first in Iowa. But a true luau needed a pig to roast, and since nobody had any money, Noyce and another student were charged with the task of stealing a pig from a neighboring farm. The two boys wrestled a twenty-five-pounder out of a pigpen and returned to campus as heroes.

The luau was a rousing success. The next morning wasn't. Stealing pigs in Iowa, like horse thievery fifty years before, was just about a hanging offense. Noyce and his cohort went back to the farmer to apologize and found themselves facing criminal charges and expulsion from school. Straitlaced Grinnell College had no compunctions about kicking out its top student for breaking the rules. Meanwhile, Noyce, the preacher's boy gone bad, suffered the wrath of the community.

But he held up, and after Professor Gale cut some deals with the cops and administrators, Noyce earned the comparatively light sentence of a one-semester suspension. It was arranged for him to spend that hiatus working in the actuarial department at Equitable Life in New York City.

Going East wasn't new to Bob. He had spent the previous couple of summers hitchhiking back to a job outside the city in White Plains carrying a tray as a waiter in a country club. His eldest brother was at the time attending Columbia, so Bob would travel down to Manhattan on his days off and explore the big city.

This trip back to New York wasn't the shock it might have been to some kid just off the farm. But it was spent under a dark cloud. Noyce had been kicked out of college in a scandal and now his only prospect was to spend the summer and fall working until the school let him back after Christmas—if he had the courage to go back and face the town.

Noyce decided to make the best of his stay in the Big Apple. He went to all the Broadway shows and still passed all of his actuarial exams. He learned the role of statistics in the sociology of aging, "little facts like how people really do unconsciously react to financial incentives: if you pay them to die, they'll die, if you pay them to live, they'll live . . . at least statistically." He also learned enough to make him suspicious about the data used in developing statistics.

The one other thing Noyce learned during his stay at Equitable was that insurance was not the place he wanted to be: "I went into it with the idea that this was a secure and comfortable place to be. I came out of it with the feeling that it was a terribly boring place to be."

The Bob Noyce that returned to Grinnell in early 1949 was a mature, professional man with a good idea of where he was going. The first priority was to graduate. Though it appeared that his classmates were now a half-year ahead of him, in reality they had only just caught up to all of the extra-credit courses Noyce had taken his first three years. So, without missing a step, Noyce marched back into school and plowed through his last semester.

This last semester was a critical time for Noyce because of the training in semiconductors he was receiving from Grant Gale. Even before the notorious pig episode, Noyce had become infatuated with the transistor and its implications. "Grant had an infectious interest in transistors that he passed on to his students. So by my junior year I began to look at [the transistor] as being one of the great phenomena of the time. And that it would be something good to exploit—well, maybe 'exploit' is the wrong way to put it—but I saw it as something that would be fun to work with."

So Bob Noyce, now twenty-two, decided to pursue the study of solid state physics at the premier school of science on the East Coast, MIT. He enrolled in the doctoral program in the fall of 1949. Unfortunately, where some backwater college in Iowa had been busily studying the implications of the Shockley-Bardeen-Brattain discovery, at the mighty Massachusetts Institute of Technology "there were no professors around who knew anything about transistors."

Instead Noyce had to pick and choose among the wealth of physics and electronics courses that could be used as background in the study of transistors. As a result, he went into physical electronics: "The major problems in the field at that time were electron emission from cathode-ray and vacuum tubes. But still they had many of the same physical properties [as transistors]; you had to learn the language, the quantum theory of matter and so on."

Equally important to Noyce's education was attending the few technical conferences revolving around transistor technology. At one of those events he got to stand, if only for a few days, right at the edge of the new technology and to meet famous scientists like Shockley and Lester Hogan.

"It was a relatively small technical community at that time. So you knew the names of the authors of the various papers being presented: you'd see them every summer. It was really quite different from now, where there's so many people working in the field, and so many different aspects to be studied. In those days it was still a question of just understanding the phenomena. The field was still virgin, so every time you did something you'd learn something new. And it was enormously exciting because there was so much to learn so quickly . . ."

Completing his doctorate (his dissertation was "A Photoelectric Study of Surface States on Insulators"), Noyce set off to find a job that would allow him to indulge his interest in solid state. And right after graduation he married Elizabeth Bottomley, whom he had met in a Tufts musical in which he was performing and she was the costume director.

At that time, just about the only places to go were large established research laboratories at General Electric, Bell and RCA. But Noyce, in a display of entrepreneurial temperament, decided not to work for any of them. Instead, he picked lowly Philco "because the way I put it to myself at the time was that they really needed me," Noyce says, with a laugh. "At the other places they knew what was going on, they knew what they were doing." An equally important reason, Noyce felt, was that at one of the large labs he would be pigeonholed into one tiny corner of technology and would miss out on the big picture. At smaller Philco he knew he would be able to wear many hats, including those of both scientist and businessman, and be able to hop around to different projects.

For that right, Noyce was willing to make some sacrifices (the Philco offer was the lowest of the group). But having grown up in a preacher's family, Bob Noyce knew always to choose God over Mammon, and he was content to make the smaller salary at Philco in exchange for the greater opportunity. ("My only real ambition was to be able to buy two pairs of shoes simultaneously, particularly after having grown up in my brothers' hand-me-downs.")

It wasn't long after his arrival that Philco, like all subsequent Noyce companies, became known as a technology-driven firm. It couldn't take on the big boys in every market, but in the one it chose, high-frequency transistors (used mainly in hearing aids), Philco took the industry lead.

Noyce stayed at Philco for three years. In 1956 he gave a technical paper in Washington. Shockley was sitting in the audience, even then plotting to leave Bell Labs and start up a new company back home near Stanford University. He was also looking for bright young scientists and was mightily impressed with Noyce's presentation. Recalls Noyce, "A month or so later he called me up and said he was starting this thing out here on the West Coast, and that he'd like to talk to me about joining him. Well, Shockley of course was the 'daddy' of the transistor. And so that was very flattering. And I had the feeling that I'd done my stint in the minor leagues and now it was time to get into the majors.

"So there was no question in my mind that that's what I wanted to do. I had a brother who was teaching at Berkeley, and, you know, his letters were stories of sunshine and lovely weather . . ."

Soon after, Noyce was out on the Coast talking to Shockley. It was a measure of what would become Noyce's famous self-assurance that he bought a house in the valley even before he had a job. In fact, he flew into San Francisco on a red-eye, drove down to the valley to meet a real estate agent, picked out and bought a house in Los Altos (for nineteen thousand dollars) by noon and made it to his interview at Shockley by two o'clock.

Needless to say, Noyce got the job. At first it seemed like a godsend. Here he was, part of a team of brilliant young scientists working for a man many considered the finest applied scientist of the age. The exclusivity of the place was confirmed just a few weeks later, in November, when Shockley was awarded the Nobel Prize in physics. Shockley took the entire staff to a champagne breakfast at Dinah's Shack, one of the valley's few serious restaurants. Now Noyce and his colleagues knew they were special; what other company was run by a Nobel laureate? They felt that they were on the brink of changing the world. And in fact they were, but not with Dr. Shockley.

"First of all, let me say that Shockley is absolutely brilliant. He was one of those people who could take a problem and just distill it down to the essence so he could work on it without getting confused by all the extraneous stuff. It was his ability to abstract and really make a significant contribution. He did not read the literature particularly, and consequently did not get caught in the traps that led other people to dead ends. He was a marvelous intuitive problem solver . . . in terms of being able to attach the mathematics to the essence of the problem and get an answer out where other people might get stuck in the complexity of the calculations . . . Shockley was an inspiring leader to work for in that he was a tremendous generator of ideas."

But Shockley's oppressive style, combined with the fact that Shockley Transistor just couldn't seem to get anything out the door, finally blew the place apart.

It was years before Shockley forgave any of the Traitorous Eight, particularly Bob Noyce, who had been Shockley's favorite. Noyce says, "I remember his wife talking to Betty, my first wife, when we were all leaving and saying, 'How could you possibly do this without telling me?' " Three years later, Noyce ran into Shockley at a trade dinner. Shockley said, "Hello, Bob," then walked away.

They would not speak again for twenty years. The occasion was a Christmas party at Les Hogan's house, when they at last had a long conversation which in the end revolved around Shockley propounding the theory of diseugenics (the race-IQ question) that had made the old scientist a bit of an embarrassment to his Silicon Valley descendants.

Despite the decades of hard feelings, Noyce holds no bitterness toward his older mentor. Like all who worked for the great scientist, he still speaks in awe of Shockley's brilliance, of how he would develop and solidify his latest ideas by patiently explaining them to a younger scientist, like Noyce. Noyce never forgets that had not Shockley decided to come home to Stanford, and had he not had the ambition to start his own firm, there would never have been a Fairchild and, by extension, never the Silicon Valley that has made Robert Noyce a rich and famous man.

But at the time, having walked out of Shockley Labs with the rest of the Traitorous Eight, Noyce found himself almost by default taking over Shockley's role at the new company, Fairchild. How he did in this new role in comparison to that eminence he had just left is apparent in the esteem in which Noyce is still held by those who worked for him. These men, many of them now famous businessmen in their own right, revere Noyce even though for many he is their toughest competitor. In the Silicon Valley pantheon of Great Men, only Noyce has been elevated into the ranks of Hewlett and Packard; he commands the respect of everyone from flamboyant Jerry Sanders to hard-bitten Charlie Sporck and the legions of new start-up presidents who long to someday be just like him.

Part of this respect is the result of sheer timing. Noyce was there at the beginning, and for many of these now powerful men, he was their first real boss. Another source of respect, particularly among people who only know the man from his reputation, is that he is one of the inventors of the integrated circuit, a founder of Silicon Valley and the head of what was once the Valley's most important company.

For those who worked for him at Fairchild, what made Robert Noyce a giant was that, when faced with the same situation as Shockley, he chose the opposite direction—toward trust in his people and respect for their abilities, toward decency and equality. He chose not to see the problem as an equation to be solved but as a structure in some way based upon the precepts his father had once preached from the pulpit. Like Hewlett and Packard before him, Noyce took the big risk and believed in the natural nobility of people.

It is easy to forget what Noyce accomplished at Fairchild, now that the firm's Golden Age has receded into myth and memory. But it must have taken a remarkable individual to hold together a company perpetually at a flashpoint with dozens of explosive and brilliant personalities. But Noyce did, and for nearly a decade—two lifetimes in Silicon Valley time—and it exploded then only because control had been wrenched from his grasp.

But for all the many fine things Noyce was, there were many things he wasn't. He was charismatic, a born leader of men, but he was not a great manager, particularly at Fairchild. The company he had built, despite its awesome array of talent, began to stagnate. Noyce was a lab man, a technical guy, not a production manager, and his company always seemed to limp along in that latter, critical, department. Part of Noyce's problem was that he erred on the side of decency. The preacher's boy who had wanted out from under the responsibilities of that title now naturally reassumed it. It was important for Bob Noyce to be liked, which paralyzed his ability to fire people, or reposition them downward, even when the company and those who worked for it were at risk. The result was that Fairchild sometimes seemed the Peter Principle in action.

Counterbalancing this "weakness" was Noyce's own recognition of it, and his unequaled skill at finding a lieutenant or partner who had the stomach for dirty work. That was Sporck at Fairchild and Grove at Intel. It might be argued that shifting the nasty business off onto some hatchet man allowed Noyce to stand in a flattering light he didn't deserve, but that's unfair. In every company, if that company is to survive, someone has to hang tough at the top. The tragedy is when that type of person is the only one on executive row. Someone who cares for employees must always be above that hard-nosed executive. Noyce understood that and always remained in command, the balancing force, the conscience of the firm.

Noyce can best be understood as the Eisenhower of Silicon Valley, keeping his egotistical and recalcitrant generals under control and coordinated as much as possible toward achieving the final objective. And, like most men in that position, Bob Noyce has an element of detachment in his personality. Many men admire him, but few seem to really know him. There is an element of reserve, of holding something back. Certainly Noyce is an affable man, a joy for interviewers, a man whose apparent humility puts even the lowliest subordinate at ease. But there is a deeper, harder part to Bob Noyce, that when the pressure is on comes to the fore with an unblinking pair of eyes and a clear, cold voice of command.

This other part of Bob Noyce comes from the preacher's boy who learned not to become too attached to a home or a school or friends, because a letter in the mailbox might be about to fling him off into another world. It is the personality of his father, whose profession demanded a friendly, engaging exterior while on the inside it required the discipline and strategy needed to save souls. It is also the young man expelled from school, facing a scandalized community and knowing that after his punishment is over he must be tough enough and sure enough to return to those accusing faces again. And it is the young man, barely out of his twenties, with little business experience, thrown into the role of chief executive of one of the important firms of the postwar world.

There is a third side to Bob Noyce, one that belies the almost preternatural calmness that seems to hover about him. Scuba-diving isn't the only Noyce leisure-time activity that gives underwriters fits. In fact, there is an odd element of danger in most of Noyce's free-time schedule: skiing, hang-gliding (a reminder of the old box-kite glider in Iowa; Noyce gave it up when a friend broke his hip and leg flying Noyce's glider), white-water rafting, sporting around in his Porsche Turbo and flying his 1947 Republic Seabee amphibious plane. Where this need for adventure comes from is difficult to guess, but apparently the same spirit that led to the stolen-pig caper wasn't purged by nine months of staring at actuarial tables.

Instead of growing easier, Bob Noyce's life in recent years has seemed to grow more complex. He has pulled away from the day-to-day activities of his new firm Intel but has not been spared the day-to-day vagaries of Silicon Valley life. In 1974, after twenty-one years of a marriage that produced four children, Robert Noyce divorced his wife, Betty. A year later, in typical Valley style, he married Intel's personnel director. Betty Noyce enjoyed one of the biggest divorce settlements in the history of California and moved to Maine.

A certain amount of fame surrounded Noyce as far back as Shockley Labs, but in the late seventies, as the world woke up to the wonders of the Electronics Revolution, he found himself pulled in every direction by people who had never heard of him a few years before. Now he was a national figure; in his mid-fifties, after decades of hard work and long hours, facing even harder work and longer hours:

> Let's see, to take a snapshot of a week or so. Last week I was in Washington at this conference on high technology, a government conference on trade and the SIA [Semiconductor Industry Association], was releasing a report on Japanese targeting. The week before that I was skiing—at least I skied on Thursday and Friday at Aspen. This week I was here [at Intel] Monday, Tuesday and Wednesday. I have a board meeting tomorrow and Saturday at Grinnell College. Then I'm heading to Japan Sunday morning for a series of conferences and meetings with customers on Tuesday and Wednesday. Then I'm leaving Tokyo Wednesday afternoon and coming back here to a University of California regents meeting Thursday and Friday . . .

At the time he was interviewed by the author in late 1983, Noyce sat on six corporate boards and two educational boards as well as helping Stanford and MIT improve their engineering curriculum. During the few times he is free, Noyce returns to the home he bought in Los Altos in 1960 that he subsequently improved with a tennis court and a magnificent pool with cascading rapids surrounded by exquisite landscaping.

Bob Noyce, who said all he wanted out of his first job was a challenge and two pairs of his own shoes, is now enormously wealthy: he has a net worth of several hundred million dollars. And like most men of his Silicon Valley generation, he has only recently begun to enjoy his fortune. How he will spend the rest of his life is still up in the air. He has ruled out politics, teaching (he finds public speaking very demanding) and, having scored big twice, ever again becoming the chief executive of a new Silicon Valley start-up.

Whatever he does decide to do from here on out—continue being the spokesman for the semiconductor industry, keep a hand in at Intel, sit on the board of a new company or two—Bob Noyce knows that he has come as close to immortality as any engineer. He played a pivotal part in the creation of the milestone invention of our time and cofounded two great companies—the first one of legend, the second among America's greatest economic weapons. And he has done all those things with grace and dignity and the everlasting respect of those who worked for him and of his competitors. In the welter of Valley life, he has set an example of success tempered with decency. In the long run that may be Dr. Robert Noyce's most important contribution.

> I never had an ambition to become an industrialist. My family had been a long line of teachers and preachers. I guess I was just following those things that were the easiest or most interesting to me. I guess those two things are congruent: what's interesting is easy and what's easy is interesting . . . the old story that you do well what you like to do and you like to do what you do well. Anyway, it just seemed a very natural thing to do . . .

3

Fairchild

Silicon Valley's most famous firm has never really existed. Rather it is an illusion, a magic-lantern show that shines memories through a small company now gone for fifteen years and projects a distorted and gigantic shadow onto the present. Sometimes, when this mythic firm is spoken of, one imagines it still alive, possessing minds of unmatched brilliance, unbeatable products and sales the sum of those of National Semiconductor, Intel, Advanced Micro Devices, Four-Phase, Intersil, American Microsystems and Signetics combined. It is the largest, most innovative and most exciting semiconductor company in the world.

This elusive, mythical Fairchild Semiconductor has nothing to do with that empty husk of a company called Fairchild Camera and Instrument Corp. that now occupies its old headquarters in Mountain View. It also bears little relation to the company upon which it is based: the Fairchild Semiconductor of 1957 to 1970. The real firm was plagued by numerous problems—weak management, poor manufacturing skills and the immaturity and inexperience of its executives. In the mythical company, these same executives are what they became with time: the leaders of Silicon Valley.

The mythical Fairchild Semiconductor is a "what if" game played by the Valley for years. It goes something like this: What if Fairchild hadn't blown up? What if, instead, all of those men, like Noyce, Grove, Moore, Sanders, Sporck, Kvamme, Widlar, Cox, Marren, Hoerni, Boysel, Lamond and all the rest, had never left? Damn, what a powerhouse company that would be. There never would have been a Silicon

Valley, just Fairchild, sitting there at the center of the semiconductor universe, big as IBM, snuffing out the Japanese and Motorola and Texas Instruments like candles. Can you imagine?

This game is reactivated every time the new Fairchild suffers another setback or the Japanese threaten the industry. And it doesn't help when Jerry Sanders says that he believes the disintegration of Fairchild didn't have to happen, or when in interviews with the Valley's great men they seem to talk as though the old Fairchild days are more immediate in their minds than whatever glorious work they're at in the present.

What was this Fairchild Semiconductor that it could hold such a grip on the minds of Valley leaders so many years and so many successes after they left it? What kind of company was it that, when it exploded, the diaspora of its talent could create several dozen major companies, the largest of them some of the most important corporations in the world?

The real Fairchild Semiconductor was remarkably small (less than $100 million even in the late sixties) and technically unsophisticated by modern standards. In an era where Steve Jobs's youth makes jaws drop, it is interesting to note that the average age for the *entire* executive staff of Fairchild in 1963 was under thirty. Even headman Bob Noyce was just thirty-six, thirty when he had helped found the firm.

There is remarkably little permanent record of life at Fairchild in the fifties and sixties, except for the reminiscences of its veterans, and mainly of those who made good. These others have disappeared—after all, not everybody who came out of the Fairchild was Charlie Sporck—drifted off into the vast international labyrinth of the electronics industry, or died from the pressure or vices created by the high-tech working life, or simply given up and moved into other professions. There are few press clippings about the firm—primarily technical articles or dull business stories; after all, no one had any idea that a revolution was being wrought out in some prune-filled California valley. *Esquire* had no reason to send a Tom Wolfe out to profile Noyce, as it would in 1983, *Time* hardly covered East Coast business, much less West Coast high technology. So Fairchild was left on its own. What sense of itself it had was created internally. As with its technology, the company's own style had to be learned from scratch.

What does emerge from conversations with its veterans is that Fairchild was a mysterious collection of contradictions. It was a company of young men who acted very old. It was the wildest-living company the Valley has ever seen, yet it was, like any good 1950s company, highly conservative and conformist. Its employees had incredible loyalty, yet it bled to death faster than most mutinous firms. The Fairchild history also seems to undermine the reputations of some of its most famous graduates. If Noyce is such a great executive, why did the company progress so fitfully, and why was it so unprofitable? If Sporck is such a manufacturing genius, why did Fairchild always have trouble getting products out the door? And if Sanders is the marketing guru of Silicon Valley, why did he have such a reputation for irritating customers?

The answer is that Fairchild was a corporate vocational school for these individuals. Here they could screw up without serious repercussions—after all, nobody else knew how the job was done either—and learn from their mistakes. That was good, because the next time around, when they were on their own, the same mistake would be fatal.

At Fairchild Semiconductor, more than HP on one extreme or Shockley Labs on the other, was the freewheeling, throttle-to-the-firewall business style of Silicon Valley forged, its best-known personalities formed. So, to appreciate Silicon Valley, one must first understand the original Fairchild.

* * *

It was September 1957, and the Traitorous Eight had just quit the greatest electronics genius of the time, had received a promise of backing from an East Coast company none of them really knew, had yet to lease a building and had only a vague idea of what kind of products they would build.

Not the most propitious start. But the men figured they had talent on their side and would just work things out as they went.

The firm that had put up money, whose name this new little California operation bore, had been founded in 1920 by Sherman Fairchild. Fairchild was a rather remarkable man—an industrialist, inventor, pioneering aviator and entrepreneur—and this unique combination of talents enabled him to recognize the potential of microelectronics while the industry was still in its infancy.

Fairchild's company had originally been known as Fairchild Aerial Camera because most of his earliest inventions (such as the between-the-lens shutter) were designed for that market. But Fairchild had other interests, notably aviation. His inventions in that field were even more sweeping, including the closed-cabin airplane, the folding wing and hydraulic aircraft brakes and landing gear. So successful were these products that he split his company in two in 1936, creating the aviation-oriented Fairchild Industries and (the name changed in 1944) Fairchild Camera and Instrument Corp., the latter the parent of Fairchild Semiconductor.

By the time Fairchild Camera and Instrument was approached by the Traitorous Eight, Sherman Fairchild was sixty years old and his interests had moved beyond the day-to-day operation of his firms, instead focusing on other responsibilities, such as his position on the board of IBM. Decision-making at FC&I was left to its young president, John Carter. As the years passed, Fairchild grew less active with his firms, until by his death at seventy-four in 1971 he was all but out of the picture. Thus, one of the biggest what-ifs in the Fairchild story is whether a younger, more active Sherman Fairchild, an entrepreneur himself, would have allowed Fairchild to deteriorate to the point where it began to unravel.

John Carter agreed to back the young group, with an option to buy in two years. In terms of product, the Eight decided to pursue a back-burner project at Shockley Labs—something called the 2N696, a double-diffused-base silicon transistor. The idea, Hoerni's, had a lot going for it, notably the use of silicon rather than the more traditional germanium. An obstacle, though, was the diffusion process, which was only two years old and, since its development at Bell Labs, had never been commercially feasible. Making it so would be the company's first goal.

Jobs were divvied up according to skills. Bob Noyce and Jay Last took photolithography: Eugene Kleiner, the ex-professor, took administration; Gordon Moore and Jean Hoerni, the two big research guns, took on the diffusion problem; Sheldon Roberts grew the silicon crystals; Victor Grinich and the company's first new employee, Murray Siegel, defined the characteristics of the finished product and developed applications.

It was truly a cut-rate, make-it-up-as-you-go operation. Siegel and Grinich designed test systems in Grinich's Palo Alto garage as there was no place else to work and there were no products on the market to do the job. Siegel: "There was no such thing as an instrumentation marketplace in those days. If you wanted something you sat down and started drawing it. Someone would look over your shoulder, make a suggestion, and you'd try it. It was that simple—and that complicated . . ."

As there were no standards, the Fairchilders made up their own, often arbitrarily, with far-reaching results. For example, a workbench: "We had no idea how high it should be," Siegel told *Circuit News* years later, "So one day in my motel room (I still hadn't bought a house yet) Vic and I took telephone books and stacked them on a table while we stood next to it. When the telephone books hit our midsections—we're both about the same height—we decided that was the height we'd want. That ridiculous bench is an industry standard today."

By the end of October 1957, the Eight were finally together in a single facility on Charleston Road in Mountain View, near Bayshore Freeway and about equidistant from Shockley Labs and the original Packard garage. Getting the company together at last was helpful, but the work environment was hardly pleasant. For one thing, the building wasn't finished yet. It didn't even have electricity. Siegel again: "We would work until dark. As the days got shorter, so did our work hours. Outside, however, there was a construction line pole with power that we attached wires to so we could at least do sawing and such. I remember Vic Grinich out there that fall with gloves on, a muffler, a hat and his pipe, with a heater nearby plugged into the line."

Trying to run a high-tech company without electricity was no mean feat, but the little firm continued to grow. One of its first (and in time most important) new hires was Tom Bay, who arrived in November 1957 to become the company's first marketing manager. The company also hired a number of Stanford graduate students as production workers.

But the main focus remained, as it should have, on building a marketable silicon transistor. They decided to build them using the "mesa" process, a new manufacturing technology. Fairchild Camera and Instrument agreed to provide financial support—to the tune of $1.5 million, big money in those days. Two teams were set up, under Moore and Hoerni, to discover the best structure for the transistor. Moore's team won because his yield rates were higher. The firm was on its way.

Fairchild Semiconductor may have been a very tiny operation in those days, not noticed by cars driving past on Charleston, but its name already was looming large in the electronics business. The big firm in those days, as it has been ever since, was Texas Instruments, founded in 1925, given its present name in 1951, and already publicly traded by 1953. But industry attention had been riveted on those brilliant young scientists out in California ever since Shockley had formed his company. Now the word was out that these guys were going to try making the first-ever mesa silicon transistors. That news was enough for the smallest company in the electronics business to attract the attention of the biggest—and in January 1958 IBM gave Fairchild Semiconductor its first order, for one hundred mesa silicon transistors to use as memory drivers in IBM computers.

Fairchild was now under way as a company, with the blessings of Big Blue itself. It was the beginning of a long relationship between IBM and Silicon Valley, and particularly with Bob Noyce and Gordon Moore.

Fairchild next proceeded to do what every high-tech firm has done before and since: reduce the cost of producing existing products by improving manufacturing, and add new products that are variants of the first. Within a year, the firm had expanded the 2N696 to include a follow-up 2N697 and then models featuring high voltages or smaller size.

At the same time, Bay was trying to stick a marketing and sales arm onto what at the core was a technology-driven company. In ten years he never quite did it, the graft never quite took, but even from the beginning he was able to get enough into place to at least handle the orders coming in.

By the end of 1958, Fairchild Semiconductor had half a million dollars in sales and a hundred employees. The latter number is more important as a comparative growth measure given the interim inflation, and by that measure, Fairchild was one of the fastest-growing companies the Valley has produced.

Fairchild also ended the year with a new general manager, Ed Baldwin, who had brought with him an intensely loyal team of managers. And for a while it looked as though Fairchild was going to smoothly make the transition to an established and mature business.

But within a year everything had gone to hell, and the company had gotten a first taste of the greed and deceit and high-rolling that henceforward would represent the dark side of playing entrepreneur in Silicon Valley.

In 1959, the year Charlie Sporck joined the firm, Ed Baldwin and his team suddenly quit Fairchild to form (with scientists from Standard Oil, General Transistor and Bell Labs, among others) Rheem Semiconductor Inc. The moving was utterly shocking to everybody left at Fairchild. Nobody knew that this would be the Valley's first true spin-off and a harbinger of things to come. The Rheem founders set an ugly precedent, creating a paranoia about technology leaks that has never stopped in the Valley. It seems that when they left, Baldwin and crew also took with them a copy of the Fairchild "cookbook," the manual describing in detail how to manufacture the company's transistors. This obviously crossed the line between quitting a company with information in your head and the theft of trade secrets.

Says Noyce, "We found out later that somebody had been hired, not from Fairchild, but a high school teacher or something like that, who was asked to sit down and study the book and we got that testimony. So it was a pretty flagrant case."

Fairchild sued in the first of many such lawsuits that pepper Silicon Valley's history. But in reality, as in many such cases, Rheem had less reason to worry about the suit than about a far more destructive force in Silicon Valley competition: technological change.

While Rheem was poring over the Fairchild cookbook trying to figure out how to copy its competitor's technology, in the back labs of Fairchild a development was taking place that would render Rheem's secrets, and everything else in semiconductor technology, obsolete. And Rheem, smug in possession of what it thought was the crown jewels of high tech, would be dead and sold within two years.

Like most great inventions, the integrated circuit seems to have been an idea whose time had come. In Dallas, at Texas Instruments, Jack Kilby took advantage of a companywide vacation in the middle of July 1958 to work out some ideas he had about putting multiple transistors on a single silicon chip. Critical to his plan were three features: "recognition that all of the required circuit elements could be made from the same material; electrical isolation of these circuit elements so that they could operate independently, and all of the circuit elements constructed in or near one main surface of the semiconductor wafer, so as to take advantage of advancing semiconductor technology and permit their interconnection."

The same idea was running around in the heads of scientists at Fairchild. But they were coming at it from a different direction, from solid state technology, not from electronic theory. Leading the charge was Jean Hoerni, one of the brightest scientists and most mercurial characters the Valley had ever known. Hoerni took the process of sandwiching layers of oxides on the surface of silicon and ran it as far as it would go, until he came up with a transistor that had been flattened out into two dimensions, a plane—"planar," the process would be called—that looked like a bull's-eye with the outer ring pulled out at one point to make a teardrop.

But that was just the start. Astute scientists that they were, the

Fairchilders quickly realized that with photolithography this same transistor could be repeated over and over again on the surface of a silicon chip in a systematic manner and with built-in interconnections between them. Said Bay, "As soon as the planar process was developed, we were all saying that now we can put devices on a chip, interconnect them and not have to worry about shorting out the junction."

It was as if a door had been flung open. The scientists at Fairchild suddenly looked down into a bottomless abyss microscoping from the visible world into that of atoms—an abyss that promised blinding speed and power, the ultimate machine. When they let their minds wander they realized that not just one transistor could be put on a chip, but even ten, maybe a hundred . . . for Christ's sake, *millions*. It was dizzying. And it was thrilling as hell.

Kilby was also looking into this new world from his office in Dallas. Despite a personal preference for silicon, he had built his circuit on germanium. It worked and in February 1959 he applied for a patent for "Miniaturized Electronic Circuits." Not long afterward, TI proudly announced "the development of a semiconductor solid circuit no larger than a match head" for $450. Noyce didn't file for his patent for an integrated circuit using the planar process until the end of July 1959.

The difference in the filing dates led to a battle that has continued to the present. Who really was the inventor of the integrated circuit? Kilby had the first patent, but his design was never practical. Noyce's planar design became the basis for the subsequent microelectronics revolution, but his filing was second. Besides, he wasn't even alone at Fairchild in developing the circuit or in designing it. It may sound like a clash of egos (and there's nothing wrong with that: who wouldn't want to be the inventor of one of the most important products of the twentieth century?), but in the competitive world of high technology, it also meant money. A lot of money.

That's why Fairchild and TI sued each other throughout the sixties. In the end the courts awarded the invention of the integrated circuit to Kilby and the crucial interconnection patent to Noyce. That meant that TI and Fairchild split up the royalties from all of those new semiconductor companies forming about that time. The Kilby patent also enabled Texas Instruments to all but blackmail its way into the Japanese market, and the royalties from the Noyce patent kept Fairchild afloat through the dismal seventies. Kilby made the National Inventors Hall of Fame and Noyce became a legend. All in all, everybody came out quite well on the deal.

Well, not everybody. It seems that at the same time Noyce and Hoerni were inventing the integrated circuit in the back room, Baldwin and his boys were sneaking out the front door with the Fairchild cookbook. Rheem thought it had the keys to the electronic kingdom, only to discover that all the secret information they had was now obsolete thanks to Noyce and Kilby's new invention. Rarely has justice been so accurate or well timed in Valley history.

Ironically, despite the fact that it precipitated a technological revolution that will echo well into the next century, probably the biggest cause for rejoicing at Fairchild in 1959 was the word that it had beaten the invincible Texas Instruments for the contract to provide transistors to the Minute Man I missile program. Now *that* was cause for celebration.

The year 1960 saw continued growth and success for young Fairchild. The big event of the year was Fairchild's decision regarding a buy-out. Needless to say, they bit, for $3 million. The Traitorous Eight each found themselves suddenly holding $250,000 in Fairchild Camera and Instrument stock—and thought themselves rich beyond their wildest dreams. But what seemed at the time to be welcome financial support to get this hot young company on its way would turn out an unacceptable burden, a source of seething resentment.

At the center of the problem was John Carter, the man who had taken the risk with the Eight in the first place, but who now seemed to be stealing profits out of Mountain View to support the rest of Fairchild Camera and Instrument—as well as to back his unsuccessful follow-ups to Fairchild Semiconductor. Furthermore, after the initial buy-out, Carter became tight with company stock, apparently unable to recognize that this was the only legal tender that counted in the Valley. Noyce, now in charge of Fairchild Semi, found himself without any incentive to keep talented people from running off and trying to make their own fortunes.

First to go, angered by what they saw as increasingly shabby treatment by the parent company, were three of the original Eight—Hoerni, Roberts and Kleiner—to found Amelco. It was bought by Teledyne Semiconductor in 1972. Kleiner went on to become a venture capitalist. Hoerni left Amelco just two years after its founding—as would be his habit—to become the most prolific (if not the most successful) entrepreneur the industry has seen, creating at least a dozen new companies.

Also that year, four other Fairchild employees quit to found Signetics, with the help of Corning Glass. Signetics, now partly owned by Philips Electronics of the Netherlands, is at present the fourth largest semiconductor company in the Valley, almost invisible until the late seventies, when a toxic-chemical scandal thrust it into the limelight.

Fairchild, despite the myth, wasn't entirely operating in a vacuum. There were other events taking place in Silicon Valley at this time. Over at Hewlett-Packard, HP Associates had just gotten under way building chips for its parent as one of the first in-house ("captive") semiconductor operations. Not far from Fairchild, a competitive chip company named Siliconix was being founded by ex-TI scientist Richard Lee and William Hugle from Westinghouse. Siliconix, though never a major force in the Valley, is still around and thriving. (Hugle is also still around—to the anger of the Federal Bureau of Investigation, which keeps trying to put him in jail for international espionage.)

But, for the time being, Fairchild was the hottest new company around.

*   *   *

The period from 1961 to 1963 was the critical time for Fairchild Semiconductor. There was one more spin-off during this period, Molectro; but in keeping with the style of its predecessors it was soon in bad shape. This period also saw, in 1962, the TI suit over the integrated circuit.

But what makes this era important is that Fairchild became big enough and important enough to begin attracting the most talented people in the high tech industry. And for that reason, this was the era in which the "true" Fairchild, the source of the myth, began to form.

The talent came from all over. Charlie Sporck and Don Valentine were already there. Jerry Sanders arrived in 1961. Marshall Cox and Bernie Marren came in 1962, along with Roger Borovoy, the premier lawyer of Silicon Valley (he would spend the rest of the decade fighting the TI suit and chasing down patent royalties for Fairchild). The next year saw the arrival of Floyd Kvamme and scores of others who would make up the semiconductor industry of the 1970s. Thus, in these three classes were probably three dozen future Valley presidents or vice-presidents and an untold number of future millionaires.

All of this talent and youth combined with a business so new it had no rules, and the result was barely controlled chaos. Everyone who survived that period has a different memory, many of them having to do with being hired.

Marshall Cox: Like any dumb, naïve M.B.A. student can do, I analyzed the thirty major industries in the world. I did a thesis on it. And I picked electronics. I forget the reason why, but it was a pretty objective review.

Well, I knew no one in electronics, so I went to a head-hunter—this was 1962—and I said I want to get into electronics, can you get me a job interview?

Well, one of them was with this company I had never heard of before called Fairchild, which at the time had a little less than $20 million in sales. I was told they were looking for B.S.E.E.s only. I wasn't one of those. And I was told to bring my résumé, and I forgot it. And then I had a three-o'clock appointment and I had a flat tire going over there, so I was late.

I showed up at the interview about three-thirty and I was just livid. I figured that it was a total waste of time at that point, so I barged in the door and said to Don Valentine, who was the regional manager, "I'm the three-o'clock appointment, I'm thirty minutes late, I don't have a résumé and I'm not a double-E [bachelor of science in electrical engineering]. If you want to end it right now I don't give a shit, but enough's enough."

Which was exactly the kind of guy they were looking for. He hired me on the spot. Which bothered me, because in graduate school you're trained that any company that would offer you a job on the first interview has to be a crappy company . . .

The first week I was at Fairchild was the week of the national sales meeting. I was in L.A. Well, what Fairchild did in those days was to have all the nonlocal guys fly to the plant as part of the sales meeting so they could see the facilities and then go to the sales meeting. None of the L.A. guys went to the plant tour, so I was all alone. Didn't know anybody.

Well, we went on a tour of the main plant in Mountain View and then went up to the San Rafael plant—where they made diodes—for a presentation.

By five o'clock all the presentations were over and we went upstairs for refreshments. Now the second floor wasn't finished at this time, so it was like a big attic upstairs filled with about fifty or sixty guys—and the company served us brownies and scotch. That was it: brownies and scotch. I thought, boy this is some weird company. And my kind of guys . . .

. . . So the next day we all flew down to San Diego to the sales meeting. There was a delay in the flights getting down there so I missed all the kick-off talks by Noyce and Charlie Sporck and Tom Bay and rolled in just in time for a presentation by Mel Phelps, the hybrid product marketing manager.

Mel introduces himself, turns off the lights and starts showing these slides. The first one is this great huge round thing that's kind of gold and has a couple of square black chips inside of it. Now I have absolutely no idea of whether this product we're supposed to be selling is sixteen feet in diameter or .16 inches or what. And at that moment I'm seriously considering driving home.

But then we have a coffee break and the guy I was sitting next to comes over to me and says, "How's it going?" and I say, "Boy, I really don't understand any of this."

And he says to me, "Don't sweat it. I've been in this business for two years and I still don't know what the hell they're talking about. But, man, if you can sell you can sell this stuff."

Cox apparently caught on quick, because a year later, he was part of another recruiting program: Recalls Floyd Kvamme:

[I was working as a project leader at Space Technology Laboratories.] Well, one day I was looking for a diode to do a certain kind of thing in a certain application and I called around. I called the Fairchild guy, who I had never met before, and I asked him if he wouldn't mind calling his home headquarters to see if anyone knew what their forward recovery time coefficient on this diode was because I was interested in its charge analysis aspects.

Well, this guy was a heckuva salesman. He shows up and brings with him this guy who he introduces as the chief engineer from the diode department, and who's the authority on charge analysis.

So I asked this guy a whole lot of questions. But every time I asked him one the salesman would butt in with the answer. Well, all the way down to the lab this salesman, Chas Haba, won't let me get a word in to this expert . . . I never did talk to the diode guy.

As it turned out later, this so-called authority on diodes was actually Marshall Cox. Marshall told me later that on that day he had made four calls with Chas Haba. One time he was a legal expert, then a financial guy, and then something else, and with me he was the diode expert. Marshall told me, "Floyd, you could've talked Greek to me that day, I didn't have the foggiest idea what you were talking about."

A few weeks later Chas came back and said, "Hey, what the heck are you doing here with your semiconductor background?" That's when I went to work at Fairchild.

Fairchild's recruiting methods were an apt prelude to its daily business style. It was a high-pressure, long-hours place, where employees were expected to exhibit almost superhuman endurance and energy. Then, when the day was over, everybody retired to a nearby restaurant-bar, the Wagon Wheel, and boozed and talked business until all hours of the night. It was not a way of life conducive to marriage (and few marriages survived) or a long life-span, but it was perfect for the time and place. It gave Fairchild the bravado it needed to take on the world, and the intense loyalty it had to have to stay together long after there was every reason to quit.

And oh was it a wild time:

Charlie Sporck: It was a very exciting, very high rapport kind of environment. We worked very hard, played very hard. It was frequent nights that lasted all night long. Very difficult on families. Frequently one would stop at the Wagon Wheel on the way home and consume vast quantities of beer before going home or decide to stay up the rest of the night.

Jerry Sanders: I think everybody was drunk most of the time in the semiconductor industry. But I think it was only because we worked so hard. I think it was just conviviality. I think it was just good times. I think we really worked hard and we played hard. I mean there was semiconductors, semiconductors and semiconductors. And the guys who didn't know they had to work hard to drink hard didn't make it. So a lot of those guys just fell out. But, no, I think we were a hard-charging gashouse gang. We were fantastic. But we worked our asses off.

> *Bob Freund:* Up at the San Rafael plant we called ourselves
> the Midnight Raiders. We couldn't get all the equipment we
> needed to do our work from headquarters, so one night
> Hoerni and I and a couple of other guys from the plant drove
> down to the Palo Alto research lab—and while those guys
> were having their Christmas party we stole all the equipment
> we needed.

Still, for all of its craziness, Fairchild still was a product of its time.
While heavy boozing was accepted as part of the life-style, nonconformity was for the most part frowned upon. One looks at the old photographs expecting to see the wild men of the stories and instead stares in
disbelief at sober, Christian-looking men in crew cuts, white shirts and
ties; one sees more sartorial anarchism in a single office at Apple Computer.

Still, Fairchild did tolerate eccentricities in some of its key employees
better than most companies of the era. For example, there was Hollywood Jerry Sanders, with his black Cadillac and long hair and house in
the Hollywood hills. But even he had to face a continuous underground
resentment over his dissolute ways—which surfaced in the notorious
"pink pants" episode, where it was claimed that Sanders had worn just
such an item of apparel into, of all places, IBM.

> *Tim Barry:* I was standing in the hallway and all of sudden
> here comes this guy wearing—I swear to God—bandoleras,
> sombrero and a machete! He was on his way to a staff meet-
> ing. I turned to the guy I was with and said, "Who the hell is
> that?" And the guy said, "Oh, that's Norman Doyle, director
> of linear products . . ."

But if there was one individual whose bizarre behavior was not only
tolerated but admired it was the legendary Bob Widlar.

If brilliance is measured by creativity, then Bob Widlar is one of the
few true geniuses Silicon Valley ever produced. And he picked the right
business: linear circuits, those physically simple but technically elegant
devices that control the flow of electricity into and out of integrated
circuits and other "machines." Unlike digital integrated circuits, which
are the product of scores of designers laying out vast collections of
circuits on charts that look like a wiring and plumbing diagram for a
Midwestern city, the design of linear circuits is an almost private art, an
act of creation like a beautiful miniature toy.

And no one has ever been better at designing linear circuits than Bob Widlar. The list of his inventions reads like the linear circuit hall of fame. Says Kvamme, "Bob was wonderful to work with from a marketing guy's perspective. Yes, he wanted to do a lot of things for himself, but (a) he's a genius, and (b) he's a perfectionist, and therefore what you wanted to do to get maximum utilization out of Bob was to stimulate him and then get out of his way."

As one might imagine, any man with that much talent in such an individual art would have to be very much an independent soul. At Fairchild Widlar was already beginning to make a name for himself as a technical genius and human oddball. For one thing, Widlar kept in his office a big ax. Some claim that whenever he got frustrated he would take the thing and start chopping the hell out of local trees. He was also famous for his capacity for liquor. Bob Simko remembers wandering with Widlar blind drunk down the middle of a deserted Fifth Avenue in a snowstorm trying to figure out how to walk to a sales call in New Jersey.

All the more remarkable was that Widlar's boss was John Hume, a tall, thin, dignified Mormon who eventually worked at HP and then Siliconix. The two worked terrifically with one another because of mutual respect. It was one of the few times Widlar ever worked *with* anyone.

In 1966, in the first of Fairchild's great defections, Widlar quit to try his hand at tycoonship with a faltering little Santa Clara company called National Semiconductor. His exit interview from Fairchild captures the essence of Bob Widlar, and perhaps Silicon Valley.

Fairchild required all of its departing employees to fill out a six-page questionnaire containing detailed questions about their experiences at Fairchild Semiconductor and their future plans. Widlar neatly cut through the horseshit. On each page, in giant block letters, he scrawled one word: I WANT TO GET RICH "X" (he never signed his name). And then he was gone, to reappear several years later with even more outrageous antics at National Semiconductor.

* * *

Despite the stories, Fairchild Semiconductor was an intensely serious company. It had to be. The semiconductor industry was heating into a blast furnace in which a company had to innovate or die. The competition was fierce. Texas Instruments was not only much bigger but a whole lot nastier, with an ugly desire to be a monopoly in every market it entered, even if it took horrendous losses. Down in Phoenix, a former Harvard professor named Lester Hogan was turning Motorola into the hottest firm in microelectronics, at times eclipsing Fairchild.

It was pressure-cooker time at the Mountain View company and though Charlie Sporck has gotten the rap as a shouter and a table pounder, that behavior was apparently standard operating procedure at Fairchild. Says a former employee: "Hey, everybody was a *bam*, smash-the-podium kind of operator. We'd throw chalkboard erasers. You wouldn't believe the shit that went on."

Fairchild, for all of its well-deserved fame for inventiveness, was struggling. Mind you, it didn't necessarily show on the consolidated statement of earnings. By the mid-sixties the company had grown to annual sales of $130 million and employment to twelve thousand, with plants in Maine, north of San Francisco in San Rafael and, in a trend-setting move, an assembly plant in Hong Kong.

All of that meant little, because in high tech extraordinary growth is the norm. What is more important is *relative* growth: how fast you are going compared to your competition, how your upcoming products stack up with theirs, how you are doing in direct competition with them for the big contracts. If your company is "only" tripling in size every year while your competition is quadrupling, then you are falling behind.

Fairchild wasn't falling behind yet, but even by the early 1960s there were signs something was amiss. Certainly there was no shortage of talent, but some glaring missed signals indicated that all of these blue-ribbon employees weren't working as a cohesive team. Little resentments were piling up in the minds of employees in unconscious preparation of some future flash point.

In the marketing department, Bay and Valentine were shuffling the deck as fast as they could, searching for new management combinations to attack ever shifting markets. In 1964, recognizing that 90 percent of Fairchild's business was West Coast and military, and that demand was growing for less expensive ("down and dirty") consumer versions elsewhere, Valentine created regional sales operations in the Midwest (Bernie Marren) and the East (Jim Martin), as well as the West (Jerry Sanders). All were highly successful and Fairchild began to reassert itself. For a time it looked as though the growing feuds between the company's sales, manufacturing and research departments might be sublimated to a revitalized corporate esprit de corps.

But it wasn't to be. Within a year, Bob Noyce was promoted to

Fairchild group vice-president and given added executive responsibilities over instrumentation, graphics products and several other divisions in addition to semiconductors. Bay, the beloved marketing executive, left Mountain View and was given charge of instrumentation and the other "funny" (i.e., lesser) divisions. Charlie Sporck was named general manager of Fairchild Semiconductor.

In retrospect, this move, which probably seemed so logical at the time, was the worst thing that could have happened to Fairchild. Before, each of those individuals was in a position to make best use of his strengths while minimizing his weaknesses. Now they were being thrust into roles where just the opposite was true.

Bob Noyce, for example, didn't seem to enjoy running a very large company, and his natural bent toward research had been at the cost of Fairchild's manufacturing ("Noyce always gave priority to Gordon Moore in R & D over Sporck in manufacturing," says an insider). But, as Cox says, "Bob had it all. He had the charm, the charisma, the personality, to absolutely knock off most customers in terms of winning them over. He had vision."

Noyce alone could keep Fairchild together. No matter what the frustration felt in a particular department, everyone worshipped Bob Noyce.

But now Noyce, the glue holding the entrepreneurial spirits of Fairchild from flying apart, was gone, kicked upstairs to a corporate job. And Sporck was in the general manager's chair.

Charlie Sporck was never what could be called a charismatic personality, but he was a pro—and a better line manager than Noyce. He knew how to run a company to make it competitive again. One of his first steps was to build up the operations wing of Fairchild with some powerhouse talents like Pierre Lamond and Roger Smullen, beefing up the production side of the firm in a way he had been frustrated from accomplishing before.

But Charlie was not the type of guy to be dealing with an old-line East Coast corporation. What had been built at Fairchild was a new type of corporate culture that mixed the casualness of California life with the youth and boundless energy of young electronics whiz kids. Tom Wolfe captured the differences between Fairchild corporate and Fairchild Semiconductor well, if a bit hyperbolically:

> One day John Carter came to Mountain View for a close
> look at Noyce's semiconductor operation. Carter's office in

Syosset, Long Island, arranged for a limousine and chauffeur to be at his disposal while he was in California. So Carter arrived at the tilt-up concrete building in Mountain View in the back of a black Cadillac limousine with a driver in the front wearing the complete chauffeur's uniform—the black suit, the white shirt, the black necktie, and the black visored cap. That in itself was enough to turn heads at Fairchild Semiconductor. Nobody had ever seen a limousine and a chauffeur out there before. But that wasn't what fixed the day in everybody's memory. It was the fact that the driver stayed out there for almost eight hours, *doing nothing . . .* Here was a serf who *did nothing all day* but wait outside a door in order to be at the service of the haunches of his master instantly, whenever those haunches and the paunch and the jowls might decide to reappear. It wasn't merely that this little peek at the New York-style corporate high life was unusual out here in the brown hills of the Santa Clara Valley. It was that it seemed *terribly wrong.*

Fairchild wasn't in the hills, and the Valley had seen limousines before, and with typical American interest in the gentry, the Fairchilders probably looked at the limousine and driver with as much awe as disgust, but Wolfe does capture the glaring difference between the caste-oriented East Coast way of doing business and the (at least at the time) more egalitarian Silicon Valley style.

No one had that Everyman style more than Charlie Sporck. Even the fact that he preferred to be called Charlie is indicative of how Sporck felt about executive rows and conspicuous consumption and putting on airs. And now, Charlie Sporck, who didn't toady to anyone, suddenly found himself answering to the upper-crust corporate headquarters in New York. It wasn't long before he was looking for a way out.

Meanwhile, the rest of the company was adjusting to the new changes. Most were positive, so morale stayed high. Besides, if one wanted to stay in the Valley there really wasn't much choice. Defections were rare because all of the previous attempts at start-ups by "Fairchildren" (Adam Smith's phrase) had been singularly unsuccessful. The last big one had been General Micro-Electronics, founded by three Fairchild employees and a Marine Corps general. GME is important to the history of the Valley for two reasons: first, because it attempted to make integrated circuits using a new technology called metal-oxide semiconductors (MOS), which in time would become the industry standard (GME, unfortunately, was ahead of its time), and second, because although it fell on hard times and sold out to Philco-Ford in 1966, it nevertheless made millionaires of its founders—a lesson for budding entrepreneurs at Fairchild.

Fairchild Semiconductor was adapting to the changes resulting from promotions at the top. The critical adjustment was in finding a new director of marketing to fill Tom Bay's slot, and the race was between Bob Graham, the product marketing manager, and Don Valentine, the national sales manager, two of the better businessmen in the company. Valentine won and Graham quit and left for ITT, diminishing the company by one more talented individual.

The difference between the departing Bay and his replacement Valentine was like day and night. Bay was a mediocre manager but a superb leader, the mentor for many of the Valley's leaders. A tall, handsome, well-dressed man, Bay represented to these young salesmen everything they wanted to be: brilliant, assured, yet one of the boys. For Marshall Cox, on whose board of directors Bay now sits, Tom Bay "was probably the industry's first great marketing guy . . . almost like a god, that was available, you know, to drink with you, and get drunk with you and chase broads with you." For Jerry Sanders, "Bay was a real counselor, a big brother to me."

Valentine was none of these things: "the straightest guy in the world" according to one report, "a real taskmaster" according to another. He also was probably the least sales-oriented marketing manager that ever lived. He almost immediately alienated Jerry Sanders, creating a feud that lasts until this day. But others he quickly impressed with his integrity. And whatever charm Valentine lacked, he made up in smarts. For years, Valentine had dreamed about how he would reorganize Fairchild's marketing operation if given the opportunity. Now at last he had that opportunity, and the organization he put together not only kept Fairchild together for years but has been successfully imitated and taught in business schools ever since.

Organizing by market it was called, and it consisted of turning the marketing operation into four little independent companies. At the top of these groups were the Four Horsemen, Martin, Sanders, Cox and Marren, assigned to, respectively, the industrial, military, computer and consumer markets. Each group in turn was fully staffed with its own sales, product marketing, engineering, even advertising and legal departments. Making it all the more remarkable was the age of the Four Horsemen.

> *Marren:* The thing that amazed you in 1965 was that I had just turned thirty, and Jerry Sanders was twenty-nine, and Cox was thirty and Jim Martin was thirty-one. Noyce was thirty-seven and he was among the oldest guys at Fairchild Semiconductor. It was amazing. I'd never gone into a large company before where nobody was old. Nobody was even forty and the girls on the production line were about the same age as the managers of the company.

The new arrangement was not only revolutionary, it actually worked. Until that time corporate research and development had talked primarily to operations and not to marketing/sales. This was a major bone of contention. One case in point was the computer market, where a particular Fairchild diode would have been the hottest thing around except that it was the wrong voltage—nobody had checked to see what the computer industry wanted—so there was no market for it.

Another source of contention, and one that was never solved during the original incarnation of Fairchild, was MOS. Even with the reorganization, the sales people, seeing the growing market demand for it, pleaded for Fairchild R & D to add MOS products to the existing and competing bipolar-type integrated-circuit line. Noyce and R & D director Gordon Moore never got behind the idea—remarkably, as when they founded Intel, the new firm was dedicated to MOS. Said one Fairchilder, "Everybody knew that MOS was the wave of the future. It was obviously the technology for goddamn calculators. Everyone could smell it. And yet we couldn't get anybody to work on it."

Nevertheless, the new marketing organization, to Valentine's credit, worked brilliantly, the corporate backlog of orders growing rapidly. The only hitch seemed to be the company's product marketing department, devastated by the departure of Graham. But that problem seemed to disappear when the product marketing people were shifted under the Four Horsemen.

Then, all of sudden, Fairchild's manufacturing wing began to unravel. Many have speculated on how that happened, particularly with manufacturing king Sporck at the head of the company. Perhaps Sporck had his mind on other problems, or maybe manufacturing needed his day-to-day attention to function, or, as some guess, years of neglect by corporate headquarters finally caught up with it. One might even offer the possibility that the industry was suffering the first of the delivery-time slippages that have dogged it ever since.

Whatever the reason, manufacturing was suddenly unable to keep up with the orders coming in from the new powerhouse marketing operation, which now, for the first time, was working well with R & D. Thus, the labs were devising what the customers wanted, the sales people were getting the orders and now Fairchild couldn't build the product.

It was now 1966. The next blow was the departure of Bob Widlar and his linear team. Brilliant, crazy Widlar, the genius, the madman, who epitomized Fairchild's innovative greatness and its hell-raising style. It was clear to everyone now that Fairchild Semiconductor was no longer the mischievous child prodigy of American business.

At the top, Charlie Sporck was doing everything he could do to keep the company together. "One of the things we tried to do was convince [Fairchild corporate] that they should lay more stock options on these technical people inside the corporation to increase the desirability of staying with the company. But they could never see that to the extent that we wanted it. I don't think they really understood the environment that existed out here."

Something was clearly happening in the marketplace. The entrepreneurial urge was beginning to bite everyone. So bad did it become that at the 1966 Institute of Electrical and Electronic Engineers (IEEE) conference, recruiting was barred for fear it would turn the meeting into a riot. Nevertheless, according to *Electronics* magazine, "One company official summed up the intensity of the talent search when he said: 'The show was a success. Our company only lost three men.' "

None of this was lost on a frustrated Charlie Sporck. "It started to dawn on us that hey, you know, fifty million Frenchmen can't be wrong, that maybe there is something to this starting up a new company.

"I basically came to that conclusion in 1966. But I looked at it a little differently, that the strength I had was for management, that it would make more sense for me to join a company that was in trouble."

He found that company in National Semiconductor. And, in the blow that ended Fairchild as a viable force in the semiconductor industry, Sporck and a group of four other executives walked out of Fairchild in February 1967.

Floyd Kvamme was the junior member of the group, which included Sporck, Fred Bialek, Roger Smullen and Pierre Lamond. Recalls Kvamme:

When we started to get together, when I was approached relative to joining "the National team," I really didn't even know who was on the team. Pierre pushed me. He said, "Hey, you know, just key guys, I can't tell you anything more." So I basically found out that I was resigning from Fairchild the Sunday afternoon before the Monday it happened.

The way it happened was that Charlie resigned for all five of us. That was on Monday and here I am sitting next to Jerry Sanders my boss and he doesn't know I've resigned. Heck, I'm not even sure I've resigned.

So, Monday went by, and nothing. Tuesday went by, nothing. Finally on Wednesday afternoon, Jerry walks by my door and looks in with this strange look on his face. That's when I knew that he knew.

Jerry never talked to me about it. But Tom Bay tried to talk me out of it, because I was the junior member and they probably figured that if they could knock one guy out of it they could break up the team.

By Thursday afternoon I decided I'd better disappear. What I really did was go over to the Stanford library to get some work done. While I was there I thought about what I was doing and I said, hey, I'm going to do this. I don't see anything wrong with doing this. I realized, yeah, there's a risk, but I had taken risks before.

. . . You have to realize that other than the group that had gone to ITT, no one had broken away from Fairchild for years. Nobody had done it. And the guys were saying, "Hey, man, you gotta be crazy. What makes you believe that somebody else can make it?" The headline in the *Business Week* article when National broke away was "What's a Five Million Dollar Company Doing with a Hundred Million Dollar Management?"

What Kvamme didn't know at the time was that Sanders had actually done everything he could to keep Kvamme, the only émigré from the marketing department around. Says Sanders, "I enlisted Bob Noyce's aid, but he was no help; he called him the wrong name. He called him Cloyd, for Cloyd Marvin.

"Now don't get me wrong, we couldn't have turned Floyd Kvamme around if Bob Noyce had legally adopted him. But it was just a little thing I remembered, because I was so sales-oriented, and, you know, we were telling him how important he was and he got called by the wrong name."

Sporck's resignation hit Fairchild like a pickax blow. It was a self-induced coup d'état. If the head of the company saw greener pastures elsewhere, why shouldn't everybody else? After all, maybe he knew something.

The company went into temporary shock. It was more than just the departure of the general manager, it was the idea, still common in those more innocent Silicon Valley days, that you stayed with a company for a full career. Some guys may have quit because they didn't see any future, and Widlar . . . well, Widlar was Widlar. But for Sporck, who had made it to the top, to suddenly pack it in for more money assaulted everything everyone had learned about business etiquette and career planning. Says one former Fairchild employee: "I was somewhere between stunned, scared and brokenhearted."

Says Jerry Sanders:

> So we were plowing along at Fairchild, you know, number one in the world in integrated circuits. And then Charlie Sporck did something that shocked me to my boots. Charlie Sporck resigned. I couldn't believe it. I remember it so well. I just could not believe it. I mean, to me, you didn't resign from a company you believed in. I mean, you know, this was a lifetime thing, I was convinced that someday I would be the president of Fairchild, whenever my turn came up. Certainly I'd be in my sixties, but someday I'd be president . . . So I said to Charlie, "I'm going to paraphrase what the kid said to Shoeless Joe Jackson. Charlie, say it isn't so."
>
> And he said, "Well, it is so." Which was Charlie, you know. And I said, "Why?" And I remember what he said, and I never understood it. He said, "I don't want to feel like a kid pissing in his pants." I thought "Huh?" And he said, "I want to run my own show, I want to do it my way and I don't want to be shaking in my boots feeling like a little kid. And treated like a little kid."

Perhaps most devastated by Sporck's departure was Noyce himself. After all, Charlie was in many ways Noyce's right-hand man, the foundation of the company, the man to whom Noyce had entrusted Fairchild. Says Noyce:

> There had been a number of defections and they started to get to me after a while. There was no way I could keep Charlie Sporck there, the offers from the outside were too substantial. [Charlie] was well liked. Very well liked. He was a straightforward person. And I suppose I essentially cried when he left. I just felt that things were falling apart, and I just felt a great personal loss, frankly. You know, working with people that you're fond of, then having them break apart, was I would almost say devastating.

Sporck himself dismisses the importance of his departure: "I agree that what I brought to Fairchild was an excellent manufacturing reputation. Manufacturing was a shortcoming of the company, but it was a very, very excellent organization. I would say Fairchild became a strong manufacturing organization, and I would take credit for that. But I don't agree [that my departure crippled the firm]. It was later when the rest of them left."

From the day of Sporck's departure, Fairchild began to hemorrhage talent. After the initial shock, the company tried to piece itself together. The operations department was devastated. The jobs there were filled by "second-stringers" who never quite caught up to their predecessors. Don Yost, the company's superb linear manufacturer, became head of IC production, an area he knew little about.

Most importantly, Tom Bay was brought back from the East Coast to be general manager. It was a welcome homecoming for the Four Horseman and the rest of the marketing department. Cox: "We were all thrilled and grateful for that. At least, you know, good ol' Tom is back, so it isn't so bad, now we're really going to let her rip."

But Fairchild didn't move. For the three years between 1965 and 1968, Fairchild effectively froze in the marketplace as it tore its insides out. Sales had been flat at $120 million, and starting in mid-1967 the company was unprofitable for more than a year and a half. During this time, TI and Motorola both passed Fairchild in sales and profits. From Phoenix, Motorola president Lester Hogan watched the disintegration of Fairchild with amazement, trying to figure out what was going on:

> The main problem was factory facilitation. They had a very low yield and low productivity in their factories because they had not spent the capital wisely in modernizing the factory. The technology, though, was superb. At the time I considered Fairchild to be the technology leader and I got some glee out

of burying them alive when I didn't have the technology they had. [By 1968] Motorola had probably 60 percent of the worldwide sales in silicon planar transistors, even though they had been invented at Fairchild.

For the time being, the company was in the hands of Tom Bay. It would have taken a management genius to put Fairchild back together at this point and Bay, the great marketing guru, was just not up to the task. It only made things worse that he was generally loved.

Meanwhile, National was stealing Fairchild blind of its top employees. Every time one of the National defectors showed up at one of the favorite local wateringholes, the Wagon Wheel, Chez Yvonne and Rickey's, they would be pelted by résumés from their old compatriots. To keep from getting sued, National agreed not to hire directly from Fairchild; but for those people they wanted, like Jerry Sanders, they cheated by getting the person hired somewhere else first and then bringing him into National several months later. Fairchild did not react. Noyce, whose future company Intel would be notorious for suing the bejesus out of spin-offs, will say only that he saw no reason for a lawsuit: after all, Sporck "took absolutely nothing in terms of proprietary information."

> *Cox:* You know we had terrific guys in R & D at Fairchild then. We had terrific guys in marketing, we had terrific guys in legal counsel, industrial relations, a lot of activities. But the one place we were weak was manufacturing and that was the direct, devastating result of having those terrific guys leave and go to National. I mean, who's kidding who? What Fairchild should have done when those guys left is what everybody does now when somebody important leaves: sue their ass.
>
> It had a real funky kind of effect on everybody at Fairch. We used to go to the Wagon Wheel on Friday night, and it slowly turned into "Well, it's Friday, who did National grab this week?" Son of a bitch. They always got some good engineering, some process guy or something. It really was a negative. It was like, "Jesus Christ, Tom [Bay], sue their fucking asses, what the hell's wrong?" But he wouldn't.

Not long after Bay's ascension, Noyce too got tapped, this time to move up into a triumvirate to run Fairchild Camera and Instrument. Noyce wanted no part of it.

> I guess I simply didn't want to move up into that sort of environment. I wanted to stay in California. The corporate headquarters were in New York. Besides, Fairchild Camera had a number of businesses in it that I wasn't particularly interested in—like the reconnaissance business, the printing-press business, things like that. And also, just looking at my personal life, I had gotten a lot more enjoyment out of starting things from scratch than running a large company—and in a real sense I still do. The other personal motivation was simply finding out by myself whether the success of Fairchild had been a lucky fluke or whether it was something I had done well.

In June 1968, Noyce announced his resignation from the company he had founded and made great. He agreed to stay on long enough to find a replacement, at last leaving in August, taking with him R & D boss Gordon Moore and process development expert Andy Grove.

With Noyce and Moore went the last of Fairchild Semiconductor's original founders.

The Fairchild Camera executive troika set about looking for a new chief executive officer to replace Noyce. According to corporate counsel Roger Borovoy, they considered executives from Alloys Unlimited and Fairchild Industries but in the end followed Noyce's suggestion and offered the job to Fairchild's greatest competitor, Dr. C. Lester Hogan of Motorola. Thanks to an extraordinary compensation package, Hogan accepted.

On the day the announcement was made, August 8, 1968, as a sign of how relieved the market was to see a sign of organization at Fairchild Semiconductor, Fairchild Camera and Instrument stock jumped 20 points. And as an indication of the respect for Hogan, Motorola's stock fell 15 points. Less than three weeks later, Motorola filed a suit against Fairchild that kept Borovoy busy for six years.

Hogan's arrival was met with fear and dismay at Fairchild. After all, he was a hated competitor. It didn't help that immediately on his arrival he fired Bay. It was probably a necessary move, one Noyce had not been able to bring himself to do, but to have this usurper do it was almost unbearable.

The sales people were in Hawaii on a meeting when they heard of Hogan's hiring. They prepared a big sign saying "We love you Les" (it was Sanders' idea) and were photographed holding the sign while wearing beach clothes. They knew they were smiling in the teeth of disaster. Bay, who was at the meeting, had already flown home and been fired. The sales and marketing executives had already heard of "Hogan's Heroes," his team of managers that he was bringing with him—and they figured that their heads would be the next to roll.

They weren't far off. In fact the arrangement would be worse than that: the Heroes were to be inserted above all of the old Fairchild executives.

Marshall Cox tells the story of those early days best:

> I can vividly remember Les's executive staff meetings. It would be like all the directors of Fairchild on one side of the table and all the new guys from Motorola on the other. It was like the Gaza Strip down the center.
>
> So Les says, "Listen, gentlemen, I know there's been a lot of rumors relative to tons of people coming up from Motorola. I want you to know it's all bullshit. The staff you see here from Motorola is the last of the, uh, Motorola types coming in— Excuse me a second, the phone's ringing . . . Hello? They're in the lobby? There's seven of them with suitcases? Just tell them to wait there for a few minutes . . . Now, gentlemen, there's no truth whatsoever— Excuse me a minute . . . There's five more in the lobby?"
>
> I mean, it was like the Katzenjammer Kids. It was that gross. He must have had ten phone calls from the receptionist wanting to know what to do with all these guys showing up.
>
> To make matters worse, a lot of these guys were guys we had fired in the past because they were noodles and now they were coming back to be our bosses. It was unbelievable.

The situation only grew worse. Obviously the company wasn't going to survive like this. Within weeks, key Fairchild employees were diving out of the firm. Of the marketing people who had held up the sign greeting Hogan, all were gone within six months. Perhaps the saddest case was Jerry Sanders, who had once worked for Les. Still hanging on to the illusion that one should be loyal to one's company, Sanders stayed longer than most—only to suffer the ignominy of being fired. "I saw Jerry over the holidays," Cox recalls, "and he was lower than a snake's hips because he had just gotten dumped; he had gotten fucked over like everybody else. By then a five-year Fairchild pin had turned into a handicap, not an asset."

Fairchild had now sprung leaks from every department, from every office. By the time Hogan learned of his error, it was too late. The legendary Fairchild Semiconductor had died—to be replaced by a ghost. The many employees who had left were now finding work at Sporck's National Semiconductor or Sanders's Advanced Micro Devices or Noyce's Intel. Others were trying their own hand at entrepreneurship, with companies like Four-Phase Systems Inc., Cartesian, Precision Monolithics, Computer Micro Technology, Qualidyne, Advanced Memory Systems and Integrated Electronics. Soon they were involved with the pressing business of keeping a new company afloat, and the memories of Fairchild receded, to be wrapped in myth.

Marshall Cox, who later would be president of Intersil and then cofound (with his old counterpart Bernie Marren) chip distributor Western Microtechnology, would before he left in September 1968 see the last gasp of the old Fairchild panache—this time Hogan style:

> On my last day at Fairchild, Les calls me into his office and says, "Well, whataya going to do?" And I said, "I'm going to go. I've thought about it and I just think it would be better if I go." And he said that he didn't want me to go and that he wanted me to be *the* marketing guy and all that, and I said that I just wanted to leave.
>
> So Les—this was really great—calls to his secretary and says, "Please come in here with the corporate checkbook."
>
> So she puts this corporate checkbook in front of Les and with a flourish he writes the check to me, dates it and signs his name, then turns the book around to me and says, "Fill in any number you want to make next year." Now at that time I was probably making maybe fifty grand and I knew I could have written in two hundred thousand and Les wouldn't have blinked an eye. I told him that there ain't no number big enough to keep me and that I knew I had to go.
>
> But I've got to give Les credit. I was really impressed. I mean that was something Cash McCall would do, baby . . .

*   *   *

So ended the original Fairchild, like most companies, on a downbeat —but with a certain brash style. As time passed, and the Fairchildren began to identify with their new companies, the pain of their final years at Fairchild Semiconductor diminished. So did the feuds and rivalries— mainly because they had been supplanted by new feuds and rivalries.

For the leaders of Silicon Valley's semiconductor industry, Fairchild was like a college, where with comparatively little risk they could practice the techniques that would mean corporate life or death when they were on their own. And like college, Fairchild was looked upon fondly as a simpler, purer time.

So, with time, the old Fairchild Semiconductor began to take on a new image: that of a corporate Paradise Lost—and, by extension, youth and innocence gone forever. In memory, Fairchild, which only in the beginning had the great success attributed to it, began to take on the trappings of a supercompany, greater than any company that would ever follow. At Semiconductor Industry Association meetings or cocktail parties or chance meetings in restaurants or at conferences, its alumni, the aging Fairchildren, would reminisce about the good times, mourn the dead or missing and play their own game of "what if." And together they would remember a time when everyone they respected and cared about worked in one shiny new company with infinite potential and the opportunity to make up the game as they went along.

> *Marshall Cox:* It was like there was a semper fi. There was pride, there was the awareness that you were really working with sharp guys, fun guys, sophisticated, professional guys . . .
>
> What I liked most about it was that from the day I showed up at Fairchild I could be just me. They liked me just being me. I didn't play a role and be something I wasn't. I really felt natural.
>
> I think it was that way for everybody and it started with the awareness that Noyce was a nugget, Sporck was a nugget, Bay was a nugget, Valentine was a nugget and the people they hired were nuggets too. It was just an unbelievably high percentage of really outstanding people at one place—and we knew it. There was a prestige to being there—particularly when you keep in mind we were so damn young. It was just an incredible happening, and it will probably never happen again . . .

PROFILE
The Grand Old Man

C. LESTER HOGAN

Dr. C. Lester Hogan sits in his spacious office like an old king stripped of his kingdom and his subjects. He is a big, heavyset man with a large stomach, a thick neck and smooth, pink skin. He has gray, thinning hair, wears tortoiseshell glasses, pulls on a cigarette and speaks in a slow gravelly baritone that puts his every word in Barnum typeface.

There is a sadness to Hogan's presence in this room at Fairchild Camera and Instrument Corp. If the man has had one failure in his distinguished career, it was here. The collapse of Fairchild, one of the most important firms in American business history, is often, at cocktail parties and in private conversations, blamed on Hogan. After all, the argument goes, didn't Hogan's arrival at Fairchild precipitate the great loss of talent that created the modern Silicon Valley? And wasn't it Hogan's fair-haired boy, Wilfred Corrigan, who took over the firm, cynically ran it into the ground, then sold off the empty husk to Schlumberger—French, of all things, and not even an electronics company?

But it is the counterargument which Hogan is convinced the Valley really accepts: that he inherited a company already in deep trouble and breaking up, did the best job he could to get the firm on its feet and was about to be successful when Corrigan stole the firm away and turned him into an impotent figurehead.

Which story the Valley leaders really believe is arguable. Perhaps they believe both. Hogan is treated with considerable respect, with the honorary titles and speechmaking opportunities afforded to a Grand

Old Man of the industry. Yet at the same time there is a subtle distance, a coolness, when the leading lights of the local semiconductor houses talk of "Les"; one mustn't forget that many of these middle-aged chip tycoons were talented young men with dreams when they dove out of Fairchild or were fired by Hogan.

Les Hogan continues to sit in his office at Fairchild because he has been asked to by Schlumberger. Officially he is an adviser to the firm. But there is more to it than that. Hogan has had many victories in his life: he is a famous researcher who invented an important electronic device, a highly respected professor of electronics at Harvard and a hugely successful director of Motorola's semiconductor operations in Arizona.

Even now, Hogan is scoring impressive victories. By being an early and prescient investor in one of the most exciting electronic firms of the 1980s—Rolm (digital PBXs)—Hogan has continued to extend his influence as well as make many millions of dollars. Hogan's initial investment of $36,000 in Rolm has turned into $3 million—more money than he ever made at Fairchild. (He has also had failures, too, notably an investment in the ill-starred Osborne Computer.)

But the blot on Les Hogan's name, what should have been his crowning achievement, is the smoking black hole of Fairchild. That may be why, though fame rests elsewhere, Hogan sits in his office at Fairchild. It may not be vindication, but to Hogan somewhere in there may be a measure of justice.

Lester Hogan was born in 1920 in Great Falls, Montana, one of many Silicon Valley tycoons born in Middle America. Great Falls had a population at the time of about thirty thousand, a good-sized, self-contained prairie metropolis: "You know where the city limits are. You don't have to put up a sign because it's a hundred fifty miles from there to the next house . . . not like we do here on the peninsula where you have no idea whether you're in Sunnyvale or Mountain View—and it really doesn't matter anyway because all the cities are all glommed together."

Hogan attended public school in Great Falls and, like most kids of his era interested in electronics, he built radios as a hobby. In high school, Hogan's favorite and most inspiring teacher was a chemist, so when Hogan was accepted to Montana State University in Bozeman, he decided to study chemical engineering.

> But about midway through my freshman year, I asked myself, what in the hell am I doing in chemical engineering? This

is really not where I belong, but I don't know where I *do* belong. So I asked for an appointment with the dean of engineering—not knowing that he grew up as a chemical engineer.

He pointed out to me that every red-blooded American boy first chooses chemical engineering and if he fails at that, he might become a [Hogan winks] journalist or something else.

Hogan laughs ruefully. "Now I was old enough and smart enough to know I was being bullshitted . . . I knew it was nothing but his prejudice, but I thought, shit, what do I do next?"

Hogan went to the school's dean of men and explained his dilemma. The dean sent the young man to the psychology department to take a battery of "interest" (as opposed to aptitude) tests.

Hogan picked businessman, college professor, research scientist and electrical engineer as potential career choices. A few days later, a stunned psychologist informed the young man he'd come out at the top of the scale in each area—something that had never happened before. So once again Les Hogan was left without a career path. He graduated from Montana State with a degree in chemical engineering.

Remarkably, in validation of those "interest" tests forty years ago, Hogan became successful in each of those careers predicted for him.

Hogan spent the Second World War working on a top-secret torpedo project, delivering the weapons to the Pacific and training submarine crews in their use. The experience convinced Hogan that his future lay in electronics.

Yet, by "a pretty good stroke of luck," when Hogan returned to civilian life to pursue a doctorate, he picked physics as his major, not electrical engineering. The decision was fortuitous, because eighteen months before he finished his doctorate, Shockley at Bell Labs announced the invention of the transistor.

Says Hogan, ". . . chemical engineering and physics—there couldn't have been a better combination in the world . . . if I had taken electrical engineering, I would have ended up learning the *Handbook of Electrical Engineering* and never would have read Shockley's paper and understood it."

After studying Shockley's transistor paper, Hogan knew where he wanted to go—Bell Labs—and he had good enough credentials to make it. He joined Bell in 1950.

Bell Labs in the 1950s was one of those remarkable places where great scientific breakthroughs are made, with a confluence of great minds, a laissez-faire corporate parent and corporate pockets deep enough to support tangential forays into theoretical projects with little prospect of ever paying off. Such flowerings of creativity are necessarily rare and ephemeral. Great minds are usually fragile and quickly chafe in even the least organized surroundings. The company itself is perpetually on a tightrope, sober minds constantly questioning how long the firm can continue underwriting arcane—and often incomprehensible—research with little chance of ever improving the bottom line. Changing the world is nice, but shareholders and market analysts focus on quarterly profit-and-loss statements.

Hogan got a taste of the Bell Labs environment the day he arrived: "I asked my boss, 'Well, what do you want me to work on?' And he said, 'Why don't you go down to the library and spend a week or two and go through the literature and see if you can find something that tickles your fancy!'"

It was a pleasant, if somewhat mystifying, assignment. To have the opportunity to do anything offered the added risk of becoming paralyzed with indecision and doing nothing at all. Hogan decided that to help narrow down his options to a manageable size, he would choose a physics project—and with that infinitesimal constraint, he embarked on a survey of recent literature in the field.

After a few days, he came across a technical paper written by a scientist named D. D. H. Tellegen, a researcher at the Philips Research Laboratory in Eindhoven, Holland. In the paper, Tellegen started with Maxwell's equations, the centerpiece of all modern electromechanical theory, and extrapolated from there.

"His article was purely mathematical," Hogan recalls. "He had no engineering intuition at all."

What Tellegen had done was to show that the four known building blocks of electrical circuitry (resistor, capacitor, inductor and transformer) and their properties could be derived directly from Maxwell's equations. That was impressive enough, but the Dutch scientist had an even bigger card to play:

"He said, you know, Maxwell's equations predict yet *another* circuit element!

"Now to us, you know, to electrical engineers, Maxwell's equations are what Matthew, Mark, Luke and John are to theologians. They're the Bible. That's where we start. If Maxwell's equations predict that something funny is going to happen, it's got to happen, and we've got to figure out what it is."

This fifth circuit element, Tellegen predicted, would have some strange properties, much like that of a mechanical gyroscope. For that reason, Tellegen called this as yet unbuilt circuit a gyrator. As a final kicker, Tellegen said that Maxwell's equations indicated that if such a circuit could be built it would violate the theory of reciprocity.

It was this last statement that stunned and then excited Hogan. As the four known passive circuits upheld reciprocity, this so-called gyrator would certainly be a breakthrough, almost of the magnitude of the transistor.

To appreciate why Tellegen's prediction was important it is necessary to understand reciprocity in the technical sense. An optical analogy is helpful: if you were to set up a series of mirrors, concave and convex lenses, crystals and prisms in such a way as to create a path for a beam of light, after being reflected and refracted the light beam would emerge from this optical gauntlet always in a certain form and at a certain location. If you were then to go to this exit point and place a mirror to bounce the light back through in exactly the opposite direction, the beam would come out of the original entrance in exactly the form it entered.

Now here was this thing called a gyrator that, it was claimed, would break this law. Says Hogan: "I thought, I've got to find out a way to do this thing; that's what I want to do. So I went to my boss and he said, 'Sounds exciting.' "

Now, Hogan suddenly realized, all he had to do was invent the fifth building block of electronics.

The first step, he decided, was to sit down and brainstorm out all the possible solutions he could imagine. He came up with fourteen, but after doing the necessary mathematical analysis he concluded that not a one was practical.

That failed, Hogan asked himself what other natural phenomena violated reciprocity. He thumbed through all of the physics books he could find. The search took fifteen weeks, but Hogan found his answer. A polarized beam of light rotated axially by a magnetic field along the beam's path was unique in all of nature for violating reciprocity. The twisted light beam would come off this "faraday rotation" at an angle X, a function of the polarizing material and the strength of the magnetic field. Putting a mirror at the beam's exit point would result in a returning beam at the entrance, not back to its original form, but twisted still further to an angle of 2X.

Perfect. After all, weren't microwaves—a hot new area of electronics after the war—simply high-frequency light? Now, Hogan decided, all he needed to build a gyrator was the right polarizing material to give the waves a shift of, say, 45 degrees. He wrote up his discovery in his notebook and had it witnessed.

It wasn't until later that Hogan discovered how difficult achieving that 45-degree twist would be. For example, using a liquid called carbon disulfide, a material well known for its very high faraday rotation number, he would still need a tube filled with the stuff approximately a half mile long—not exactly practical for an airplane radar or a portable microwave communications transmitter.

So obviously that wouldn't do. Then Hogan remembered that some optical work had been done with magnetized-iron film spread so thin that it was almost transparent. When tested, these films twisted light just a fraction of a degree—but given the thinness of the film, that amounted to several thousand degrees per centimeter.

"So," Hogan recalls, "all I needed was something that was magnetic and yet transparent to microwave frequencies." He found the material, of all places, at Tellegen's own company, Philips. It was a magnetic ceramic called a ferrite.

> An interesting thing: Philips Labs invented and developed ferrites in World War II. They were the source of all knowledge about ferrites. When the war was over nobody knew anything about ferrites except Philips. They had kept it secret from their German masters . . . They developed this brand-new magnetic material and the world found out about it when we sent our troops through—because right behind those troops were our scientists, who asked the Philips scientists what they had.

After cajoling Bell's ferrite scientists and microwave engineers to develop for him the right materials and set up the proper equipment, Hogan was ready to test his theory.

He went to see the Great Man himself, Dr. William Shockley. "I asked him if there were any flaws in the material—and that guy's brilliant, he's absolutely brilliant; he jumped up to the blackboard, worked through the equations and said, 'You know, this is amazing.' "

That was all Hogan needed to hear. He now sat back and waited for the different parties to bring together the pieces of his invention. "All I was was a synthesizer. I didn't build a single thing. People at Bell Labs headquarters built the wave-guide plumbing for me, the metallurgical department built the ferrite and it was all [a microwave scientist's] equipment. The day before it all came together, we tore down his project and got things set up for my project. And *he* did most of that. All I really did was when the parts arrived I went over there and we plugged it in.

"On November 1, three months after I arrived there, I built the world's first practical, nonreciprocal passive circuit"—the gyrator. "Today there are several hundred different types. You can't build a microwave circuit today without one of my devices." For example, there are an estimated two hundred gyrators (and the related isolators and inductors) on the IntelSat 5 satellite. Acclaim came quickly. "Here I am internationally famous and I've only worked there three months. Bell Labs thought I was a genius, but it was luck."

Les Hogan was now thirty years old. He had worked in the corporate world for 180 days and already he had invented a multimillion-dollar product. It looked as though he had embarked on an impressive lifetime of laboratory work.

However, Hogan would never conduct pure research again.

There was a lot more work to be done in ferrite technology and in refining the function of the gyrator. But Hogan didn't have a chance to do much of it. The world had heard about this fifth circuit and wanted to hear from its creator. Hogan was sent on a lecture tour that took him throughout the world. "Everybody had to hear about it, you know? It wasn't as important an invention as the transistor but in some ways it was even more exciting because it appeared to violate the second law of thermodynamics . . . and anything that appears to be that weird, of course, excites engineers the world over."

In the next two and a half years, Hogan talked about his invention to ready audiences and in between worked on perfecting it. If the technical conferences and faculty speeches kept him from his research work, they did offer Hogan the chance to meet some of the leading lights in the electronics world—some of whom he would later employ.

One of these speeches, at Harvard in 1953, found Hogan his next job. After that speech, he received a phone call from John Van Vleck, dean of the School of Engineering and Applied Physics. Van Vleck was one of the most distinguished scientists in the world. Within three years he would win a Nobel Prize. He offered Hogan a faculty post.

Upon giving notice at Bell, Hogan was hustled into the office of the company's executive vice-president. The exec V.P. noted the precedent of the lab's newly appointed president, who had left Bell Labs for a few years of teaching at Harvard. "He said, 'All I can tell you is that of all the young guys we've hired in the last five years you have the best chance of being president if you want to stay. And if you leave you probably still have a chance.' He said, 'I'll tell you what: we'll give you a year's leave of absence and if after a year you want to come back you come back and frankly, my friend, you don't lose anything.' "

But Hogan never went back to Bell Labs. After a year, he informed the labs that he planned to stay at Harvard. "I loved Harvard. I loved the atmosphere. I had five graduate students who wanted to do their doctoral theses under me and I was busier than a cat covering shit on a tin roof."

As a professor, with some experience in management, Hogan was a perfect target for the raids by industry on academia common in those early transistor years. In his five years at Harvard, Hogan received many such offers. The most aggressive was Texas Instruments, then just becoming a power in the transistor industry. TI actively pursued Hogan throughout his Harvard tenure, at times offering him triple his salary as a professor. But Hogan wouldn't budge.

Then, in December 1957, Hogan received a long-distance call from Dan Noble, executive vice-president of Motorola, based in Phoenix. Said Hogan:

> [Noble] had been founder of Motorola's communications division, their military electronics division and their semiconductor products division. The first two were howling successes. But the semiconductor division was a bag of worms. It had been in existence for four years and had $3 million in sales and a $4 million loss. And the board of directors had told Dan, just a week before, "We'll give you one more year to make the thing profitable or we'll lock the door and throw away the key . . ."
>
> I said, "Dan, I've turned down five good jobs. I know I could go over to TI tomorrow and they'd give me almost any job I wanted. And I don't think I want it . . ."
>
> . . . And he finally said, "Look, you have a Christmas vacation coming up. . . . We would like you to come to Phoenix, bring your family, at our expense."
>
> I said, "Dan, just so you know that when I get on the airplane to go home and leave Phoenix I'm going to tell you

no." He said, "Les, if you're willing to come I'm going to take that gamble." And I said, "Fine, I'll be there."

   . . . It was the mildest winter Phoenix had in forty years . . . When we got on the plane in Boston my wife started crying. I said, "Why are you crying?" She said, "Are you serious? Would you really go down to that desert, that wilderness?" . . .

So Dan took me through and showed me everything at Motorola, and he of course wined and dined us and partied us. We went swimming every day. Picked up a hell of a suntan . . .

So we got on the plane [home], and it was supposed to be nonstop from Phoenix to Boston. But we landed in Hartford. The Boston airport was closed—six feet of snow on the runways. The worst goddamn blizzard they'd ever had in their history. It was midnight when we finally landed in Hartford. Took 'em an hour to unload the plane and get the baggage out. They put us on busses and took us into Boston. Then I had to get a taxi to get us home to Lexington. We got home at four o'clock in the morning, freezing to death.

When we were in bed about to turn off the light, my wife said, "You know, when I got on the plane I didn't want to go home. I don't want to influence you, but anytime you want to go to Phoenix, I'd be happy to go with you."

Eight months after Hogan's arrival in Phoenix—two months after the original deadline, Motorola was profitable. In 1958, the year Hogan arrived, the Motorola semiconductor division had sales of $3 million and a net loss of $3 million. The next year the division had sales of $10 million and showed a small profit—one of the more remarkable turnaround stories in the history of the U.S. electronics industry.

When he left in 1968, after ten years, Motorola was a $200 million company with $30 million in pretax profits. Further, Motorola had become the second largest semiconductor maker in the world, breathing hard on the neck of the leader, Texas Instruments.

Hurrying Hogan's departure were strained relations with Motorola president Robert Galvin, who had inherited the presidency of the firm from his father, the latter having died of leukemia not long after Hogan arrived in Phoenix. It was dislike at first sight. "A spoiled kid," Hogan says of Galvin.

Thanks to his impressive track record, other firms had started approaching Hogan about joining them. Once again Texas Instruments was the most aggressive—and once again (as they made their pitch in 1963) premature.

By 1968, though, Hogan was ready to go. "I took Motorola in '68 to at least a tie for number one in sales and with three times the profits that TI reported that year. So by that time I could leave."

When the call came from Walter Burke, the financial adviser of Fairchild Camera and Instrument, Hogan was ready.

Burke also laid out for Hogan a picture available to few corporate executives: the complete corporate financial picture of a competitor. The numbers surprised Hogan. After all, during this period Fairchild Semiconductor was generally considered to be one of the most innovative technological business entities on the planet. But what Hogan found was that "the [Fairchild] semiconductor division hadn't done too well the last three years. It turned out their sales had been flat at $120 million for three years and the semiconductor division had been unprofitable for eighteen months. Those were facts I didn't know because they had been buried in the whole corporate picture."

Noyce himself paid a visit to try to talk Hogan into taking the Fairchild presidency. Hogan was confused. After all, wasn't Fairchild Semiconductor Noyce's child? "I said, 'You're nuts, you should be the president of the company.' And Bob said, 'I'm quitting. I'm going to start another company.' And I said, 'Why? What you've done is good, you may have some problems but they can be fixed.' But Noyce was adamant."

Hogan took the job, which had one of the largest compensation packages the industry had yet seen: $120,000 in annual salary and 10,000 shares of Fairchild stock, plus a $5 million loan to acquire 90,000 more shares. So spectacular was this amount for the era that it came to be known as a "Hogan," a standard unit by which other salaries were compared.

With his departure for Fairchild, Hogan left a meteorological desert for a metaphorical one. When he was forty-eight, his life a continuous string of successes, his reputation apparently sealed, Hogan's career was suddenly about to enter an early twilight. Fairchild wasn't Motorola. It wasn't the sick fragment of a firm in the early days of an industry. Rather it was a $100-million firm leaking at every joint while the competition was running away with the market. Furthermore, when Hogan arrived at Motorola, he came from academia to a firm on its deathbed.

The Hogan who arrived at Fairchild in June 1968 was a hated competitor coming to a firm with little idea how sick it really was.

The Fairchild Hogan inherited was bleeding talent from every division, every department, every office. The departure of quality personnel, which had begun with Charlie Sporck in 1967, was now a slow, steadily growing trickle that included the cream of the company's executives.

But instead of stanching the flow by diminishing the impact of his arrival, Hogan did precisely the opposite: clearing the decks for action, making pronouncements about turning around the company, preemptorily firing the beloved semiconductor general manager Tom Bay in the first week and generally throwing longtime Fairchilders into a panic.

But Hogan's most disastrous move, the one he most regrets, was to place his own people from Motorola—Hogan's Heroes—into executive positions at Fairchild above the existing managers. As Hogan himself now admits, the move "destroyed" whatever morale remained at the company. Fairchild, already the target for every recruiter in the Valley, began to collapse inward on the vacant positions in the corporate hierarchy, a crippled giant.

The record belies this, at least during Hogan's tenure as president of the company from 1968 to 1974. In that period, despite the obvious handicap of lost employees, Fairchild's sales tripled. Further, "the highest profit that had ever been reported at Fairchild before I arrived was $3.30 a share; during my last two years as president we reported $5.00 a share."

And even those numbers understate, as frequent trips to the equity market during the Hogan era increased the total number of outstanding shares and diluted per-share earnings—so total profits were much greater than those known by the legendary Noyce Fairchild.

However, in a more global sense, the myth of Fairchild's disappearance from the limelight is an accurate one. Until 1967–68, when the firm exploded like a seedpod and scattered the germs of new firms throughout the Valley, Fairchild may have been the most important firm in America, the country's dynamo of technological change. The Hogan Fairchild operated in a drastically different environment—most of it of the company's own making. There were still the industry giants, TI and Motorola, beyond the horizon; but now there also were dozens of little companies, filled with ex-employees, springing up in Fairchild's own backyard. It was to these new little firms, National Semiconductor,

Intel, AMD and Intersil among others, that the spark of innovation had gone forever.

Certainly it was impressive that a big firm like Fairchild could grow 300 percent in six years—but among some of the new little semiconductor firms that kind of jump was exceeded in eighteen months. And though Fairchild in some respects remained an innovator—notably pioneering the oxide isolation process of making chips—down the road at tiny new Intel, Ted Hoff and his team were inventing the microprocessor.

Hogan admits now that Fairchild might have remained more in the industry eye had he been willing—as Noyce did—to do the corporate and product promotion ("the song and dance") necessary to keep security analysts, investors and customers aware of the company's progress. That, he says, "was my biggest mistake."

But Hogan is incorrect. In truth, with the Hogan's Heroes episode, Hogan started rolling a force that would destroy his reputation and darken his impressive presidency at Fairchild with the bleakness that fell over the company immediately afterward under Wilf Corrigan, a lesser Hero who in 1974 went around Hogan to the Fairchild board and convinced it to award him the presidency—leaving Hogan in the titular position of vice-chairman.

Five years later, Hogan sat on the dais at Fairchild's final stockholders' meeting. In the intervening years, Fairchild had fallen into the dustbin of Silicon Valley history. From 1974, when it was third in the industry and gaining on second-place Motorola, Fairchild had fallen to sixth. The firm's products were increasingly uncompetitive, its recent contribution to technology all but nil and the firm was nearly reduced to living on patent royalties from the Noyce era. Corrigan had awarded himself a bonus for a job well done and Fairchild—after treating its employees like vermin through the 1974–75 recession—had become (replacing Lockheed) the most despised company in the Valley.

"It was a bad scene," says Hogan.

There on the dais, many emotions were going through Lester Hogan's mind, and they were betrayed by an inscrutable expression on his face. The Corrigan era is still something Hogan rarely talks about, but when asked about that strange look on his face as he watched his company being sold, Hogan replied, with a similar look combining anger and joy, "I couldn't believe the arrogance of the man who had destroyed the company in such a short time. That's what it was, I just couldn't believe the man . . . And I was relieved to know somebody was going to buy the company, it didn't matter who; but I think we have the best of all possible owners."

Fairchild asked Hogan to stay on, and so he still goes to his office, his Waterloo, nearly every day.

> Since '79, I've had a contract with the corporation for half time at Fairchild. Actually I spend more than half time, like three-quarters time, as consultant to [president] Tom Roberts to help and advise when he just wants an intelligent ear to bounce off of. He's also asked me to be the senior person at Fairchild to rebuild the bridges with universities which Corrigan burned—along with all the other things he destroyed. I enjoy that, and having had a university background at one time, it's an easy bridge for me to build.

Hogan is also, in his role as Grand Old Man, often in demand as a speaker. He gives two reasons: "One is I'm a good speaker; I can give good speeches. But number two, I'm brutally honest . . . I won't bull-shit people."

More interesting—and ironic—is what Les Hogan now does with the rest of the time: he helps new firms. He is permitted to make investments in and join the board of any firm that does not directly compete with Fairchild.

When will he retire? Where does Hogan see himself in ten years? "My wife asked me that. You know what I told her? 'I'm going to chase girls.' "

Academia? "Yeah, I've thought about it. I've been offered the dean of engineering job at some big schools. But I don't want to, because I'm in a new thing I'm enjoying very much."

Perhaps, as he sits in that Fairchild office, C. Lester Hogan believes that, before he can go on, there is still that skeleton, the disintegration of Fairchild under his command, that must be buried forever.

4

Rich Man, Poor Man,
Beggar Man, Thief

The explosion of Fairchild threw some of its top talents farther than others. Some, like Charlie Sporck, landed in existing, if faltering, companies. Bob Noyce had a sterling reputation and investors crawled all over themselves lining up to give him money. Jerry Sanders, still a relatively unknown quantity, had to pound on doors for months to get backing. Others, without the entrepreneurial ambition or the necessary pedigree, jumped into the executive ranks of established firms and began a hopscotch of Valley jobs, biding their time until the day they could start their own firm. Finally, some stayed behind at the shattered Fairchild, hoping to make a place in the new order under Hogan, still believing that company would regain its old glory and they would be duly compensated for their loyalty.

As noted, Charlie Sporck had been the first top executive to go during the big Fairchild breakup of the late sixties—some would say he precipitated it. With his team of Bialek, Lamond, Kvamme and Smullen, Sporck walked out of Fairchild and into National Semiconductor.

National at the time was based primarily in Danbury, Connecticut, with an operation in Santa Clara. National was almost as old as Fairchild, having been founded in 1959, but had never seemed to come together. It had only $7 million in sales and was losing money.

Still, the company had two things going for it. The first was Peter Sprague, scion of the Sprague Electric fortune. Sprague had a board position at National, obtained while still a graduate student at Columbia University, and in the mid-sixties, when the firm was about to sink into receivership, he had been asked by the other board members to guarantee some loans. In doing so he became a major stockholder and chairman (a title he carries to this day).

In this new role, Sprague set out to hire the best in the business at whatever salary or stock was required. In early 1967, he made his first big score: Fairchild circuit design genius Bob Widlar and his linear staff. Widlar et al. were the second feature that made National appealing to Sporck; after all, he had been their boss and knew just what a peerless design team they really were.

So when Sporck and his handpicked team went down the list of prospective semiconductor companies they could step into and run, National seemed the likeliest prospect. Here was a crippled company ripe for a turnaround with a young, ambitious, free-spending chairman, and the best linear circuit team in the world. Sprague sealed the deal with stock.

The ex-Fairchild team arrived on a Friday. Says Sporck:

> The company was losing money fast. So the first thing we did—that weekend—was to fly back to Danbury. There was some six hundred employed there building transistors. And we knew that there was only one way we could go: we had to somehow get the transistor operation into a profitable mode there so we could fund our penetration into linear circuits out here.
>
> So we immediately laid off three hundred of those six hundred people. The whole company turned profitable almost immediately. And our sales began to grow, even though we had only half the people we had before.
>
> So, very shortly after we arrived the company made a profit —and it's been profitable ever since.

Thus, in that first weekend, Sporck set a slashing, bottom-line-oriented, pragmatic-to-the-point-of-callousness style that has characterized National Semiconductor ever since.

Still, the company was a long ways from being on dry land. On weekends even Sporck would come in to hand-pack shipments. The firm's financial situation remained dicey for a long time and forced the new management team to do some perhaps illegal, or at least unethical, corner-cutting. Sporck won't talk about these moves other than to say, "We had a lot of harrowing experiences, a lot of months when we couldn't meet the payroll. We did the strangest things." When it was suggested to him that any acts were now beyond the statute of limitations, he replied, "You're right, except people would suspect we might do it again."

National's extreme poverty led to a classic Widlar story. Kvamme tells it:

> In the early days we didn't have a lot of budget and during one of the recessions about 1969 we had to shut off the gardener. He started coming once a month instead of once a week. So the lawn in front of the [Santa Clara] building got very very long.
>
> Well, one morning Widlar tools up in the Mercedes-Benz convertible he always drove, opens the trunk, and, son-of-a-gun, he pulls a goat on a leash out of the back of the bloody thing. And he ties the goat on a long tether to the bumper of his car.

Widlar then calmly sauntered into the building and his first move was to file a requisition for a bale of hay—which arrived atop his desk the next morning from a bemused Pierre Lamond.

At the end of the day, about the time the San Jose *News* was running a picture of the goat in the evening paper, Widlar and Dobkin loaded the animal back into the Mercedes, drove to a nearby bar, got crazy drunk and auctioned the goat off to the highest (literally) bidder.

But it wasn't all fun and games at National, particularly not with Charlie Sporck at the helm. Widlar got away with his outrageous behavior because he was a genius, and because Charlie needed competitive linear chips to keep the company afloat and only Widlar (and Dobkin) could provide them. And he did. Kvamme says:

> His competence was so great and he was so knowledgeable about how to get something done. He was absolutely incredible with customers. I never saw him in a situation where he was stumped with a question. He would tell you afterward if the customer knew what he was talking about or didn't, although he never ever told a customer where to get off. But he would tell people in the company to get off if he didn't think they were competent. He was very hard to work around if he did not think you knew what you were talking about.

Widlar's department's inventions were critical to Sporck's strategy to drive National like a wedge into the semiconductor business. He knew that once linear devices started making money he could use those profits to bootstrap National's attack on the digital logic chip business—which Sporck rightly recognized as the next big business in semiconductors.

Once in the digital logic market with the right products, Sporck knew he could bring his unmatched manufacturing skills to bear and start forcing prices down until the competitors screamed and got out of the way. It was here that National first earned its nickname, "the Animals of Silicon Valley." To hear Sporck describe it is to understand the source of his nickname, "Attila the Sporck":

> We chose after linear circuits to enter digital logic in the 1969 to 1972 period. There were a lot of companies [in digital logic] then: Motorola, TI—which was the biggest—Fairchild, Signetics, GRE, Harris, Rockwell; everybody made them. We entered fairly late in the game, but we entered with our eyes open saying to ourselves, "We're going to have to do two things to penetrate this market: we're going to have to introduce some unique products and, in addition, we're going to have to be very price-aggressive.
>
> And we went into the market with a vengeance. We were just plain heartless on price. We kept driving the price until one by one the other guys started leaving the game . . . We now had a sizable market share that gave us an economic scale so we were no longer at any disadvantage.
>
> After that there were a lot of stories about how tough we were in attacking that market. The image stuck—and indeed we promoted it. We liked it because it helped us get a lot more recognition from our customer base than our size warranted.

In fact, they liked their reputation so much that when *Fortune* wrote an article using the nickname as its title, the company ordered thousands of reprints and conducted an in-house motivational campaign around it—even preparing a mirrored poster in which an employee could see his or her own reflection under the title "Animal of the Month." Years later, when government investigations and chemical leaks and drug exposés cast National in an unfriendly light, the firm would come to regret the image it had tried to foster. P.R. director Mike Ayers would say, "It's very fashionable to kick us. We're not the glamour boys of the industry. We've played hardball and now it's come back to haunt us."

But in the early 1970s, National was the underdog, not the giant, scratching for recognition, and anything that kept it in the public eye seemed worthwhile. It seemed to work, because by the early eighties, 80 percent of National's component business was logic chips.

It was during this era that National was first stigmatized as not being an innovative firm. Sure there were Widlar and Robert Dobkin, but that was linear, the new game was digital circuits and National had made its entrance armed with "second-source" agreements to produce the chips other firms had designed. There were even unproven rumors that National had gotten into the microprocessor business by stealing an Intel chip on display at a conference at Foothill Junior College and then reverse-engineering it.

Sporck burns when he hears things like that: "The only companies who have succeeded in semiconductors are innovative companies. Innovation is everything." But still the image stuck.

Certainly, it didn't hurt to have a legend like Widlar around, particularly with his penchant for adding to that legend. For example, Widlar still had the big ax, and when he was frustrated he'd whack big chunks out of his linoleum floor. Floyd Kvamme, a conservative and religious man, often acted as Widlar's chaperon and confirms many of the more remarkable stories.

For example, there's the time at the Solid-State Conference in Philadelphia when Widlar got into a disagreement that dissolved into a rip-roaring fight in which Widlar's head was all cut up and bloodied and Kvamme had to keep him from being arrested by the police. ("Here I was in the middle of the night dealing with these guys who were trying to get Widlar, you know, trying to protect the company's assets.) On another occasion, Kvamme had to pull a smashed Widlar back from the edge of a Paris subway siding when the latter was trying to see how far he could get his feet over the brink without falling and electrocuting himself on the third rail.

In Europe especially, Widlar was a huge draw, his skills as a communicator almost as great as his technical expertise. (However, when he was speaking before a foreign audience, Kvamme would have to translate for the translator Widlarisms like "snakey.") It was at one of these seminars, in France and attended by National's top brass, that Widlar probably had his most anarchistic moment. Widlar got "absolutely thick-tongued, pie-eyed" during the luncheon for this seminar, which included hundreds of attendees. After lunch came a question-and-answer session in which Widlar was to sit at the dais.

As Kvamme describes it, before Widlar walked up to the front he made a pit stop at the bar and filled up a water glass full of scotch to tide him over. Sporck spotted this, nudged Sprague and whispered "Go get that away from him."

Sprague met Widlar in the aisle and, thinking quickly, asked, "Say, what's that you're drinking, Bob?"

"Scotch," Widlar replied.

"Mind if I have a sip?"

"Sure."

At that point, Sprague proceeded to chug-a-lug the entire glass. Widlar made it through the presentation; meanwhile the chairman of the board was in the bathroom throwing up.

Widlar's counterpart Dobkin was a practical joker. His best trick was the sabotage of Pierre Lamond's clock-radio. The electrical power in the United States is kept in synch at 60 hertz (cycles per second), and electric clocks over the long term maintain almost perfect time. Dobkin, however, built a circuit that would pull one cycle per second out of the electrical line feeding into Lamond's clock-radio. So the top technical guy of one of the world's leading high-tech companies suddenly had the only electric clock in America that wouldn't keep the right time. Lamond nearly went nuts trying to figure out why.

Widlar and Dobkins weren't just exceptions at National, they were the *only* exceptions. And even they in time found the company's environment unacceptable. Widlar left in the mid-seventies and moved to Mexico. Five years later he returned, signed a consulting agreement with National and from that point on would design products from his south-of-the-border home and periodically fly up to Santa Clara to deliver them. In 1982, Widlar and Dobkin left National for good and, with some other linear heavyweights, founded Linear Technology. National sued, of course.

In truth, National was a lousy place to work. Its offices were crowded and ugly, the huge, factorylike assembly buildings were the closest thing in the Valley to sweatshops—jammed, unpleasant, a perpetual pressure cooker riddled with drugs. Worst of all, the company to save energy installed sodium lamps, whose yellow light drained all colors into a monochrome and whose stroboscopic effect were enough to drive you half insane—perfect for the Animals of Silicon Valley, and they wore their no-frills approach like a badge of honor.

If the atmosphere was horrendous, it was nothing compared to the daily pressures of dealing with management. As John Nesheim told

Fortune, the day he arrived at the company in 1976: "I was terrified. There was so much table-pounding and yelling at meetings that I thought the company was falling apart."

And at times it seemed it was. In 1973, as National was beginning to assert itself in the marketplace, it launched into a doomed foray into consumer end products. It wasn't alone: at the time it seemed that every chip house in America was trying its hand at this new market. Recalls Sporck, ruefully:

> The consumer business was a very good one when we first went in. We entered it by and large, I must admit, because everybody else was, and at that time, you know, semiconductor people were overimpressed by their own competence. They really viewed themselves as more competent than management in other industries. We thought ourselves invulnerable.
>
> So we all plunged into the calculator business and the watch business with the idea that we were bringing technology to these incompetent types. And indeed, when we first started, we brought out this very low-end calculator that was essentially based on one chip and it sold like gangbusters.
>
> But in the long term we in the semiconductor industry were vulnerable in the consumer business because we really didn't understand it. In semiconductors and electronic goods it is a price-performance business. You give a guy a certain amount of performance and for that performance you charge a certain price. The consumer business is much more based on the perception of the buyer and that is influenced by advertising and a hundred other different things, none of which was our cup of tea.
>
> Anyway, the bloom quickly wore off and one company after another got into serious trouble in the consumer business and started jumping out. Mostek, Motorola, Intel, AMI, Rockwell, Litronix, you name them, they all took a swing at it. We kept swinging longer than any of them and indeed we got it to the point where we did a resonable business in watches and calculators. But after having gotten there we asked ourselves, "Who needs it? It's a really tough business, one that we're not good at, so why are we beating ourselves?"
>
> So we bagged it.

He adds: We're all like lemmings in the semiconductor business. If one of us goes into a business, we all go in. When one of us went into the consumer business we all went in. And we all got burned.

If that sounds impulsive, it's because it was and National became somewhat notorious for jumping into new markets almost without a second thought. Said one business consultant, "Their product strategy is a zigzag, the result of somebody's having come up with a bright idea at the last minute."

National spent a decade struggling to make its point-of-sale super-market check-out machines profitable after representatives of a grocers' cooperative offered in 1971 to sell automated checkers if any Silicon Valley firm wanted to build them. In this case, as well as in calculators, the unseen force that kept the division alive was the invisible member of the original group of Fairchild expatriots, Fred Bialek. Bialek, a bald New Yorker so cold-blooded as to make Sporck look like a pussycat, was the production specialist at National. It was he who moved much of National's operations offshore to Southeast Asia, setting an industry trend.

National's entry into IBM-compatible memory was typically haphaz-ard. It began with a memorable, if uncharacteristic, ad, showing Charlie Sporck, chomping on one of his ever-present cigars. The copy read: "National Semiconductor is crossing the Rubicon. We are entering the computer market with a range of sophisticated, system-level products."

Sporck:

> Back in the early seventies the semiconductor industry started making memory devices. There was AMI [Advanced Memory Systems] first, which is now Intersil, Intel, Mostek (Texas) and ourselves—and it occurred to us that there was one very large market for memory devices that we didn't have a chance at, and that was the mainframe business of IBM. IBM didn't buy memory on the outside, and they were the biggest single application of memory.
>
> Well, somebody at AMI came up with the idea that the way to address this problem is to put our devices into IBM-com-patible add-on memory. And they did very well. Then Intel started doing it. Then Mostek and ourselves. It was a very profitable business . . .
>
> Then a couple of years later we were approached by Itel [not to be confused with Intel] with the idea that, hey, the

business we ought to be in is IBM-compatible mainframe computers . . .

With the memory add-ons, National sold its products through middleman Itel, buying up a company in San Diego that was in the process of developing just such a computer.

The equipment sold very well, it was very profitable; as a matter of fact it was outstanding. And that went on for a couple of years, to about 1978. And then Itel started running into financial difficulties of various types . . . then IBM brought out the E Series computer and sales sort of stopped until the world could figure out what it was. Well, Itel just plain could not afford sales to stop and they got into very serious trouble.

We were faced with three alternatives. Either to get out of the business—which we didn't want to do because it was very strong for us—build up our own sales and service organization—which would take years to do and be very expensive, or absorb a portion of Itel . . .

It is important to note here what Sporck isn't saying. Itel was indeed in serious trouble, right on the edge of what would be one of the biggest bankruptcies by a U.S. firm in this century. But as things began to fall apart and the demand for its computers disappeared, Itel frantically cut deals with its suppliers and creditors, and all agreed—except National. Both National and another computer supplier, Hitachi Ltd., had contracts to supply Itel with a certain number of machines. Itel begged to be let off the hook. Hitachi agreed. National, to which Itel owed $18 million, refused. Itel, dangling by a thread over a precipice, watched as National swung the sword and let its old partner fall. Itel, broken, sold its computer operation to National at bargain-basement prices, and the new owners dubbed the operation National Advanced Systems. One Itel executive, who refused to work for National, said privately a few days after this debacle, "If National had just given us a break like everybody else, Itel might still be alive. Instead, they fucked us."

(Itel's old competitor, IBM, would even the score a few years later, when it sued National Advanced Systems for billions of dollars over the stolen secrets involved in the Japanscam case.)

Despite all of these forays into systems, National consistently proved to everybody but itself that semiconductors were and would always be the business in which it truly belonged. The company came late to the microprocessor revolution, and as late as the mid-eighties it was still a half step behind the market leaders like Intel. Part of this may have been due to the three-year departure of tech boss Pierre Lamond beginning in 1974. It was during that period that National suffered its worst era as a mature company.

The firm had endured the 1974 recession well, despite a 25 percent industrywide drop in chip shipments, thanks to the temporarily booming sales of consumer products. But the bad times finally caught up with National in mid-1976. Everything seemed to go wrong at once. Semiconductor sales were still flat for the industry, the consumer business was slipping and what there was National had trouble reaching because of production problems in Connecticut, material shortages in Utah and a strike in Malaysia.

In response, National laid off 350 nonproduction employees (a fact the company tried to cover up for years), a stupid move at a time when the rest of the semiconductor industry was learning the lessons of layoffs, and one that hurt National's image for many years. In 1977, National's earnings fell from $18 million to $10 million.

By the next year, the industry was rolling again, and National was making money hand over fist. Lamond was back and not only did investments in microprocessor development rise, but the technical chief also took National into the growing field of MOS-type semiconductor manufacturing. It was a brilliant move. Within two years MOS would be the predominant type of chip and National would be at the forefront of a new industry.

By 1981, National Semiconductor, the company that had been counted out or tossed into the pile of second-rate companies many times, became the first semiconductor company in Silicon Valley to achieve a billion dollars in sales. Despite sidetracks and false moves, the Animals of Silicon Valley had won the race.

*   *   *

Given the reputation and the personalities of its founders, Intel Corp.'s birth was far more genteel than National's.

Recalls Bob Noyce:

> I remember standing out in my front yard talking to Gordon [Moore] and telling him that I was resigning [from

Fairchild]. He was probably the closest person left in the organization to me; I mean, he'd been part of the original founding
team of Fairchild and I felt that I had to tell him about it.

And we got discussing, you know, "What are you going to
do?" that sort of thing, sort of speculating on what would be
the next big thing in this field. And that sort of planted the
seeds in our minds that it might make sense to do something
together.

A month after Bob Noyce resigned as head of Fairchild, Moore also
quit the company as its chief technical wizard, bringing with him an
almost unknown applications expert from Hungary named Andy
Grove. The three agreed that the one semiconductor market offering
the greatest potential to growth was computer memory chips. One reason that market appealed to them was that it was almost entirely technology-driven: you stuffed as many circuits onto a chip as possible, and
whoever had the most at a given point was the industry leader. It was
the one area where this new company could take on the big boys, as
well as manufacturing marvels like Sporck's National, and still hold its
own.

The first step was to go to see the king of venture capitalists, Arthur
Rock, the man who had first made his name backing Noyce and Moore
and the rest in the creation of Fairchild. Noyce and Rock were by this
time good friends. It wasn't too long before Rock came up with the
necessary bucks to get the new company, to be called Intel, off the
ground. Noyce would later joke that it took him all of five minutes to
raise the venture capital Intel needed, and he wasn't far off.

The three founders discovered a facility in which to make their start.
Significantly, it was the old Union Carbide Electronics building, not far
from Fairchild in Mountain View. UCE was one of the companies that
had been founded by another member of the Traitorous Eight with
Moore and Noyce, the prolific entrepreneur Jean Hoerni, and had
moved to San Diego in 1967. Now it was home to a second Fairchild
spin-off.

The three men and their staffers (a dozen by the end of 1968) decided
to keep themselves unattached to any particular technology or product
line, but rather, in the words of Noyce, "to take a snapshot of the
technology of the day, trying to figure it out, what was going to work,
what would be the most productive." The company had time, talent
and money and it refused to be rushed. "We didn't have some commit-

ment that we had to keep some manufacturing line going for," said
Noyce, "so we weren't locked into any of the older technologies."

As a result, when it was finally ready to start introducing products,
the tiny start-up had a breadth of technology and design innovation
almost unmatched by some of the biggest firms in the industry. In the
spring of 1969, a year after its founding, Intel introduced its first product, a bipolar-process 64-bit (that's *64* units of memory, compared with
the modern 64,000) memory chip. Soon afterward, the company introduced a 256-bit MOS-process memory chip. In other words, little Intel
the technology powerhouse, had bracketed the entire computer memory
business with its first two product introductions. Some other firms in
Silicon Valley would not be able to get both MOS and bipolar operations running until the 1980s.

This was a spectacular start, and the handful of workers knew it.
After the first shipment of the first product, all eighteen or so employees
of the Intel met in the tiny company cafeteria and toasted each other
with champagne. It was a measure of the relative youthfulness and the
California life-style that at that congregation three employees were in
leg casts, including Noyce with a broken leg from skiing at Aspen, and
another employee who had broken his ankle on his ninety-ninth para-
chute jump. One of the employees at that celebration, Intel employee
number 12, was a young, very bright ex-Stanford research associate
named Marcian "Ted" Hoff.

Intel was in the memory business for now and had to scratch a living.
For the three founders it was a long ways from Fairchild, and for Noyce
and Moore it was back to the early days with Shockley, trying to carve
out a place in the electronics world. The start-up money wouldn't last
forever.

According to one Valley veteran, the event that put Intel on its feet
was a deal with Microsystems International of Ottawa, a subsidiary of
Bell-Northern. They were interested in Intel's newest line of 1K ran-
dom-access memory chips, perhaps as a second source manufacturer.
But Intel turned the process inside out, cutting a deal with Microsystems in which, for a sizable hunk of change, Intel would not only
license the Canadian company the rights but would also build its chips,
remarking them with the Microsystems label. It was the kind of sweetheart deal one might expect of Charlie Sporck.

As it turned out, Intel didn't need to depend so much upon the
income from its memory chips. By then, engineering genius Ted Hoff

was working with an engineering team from a Japanese firm to see if the custom chips they wanted Intel to build were viable.

The Japanese company seems to have gone by a lot of names, including ETI, Nippon Calculating Machines and, eventually, Busicomp. Whatever its name, the company made calculators, and in 1969 it contacted Intel about the possibility of the American firm's helping it to design and build some custom circuitry. Intel, trying to build up its line of proprietary products, agreed and the Japanese sent over a design team to meet with Hoff.

Hoff was intrigued by the Japanese proposal but he also had serious doubts: "They had an interesting design, but it was going to involve a lot of chips and the chips were going to be quite complicated and they were going to be in rather large packages and [Busicomp] had some pretty aggressive cost targets."

What the Japanese engineers visualized was anywhere from six to eight chips per calculator—a sizable number, and that would make the members of the proposed calculator family quite expensive. The reason for so many chips was that in the technology of the day, each chip had to be assigned a distinct task. For example, in the Busicomp calculators there was to be a chip that controlled the keyboard, and another to control the printer (these were desk-top calculators; pocket machines had not been invented), another to do arithmetic, still another to handle memory.

All of these "dedicated" chips made a sizable bundle, and Hoff began to wonder if there was another way. He had long been curious as to why electronic calculators were so much more expensive for their performance than minicomputers.

Minicomputers, Hoff realized, might be the key. In particular, he had been working with a Digital Equipment computer doing circuit design and he was impressed by how the machine had such a simple instruction built into it and how with outside software the computer could be made to perform extraordinarily complex tasks. Why, Hoff, asked himself, couldn't the same thing be done with an integrated circuit, stuffing all of the calculator's logic on a single chip of memory programmed with a simple but universal instruction set?

This was the theory behind the first microprocessor.

> *Hoff:* So I made some proposals to the Japanese engineers to do something along these lines—and they were not the least bit interested. They said that they recognized that the design

was too complicated but they were working on the simplification and that they were out to design calculators and nothing else. They simply were not interested.

It was now July 1969. Frustrated by the Japanese lack of interest in microprocessors (times would change), Hoff went to Noyce and Moore and told them his ideas and his reservations about the Japanese. Noyce and Moore told Hoff not to worry about Busicomp and to keep working on his idea. Enlisting the help and the refinements of a new employee, Stan Mazor, Hoff continued perfecting what would be the 4004 arithmetic chip. Says Hoff:

> It finally came to a point in October 1969. We held a meeting in which the managers of the Japanese company came over here for a presentation by their engineering group and by a group representing our firm. At that time we presented our idea, that our new approach went well beyond calculators, that it had many other possible applications.
> They liked that and they went for our design.

At this time, in an unrelated activity, Intel was contacted by another company, Computer Terminals Corp., now called Datapoint, about the prospect of Intel building for it a custom chip that would take on some of the work of a central processor in its new computer terminal. Hoff and Mazor looked at the proposal, remembered the breakthrough they had just made with the 4004 and decided: why not go one step further and put the entire central processor on a single chip? The result was the first true microprocessor, the model 8008. (It was given that number because the 4004—its designation had been a lucky coincidence— "thought" in units of four bits, the 8008 in eight.)

The man who was crucial to the design of the 4004 was Federico Faggin, who had recently been hired away from Fairchild. He was the chip design expert, with a knowledge of the inner workings of semiconductor circuitry Hoff and Mazor didn't have. (In 1974 he would leave to found the Exxon-backed Zilog, the last mass-market chip house in Silicon Valley.)

The 4004 chip set was delivered to Busicomp in early 1971 and immediately ran into resistance from the Japanese firm. The calculator market was heating up with prices falling rapidly, and to Busicomp the year-old contract was now too high. It wanted the prices renegotiated:

Hoff: That's when all of us, Mazor, Faggin and I, went to our marketing people and said, "Get the right to sell to other people!" And there was a reluctance on the part of marketing to consider that. Intel was a company that made memories; these were custom chips. Marketing was very much afraid of the computer business, and they came up with arguments as to why we shouldn't go into it.

In fact, one of the marketing people at the time told us, look, [computer companies] sell 20,000 minicomputers a year. And we're latecomers to this industry. If we're lucky we'll get 10 percent. At 2,000 chips a year it's just not worth all the trouble.

This was reminiscent of the argument made in the late 1940s that the entire world could at most use ten computers. Needless to say, that marketing man is no longer with Intel, which now annually ships millions of microprocessors.

Anyway, the right to sell the 4004 to the outside was obtained from Busicomp in May 1971 and by midsummer most of the marketing department had been replaced. The new head of marketing was Ed Gelbach, from Texas Instruments. Hoff: "Coming from TI, which was in the logic business, Gelbach did not have a bias against offering logic products. So he was an important factor in the decision to release the new product.

"And there were many valid concerns about releasing it. For example, providing support was going to be an enormous problem."

But Intel went ahead, and the computer-on-a-chip revolution began. With the symmetry that seems to consistently assert itself in Silicon Valley, Intel's gain by landing Gelbach was balanced by TI. For one thing, Gelbach's success led other TIers to come out to Intel, and, as with Apple years later, rapid growth left little time for assimilation of outsiders. The result was a TI clique that reportedly operated with their old company's repressive style for more than a year before they learned the Intel culture.

More important, TI joined battle with Intel over authorship of the microprocessor. It seems that Computer Terminals, to cover itself, had also gone to TI with its plans, in hopes of making it a second source. The people in Texas came up with a different design than Intel's, more specific to the Computer Terminals planned product (Intel was working on a more general-interest design), but it took up three times the area of the Intel chip. TI got the assignment later, but because it used semiautomated design procedures, it beat Intel to the punch.

At least that's what TI claimed. It's all rather complicated, and it would give Roger Borovoy, Intel's counsel, a new job, now that he had finished Fairchild's similar suit with TI over the invention of the integrated circuit. Noyce, who had been through this once before, must have thought history was repeating itself.

It went like this:

> Texas Instruments officially announced its new microprocessor in early 1972. Intel didn't announce the 8008 until April. But Intel had mentioned the product in a copyrighted brochure called *The Alternative* in late 1971. TI claimed it had made references to its designing a computer on a chip for Computer Terminals in June 1971. Intel claimed what counted was a working chip and that the first deliveries by TI to Computer Terminals in June 1972 were composed of dead chips—and besides, it argued, the 4004 was really the first microprocessor . . .

And so it went. In the end, Intel filed a few patents on microprocessor design but, said Hoff, "did not take the attitude that the microprocessor was something that you could file a patent claim on that covers everything."

As it turns out, it didn't much matter anyway, because only a handful of firms ever really got up and running in microprocessors (now called microcomputers because of their complexity) and they were just about impossible to catch—even by the Japanese, who, despite their damage to the rest of the semiconductor industry, have yet to achieve a serious presence in this market.

It is important to remember that in 1972, Intel, the inventor of the microcomputer, the firm that would soon be called (by analyst Ben Rosen) "the most important company in America," was still a tiny little shop. It had just moved to a new headquarters in Santa Clara and its sales were only about $18 million, about a tenth the size of Fairchild at the time, and about what Intel now takes in each week.

It had two revolutionary new products, the 4004 and the 8008, but no real market for them. In fact, as with many breakthrough products, its inventors had little idea what they could be used for. Smaller minicomputers probably, consumer products definitely, but that was about it.

Noyce and Moore had been down this path before with the integrated circuit. But the microprocessor, because it also opened the world of software, was even more imponderable. Still, the first thing they knew had to be done was to educate the marketplace—let the people figure out how they wanted to use it. So Hoff and Mazor were sent out on the road to give seminars to engineers and get the word out. The two also gave speeches and published technical articles—until it got to the point that Hoff was convinced he and Stan had been seen or read by every even remotely interested technical type in the world.

Even then it was a difficult job getting the idea of the microcomputer accepted. The technical press first noticed the microprocessor in late 1972, and by early 1973 the electronics magazines were filled with articles about this new wonder. But by mid-1973 there appeared a growing number of articles describing "paper tiger" products: most of the semiconductor industry had been caught with its pants down by the introduction of the microprocessor, and in order to buy some time and keep the market uncommitted to a particular line, announced products that in reality had progressed little beyond the dream of some design engineer. Intel found itself in comparison studies with products that didn't even exist.

But confusion wasn't the only resistance Intel ran into while trying to legitimize the microcomputer. There was also a 30-year customer mindset over just what a computer should be.

> *Hoff:* People were so used to thinking of computers as these big expensive pieces of equipment that had to be protected and guarded and babied and used efficiently to be worthwhile and cost-effective. So there was a built-in bias in people that any computer had to be treated that way. I remember one meeting in which there was all this concern about repairing microcomputers and I remember saying, "A light bulb burns out, you unscrew it and throw it away and you put another one in— and that's what you'll do with microcomputers." But they just couldn't accept doing that with a computer.

Even the young had trouble visualizing a future in this new technology. . . . It's also important to remember that in those days prestige in computers was associated with their bigness and their power and their speed. I actually had a case where a guy came in interviewing for a programming position and asked what size [IBM] 360 we had—and once he found out that we didn't have a 360, in fact I think he would only consider a Model 65 or higher, he said that he just wasn't interested.

Remarkably, and this may be indicative of the kind of paradigm model about which philosopher Thomas Kuhn wrote, once the market embraced the microcomputer as the wave of the future, once it made the mental shift into thinking "micro," then all of a sudden the same people who couldn't accept the idea of a minicomputer on a chip now expected these new little wonders to exactly duplicate the functions of their refrigerator-sized counterparts.

Intel tried to tell its customers that they could hardly expect the range of functions available on a $50,000 minicomputer from a chip costing only a few hundred dollars (these days it would go for less than $10). But the newly enlightened apostles of microcomputing would have none of that, especially because the 8008 had certain rudiments of minicomputer operations.

In response to this, Faggin proposed a reworking of the 8008 in a different process technology to increase its performance. Mazor and Hoff agreed, but decided, what the hell, if the chip was going to be laid out again, then why not go ahead and implement all the additional functions customers were clamoring for?

The result, introduced in 1974, was the Intel Model 8080. It may very well be the landmark invention of the last quarter of the twentieth century. This was the chip that turned the corner. It and its second source copies and imitators sold in the millions and reshaped the modern world. The Intel Model 8080 and its direct descendants, the 8086 and 8088, were soon found in automobile engines, in video games, in the digital watch on the wrist of some peasant farmer in Africa, in the nose cones of American and Soviet ICBMs, in the last four digits of the Intel phone number, and, of course, right at the heart of many models of that seminal product of the consumer electronics era, the personal computer.

Intel was now more than just on its way. Sales were doubling every year. But more than that, the company came to be looked upon as the world's leader in high-technology innovation, the place to watch for a sneak preview of the future.

Intel was more than just changing the technological landscape. It was also trying its hand at social engineering. The company attempted to create a new kind of company, one that combined the casual but ambitiously self-driven nature of the old Fairchild with the careful strategic planning of older East Coast establishment corporations, producing what might be called a sublimation of personal ego—a communal attitude fostering innovation and creativity, yet at the same time keeping away the sort of entrepreneurial selfishness and egocentrism that had torn up Fairchild. If that seems both contradictory and ineffable, it's because it is. What Intel was trying to do was to create a company of brilliant, creative people who nevertheless felt little need for admiration or self-aggrandizement or the chance to be their own boss.

The Intel philosophy was a little like HP's, but with some crucial differences. Where HP had the self-image of a family, an Ozzie and Harriet perfect TV family, in which there was ambition but no backstabbing, in which differences were worked out quietly, like Ward Cleaver with Beaver, Intel seemed to see itself as one big research team. Corporate communism it might be called, ironically targeted at the capitalist goal of higher profits and greater market share.

The image of a giant research team is important to understanding the corporate philosophy Intel developed for itself. On a research team, everybody is an equal, from the project director right down to the person who cleans the floors: each contributes his or her expertise toward achieving the final goal of a finished, successful project. In this schema, little else matters besides the final victory—not the bottom line per se, but the new chip, the new growth goal, the victory over a threatening opponent. If the employees need a Jacuzzi to accomplish this, then fine, whatever the cost. But if it also means that they must work seven days a week, fourteen hours a day, for several months, well, that's the cost too.

The operative word here is *performance*. Screw up at National Semiconductor and you're on the street. Do the same thing at Hewlett-Packard and you're taken aside to a private conference room and told you seem to be having a little problem fitting in. At Intel you're screamed at for not exhibiting the proper level of performance and the next day are back on the job working twice as hard as ever to regain the respect of your peers and the matter is never mentioned again.

At Intel, the codification of this philosophy began almost at the beginning. Initially the chief figure was Noyce, he after all having been the headman at Fairchild. It was Noyce who instituted the Big Research Team concept, the one he had seen work so well in the early days at Fairchild. It was Intel that cast into stone the idea of an office without walls, a maze of dividers filling one large room. HP had something like that and so did National, but the former was much more of a stratified traditional company and the latter did so because Charlie Sporck found the trappings of success counterproductive. At Intel, the format only amplified the corporate philosophy—and the result was like a huge high school language lab with everybody in his own cubicle but listening to the same tape, only this time the program was on technological and financial success.

That was only the start. One of the problems with a corporation was that any kind of corporate hierarchy quickly became ossified into rigid lines of communication and smug protocols of who can talk to whom and who can have a credenza in which office. Pretty soon, in the general spirit of covering one's ass, corporate development grinds to a halt in a flurry of phonied-up reports and empire-building and backstabbing. Intel resolved to solve all of this by counteracting the inevitable top-down structure of management with a lateral one, a system of interdisciplinary groups that ran sideways through the corporation with an itinerary sometimes at odds with the needs of the traditional company product divisions: As Tom Wolfe describes this system and the meeting-oriented style that arose from it:

> At Intel, Noyce decided to eliminate the notion of levels of management altogether. He and Moore ran the show; that much was clear. But below them there were only the strategic business segments, as they called them. They were comparable to the major departments in an orthodox corporation, but they had far more autonomy. Each was run like a separate corporation. Middle managers at Intel had more responsibility than most vice-presidents back east. They were also much younger and got lower-back pain and migraines earlier. At Intel, if the marketing division had to make a major decision that would affect the engineering division, the problem was not routed up the hierarchy to a layer of executives who oversaw both departments. Instead, "councils", made up of people already working on the line in the divisions that were affected, would meet and work it out themselves. The councils moved horizontally, from problem to problem. They had no vested power. They were not governing bodies, but coordinating councils.
>
> Noyce was a great believer in meetings. The people in each department or work unit were encouraged to convene meetings whenever the spirit moved them. There were rooms set aside for meetings at Intel, and they were available on a first

come, first served basis, just like the parking places. Often meetings were held at lunchtime. That was not a policy; it was merely an example set by Noyce . . .

If Noyce called a meeting, then he set the agenda. But after that, everybody was an equal. If you were a young engineer and you had an idea you wanted to get across, you were supposed to speak up and challenge Noyce or anybody else who didn't get it right away . . .

This is generally true, except that Noyce is given far too much credit as the locus of Intel daily life. In reality, particularly by the late seventies, it was just the opposite: Noyce began to drift away from the daily operation of the company as the national and international arena called to him.

The truth was that since the beginning, Intel's top management was a perfect triumvirate, in which the personalities of Noyce, Grove and Moore dovetailed so seamlessly that without one of them the company would probably spiral down and collapse. Despite the musical chairs the three constantly played involving the titles of president, vice-chairman and chairman, the roles each played were pretty well set within the first five years of the company.

Noyce, of course, was the most visible, the legendary inventor, the president of Fairchild, the statesman of the semiconductor industry. He was the face of Intel. But the heart of the company resided with Gordon Moore. Moore is the great faceless figure of Silicon Valley history, perpetually overshadowed by partners throughout his entire career. But in Silicon Valley, and particularly at the company, Moore is the most admired of Intel's founders, and the most respected scientist. More than anyone else, he exemplifies the model Intel employee—brilliant, soft-spoken, self-effacing, placing the company before his own need for acclaim. Only a well-developed wit distinguishes Moore from many of the people who work for him.

Without Noyce, Intel would not be a great and famous firm. Without Moore, Intel would not have the inner strength and morale it has needed to stay on top. But without Andy Grove, Intel would not even be a company. For all of their strengths, Noyce and Moore both suffer from the one weakness that is unacceptable in an entrepreneur trying to build a large and successful company: they lack the steeliness needed to slash away any body or any program that is hindering the progress of the company. Noyce proved he lacked that toughness back at Fairchild.

Moore was a great lab man and unmatched long-term visionary, but never an ax wielder.

Grove is. He is the key factor in the sustained success of Intel. He plays hardball; oh boy does he play hardball. As Lester Hogan of Fairchild has said, "Andy would fire his own mother if she got in the way." Hogan is not being derogatory but respectful, even a little awe-struck, about Grove's single-minded purposefulness. As Marshall Cox said, "You have to understand. Bob [Noyce] really has to be a nice guy. It's important to him to be liked. So somebody has to kick ass and take names. And Andy happens to be.very good at that."

The ascendancy of Grove, with his muttonchop sideburns and Engelbert Humperdinck sartorial stylings—the "mad Hungarian" he is called —is a perfect example of a man finally finding his niche and blossoming. At Fairchild he was all but invisible, except when he took blame for the research and development department's coming up with some impractical product. He was never thought of as anything but a laboratory man, never as a line manager. Recalls Cox:

> Andy had kind of a funny rap at Fairchild in those days because as an operations guy his position was in process development and those guys were always developing these processes that when you put them into a real production environment they wouldn't work. Now, R & D's position on all this was: "Hey, if you guys weren't such douche bags you could absolutely take this process and put it into production." Well, Grove, because he was a process development guy, got a lot of nailing for being a guy who didn't develop practical kinds of things; they said he wasn't an operations guy. But hey, let me tell you, I think the sonofabitch proved his point at Intel. He's a great operations guy.

One of the best, in fact. It was Grove who took what were blue-sky designs and apparently impossible-to-reproduce prototypes and wrestled them into mass production. It was Grove who implemented the Intel philosophy. And for better or worse, it was Grove's personality that defined Intel in the late seventies and early eighties.

The strengths and weaknesses of Grove's style are summarized in the title of his book, *High Output Management,* published in 1983. (A Silicon Valley irony: the man whom nobody considered to have managerial potential wrote the book exemplifying the Valley's management style.)

The phrase "high output" has several connotations, and Grove's management style included all of them. First there is the idea of production, of producing large volume in relation to one's physical plant. It also means the most effective use of an employee's time. And finally, on a darker side, "high output" can also mean a sustained, unrelenting pressure on employees to produce.

Intel was all of these things. It was quite simply the best semiconductor company, and perhaps the best electronics company, in the world. But it took a very special personality to work there, and if you didn't have it the place could be a pure hell. A case in point was one middle-aged engineer with a heart condition who finally quit because of the alienation he encountered for not being able to make Sunday morning meetings. During boom periods the Intel parking lots seemed perpetually full, morning and night, weekday and weekend.

Long hours were only part of it. Grove was hell on wheels, running around making spot inspections, taking "creative confrontation" (Intel's euphemism for screaming) to new heights, implementing an employee-rating program that was right out of parochial school. During the 1982 slowdown, Grove unveiled the "125 percent solution," a program that claimed that even though Intel employees were already working at full efficiency they would have to give just that much more if Intel was going to weather the recession, beat the Japanese and come out on top. This was the genesis of the Late List. Now, everybody was expected to put in ten-hour days, instead of eight (though few put in less than ten or twelve anyway) and anybody who showed up after eight-ten in the morning had to sign the guard's Late List. Grove said nothing ever came from these lists (and, to his enormous embarrassment, even he was caught one morning signing in late by a New York *Times* reporter), but the point was made to the employees, particularly when, if 7 percent or more were late for three months, the whole section had to sign in. The point was not that Intel didn't entirely trust its own people (though the management argument was that a true Intel employee would never be late), it was that no one seemed to object to these rather childish measures.

No one objected because by 1982 the company had developed pretty much a homogeneous work force of people who matched the Intel profile. What kind of people were these? A lot like the Hewlett-Packard employee: loyal, upstanding, very bright. But the Intel employee was younger, more aggressive, less likely to have a rich private life and, like a true child of the seventies, in love with achievement for its own sake.

Intel was not warm like HP or spirited like Sanders's AMD or hot-blooded like National (except of course for Grove). Rather it was *efficient* in a manner that wasn't entirely human.

Intel was in many ways a camp for bright young people with unlimited energy and limited perspective. That's one of the reasons Intel recruited most of its new hires right out of college: they didn't want the kids polluted by corporate life. The more cynical suggested that, as in the Marines, only children would stand for this kind of horseshit because they didn't know any better. But there was more to it than that. There was also *belief,* the infinite, heartrending belief most often found in young people, that the organization to which they've attached themselves is the greatest of its kind in the world; the conviction they are part of a team of like-minded souls pushing back the powers of darkness in the name of all mankind. Corporate Moonieism, if you will, but with both feet planted firmly on the ground, and leavened with a bit of California soul.

One had only to sit in on a sales meeting, five hundred strong, at a hotel near Intel's plant in Phoenix, and watch Andy Grove, so small he could barely be seen, the traces of his Hungarian accent twisting the occasional word, as he figuratively wrapped himself in the American flag and intoned that Intel stood as the last great hope of American industry against the onslaught of the Japanese electronics industry. One could feel the adrenaline rushing through the veins of the hundreds of young men and women, get caught up oneself in this sense of shared destiny, be willing to accept any sacrifice needed to uphold this solemn responsibility and ready to go out there and sell those chips as America's last hope against the foreign hordes.

And perhaps it was.

But all the hard work and self-sacrifice and technical genius in the world is wasted if the company is sent charging down the wrong path, as Intel (like everyone else) was in the early seventies with the watch business. Intel's watch subsidiary was Microma, and it did as badly as all the other semiconductor company ventures into consumer electronics. Intel eventually bailed out with losses. Noyce: "When we went into the watch business we saw it as a technical problem and we felt we knew how to solve the technical problems. But, in a sense, we solved them so well that they stopped being a factor of importance. It turned into a jewelry business and we didn't know anything about jewelry."

That mistake can be forgiven as marketwide youthful enthusiasm. Overall, Intel has been the most consistently successful company in the semiconductor business. It is the Dallas Cowboys of the chip industry, always in or near the winner's circle, its mistakes small. And like America's Team, Intel, which might be called America's Company, has had to make sacrifices to achieve this consistency: like a lack of personality beyond the elegance of perfection, a discipline that makes few allowances for nonconformity and a reputation so great that the slightest mistake is blown out of proportion both internally and by outside investors. In other words, to become the shining example of what an American company can be, Intel has eschewed many of those traits that are synonymous with being American. To beat the Japanese—which it thoroughly has beaten to date—Intel has had to become almost the ultimate Japanese firm.

When Intel has been right, it has been very, very right, as it was when it moved in the early eighties toward creating the true computer-on-a-chip, the microprocessor. These have been breathtaking strategic shifts, carrying with them both the thrill of forcing back the frontiers of technology and of betting the company on faith in something that has yet to be invented.

But at what cost? What have Noyce and Grove and Moore wrought? Intel is the class act of the semiconductor industry, the firm with a reputation for quality and decency in the same league with HP. But it is a company of unique requirements, so special it may be impossible to duplicate: there may not be enough people out there who are entrepreneurial yet conformist to build even one more Intel. Certainly most Americans don't fit in the Intel mold, yet those many theories that speak of reindustrializing America along an Intel-like format don't seem to recognize that reality. In fact, so special is the Intel personality that privately, many of the company's own leaders will admit that were a young Bob Noyce to apply for a job at Intel, he probably would not fit in. The fact that one of the greatest men Silicon Valley has produced does not really belong at the company he founded is a telling fact about Intel—and the cost of success.

There were other semiconductor companies besides Intel and National Semiconductor, of course. For one thing, there was still Fairchild, though as the years passed it became less and less a force in Valley life.

From the moment Les Hogan took over control, Fairchild's collapse was just a matter of time. Not that Hogan was a bad manager; in fact he improved the corporate financial picture. But he was plugging holes. Fairchild was like a big Gothic cathedral in which half the stones had been removed. It was still a building, and one might add a little to the spire, but it would be lying to call the place sturdy or safe. The soul of the company was gone and no one could get it back.

Nevertheless, Hogan might have put Fairchild back together. He had, after all, done a far greater turnaround at Motorola. At Fairchild he had a much larger company with a good reputation, a few key people left, his own high stature in the industry and, best of all, the key patents in integrated circuits to provide a huge source of royalties for years to come.

Hogan did the best he could. As noted, in the six years of his tenure, the company tripled sales. That didn't earn him many admirers, but it did earn respect. During Hogan's presidency, he regained its position as number two in the semiconductor industry behind Texas Instruments, and to the start-ups like Intel and National Semiconductor, Fairchild still represented a dangerous business threat in Silicon Valley.

Given his success with a crippled company, it is interesting to speculate what would have become of Fairchild if Hogan had stayed in charge. Perhaps the firm's weaknesses would have caught up with it. But on the other hand, given its head start, the company might also have become by now—given comparative growth with the other Valley leaders—a $3 billion chip company, which would have made it an enormous power in the world's electronics market.

But Hogan didn't stay on top. He knew almost from the moment he arrived at Fairchild in 1968 that he'd made a mistake. In 1974 it became a fatal one, when, in a power play run through the East Coast board of Fairchild, Hogan was replaced as president (and later chairman) by one of his "heroes": Wilfred Corrigan. From that point on, Hogan sat as vice-chairman and sadly watched the dissolution of the great company he had almost restored.

Corrigan, thirty-six at the time he took over and addicted to gangsterish chalk-stripe British suits, came from the Liverpool docks and was as tough a character as the Valley had seen. He was very bright, but with an edge of meanness about him. Corrigan arrived in the president's chair at Fairchild and presided over a disgusting moment in Valley history—when Fairchild laid off numerous employees alphabetically over the loudspeaker. The image is indelible, hundreds of engineers and managers sitting at their desks, listening to the names being read, beginning with the *A*'s, hearts in their throats, waiting for their letter to come up, praying to heaven that their name wouldn't ring out so they would have to walk past their relieved peers to pick up a cardboard box in which to empty their desk drawers and trudge out to the parking lot with the box in their hands and their last paycheck in their pocket and wonder what in God's name they were going to do now . . .

The Corrigan Fairchild treated its people badly, leading to a second exodus. Further, according to *Business Week,* quoting a competitor, "Wilf put people in the position of agreeing with him or leaving." The author, as a *Mercury-News* reporter, remembers sitting at lunch with Corrigan and several of his vice-presidents and feeling a terrifying tension in the room, watching as the vice-presidents watched Corrigan for signs of when to eat, when to talk, when to laugh. This was not Silicon Valley, this was some senile old smokestack firm whose only reason for existing was to provide a pleasant income for the headman.

Being a callous, indifferent executive would have been of less importance if Corrigan had made Fairchild a success and spread some of the largesse to the staff. But he and his people all but ran the company into the ground with some ill-advised moves into consumer electronics and computers. Even these fiascoes might have been overcome if the company had just kept up its development in semiconductor technology. The company didn't even do that, never developing the ability to design its own MOS-type circuitry, instead second-sourcing others' designs.

By the end of the seventies, Fairchild's most important source of revenues was the integrated circuit patents of Noyce from the late fifties, and even these were about to run out. The only other bright light in the company's entire line was an automated system for testing integrated circuits, which by the end of the seventies accounted for 75 percent of all the company's profits—and even it was beset with defects. Nevertheless, in 1977 Corrigan was made chairman of Fairchild Camera and Instrument. Now, nothing could stop him.

What sometimes counts in business is not how one runs a firm but how one sells out. And despite being a disaster as Fairchild's head, allowing the company to slump from second place to sixth in the semiconductor market in just four years, Corrigan sold out in style.

The trick was to find the right sucker, and in the late seventies, with every large company in the world drooling over the chip industry, Corrigan had a lot to choose from. The firm he found was Schlumberger Ltd. of Paris and New York, a $2.1-billion oil services company enjoying a fat $600 million in profits. So Schlumberger had money to burn and the chip industry looked like the place to do it. After all, weren't semiconductors the wave of the future? And wasn't Fairchild the biggest name in chips? And here it was for sale for just $400 million.

In the summer of 1979, Schlumberger took the bait. Corrigan happily turned over the gutted skeleton of what had once seemed America's greatest company. Happy shareholders walked away with their $66 a share, blessing Corrigan's name. Corrigan himself left a few months later, several million dollars richer. And Schlumberger discovered it had bought a pig in a poke.

With that the curtain fell on Fairchild. Schlumberger put the company under wraps while a new president, Thomas Roberts, tried to sort things out and get the company turned around. There was talk at one point, when much of the artificial-intelligence group at think tank SRI International jumped to Fairchild, that the company might go into robots—but nothing came of it. In fact, nothing came of Fairchild. By the mid-eighties, the company still hadn't reemerged from its decade-long decline, and by now few thought it ever would. There were reports that Schlumberger was trying to sell.

So ended the spectacular rise and pitiful fall of Fairchild.

In addition to the Big Three, there was a raft of what might be called second-tier firms, companies that had started out as equals with the leaders but for one reason or another—inadequate financing, unambitious management or a wrong marketing hunch—had ended up dropping out of the mass-production race to find security and solid growth in some nice market niche. Some of these firms, like Intersil, American Microsystems and Precision Monolithics, found a business in custom chips, limited-production products made for individual industrial customers at a premium price. Signetics, one of the few early (1961) Fairchild spin-offs, was first backed by Corning Glass and then by the Dutch electronics giant Philips. It found its corner selling primarily to the military market, where its weakness in getting MOS up to speed was not so debilitating because bipolar technology better met Defense Department radiation "hardening" requirements. Another of the Valley's oldest chip firms, Siliconix, founded in 1969 and run ever since by Richard Lee, formerly of Texas Instruments, made the papers twenty years later when it was noted that Lee had cofounded the firm with the increasingly notorious William Hugle, of the Harper espionage case fame (see Chapter 6).

Perhaps the most interesting of the little chip houses was Monolithic Memories (MMI), founded in 1969 by a flamboyant Israeli from IBM named Zeev Drori. Drori was a loud, passionate character with a fancy for expensive cars. He was not a great manager, but he had style. One morning in the early seventies he called into the office to say he wouldn't be in for a few days, then left to join his unit in the Israeli Army for the Yom Kippur War. Drori exhibited another trait that to date has been lacking in some of the other Valley leaders: he knew when to give up. In the late seventies he turned over the reins of MMI to Irwin Federman, a likable, enthusiastic man who became the first non-technical person to take over a Silicon Valley semiconductor firm. It was thought at the time that Federman represented a new wave in Valley leadership, a transfer of power from the first-generation scientist-pioneers to a second generation of professional businessmen. However, by the mid-eighties, Federman (who, by the way, had done an excellent job—despite suffering the largest robbery in Valley history) was still all but alone; the old guard wasn't going to give up so easy.

A last group of Valley firms chose to stay in semiconductors but to fight in a different arena. These were the microwave chip firms, like Avantek. This was a different world, all but alien to the more famous digital chip houses, with a distinct market that included the telephone company and telecommunications networks. In fact, so different were these firms that their cycles of boom and bust were perfectly out of synchrony with the rest of the semiconductor industry. Thus, in 1974, when the other chip houses were laying off employees left and right, Avantek was hiring. It had a crowded lobby there for a while.

Still, Intel and National Semiconductor are Silicon Valley's two great victors in the semiconductor wars. And nothing could be more fitting, because they are the yin and the yang of corporate cultures, the clean, bright, colorless, perfect company with the immaculate reputation versus the dark, dangerous, wonderfully earthy company that is the constant source of rumor and curiosity. They are, and have been since the beginning, the twin poles of Silicon Valley life. Like Cain and Abel, the sons of the patriarch, Hewlett-Packard.

There is a third winner in this game, the wild card: Advanced Micro Devices. Like its two larger counterparts, AMD is a manifestation of the personality of its chief founder, the flamboyant, complex and ultimately endearing Jerry Sanders.

For much of the seventies, AMD was a hidden firm. Because Sanders had a much slighter track record than Sporck or Noyce, it got off to a slow start. It was initially more than a little schizophrenic, its dozen founders a pickup team of ex-Fairchilders looking for a new place to play. And AMD probably would have either blown up or ended a second-rater with the many other Fairchild spin-offs of the late sixties, had it not been for the unknown and always unpredictable factor of Jerry Sanders.

Sanders is Bob Noyce without the Midwestern repressiveness, Sporck with style. Rather than avoiding the trappings of success or pretending to hate it, Sanders revels in it, flaunts it, bares his naked materialism to the world. It was a refreshing change from the sobersided style of Silicon Valley in the early years, even if it was a bit of a fraud, the product of one of the most complex and powerful minds in the industry. Jerry Sanders can be outrageous because he is smart enough to be very good at what he does and at the same time to make light of it.

Sanders was smart enough to know that whatever distance lay between AMD and its two big local competitors, he could make it up by sheer personality alone. Throughout the seventies, Sanders performed one of the great tours de force in business, nearly on the level with Lee Iaccoca's a few years later at Chrysler. While AMD was little more than a moneymaking second source for other companies' chips, Sanders was single-handedly keeping the firm in the forefront of the public eye through a combination of charm, swagger, wit and calculated craziness. This bigger-than-life Jerry Sanders made AMD look larger than it really was. So, when the firm really belonged down with the Intersils and AMIs, the world still consistently thought of AMD as in the class of National and Intel. Why? Because Jerry Sanders said it was, and by God, he sure seemed more on top of things than Noyce and Sporck combined—or at least he sounded that way.

Unlike Noyce, who started Intel with considerable funding, or Sporck, who had an established company at National Semiconductor, Jerry Sanders started AMD with almost nothing. Despite the way the cards were dealt, the companies that arose were perfectly matched to their founders. Noyce, the scientist, got the money he needed to design the latest technical breakthrough and his company is famous for its innovation. Sporck, the manufacturing guy, got all he needed—an assembly line manned by people—and the company he built is best known for its manufacturing. All Jerry Sanders, the king of salesmen, had was his talent and style, and AMD's greatest strength is its sales and marketing.

An example of the AMD style as reported by *Forbes:*

> Sanders, ever the wise huckster, knew he would have to give
> his sales force a selling edge. Advanced Micro Devices, San-
> ders told the world, would build its products to something

called Military Standard 883. Simply, that meant AMD tested and inspected parts more carefully than the competition. This was important in the late Sixties when the technology was still new and computers were regularly being fouled up by defective chips. Sanders also concentrated on customers for whom high reliability was so important that he could tack an extra dollar or two on to his selling price. Makers of digital watches or calculators might not be interested, but customers in the telecommunications, computer and instrument industries were. So AMD was able to keep its average selling price well above the industry average. And since most of its customers were growing rapidly, AMD could ride on the momentum.

Another example was the AMD ad campaigns. One, for television, showed a young man in a business suit astride a surfboard with a bunch of similar types. A breaker rolls in and the young man alone catches it and, with tails flying, triumphantly shoots the curl. The slogan, one the company used for years, was AMD: Catch the Wave.

Then there was the notorious ad, based upon the Silverstein cartoon of Manhattan as the center of the planet, transferred to Silicon Valley. Needless to say, this one showed AMD as the center of a Silicon Valley populated by Intel, National and, cruelly (Sanders never forgets), Fairchild as a false front propped up by sticks. Far off, as insignificant bleeps on the horizon, lie (geography be damned) Motorola, Texas Instruments and Japan.

Sanders wasn't above verbal shots at his competition. In 1982, while the rest of the industry was in a recession, AMD was thriving, its 17 percent revenue growth even greater than Intel's. Sanders took the opportunity to say, "While other [semiconductor companies] have had declining sales and have generally been making apologies for how inept they are, AMD grew—and we're making money."

But Jerry Sanders was more than just a great huckster. There was something else going on at AMD. The three descendants of Fairchild had each gone their separate ways, following their own unique itineraries. These different paths also included distinct management styles. National's was the hardheadedness of the shop floor, Intel's the dry, think-tank style of a research team. AMD's was neither of the two, nor anything in between. It also wasn't HP.

Instead it was something rather remarkable, something that went unnoticed by the legions of sociologists and management theorists who swarmed to Silicon Valley to study Intel and HP.

In some ways the AMD style could be called a cult of personality, wrapped around the shining figure of Jerry Sanders, with his obvious relish of being rich and his comments like "I love money" making him sort of a high-tech Reverend Ike. The message was: Be like me, be like Jerry Sanders, and you'll be rich and happy, wise, handsome and witty.

There was more to AMD's style than the apotheosis of Jerry Sanders. For one thing, Sanders always had too great a sense of his own absurdity to carry off being a cult figure without his tongue firmly in cheek. But more important, there is an attitude at AMD, perhaps an outgrowth of Sanders's difficult childhood, of respect for the lowest people in the organization. Structurally, AMD is a very centralized, top-down company, just the kind of organization that Intel tried to escape. But instead of imitating Intel by creating new structures to counteract hierarchism, Sanders has chosen a different path, a more humane arrangement, and one that is very Jerry Sanders. Simply, he short-circuits the company's own structure by circumventing it, by going right down to the lowliest employee.

He accomplishes this in several ways, each designed to increase employee morale yet serve Jerry's own need for self-dramatization. The speech above about the ineptness of AMD's competitors was given at the annual AMD Christmas party, an event covered by the local and national press. While other firms have office parties and maybe a few cookies and a cup of booze in a conference room, Sanders each year invites the entire company to a monstrous Christmas party at one of the nicer settings in San Francisco. In 1982, for example, the event was held at the Galleria, a collection of decorator showrooms, and featured entertainment by pop-rock star Kenny Loggins. The entire event cost four hundred thousand dollars.

Another morale builder came in 1980, when AMD declared an "American Dream Christmas in May" and gave away by raffle a thousand dollars a month for the next twenty years to a company employee. The winner was a twenty-one-year-old Filipino woman holding one of the lowest positions in the firm, who had worked for AMD for just fourteen months. On a Saturday morning, Sanders, flanked by camera crews, delivered the prize to the woman.

This was pure bread and circuses, of course. Sanders knew it and the employees knew it and they reveled in it together. This wasn't National, where the atmosphere was "business is business," or Intel, with its intimations of immortality, but Jerry Sanders saying, "Look, I got into this business to make a lot of money and to have a hell of a good time and there's no reason that you shouldn't too."

Of course, all of this could have a dark side as well. After the big Christmas party Sanders could fly home to his house in Malibu, but for some workers it was back to their ramshackle apartment in East Side San Jose and the hope that the Christmas tree hadn't been stolen.

But it worked. Sanders, more than the rest of the Silicon Valley pioneers, had sweated the Silicon Valley Dream from the very beginning. Just like the people who worked for him, he had once dreamed of the Big Score and lived perpetually in hock achieving it. Now he had done it, and his success and his apparent though not necessarily real enjoyment of it gave AMD employees hope.

It was that hope, translated into hard work and loyalty, combined with AMD superior salesmanship and, remarkably, its relatively backward product line (it took years for AMD to get into MOS technology), which kept the firm from heading off on expensive tangents and AMD in the running long after its counterparts had fallen off. By mid-1983, AMD was a $350 million firm, its stock at an all-time high. And though it was still one third the size of National, it was coming up fast and seemed on its way to achieving Sanders's dream of a billion-dollar company before the end of the 1980s. It appeared that only the general hardening of the industry into giant conglomerates might stop it—and even then, no one would dare count sly Jerry Sanders out of the game.

*   *   *

The eighties saw some important changes in the semiconductor industry. For one thing, the ante changed. In the early 1960s, an entrepreneur could start up a full-line semiconductor wafer fabrication facility for about $250,000. By 1980, such a facility, with all of the new very large scale integrated-circuit manufacturing equipment, robots, pollution-control equipment and computers, would run upwards of $100 million.

That's a lot of capital equipment, particularly for a firm only selling a billion dollars' worth of chips right now. Unfortunately, by the mid-eighties, the multiple-hundred-million-dollar-facility chip company was a reality. And to make matters worse, the Japanese, with their vast conglomerate corporations, had that kind of money and were willing to spend it. The American firms knew that they had to match the Japanese bet or leave the table. But no venture capital was available. So, for the smaller companies that meant only one thing: find a sugar daddy.

That's just what happened throughout the late seventies and early eighties. Siemens of West Germany bought Litronix and 20 percent of AMD. Northern Telecom took 24 percent of Intersil and eventually turned around and sold its share to General Electric. Electronic Arrays was sold to Nippon Electric (NEC). Honeywell bought Synertek, Bosch got 25 percent of American Microsystems, which it kept until Gould bought the whole place; Philips already had Signetics and Westinghouse bought Intersil. Finally, in the biggest deal of all, in December 1982, IBM bought 12 percent of Intel for $250 million and an option to buy as much as 30 percent of the Santa Clara firm—which it slowly exercises.

On the one hand, these investments were good, giving the semiconductor houses the necessary capital infusion they needed to stay competitive. But on the other hand, particularly in the cases of buy-outs, there was the nagging precedent that no chip company fully acquired by a large outsider ever remained a viable force in the industry. It seemed that running a semiconductor company required some unique skills and considerable experience as part of the Valley chip "family" before one fully understood the nuances of the business. Most of all, semiconductor companies needed the freedom to move fast, to make split-second decisions, to bet the store on a hunch, to embark on new projects without having to worry about clearance cycles or stepping on some executive's toes or doing precise market research—all difficult for established, giant corporations. Like Lenny in *Of Mice and Men,* the big industrial monoliths would take up a fragile Valley chip firm and, in trying to protect it and nurture it, would instead crush and suffocate it. That's why many chip firms danced on a razor's edge, trying to remain competitive without selling themselves out. How many would make it was the subject of considerable speculation.

Other things happened in the Valley semiconductor industry in the 1980s. Intel suffered a wave of defections, notably in its systems program (products built around its computers on chips), where disenchanted managers saw entrepreneurial opportunities elsewhere. Not only did this tarnish the image of Intel as the perfect employer, it also led Grove and Moore to make unseemly remarks about "vulture capitalists" and then rationalize how the new loose investment money was different from the money that had led them to jump from Fairchild.

Over at National, Charlie Sporck lost original partner Floyd

Kvamme to Apple Computer. Kvamme was only one of a growing number of chip people who had jumped to the personal computer business as a wave of the future. (Over the years Apple alone had gained Kvamme and Gene Carter from National, Ken Zerbe from American Microsystems, and of course, Apple cofounder Mike Markkula, from Intel.)

The 1980s was also the decade National was thrown into the limelight Charlie Sporck had always feared. First there was the Japanscam scandal, in which some of the stolen IBM manuals turned up at National's subsidiary, National Advanced Systems.

That was just the beginning. In early 1984, National admitted to taking shortcuts testing chips destined for use in everything in the military inventory from walkie-talkies and Jeeps to fighter aircraft and battleships. National admitted to a few hundred thousand; insiders said the number was more like 26 million. The Justice Department went after Sporck and the top management but found no implicating paper trail to the top; so it settled for a hand slap: several million dollars in fines and a blacklisting of low-level department heads.

National barely blinked. It knew it had the government where it wanted—and within months the Defense Department was again buying from the sole source of many key chips: National Semiconductor, of course.

The most important change in the semiconductor industry in the 1980s was the rise of a number of new semiconductor firms. Because of growing facilities costs it had been generally assumed that the semiconductor industry was as good as sealed off by about 1974, with Exxon-backed Zilog (cofounded by Federico Faggin of microprocessor fame) one of the last to slip in under the wire. And even Zilog appeared to have jumped in too late, as it remained unprofitable nearly a decade after its founding.

By the beginning of the eighties, a new semiconductor process had been invented. It was called a gate array and it consisted of a standardized chip (which could be ordered from large chip houses) whose functions could be defined by the turning off or on of the dozens or even thousands of separate circuits on its surface. What this meant was that a customer could obtain through gate arrays a semicustom circuit at a fraction of the price of a fully custom chip and almost in the volumes of a general-use chip. Further, the cost of setting up a gate-array operation was a small percentage of the cost of a full-blown chip facility.

Not unexpectedly, this newly opened doorway into the semiconductor industry was quickly jammed with start-ups. As a measure of just how hot these companies appeared, most sported heavyweight founders and equally heavyweight investors. For example, VLSI Technology, Inc., was founded by three of the founders of Synertek and eventually run by a former vice-president of Motorola, Al Stein. Bendix; Olivetti; Kleiner-Perkins; Caufield & Byers; and others put up $40 million to get the company started. LSI Logic was founded by the one and only Wilf Corrigan with $90 million in start-up money. By 1983, there were at least a half dozen other gate array firms springing up in Silicon Valley, including SPI, one of the latest of Jean Hoerni's (one of the original Shockley Traitorous Eight) endless number of new companies. SPI, in a slight departure from the Valley garage myth, started up in a house trailer.

These new firms got a faster running start than their predecessors. VLSI Technology grew more rapidly than Intel had done fifteen years before and had its first public sale of stock in February 1983 after just three years in existence. Despite the fact that it had yet to turn a profit, the company was suddenly worth $66 million—and president Al Stein had a paper value of $15 million for just one year's work.

There were even more wonders in the offing. Nineteen eighty-three saw the announcement of several new chip-etching technologies, such as the focused ion beam, that offered the prospect of reducing a hangar-size chip fabrication laboratory to the size of a transportable semitruck trailer. Semis from semis, so to speak.

More than a technological breakthrough or the latest entrepreneurial outlet, the rise of gate arrays and new processing technologies signaled something else—something far more important.

It was that the semiconductor business, now one of the oldest and most mature of electronics industries, at the time when it seemed moribund and stagnant in the fresh current of new business activity, had suddenly been revitalized. It had been reborn by its own technological innovation; the semiconductor industry had come full circle, from youthful exuberance to the responsibility of maturity to a second childhood. One had to ask, if it happened here, could it not happen in all of the scores of other electronics industries—and in each one over and over again?

PROFILE
The Clown Prince

JERRY SANDERS

Who else would be filmed for "60 Minutes" driving his convertible Bentley, long silver-blond hair blowing in the wind? And when asked by Morley Safer about his wealth would first feign modesty and then compare himself with Aristotle Onassis? Who else would nakedly tell the San Francisco *Chronicle,* "I love money?" Or bring his wife to the company annual meetings and conferences, the latter looking wildly out of place in the latest Parisian high fashion—including on one occasion, a doeskin outfit that earned the nickname Princess Minnehaha? Or hold a quarter-million-dollar annual party for employees in San Francisco? Or run a raffle to give an employee twelve thousand dollars a year for the next twenty years and then deliver the award to the stunned, bathrobed young woman on a Saturday morning as the cameras turned? Or build a multimillion-dollar advertising campaign around the lowly asparagus or a young besuited executive looking a lot like Jerry riding a surfboard? Or who commutes every weekend to his home near Hollywood, not far from where he used to hang around Muscle Beach in hopes of being discovered and becoming a movie star?

Who else but the flamboyant clown prince of Silicon Valley, Jerry Sanders?

But there is another Jerry Sanders. This is the boy who collected stamps, the young executive whom as sober and calm a personality as Floyd Kvamme can call "the best boss I ever had"; the tycoon and industry titan who still worships his mentor, Robert Noyce, though to the outside world they seem peers. The man who has special spots in his garden for private talks with each of his three daughters. And the man who was so devastated by his divorce that even today mention of it brings tears to his eyes.

It is too easy to dismiss the florid side of Jerry Sanders as just a public persona, constructed for both personal and corporate promotion. Rather the public and private Jerry Sanders are part of a single man, and they have been there since his childhood, the product of an incredibly complex mind. The parallels to a movie star are obvious: his youthful dream of Hollywood has come true, only on a different stage where he is allowed to play himself. P.R. guru Regis McKenna is probably correct when he says that of all of Silicon Valley's "great men," Jerry Sanders may be the most brilliant—and the most insecure.

Certainly Sanders's difficult upbringing is unique among the generally sedate childhoods of the men who built Silicon Valley. He was born at home in a little house on South Winchester Street in Chicago on September 12, 1936. It was his grandfather's house, and Sanders would live there until he left for college.

Sanders's father was a twenty-year-old workingman, an electrical worker who started out stringing high-tension wire and eventually became a traffic light repairman. His mother was fifteen.

Jerry's parents' marriage was a stormy one, with his father often away on work or just away.

> My earliest remembrances, which are before I went to kindergarten, were of looking forward to the time I could spend with my paternal grandmother and grandfather, because up until about that time I was being cast about in various apartments where my mother and father lived together for a while or when they were apart for a while when my father was out on the road as a lineman. So those are not very happy memories.
>
> My grandparents sort of became my de facto parents when I was about four and a half or five years old. My mother decided once and for all that the marriage wasn't going anywhere, so there really was no place for me, no family homestead. So my paternal grandparents took me in and my maternal grandmother took my kid brother in.
>
> Looking back, I think it's just an amazing act of good fortune the way it worked out, because my paternal grandmother and grandfather were somewhat upscale—that is, middle-class —from my maternal grandmother. She was the widow of a

policeman who had been killed in the line of duty, and so she was living on a policeman's pension and was trying to raise her own kids. As you recall, my mother was only fifteen when I was born, so my grandmother still had kids living at home or living off her. It was pretty rough.

Whereas my grandfather, my paternal grandfather, was a college graduate, improbably enough in electrical engineering. He was sort of my role model, at least in the early days. I grew up under the assumption that you had to get to college, that you had to graduate from a university.

In fact, Sanders's grandfather was one of the first graduates in electrical engineering, earning his degree at the Armour Institute of Technology (now the Illinois Institute of Technology) about 1905. EE's of that era—not surprisingly, given that it was just a few years after Edison's research in the field—specialized in the distribution of electrical power and studied the exciting new discoveries in the theory of alternating current.

Finding a stable home life didn't solve all of Sanders's problems.

I was always kind of a brash kid and never seemed to be able to keep my thoughts to myself. That resulted in a certain amount of friction in my schooldays. I was extremely bright: I was valedictorian in my high school class and also a year ahead because of a promotion. So I was younger than my classmates, which means that I was also somewhat smaller physically and not as mature emotionally. I seemed to have a difficult time learning to keep my mouth shut, so I used to get into a significant number of fights.

Now the only problem with getting into a significant number of fights is if you have a tendency to lose. And it seemed to me that I was getting into a significant number of fights that I was losing.

But I was always very objective-oriented, and I decided we had to change that, so I started lifting weights in high school and got involved in a weight training program and trained myself from the proverbial ninety-eight-pound weakling to someone who looked pretty good.

Besides earning A's and picking fights, Sanders had other pursuits. He was never much at sports though he did go out for sophomore football—but very quickly dropped it. "Since I was such a smartass and people could smear me pretty well on the football field without any recriminations, I decided football wasn't too smart of an idea."

So the lonely young man found something he could do on his own: stamp-collecting. "I was a philatelist . . . It's really quite the antithesis of what I'd be interested in now—and yet it isn't because I still like beautiful things. I think I was just enamored of the beauty of a stamp. I used to collect British Colonials and other tropical stamps from places like Mozambique, whatever Mozambique is called today—certainly it was a much nicer place when it was called Mozambique."

It was stamps that led the fifteen-year-old into his first entrepreneurial venture: Walter J. Sanders, Stamps for Collectors.

> I used to buy stamps on approval, you know, write to magazines and they'd send me stamps. You pick out the ones you want and send them money for the ones you want and send the rest back. I decided that was a pretty simple way to run a business . . . I printed up a rubber stamp and stamped a lot of envelopes, bought some papers, bought stamps in bulk and sorted them out and ran ads in the newspaper.
>
> It was kind of fun. It was also a real insight into human nature. Some people paid, some people never paid and some people never even sent the stamps back. I never really did learn to write threatening letters. I guess I should have. It's funny, but I always paid my bills promptly—part of my Puritan ethic—so I never got the nasty letter to use as a model.

Sanders graduated from Lindblom High, a block away from his home, and was accepted to the University of Illinois at Navy Pier (now Chicago Branch), at the time a two-year school. He decided to major in engineering.

Before the young valedictorian had finished a single semester, he ran into the most devastating experience of his life, one that shattered many of his dreams and so derailed his life that the bright young man who had once skipped two years of school didn't graduate from college (University of Illinois/Champagne-Urbana) until he was twenty-one. Sanders cannot discuss the experience today without becoming visibly upset.

As usual, Sanders tells his own story best:

What happened was that I was at a party, a perfectly innocent affair after a football game. The football game was at the school where I had gone to high school and I got invited to the party along with some other guys. That was a mistake because it really wasn't a Lindblom High School party and there weren't many people there I knew. I didn't have a lot of friends there, to say the least—not that I had any enemies, but they were just strangers to me.

Now, one of the guys I had gone with was an extremely aggressive and self-proclaimed ladies' man and he managed to go after the date of the leader of a gang which I learned later was called the "Chi Nine." The leader's name was Bob Biocek [Sanders's voice breaks]. I'll remember that name forever.

Well, Jim Naumczik, the guy I was with, put a heavy press on the young lady, who was apparently the girlfriend of Biocek. So the party got kind of ugly and we started to leave. Somebody threw a beer bottle at the back of the car we were in. My judgment told us to keep moving, but unfortunately the group I was with thought this was an insult to their honor [tears in Sanders's eyes]. So we stopped the car and a discussion commenced by Jim Naumczik over who threw the bottle. And Bob Biocek stepped forward and it was going to be a real duel of the giants in the city streets of Chicago.

And so they began to fight. It seemed a reasonable thing to do, that's what they wanted.

Unfortunately— I'm a little sensitive on this subject; I'm amazed this can still bring out emotion in me. Unfortunately, Bob Biocek wasn't winning. And that was his group there, so a couple of the guys jumped to his aid to hold Jim while Bob was going to beat on him. My innate sense of fairness did not manage to be suppressed by my brain that particular day, so I went to the aid of Naumczik—something I incidentally wouldn't have done if I didn't think Jim and I could take those guys.

Well, it turns out that we'll never know if we could have or not because as soon as I pulled the guys off Jim he ran, leaving yours truly there.

I was doing all right for a while until somebody tackled me around the feet and got me on the ground. Then they proceeded to kick my head in. They broke my nose, they fractured my jaw, they fractured my skull, they broke my ribs and then, for a little local color, they carved me up with a beer can opener.

Then they left me on the street, presumably to die. And through good fortune, my next-door neighbor, a guy named Roger Iser, was kind enough to throw me in the trunk of his car—he literally just opened the trunk and pushed me in— and drove me to the Little Company of Mary Hospital, out on Ninety-fifth Street, somewhere between Ashland and Western. He drove up to the emergency ward, literally set me on the sidewalk and ran inside and said, "There's an accident victim out there."

. . . Thanks to Roger I'm alive, because I was in pretty bad shape. I'd lost a lot of blood. They even brought in a priest and gave me last rites . . . Because I was in good physical condition, because I didn't smoke or drink, the doctor subsequently told me, my system survived.

So I survived. I've still got a nose that's crooked and I've still got a depression in my forehead where they took the bone out to kind of fix my nose. All the other scars were emotional.

It was months before I could actually get around. I lost a semester of school over that—but it was a lesson well learned. I learned better where to put my loyalties. It turns out that those guys weren't worth my loyalty.

As it turned out, Sanders wasn't the first person the Chi Nine had beaten. The members were all on probation or parole. Years later, Sanders learned that Bob Biocek had been killed in a bar fight in Denver.

"I was your sandy-haired, blue-eyed college kid who thought because he could bench-press his own weight he was going to make the world safe for democracy. I was going to kick ass."

Sanders confesses that he still has a tendency "to step into crowds when I think things are unfair" but lately the prospect of lawsuits preys upon him: "In that regard I'm going to get smarter . . . I have to remember that I have deep pockets."

Finally, after that horrendous start, Jerry graduated from the University of Illinois in 1958 with a bachelor's degree in electrical engineering. He immediately went looking for work in Southern California. He had visited there once during his college years, hung out lifting weights at Muscle Beach in Venice and decided that was just the place for him.

He found a job at Douglas Aircraft Co. (now McDonnell Douglas) right in the midst of the aerospace boom. "I went there for a very simple reason: It was close to the beach. In those days I had this— what's the best way to put this?—romantic idea that I was going to get into movies. I thought that sounded like a great thing: I'll be an actor, make lots of money, have lots of beautiful women."

Sanders became all the more convinced that movie stardom was his destiny by an odd coincidence at Douglas.

> The desk I was assigned was in this general bullpen area, which would dehumanize anyone—hundreds of desks all with graduate engineers. But it turned out that the guy who had my desk before me was *Ty Hardin!*
>
> Ty Hardin had been an engineer, an awful engineer I might add from everything people told me, but he was an extremely handsome guy. Well, he was going over to, I guess it was Warner Bros., to get a costume to go to a party and when he put on some Western clothes somebody spotted him and said, "We need you." Clint Walker had gone on strike from "Cheyenne"—and Ty Hardin went on as his substitute.
>
> So those were heady days. It could happen. I mean, here was a guy working at this desk and now he's a TV star . . . the problem was that I wasn't nearly as good-looking as Ty Hardin.

But Sanders clung to his dream of movie stardom for some time. Finally, one weekend he was invited by a workmate to brunch with an elderly woman, the widow of a man who had spent many years in the film business. The old woman quickly appraised Sanders and informed him that he would never make it in the movies unless he got his nose fixed. The prospect didn't appeal to Sanders. Even with the surgery, the woman continued, "you don't look like a leading man, you look like a cowboy," and suggested that if Sanders learned to ride a horse he might get some work.

Finally, disintegrating Sanders's dream forever, the old woman pulled out a photograph of a good-looking young actor who had been trying for ten years to make it in Hollywood and thus far had only landed a few second and third rate parts. "It was Efrem Zimbalist, Jr. . . . and I agreed, he was pretty goddamn good-looking. So, I thought, well, the odds are pretty long against Jerry Sanders being a leading protagonist in the movies."

Now the disappointed young twenty-one-year-old had to decide what he wanted to do with his life. One thing he knew for certain: he didn't want to be a desk engineer. He wanted to be a boss and make enough money to keep up with his ever growing standard of living.

Douglas gave Sanders his first shot at management, directing a project to design the air-conditioning-control system on the DC-8 jetliner. "It worked and everything," Sanders says proudly of his one important engineering job. In the process of developing this control system, Sanders worked with his first semiconductor products, diodes, which Douglas bought from the Arizona firm Motorola. And as he dealt with the Motorola sales people, "I learned something very quickly: they didn't know anything about their products, they made more money than I did, they drove company cars and they had expense accounts. And I thought, this is crazy—so I applied for a job as sales engineer [salesman] at Motorola." Sanders had found his home. Whether it was chips, companies or himself, no one could sell it better than Hollywood Jerry Sanders.

He moved to Phoenix in August 1959 and went to work for Joe Van Poppelen, then Motorola sales manager and now a vice-president of National Semiconductor. He also met for the first time the general manager, Lester Hogan, who would one day fire him in the turning point of Jerry's career.

The young man rose quickly up the corporate ranks, from sales engineer to district sales manager in just two years. Unfortunately, Motorola had assigned Sanders back to his hometown of Chicago, a location about which he had been indifferent at first but which in time made him increasingly unhappy.

Nevertheless, Sanders was quite successful as a salesman and his talent was noticed by competitors, in particular by the local salesman for a young northern California company, Fairchild Semiconductor. Despite his disappointment with his beat, Sanders had no intention of leaving Motorola. However, when Fairchild offered him a free weekend trip out to the Coast to see the plant, Sanders jumped at the chance—figuring that if nothing else, he'd stop over and have some fun in Las Vegas.

But Fairchild was more than Sanders had anticipated, particularly its two top men: Bob Noyce, general manager, and Tom Bay, director of marketing. "They were quite impressive guys." After years of looking, Sanders had at last found his role models. Fairchild made him a job offer that weekend and Saturday night the Chicago Fairchild salesman, who was also there, "took me out on a typical recruitment evening, which meant get me drunk and get me to accept."

Sanders took the job, but in doing so threw down his trump card. It would be the Southern California beat or nothing. Fairchild gulped and agreed. So, in April 1961, Jerry Sanders finally made it, albeit through a different door, to Sunset Strip—actually a little four-story building with an outside elevator which Fairchild leased as a sales office. Hollywood Jerry Sanders had come home.

Unfortunately, it didn't last. Within a year, as reward for the excellent job he was doing selling Southern California, Sanders was asked by Fairchild to take the firm into the consumer business—which in those days meant television.

With little enthusiasm, Sanders moved up to San Francisco and set about selling Fairchild transistors to TV manufacturers. He was also made Northwest sales manager for all Fairchild products.

But he hated the work, particularly the consumer business—even though Fairchild quickly dominated 90 percent of the market. "I didn't like the customers . . . I just thought it was a dirty market. Suede shoe. I wanted to be at the forefront of technology. I saw the growth in computers—by that time Fairchild had introduced its first family of integrated circuits—and I wanted to get back into that. It just seemed to me that was where the future was."

Luckily about that time Don Valentine (now a leading venture capitalist) was made company sales manager. Sanders saw his opportunity and cut a quick deal. In a short time he was back down in his beloved Southern California, now as a sales manager for eleven Western states.

With a good salary and an executive position, Sanders's natural bent toward living beyond his means could come to full flower. By assuming a little debt he could now live like a movie star. In short order he received permission from ever flexible Fairchild and went out and "got myself the most magnificent black-on-black-on-black—black top, interior and outside—Cadillac convertible. It was a wonderful car. A great car. It was an *event.*"

Sanders also bought a stunning cantilevered house on Kings Road ("which was appropriate") in the Hollywood Hills. But the house didn't quite match Sanders's aesthetics or self-image: he concluded that what it needed was a brick façade on the wall of the living room that jutted out over the hillside. But rather than merely buying a brick façade, Sanders decided to call in a bricklayer and build a real wall.

The weight of this real wall was so great that it nearly tipped the house over and sent it crashing down the mountain. "So I wound up having—this is another insight into my personality I think; the average person would have just said to hell with it and taken the brick out, but Jerry Sanders wanted the brick wall on the fireplace—so I put concrete piers under the beams, jacked up the house and put steel beams underneath it.

"So I had the most expensive brick façade you ever wanted to see, but it was gorgeous." Between the Cadillac, the teetering house and the increasingly long hair, Sanders's reputation for flamboyance was already well established by the mid-1960s.

By the fall of 1965, when Valentine was promoted to director of marketing, Sanders was the top area manager for Fairchild. Valentine asked Sanders to come up to the plant and be his number two man. But what should have been an easy decision instead became a very difficult one. The same management shuffle that promoted Valentine had also made other changes on executive row. In particular, Sanders's two mentors were made increasingly inaccessible: Bob Noyce, in recognition of Fairchild Semiconductor's preponderant contributions to the parent company's profits, was named a group vice-president, responsible for several divisions.

It was expected then, among Fairchild Semi staffers, that Jerry's other role model, Tom Bay, would step up to fill the newly opened position of division general manager. But Fairchild management back in Syosset instead chose Charlie Sporck and transferred Bay back to New Jersey, where he was to become general manager of the Instrument Division. Bay asked Sanders to join him as marketing director. With deep regret, Sanders said no. "I'd like to tell you that I didn't want to leave semiconductors, which was true, and I'd like to tell you that I wanted to stay at Fairchild Semiconductor, but the real truth was that there was no way I was moving to New Jersey. I figured that I was now a California boy: that's where I wanted to live and that's where I was going to live."

So Sanders stayed on the coast. Bay, about whom Sanders would say, "Without Tom Bay there's little chance that Jerry Sanders would ever have been president of anything," would in time come back to Fairchild Semiconductor, but by then the world had changed.

To stay at Fairchild Semiconductor, Sanders had to leave Southern California and move again back North. And there were other commitments as well. "I was a bachelor until then. A very happy bachelor, with a Cadillac convertible, a house in the Hollywood Hills and a herpes-free environment." But Sanders's girlfriend, Linda, was not about to move five hundred miles without a wedding ring. They were married in three days and two days later Sanders was at work in the plant in Mountain View—leaving Linda to come up two days later.

It was a tough time that first year. "[The factory] is very different from life in the field—and at the same time as a married man . . . The marriage was under a tremendous strain; I think the only reason that I stayed married that first year was that I wouldn't admit to failure."

The job was equally frustrating. Valentine, Sanders claims, had promised him the number two job in marketing. But soon after Sanders arrived, "Don moved in three guys at my level. Marshall Cox, Bernie Marren and Jim Martin," all of whom at one time or another had worked for Sanders. "I thought that was pretty bum and unfair . . ." But Valentine, "a master of manipulation," took advantage of Sanders's huge ego and fear of failure to keep him on the job.

Adding to the pressure, Sanders's home in the Hollywood Hills refused to sell for a year—forcing him to continue to make payments on the place while renting another house in Silicon Valley. Exacerbating this financial strain, of course, was Sanders's undying talent for living beyond his means. To quote Jim Martin at the time, "Jerry, you live as though you make twice as much money as you really do."

"It's true," says Sanders. "But I always had the belief that the future held better things . . .

"So I was under cash strains. I was having a tough time. The marriage was rough. I was in trouble and very frustrated." One day, Valentine's boss, Charlie Sporck, the new general manager, came up and asked Sanders if something was the matter, he didn't seem like himself. Sanders spilled out the entire story. "I explained to him that I was paying five hundred a month rent, making payments of four hundred a month on the house and I was only making twenty-four thousand a year . . . I was dying."

Sporck, belying his reputation as a hard businessman, arranged for the company to pay Sanders a five-hundred-dollars-per-month special housing allowance until the house was sold. "It really saved my life," says Sanders. "I mean I wasn't really asking for a lot. I had moved up on short notice, made no arrangements for compensation for selling the house. Now that I think back I was a fool . . . I was just a gung ho company man and the company didn't care for me."

Sanders also never got over what he felt had been callous treatment by Valentine both on the compensation matter and in the job promotion. They were never again close.

This period marked the beginning of the end of Sanders's career at Fairchild Semiconductor. Not only had Sanders begun to develop a growing personal resentment of his treatment at the company but "there was a thunderstorm on the horizon."

Sanders claims that he has no interest in the past, but when he begins describing life at Fairchild in the late 1960s, he grows louder, angrier and increasingly bitter over old slights. The subsequent wealth and fame seem to have put few of these ghosts to rest. And nothing stirs more anger in Sanders than memories of the blame placed at the time on the marketing department for Fairchild's dwindling market share.

"I sure would like to get one thing off my chest," he says.

> I have always known that the customer is what counts and you gotta go take care of the customer. And if you are not prepared to do what it takes to take care of the customer, then you really should have the courage of your convictions and live with the result and not look for scapegoats . . . the scapegoat being either the salesman or the director of marketing or the sales manager or somebody.
>
> . . . Jerry Sanders was the answer to a maiden's prayer. We have someone to blame, the guy who wears the pink pants into IBM. I'd never visited an IBM facility nor did I own then or have I ever owned pink pants. But Jerry Sanders was the brash guy, you know, blah, blah, let's fix the marketing problem.
>
> . . . Bob Graham used to say that Jerry Sanders wins 100 percent of the time when he's right and 95 percent of the time when he's wrong. It turns out that there was a lot of truth in that, but what I think is especially important is that when I did win an argument when I was wrong I made an enemy. So I think some of those things came back to haunt me . . . I was a brash guy and I was not a me-too guy.

Then the impossible happened. In 1968, Charlie Sporck quit Fairchild to take over National Semiconductor. It was a stunning act for a company man like Sanders. Furthermore, it not only looted Fairchild of much of its talent, but also removed Sanders's greatest champion at the company. Now there was only Don Valentine above him and their relationship had long been chilled.

Tom Bay was called back from New Jersey to serve as general manager of Fairchild Semiconductor. Though generally loved, "Tom was just not up to the job," says Sanders. For the first time, Sanders seriously considered walking out of Fairchild.

One night, Sanders had a conversation with Pierre Lamond at the Wagon Wheel, the favorite Fairchild watering hole. Lamond had just quit Fairchild to become National's top engineering man. After ascertaining the depth of Jerry's bitterness toward Fairchild, Lamond suggested that Sanders jump to National.

> He said, "We need a good marketing guy." And I said, "Hey, I thought, you know, that there was an agreement that you couldn't hire from Fairchild." Well, Pierre said, we can handle that.
>
> Well, the way they handled that was to have the guy resign and then go to work somewhere else for a few months on some arrangement—and then after a couple months the guy's in there at National. So much for fair play.
>
> I was shocked. Stunned.

But not too disgusted to meet with Charlie Sporck about a job at National. Sanders's first daughter, Laura, had just been born and Jerry left his wife and baby at the hospital one evening to go over to Sporck's house. "His wife Janice was out at choir practice and Charlie boiled some eggs and chopped them up, took some Iranian caviar that [National chairman] Peter Sprague had brought back from one of his trips —he apparently owned some chicken farms in Iran—and we drank some champagne and talked about it." Sporck offered Sanders the job as National's vice-president of marketing. Sanders said he'd think about it. That night he went back to the hospital and told his wife "that I was going to do it, that I felt I had to do it."

". . . It was pretty grim. I mean, I didn't have enough money to get her out of the hospital, much less knowing how I was going to live maybe three months on no salary. But I had a little vacation pay coming and I figured we could tough it out."

Sanders felt obliged, after seven years at the company, to notify someone at Fairchild of his intention to leave. Luckily, Valentine was on the East Coast, because Sanders didn't feel friendly enough to tell him. Sanders also couldn't screw up enough courage to tell his old hero, Tom

Bay, directly. So he sent a vague message of his desires through an intermediary.

It wasn't long before Bay was standing in front of Sanders's desk.

> "I understand you're not happy," he said. And I said, "Tom, it's beyond that. I'm leaving, resigning . . . I'm going to leave and find a job where I can be the number one marketing guy rather than the number two marketing guy." And Tom said, "What can I do to keep you?" I said, "Nothing." And he said, "I don't believe you." I said, "The only thing you can do is give me Don's job." And he said, "You got it."
>
> I hadn't counted on that. I said, "What?" And he said, "We're not happy around here with Don in that job and we've been thinking about making a change . . ."

Having made his plans on the presumption that his resignation would be accepted, Sanders decided to raise the ante. Either he got everything he wanted or he'd be out—where he'd planned to be in the first place. It was Friday, so Sanders announced that he wanted Valentine's job Monday morning.

Bay quickly agreed, saying that he would meet Valentine at the airport that night as the latter returned from the East Coast and let him know.

"Tom met Don's plane and fired him. Awful."

Next, Sanders asked for stock options. He got them.

Charlie Sporck called Sanders at home the next day, Saturday. "He said, 'You're staying at Fairchild.' It was a statement. I said, 'Well, what makes you say that? How do you know?' And he said, 'Jerry, I know everything that goes on at Fairchild.' "

Sanders says that he has never regretted not going to National—especially in light of the company's harsh personnel policies. As it turns out, despite Sporck's stated lack of interest in anyone but Sanders for the vice-presidency, he quickly hired Don Valentine.

Sanders had already settled into his new position at Fairchild when, just a few months after Sporck's departure, founders Bob Noyce and Gordon Moore announced that they were quitting to found Intel. Sporck's resignation had been a shock, primarily because such a move had so little precedent; but Noyce's departure was a body blow to Fairchild, and no one felt it more deeply than his greatest follower, Jerry Sanders.

"I felt a little bit like a Christian saying to someone, you know, you can touch my physical body but you can't touch my soul. And after they cut off two legs and an arm they asked, 'Have we got your soul yet?' And the Christian replies, 'No, but you're getting close.' "

Word soon came down that the famous Dr. C. Lester Hogan, savior of Motorola (and Sanders's old boss), was taking over the controls of Fairchild and bringing with him his team of specialists. Worse, Sanders found out from another source that Hogan had already hired Sanders's replacement, Joe Van Poppelen of ITT, who would take over for Sanders as Fairchild vice-president of marketing as soon as he could get home from Europe.

"But it turns out I was a persuasive fellow. Les Hogan quickly perceived . . . that, hey, this is a real smart guy and you don't want to lose this guy." The result was that a new position was created for Van Poppelen, inserted between Sanders and Hogan. Van Poppelen was vice-president of corporate marketing, reporting to Hogan, the company president, while Sanders was director of marketing, reporting to Hogan, the division general manager.

It didn't take long for Sanders to realize that the position he was in was little better than the one he had tried to escape. "Basically what I had—and again I was too Truth, Justice and the American Way to see it —was a guy just waiting to nail me; Van Poppelen just waiting to build up a dossier to get me out of there."

Making matters worse, National Semiconductor, agreement or no agreement, had begun its devastating raids on Fairchild personnel. Sanders remains proud of the fact that his department lost only one staffer to raiding parties—and that was an individual for whom Sanders had no job. Nevertheless, Sanders's efforts didn't save him.

"The reward for all that was that one day Les called me in and said, 'I'm replacing you as group director of marketing.' " Hogan, who still speaks of Sanders in paternal tones, has since confessed that the firing was a mistake.

"I thought I was getting along great [with Hogan]," Sanders said fourteen years later.

> What I didn't realize was that the Lester Hogan of that time frame wasn't interested in dissent . . . and I was a brash kid. I thought if I was right, the weight of my argument would carry the day.
>
> It was a very different environment. Dissent was encouraged in the Noyce environment, certainly in the Sporck envi-

ronment. Dissent was commonplace. Yelling was not uncommon. Screaming. Table-pounding. The Hogan environment was different and I didn't realize that . . .

"I was really dumbfounded by the conversation—Les saying that he was replacing me. I wanted to know why—not in an argumentative fashion at all—just because I wanted to know why. And he began to give me some palliatives and I've never been good at taking palliatives, and then he began giving me some reasons, which even if they were true were inadequate.

In particular, Hogan accused Sanders of getting the corporate parts catalogue out late—an unusual reason for firing a vice-president, and the validity of which Sanders also disputes.

"But then it really got down to something when he said, 'I really don't want somebody on the staff who's threatening me.' "

Hogan, it seems, had not forgotten the day a few months earlier when Sanders had walked into his office and announced: "I want to put my name in the running for general manager."

How's that for brash? I said, "You're looking for a vice-president and general manager? I think I can run this division. I'd like to throw my hat in the ring . . ."

So then he asked me, which I had totally forgotten, "Okay, you're in the ring. But what happens if the next general manager isn't you? What is your reaction going to be?"

And I said, as only a young, brash, asshole would say, "I can't guarantee my behavior." Right? What a dumb, childish, adolescent thing to say. It was just a brash remark that could have been dealt with if he'd been persuaded to deal with it. He elected not to.

. . . [Hogan] later told me that he kept me there to keep the sales and marketing organization together and keep the books going and keep things alive until he could get his arms around the problem. I found that to be a little expeditious and I wasn't too thrilled with it but he was charged to save the corporation and that was his job and I'm sure everybody's heard the story about Winston Churchill [who] was prepared to sacrifice Coventry to a major bombing raid rather than let the Germans know [the British] had broken the Enigma code. Well, I suppose that every corporate executive can use that as an example for what I would consider to be less than honorable behavior. But then, exemplary behavior is rare in corporate boardrooms . . .

I guess what I would say now from my vantage point, running a semiconductor company much larger than the semiconductor company Les Hogan was running at the time, is that there aren't enough really good people and therefore you have to be more tolerant of their idiosyncrasies and try to channel their energy and effort—rather than force rounded, flavorful people into dull, square holes.

High-living, free-spending Jerry Sanders instantly went from a forty-five-thousand-per-year salary (up from thirty-three thousand with Hogan's arrival) to nothing in just four months.

"There I was. I had two little kids and house payments to make. I was scared. I was shocked. It was awful. So I did what any scared, impoverished young middle manager would do when faced with the prospect of unemployment: I rented a beach house in Malibu Colony. It cost me six hundred bucks a month and I think that left me with a hundred fifty in the bank."

There was a reason Sanders returned to his heartland of Southern California. Up north, in Silicon Valley, his firing had made him a pariah. Old friends and workmates suddenly "didn't know me, they didn't want to talk to me . . . they were there huzzaing on any comments about Jerry's shortcomings.

"That really was a great experience for me, though, [because] it taught me who my friends were." But in later years, when AMD was thriving and Fairchild was sinking, Sanders hired many of the same men. "I've never held grudges. I hired them if they had a contribution to make. I just never again valued their integrity . . . I basically put it down that they were scared. I knew how scared I was."

A severance agreement Sanders had made with Hogan promised a lump-sum payment of a year's salary after the first of the year (for tax purposes). It left Sanders with two impoverished months to walk along the beach and sort out his options. One alternative was to go back to what he had been doing: "find another company, be chief marketing executive—except that I think at that point in time nobody would have touched me. I mean who would want a guy who'd"—Sanders makes quotation marks with his fingers—"alienated all the customers, handled people with a heavy hand, wore pink pants into IBM and generally was a screw-off?"

"The other thing I decided I might do was go into personnel and music management. Somebody had a bunch of talented groups they wanted managed and they wanted somebody who had a flair for that.

"I also contemplated suicide. That's a joke, but I really was low. My sense of self-esteem was in the toilet."

The thought of becoming president of his own company never crossed his mind, Sanders claims. "What did I know about being president? I didn't even know the difference between a balance sheet and an income statement." But apparently other people felt differently. Within weeks a number of groups contacted him about starting up a new semiconductor company.

The more such start-up groups approached him, the more Sanders concluded that the best business in which to start a new company would be one that built Fairchild-type products as an alternative source for customers. One team that approached Sanders was led by Jack Gifford. This group wanted to build linear circuits—an idea that had no appeal to Sanders. Nevertheless, it was a talented group and he didn't want to lose them.

About this time, Sanders was approached by John Carey, an integrated-circuit expert who had just suffered a similar fate to Sanders's at Fairchild. ("They didn't even give him a chance to say goodbye to his people, which shows you the quality of human resource management at Fairchild at that time.") Carey drove down to Malibu in his Corvette and slept on Sanders's sofa, and the two spent their days roughing out a plan for a new company.

In the end, Advanced Micro Devices was founded in 1969 by eight individuals: Sanders, Carey, Sven Siemenson, a circuit designer who had worked for Carey at Fairchild, Ed Tourney, and Jack Gifford and the three members of his team who went along with Sanders's requirement that the firm make only digital integrated circuits. Sanders was president and as the sole marketing "name" was in charge of writing the business plan and raising money.

> I saw the business as basically one of design, make and sell
> . . . [We needed] someone to design the circuit, someone to
> fabricate it and someone to sell it. To me that was the heart of
> the business. The rest could be subcontracted, hired out; now
> don't get me wrong, I had no idea how to do any of this . . .

. . . Then I did something which really stunned the group. I said, "Oh, we've got to get a sales guy." And they said, "But you're the sales guy." And I said, "No, I'm not, I'm the president. And I can't be the president and be a good sales guy."

The cofounders agreed. But Sanders still had the responsibility of raising venture money. The others figured that it would be easy for Sanders, what with his bluster and industry reputation.

However, that was not the case. Sanders's bluff had fooled his peers. "I didn't know a damn thing about how to raise money." Famous or not, Sanders knew he "was incredibly naïve" when it came to raising the bucks. It was a much smaller venture community in those days, and less sophisticated ("real oxcart stuff") and much more competitive. "Today you just have to pick up any financial magazine or newspaper and you read about some new venture capital firm or maybe a new venture capital partnership, and they've raised $5 million and there's all this money around. The world was a lot different in 1969."

Through an old Fairchild compatriot, Sanders was introduced to Capital Management Services and its redoubtable patriarch Jonathan B. Lovelace, Sr. CMS agreed to be the lead investor for AMD (that is, they would locate the other venture investors) and old man Lovelace even loaned the budding entrepreneurs fifty thousand dollars with no strings attached.

Unfortunately, Capital Management's man in charge of locating other investors "was a disaster, I mean, he just had no idea how to raise money. He took us around to a few venture capital sources and it quickly became very clear that I was raising the money."

One of Sanders's first stops on the money-begging trail was the office of Art Rock, the dean of high-tech venture capitalists and backer of Intel. "I got nowhere with him. Art Rock said to me, 'It's no time to go into the semiconductor business, it's too late for that, there's no hope in semiconductors, plus just about the only investments I ever lost money on were ones where a marketing guy ran them.' So I said, 'Thank you very much,' and so much for Art Rock."

Sanders next visited some investors recommended by Rock. "I remember the phone conversation: they asked 'How are you going to compete with giants in the field like General Electric and RCA?'" and other dinosaurs who had dropped out of the chip race before it had even begun.

"What I learned from that experience was that a lot of guys didn't even know the questions to ask. You know, they were looking for xerography and I didn't have xerography, so they'd go back to sleep . . . Bob Noyce always said that it took [Intel] five minutes to raise $5 million—well, it took me five million minutes to raise five dollars. It was just grim. But I was dogged about it. I knew I had a story. I knew we could make money."

Finally Sanders put together a team of investors: Hale Bros., Bank of America, Sprout Capital (part of Donaldson, Lufkin Jenrette) and Shroeder Rockefeller.

But even this jury-rigged team wasn't enough to get AMD over the top on its cut-off start-up capital goal of $1.5 million. In the end it was Sanders's friends who came through. "I mean former Fairchild employees, Intel employees and distributors got together and formed a limited partnership and that partnership was the largest single investor we had." Even that almost wasn't enough. The goal was only cleared by five thousand dollars. The era of the $50-million start-up investment was still a long way off.

Such peer recognition, as always, was vitally important to Sanders:

> . . . it turns out that the testimonials I was getting weren't from analysts looking over our business plan and evaluating the team favorably, but it was from people who had known me personally and were investing in me. I actually had one guy before I formed AMD who was prepared to buy 10 percent of my earnings for a period of time for cash . . . I could've lived on that and not done anything. But he said, "I know you'd never do that, that's not your style."

Those friends who backed Sanders and held on to their 30-cents-per-share founders' stock probably have never regretted their faith in him. As this is being written, thanks to a booming market, those investors have realized about a 2,000 percent return on their investments in less than fifteen years. In that time, AMD has grown from a handful of founders and that initial nest egg of capital to a New York Stock Exchange firm employing twenty thousand people with annual sales of $400 million. "The difference between AMD and a lot of other guys," Sanders says proudly, "is that we're a real company. Thousands of employees, millions of square feet of space, products, factories—a real company."

But the growth and evolution of Jerry Sanders has matched that of his company. The Clown Prince in the Cadillac and handlebar mustache has become the most lucid and respected voice in his industry. When "60 Minutes" or the *National Geographic* come to town they visit the master quotemaker himself. And what would a Silicon Valley story be without Sanders in his Bentley? And it is little Jerry Sanders now who is tapped to give presentations on the semiconductor industry before Congress or to visit the Queen of England on her yacht—not just because he is every inch the image of the young California tycoon, but because he now *is* the equal of his old heroes, Noyce and Sporck and Bay, because he has the most facile mind of any of them and because he is the finest and wittiest public speaker in the electronics industry.

This achievement has come at great cost. For Jerry Sanders is perhaps the most haunted of Silicon Valley brahmins; the flamboyance and extroversion is matched by a considerable amount of private pain. One senses about Sanders that he has yet to believe his own success, that despite all evidence to the contrary, he still sees himself as a contender and not a champion. It is apparent in his appearance, in his ostentatious and nouveau materialism, in his inability to forget old slights that should have been long lost in the noblesse oblige of victory, and in his charming disbelief that someone like David Packard would come over at the Queen's reception and actually know him by name.

Sanders is an obsessive perfectionist—as he himself is first to admit. ("I was an angry young man. Now I'm an angry middle-aged man. I want perfection and the world isn't perfect . . . I want the whole world straightened out. Jerry Sanders wants the whole world to play to his scripts, his color combinations.") He has discovered that sometimes a victory on one front demands losses on another. Building AMD has cost him his best friend, his wife and his privacy.

His best friendship, with AMD cofounder Ed Tourney, collapsed in the 1974–75 recession when Tourney demanded more money and Sanders refused, instead accepting his friend's resignation.

The marriage broke up, after fifteen years and three daughters, in 1981. It had almost come apart the first year. "I think the only reason I stayed married that first year was that I couldn't admit to failure . . . I still consider myself a failure in that my marriage finally failed after fifteen years. So again my perfectionism and my sense of loyalty. Marriage to me was a major commitment—and I don't break commitments. And I don't like having them broken to me. I don't take well to that."

In fact, Sanders was emotionally and financially devastated by the break-up. His personal fortune was neatly sliced in half, reducing it to an estimated $12 million—a miniscule amount by Silicon Valley standards and just enough to support Sanders's life-style. The bull market of 1983 restored much of the lost net worth, but it didn't recoup something far more important: equity in AMD. In the settlement, Sanders's wife obtained half of their holdings in AMD—but, thankfully, instead of using it to assert leverage on the corporation, she quickly liquidated it on the open market.

As painful as the lost wealth was ("After all, the way I look at it that half was never really mine anyway"), the shock to Sanders's personal life was far worse. He admits to having been nearly a zombie for the year between the separation in the summer of 1981 and the final decree in the summer of 1982. What finally snapped him out of it, he says, was a bonus awarded to him by the AMD board for a job well done during that lost year, a dinner put on for him by his executives, and most of all Stacy, the twenty-three-year-old Vassar grad and budding writer Sanders met at a Palm Springs hotel where she was singing in the bar and he was holding a staff meeting. As she is only four years older than eldest daughter Tracy, a USC communications major, Stacy has been nicknamed TOK—for "The Other Kid." She travels with Sanders between the Russian Hill apartment in San Francisco and the homes in Malibu and Bel Air.

While these relationships were in transition, Sanders's private life was being assaulted from another direction. After being relatively ignored for two decades, Silicon Valley suddenly became the darling of the general press—with Hollywood Jerry one of the select few at the very center. The public Jerry Sanders began to compete with the private one —the bright, vulnerable ex-stamp collector with the man asked to pose in front of the trappings of his wealth.

> I don't know how to handle that part . . . I really hate to think that the public Jerry Sanders is something created for public consumption . . . My reaction to that at first was "Gee, that's fine, because I never had my picture in a magazine before" . . . then I got into the mode of saying, I even remember this, do they want to interview me about my views about the industry or do they want to take my picture in a Ferrari? Let's get it straight. But I've come beyond that, where now I look at it as, you know, Jerry Sanders and Jerry Sanders's views are kind of intertwined. This is the whole

person . . . I do wear a Rolex watch, I do go to the South of France on my holidays, I do like to live well, and I don't see how you can separate them. The numbers speak for themselves. AMD performs very well, and the people who work at AMD think I make some contribution to that.

But the excitement of national fame, the talk of entering politics ("Why should I take a demotion?" he jokes), has brought with it equivalent fears. Like kidnappers: "I worry about it to the point that I won't let my children be photographed with me." And the anonymous fan or enemy:

I think that celebrity is really of no value at all. I would not like to be a celebrity, and whatever minor celebrity I have within my society and my peer group is more of an annoyance than a benefit. I like the respect of my peers, but we're talking about two different things. I mean I was in a bar the other night just sitting there, and some girl said, "I used to work for you and blah, blah, blah." Christ, I thought, fuck it, I don't care if you used to work for me. It's Saturday night and I'd rather drink with my girlfriend.

That happens to me more lately than it ever has before.

Jerry Sanders also knows the greatest test to his carefully constructed self-image lies just beyond the horizon. In an age of massive capital investments for each new generation of chips, a half-billion- or even a billion-dollar company like AMD might not be able to survive as an independent. Siemens of Germany, which already owns 30 percent of AMD, may choose to buy the rest, or perhaps another megafirm "angel" will be found. Either way, the days of AMD as an extension of the personality of Jerry Sanders (and vice versa) will be over. Sanders already has said that he won't stay in such a new environment. But what happens to a man who is so closely identified with his company?

Sanders says that he can live with such a parting. "If I could give up my wife," he says, "I can give up AMD." It's an honest answer, but too facile to be comforting. In the back of his mind, Jerry Sanders knows that he personifies the American dream. But he also knows that America loves hustlers, but hates a success—and that the Great American Success Story always includes a fall from grace.

"Once, to wrap up a managers' meeting, I told them: In America, people don't really like winners, you know? Even other winners don't like winners . . . whenever you stick your head above the crowd you run the risk of getting whacked back down.

"I'm sure that my approach to life has caused me some grief and it may cause me more in the future, I don't know. But it's just the way I am."

5

The Money Sandwich

It is a well-tended myth that before one can understand anything about the electronics industry one must have a working knowledge of electromagnetic theory, be able to explain the dynamics of an 8-ohm resistor and write software for a minicomputer in assembly code.

Nothing could be further from the truth. It's a smoke screen put up by insiders, mumbo jumbo to scare the tourists. The reality (as many new personal computer owners have begun to discover) is that one can gain an appreciation of how a place like Silicon Valley works without knowing the difference between a volt and an amp, an A-to-D converter and a disk drive. In fact, one can read any business article about Silicon Valley and instantly comprehend it by replacing the more arcane names with familiar ones—aspirin for semiconductors, toasters for computers and so forth. This isn't as spurious as it sounds, because close up, the semiconductor business is just another chemical industry, and from far off, the personal computer just another household appliance. Business is still business, even when conducted by twenty-five-year-olds in hot tubs.

Nevertheless, though it is true that to comprehend Silicon Valley, one need only realize it is a business like any other; to *understand* the place, one must appreciate that the dynamo that lies at the heart of Silicon Valley is technological innovation. Technology is the guts of Silicon Valley, everything else—marketing, distribution, sales, management, manufacturing—is muscle, bone and flesh to protect the guts, to give it sustenance and derive from it existence.

Except for a diminishing number of the most disenfranchised people in the most humble Third and Fourth World countries, the importance of electronic invention must by now be apparent to everyone on the planet. (And even those poor peasants are no doubt learning about smart bombs and wire-controlled missiles these days.) But for most, even in the affluent West, where we are surrounded—and often assaulted—by the fruits of the Electronics Age, the actual nature of the devices we deal with daily remains undisclosed. The recent spate of teleological tracts that imbue everything from the lowliest integrated circuit to the most powerful supermainframe computer with mystical powers, evolutionary imperative and all sorts of other anthropomorphic gibberish have done nothing to improve the matter. The Wall Street lawyer or the newspaperman or the supermarket inventory control manager has little idea what is in that word processor in front of him, but does have a vague fear that some technological "Third Wave" is about to crash over his head and wash him away to oblivion. The working mother of three teenagers goes into a computer store to buy what she imagines to be a typewriter with a TV screen, only to be assaulted by bits, bytes and bauds, RAMs, ROMs and rasters and hardware, software and firmware. Does she want 256K core with a double-density dual-sided floppy, a 10 Mbyte Winchester and serial I/O?

Much has been written about the impenetrability of technojargon, all of it true. Electrical engineers run roughshod over our language, smashing syntax, making a fetish of acronyms, using nouns as verbs and vice versa and, in the most extreme case, selling their birthrights by collapsing into what might be called "digitomorphism," describing their own (approximately) human behavior with language normally reserved for describing the mindless actions of machines. When combined with the different, but derivative, jargon employed by M.B.A.s, the result is a weird hybrid language that seems to presage what the mother tongue will be like when that much vaunted union between people and machines is finally achieved:

"So, Fred, as soon as you get a data dump on the 64K RAM burn-in scheduling input me over at my workstation. I wanna be FIFO on this sort so I can get under way fabbing some kind of synergy—'cause if we don't get this whole run-through debugged in real time and get it prioritized and spread-sheeted we're gonna have a big crash on our hands . . ."

But obfuscatory language is only part of the problem for the outsider trying to grasp high electronics tech. An even greater obstacle is the endlessly changing and often looping nature of the industry. The history of the electronics industry is not serial. Chips were not the first devices invented, to be followed in turn by increasingly complex boxes to contain them, leading up through instruments and personal computers to minicomputers, mainframe computers, supercomputers and now the so-called fifth-generation computers.

A more accurate analogy is medicine. The medical profession did not start out learning how to treat cuts and cure colds and then over hundreds of years progress to treating infectious diseases or traumatic injuries and conducting organ transplants. Certainly there was an ever rising climb to greater sophistication, but there were also areas bypassed for many years, and others treated in a comparatively primitive manner until new discoveries came along. At that point, outmoded therapies were discarded (leeches, trepanning, etc.) for more modern methods— which in turn were supplanted by even more effective methods as they developed.

The electronics revolution has followed a similar, but greatly accelerated, course. Instrumentation, telecommunications and computers all predate the integrated-circuit chip—and all in time have been enhanced by it. Further, the changing needs of these older industries have forced changes in chip design. The snake consumes its own tail and is better off for it.

Thus, there is a dilemma for anyone trying to describe the world of electronics—and for anyone trying to understand what is being said. A historical account of the rise of the industry creates confusion about the relationship between components, such as integrated circuits, and the systems (such as computers) in which they are used, because chronologically the relationship is reversed. Yet a more technical approach that follows a logical path from the simplest pieces through the most complex constructions not only creates a false impression of how each level was developed, but also leaves out now obsolete technologies (such as vacuum tubes) that were once fundamental to the development of the industry.

There's no tidy solution to this problem, but one can at least be forewarned. This book offers a compromise solution: The first half of this chapter will describe in historical terms the prehistory of modern integrated-circuit, computer and microwave technology; the second half will start at the present with a building-block approach—and chronology be damned. The rest of the book provides a historical account of the last thirty years, complete with dead ends, backsliding, rediscoveries and evolutionary change.

Since the late 1960s or early 1970s, the fundamental device in all electronics products has been the semiconductor chip. Neither "semiconductor" nor "chip" is synonymous with the phrase "integrated circuit"—although increasingly in everyday use that is the case. In reality there are several distinct semiconductor families, of which digital devices—integrated circuits—are only the best known.

Semiconductor technology, as devised by Dr. William Shockley et al., refined by Robert Noyce, Jack Kilby, Bob Widlar, Ted Hoff and hundreds of others, is the product of more than a century of research into manipulating the flow of electricity in order to find new applications. In 1821, Michael Faraday built the first electric motor. In 1879, Thomas Edison constructed the first incandescent electric light bulb. A decade later, Nikola Tesla perfected alternating current.

By the end of the century, John Fleming, by modifying Edison's light bulb with the addition of a metal plate, found he had developed a device to pick up high-frequency signals—a key step in the development of radio. A few years later, Lee De Forest added a third metal element to Fleming's diode and found that the resulting tube not only received radio signals, it also amplified them—making long-distance communications possible—and the electronics revolution was on.

For the next thirty years, vacuum tubes (those glowing bulbs in old radios) were the golden keys to electronics. With refinements in construction and design it served as the basic unit of an entire panoply of products that defined postindustrial society up through the middle of the century: television, radio, radar, test and measurement instruments and early computers.

Of course, the vacuum tube was only part of the development of these products, an important tool in the actual construction. The intellectual wellspring of all of these products was four equations derived in the mid-nineteenth century by mathematician James Clark Maxwell. Maxwell's Laws, as they're called, are (as discussed in the chapter on Les Hogan) the four fundamental rules of electronics. From them can be derived the four elementary tools for manipulating the flow of electromagnetic waves, be it electricity or radio: the resistor, which "squeezes" down the flow of current; the inductor, which produces an electromagnetic field in a neighboring body without contact; the capacitor, which acts as a "spillway" to current, accumulating charge to a certain point and then releasing it; and the transformer, which changes the flow of electricity (current and voltage) but maintains the frequency. In their most primitive form, these circuits could be created by running current through the right combination of wire-wrapped magnets and metal plates.

With these four basic blocks, plus the vacuum tube amplifier, electrical engineers were given a small but potent bag of tricks to work with. With them, in time, they could build a scientific universe some would suggest could rival what nature did with the four nucleotides of DNA.

By the time De Forest was dangling his "trusty Ingersoll" before his triode, electrical scientists already were experimenting with combinations of these circuits to produce specific functions. By 1919, British scientists W. H. Eccles and F. W. Jordan, using two resistors and two triode tubes, built the primitive bistable latch, or "flip-flop," the ancestor of the computer memory circuit. With time, such second-level circuits—about a dozen fundamental ones such as the flip-flop, the negative-feedback amplifier (1927), the phase-locked loop (1932) and the automatic frequency control (1935)—themselves became the core building blocks of more complex devices. It was in this world that Hewlett and Packard and the Varian brothers first worked. HP combined these different jigsaw pieces into increasingly complicated instruments designed to test and measure the flow of electricity through more fundamental circuits—in essence, building an empire selling products to people like itself.

Meanwhile, at the center of all of this rapid expansion in electronics technology was the tube business. By 1932, the first trade magazine in the field, *Electronics,* reported that there were as many as three hundred different tube types on the market—twice as many as the year before—ranging in size from models larger than an office water bottle down to the tiny and accurately named acorn tube. Each year, new advancements were made in tube technology, pushing upward the attainable frequencies, while, thanks to mass production, the wholesale cost fell. Each new breakthrough in power or price opened a new market. And many of these new markets transformed society. Radios became not only more powerful (the headsets finally replaced by speakers) and more accurate to tune but also more compact and portable. By the mid-thirties, radios were in almost every home in the country, and by the end of the decade in almost every car.

Tubes were finding more applications than just in appliances. In another form, the cathode-ray tube—in which, instead of being looped, the amplified signals were spewed in a controlled spray against the top of the tube—led, in the hands of many inventors, notably Russian immigrant Vladimir Zworykin and San Franciscan Philo Farnsworth, to television. And a related but more powerful tube, the Varians' Klystron, led to radar and the "atom smasher" particle accelerator.

But easily the most portentous new technology in which tubes found application was in the young-old field of computation.

Computers had been around a long time, even by the early days of radio. The abacus's origins extend back to prehistory. The great philosopher-mathematician Blaise Pascal built a primitive computer in 1642 that used marked wheels. His intellectual peer Gottfried von Leibnitz, the father of calculus, built a more sophisticated version of the device (it could not only add and subtract but also multiply and divide) thirty-one years later.

The rest of the scientific community caught up with these titans two centuries later at the threshold of the Industrial Revolution. Suddenly there was a use for such a device in several highly diverse industries. Scientists needed a means to rapidly manipulate the multidigit numbers coming from their increasingly sophisticated measurement instruments, businessmen needed to monitor multinational operations, currency exchange rates and swelling inventories, and census takers had needed to track and cross-reference populations.

A remarkable answer, the Difference Engine, came in 1824 from a mathematician, Charles Babbage. It was constructed in an attempt to help the British Navy prepare nautical maps. Like a modern computer, the Difference Engine had two main subsystems: a central processing unit, consisting of wheels and gears, that did the arithmetic operations; and, most remarkably, a memory unit of punched cards like those the Jacquard mills had used for twenty years to control looms.

The Babbage Difference Engine was a titanic achievement, an awesome leap in human thought—and it also wasn't built for 130 years, and then only by IBM as a museum piece.

Nevertheless, an idea had been put into motion. Only one more preliminary step was needed, and that was the development in 1848 by English logician George Boole of Boolean algebra, the binary mathematical system of 1's and 0's, ons and offs, that would be the heart of computer logic. By the turn of the century, adding machines, descendants of Pascal's invention, were appearing on office desks. Herman Hollerith developed a primitive digital computer (that is, it counted in distinct units like a modern calculator) to help with the 1890 U.S. Census. That same year, two future computer industry leaders, IBM and Burroughs, were founded.

A true computer could now be built; not just a bigger adding machine with a set of functions predetermined by its construction, but a true data processor in which even the operations could be defined by the user. That is, it could be "programmed." But the date of the creation of the modern computer was delayed by the same problem that impeded other inventions, like the airplane, at the beginning of the twentieth century: a source of power.

The descendants of Babbage's machine were cranky, slow, mechanical creations that were perpetually limited by the task of moving all those driven shafts and wheels in a reliable, synchronous manner. The first attempt to streamline this activity, with the introduction of a motor-driven shaft, came in 1930 with the differential analyzer (early computers had hopeful names), an MIT project backed by the deep pockets of the J. P. Morgan Co. It was a string-and-chewing-gum deal, but the differential analyzer could solve equations in calculus, and it was obvious to observers that there might be something to this newfangled computer thing—if something could just be done about those damn wheels and gears.

The breakthrough came on the eve of the Second World War, when Claude Shannon, an electrical engineer at MIT, was studying electromechanical relays and suddenly had an idea. Relays were already being used by the telephone company as switches for interconnecting phone calls (you can still hear them, as clicking sounds, on old exchanges) and in operation they were pretty straightforward, working like a telegraph key.

But Shannon's remarkable contribution, one of the wonderful inductive leaps among the engineering discoveries in his generation, was to ask if there was some sort of logic that would describe multiple combinations of two-stage relays . . . binary . . . Boolean algebra.

Bingo. Shannon had pulled off something remarkable; he had linked the controllable behavior of machines with a system of logic that encompassed all science, perhaps even all of human thought. The Age of Computers had begun—and hard on its heels the rise of information theory, the great organizer of the postwar world.

Shannon wasn't alone in defining the shape of the computer to come. In 1936, Englishman Alan Turing wrote a paper describing a universal computing machine, the Turing Machine. It too would be instructed using a language of 1s and 0s, entered into the machine via a pattern of holes punched into ribbons of paper tape.

In Germany, Conrad Zuse had, in many ways, gone even further. By the mid-1930s, using electro-mechanical relays just like the ones Shannon was studying, Zuse had actually built the first electric computer, the Z-1.

At Harvard, contemporary with Turing and Zuse, Howard Aiken made plans to build his own computer, the Mark I.

Truly this was a case of an idea whose time had come. The stage was set, the players at their places. The need now was for a massive infusion of capital to get things going. World War II would be among the best times the computer industry ever had.

By Hiroshima, a handful of computers had not only been built but had played an important role in the war effort on both sides. In England, Turing and the team of the ULTRA group had built COLOSSUS and cracked the German ENIGMA, probably the greatest act of cryptology in history. The Mark I had developed ballistic tables for the U.S. Army and Navy until it was replaced in 1945 by the legendary ENIAC, the first computer recognized by popular culture.

As for poor Zuse, he continued improving his designs during the war. His Z-3 was used by the Third Reich for ballistics research. The Z-4, before it was partially destroyed by a 1944 Allied bombing raid, was used in the development of the V-2 buzz bomb.

In the battle of electronic wits between ULTRA in England and Zuse in Germany, the British team had a crucial advantage: it had chosen to use vacuum tubes in the COLOSSUS as the on-off switches, rather than the relays used by Zuse. Not only were vacuum tubes more reliable, because they had no moving parts they were also a lot faster than relays —several hundred times, in fact.

But computers weren't the only technology that thrived in the accelerated-spending environment of a world at war. Another was the science of microwaves and its first great product, radar.

Microwave technology, as might be expected, was an outgrowth of radio. Radar itself began as an accident: in 1922, two Navy scientists, A. Hoyt Taylor and Leo C. Young, were transmitting high-frequency radio waves across the Potomac River near Washington, D.C., when a ship happened to pass between the transmitter and the receiver, interrupting the signal. The two men instantly realized that the same technique would work on enemy ships hiding in inclement weather or fog. They proposed an early warning system of two destroyers sailing at a great distance apart and firing signals back and forth at one another, noting the points of weak or scattered signal.

It was a clever idea, but Taylor and Young eventually had a better one. The trick lay in placing the receiver next to the transmitter and *bouncing* the signal off any object that came in range. Direction could be found using a precise antenna and distance by the time it took the signal echoes to return. Signals were pulsed so that outgoing bursts wouldn't interfere with incoming ones. The Navy held its first test in April 1936 and declared "radar" (*r*adio *d*etection *a*nd *r*anging) a success.

Similar experiments were taking place in Europe; in the fast-moving world of electronics, thanks to conferences and technical papers, when a technology has arrived the fact is usually known everywhere in the world at the same time. The French were first, installing an obstacle detector aboard the liner *Normandie* in 1935 and a search radar to detect ships entering the harbor at Le Havre.

In 1936, the British Air Ministry constructed a chain of five radar stations twenty-five miles apart across England. The Germans too were hurrying to bring their radar work up to the state of the art.

As with computers, here again the Second World War led to a collision of technologies. But unlike most other electronic warfare devices of the era, the benefits of radar were tangible and instantly apparent. Radar's decisive role in the Battle of Britain has been well documented.

After the war, microwave technology remained the heart of military electronics, a staple of military contractors. Though clearly related to the other branches, microwave high tech was a world in itself, with its huge satellite dishes and hollow waveguide tubing that looked like sink plumbing. It was the province of giant contractors like RCA and ITT working for giant customers like the Department of Defense, the television and radio networks and Bell Telephone.

(It remains much that way today. But with the rise of personal telecommunications, of interactive cable television and backyard satellite disks, the microwave chip may soon be as much at home in the average household as the digital chip has become.)

So, by the late 1940s, tubes were everywhere: radio transmitters and receivers, video cameras and home television sets, record players, computers, test and measurement instruments and radar. The press called it the Atomic Age, but a more discerning eye might have labeled it the Age of the Vacuum Tube. As usual, among the tube makers who had begun the thirties, names such as De Forest Radio Corp. and Crosley Radio Corp. were ghosts by the time the golden age arrived. On the other hand, the survivors (not necessarily the pioneers), such as Zenith Radio, General Electric, RCA, Westinghouse and Raytheon, made a killing, and all endure to this day.

It can be said about almost every electronics boom that on its highest peak one can usually discern off in the distance a new invention destined to destroy it. This time it would be a tiny, striped ceramic cylinder resembling the abdomen of some kind of Bauhaus wasp. It was called a transistor. Within a decade it would not only effectively compete with the tube for the same markets but in almost every business would drive tubes into museums where they would be looked upon by bored schoolchildren as if they were shards of Etruscan pottery.

Almost from the beginning, the flaws of vacuum tubes were apparent to everyone who owned a radio. They were fragile, not particularly durable (remember the tube counters at hardware stores?), took forever to warm up—and, once they did, produced a lot of heat.

These limitations were not particularly apparent to a family listening to "Amos 'n Andy" on its High Gothic table radio (after all, no one had ever seen a pocket radio for comparison), but in more complex structures these flaws became insurmountable obstacles. The ENIAC computer, for instance, because it required eighteen thousand vacuum tubes to operate, was the size of a small warehouse, baked the operators at a perpetual boiler room temperature of 120 degrees F. and blew out tubes so often that it required teams of workers to stay continuously on the run finding and replacing them.

By the 1940s it was becoming increasingly obvious to scientists at the forefront of research that the demands being placed upon the vacuum tube were approaching the physical limitations of the device itself. You just couldn't make it much smaller or faster or tweak out much higher frequencies.

It was in this climate that Shockley, Brattain and Bardeen erected the new paradigm, the transistor. The handwriting was on the wall for vacuum tubes. The Solid State Era had begun. Within a decade the transistor too would all but follow the tube into oblivion.

*   *   *

At present, semiconductor devices come in three forms. First are the discrete devices (transistors, diodes, thyristors) which are descendants of circuits one might have found in Shockley's lab forty years ago. Next are monolithic integrated circuits which include of the single-chip devices we think of when discussing semiconductors. Monolithic integrated circuits come in three types: digital (such as logic circuits and memory chips), linear (such as amplifiers and regulator—descendants of products De Forest would have used at the turn of the century) and combined digital/linear circuits (such as comparitors).

The third type of semiconductor device is the hybrid integrated circuit. Hybrids get their name because they are combinations of the first two groups—discretes and monolithic ICs combined on a single, small substrate resembling a miniature printed-surface board. Hybrid circuitry gets into the most arcane of semiconductor disciplines: microwave devices, the stuff used in telecommunications.

The semiconductor world can also be sliced another way into halves, digital and analogue devices. Discrete devices and linear ICs operate in the analogue world, where the flow of information and control is continuous, like that of a wall thermostat or a light dimmer switch or the automatic choke on a carburetor. Digital circuits, on the other hand, process their information in distinct units (the 1s and 0s of Boolean algebra), as in the thought processes of computers and video games and "intelligent" appliances.

Although each of these disciplines forms a major industry in its own right and has undergone extensive change in the last two decades, most of the focus of attention is upon ICs. (In everyday use, "IC" means the monolithic type.) This is because their impact upon society to date is the deepest and best known, and because the Valley's greatest firms belong, for the most part, in the digital world.

Integrated circuits are called semiconductor devices (or just "semiconductors") because that branch of physics is the underlying technology in their construction. Solid state physics is a rather imponderable field. Its origins lay in the mid-nineteenth century in the work of men like Faraday, Becquerel, Willoughby Smith and Ferdinand Braun, who explored the changing capacity of electrical conductors under varying external influences, such as heat, light and atmospheric purity. The average person's one contact with this new field was through the earliest radios, in which tuning was accomplished with fine wires ("cat's whiskers") scratched across the surface of a crystal. With the rise of tubes, this research retreated into only the most advanced physics labs.

But it came back with a vengeance in Shockley's transistor.

The theory behind semiconductors is that certain nonconductive materials, such as silicon and gallium arsenide can be turned into precisely controllable conductors with the introduction of exact amounts of impurities. In the case of silicon, "dopants" such as arsine, phosphine and diborane gases (ions, specifically) are used to change the electrical characteristics of the silicon. Atop this is placed the fine matrix of metal circuitry we have become accustomed to seeing in blown-up microscopic photographs of integrated circuits.

Semiconductor technology has survived as the quintessential technique for building electronic devices—though the pace of historical development would argue for a newer methodology to appear and supplant it—because it offers some distinct advantages to the user.

First of all, in a trait it shares with the transistor, the semiconductor integrated circuit is solid state (that is, it has no moving parts). It is elegant and fundamental in its simplicity, like a rock crystal or a sliver of mica. The comparison is not disingenuous. After all, silicon is the third most common element on the planet, after oxygen and carbon. The precursors of the IC were machines, like the mechanical switch. The transistor, too, is a switch—or, more precisely, an electronic "gate," opening and closing to allow the passage of current. An integrated circuit is basically hundreds or thousands of transistor "gates" arrayed on a flat silicon sheet.

An integrated circuit is also a machine, but only in the way a magnet is. Its activities take place at the atomic level, in a manner akin to nature's own elementary behavior. As a result, semiconductor devices are incredibly durable. They can operate under extreme environmental stress: in the heat of deserts and the cold of cryogenic tanks, in the pressures of an ocean bottom and the emptiness of space. By comparison, a brisk shaking of an old television or radio was usually enough to kill or dislodge a tube or two. Switches wear out, tubes burn out, but semiconductor chips are all but immortal. When they go bad it is usually because there was a flaw in the original construction or a breakdown in their one Achilles' heel: the connection to the outside world. A tiny wire snaps or a surge of static electricity melts a miniature connection or the seal breaks on the casing and a stray dust mote falls on the exposed and vulnerable chip.

But barring such accidents, the integrated circuit is as immortal a machine as human beings have yet devised. There is no reason that historians a millennium from now won't have the opportunity to play with a still working Apple computer or Hewlett-Packard calculator or a Casio digital watch. They might even try their hand at Pac-Man (one can only guess what they'll make of biorhythm computers and X-rated video games).

This durability factor alone would have been enough to have created the semiconductor revolution. But solid state electronics has yet another feature that has turned out to be far more important. Because of a chip's simplicity—after all, one is basically just scratching on the surface of a piece of glass—it can be made *small*. Very small. Most people are old enough to remember the astonishment over the early pocket transistor radios, that tubes the size of juice glasses could be replaced by transistors no bigger than ladyfinger firecrackers. But that was just a warm-up. The modern integrated-circuit memory chip the size of a little fingernail can now hold 125,000 transistors, the tiny lines on its surface less than 1/300,000 of an inch wide. By the end of this decade, a million transistors on a chip may be realized.

Every year, the degree of miniaturization increases. For twenty years now semiconductors have adhered to Moore's Law (named after the cofounder of Fairchild and Intel), which predicts a 30 percent drop in the price per bit (transistor/"gate"/unit of memory) each year. What this means is that year in and year out the power (speed/capacity) of a chip at a given price is 30 percent greater—or, conversely, the price of a chip at a certain power is 30 percent less.

This is an astonishing ratio, with no real equivalent in the history of manufacturing. Electronics people delight nevertheless in developing accurate, if outrageous, comparisons to other industries. A favorite is automobiles: if Detroit had improved its products as rapidly as the electronics industry, a Cadillac would have a top speed of five hundred miles per hour, get two hundred miles to a gallon of gas and cost less than a dollar—or something like that; the numbers seem to change with every dinner speaker.

Moore's Law has two lessons. First, it all but nullifies the durability factor. Certainly a device that can stand up to just about anything nature can throw at it will be in great demand for high-cost, high-durability items such as military aircraft, space capsules and large computers. But in consumer goods, great durability at such a low cost is actually a handicap. At fifteen bucks for a digital watch, the chip will have paid for itself many times over in usefulness in the first year. Any built-in obsolescence to propel a sizable replacement market must be created by weaknesses in packaging—case, keys, display, etc.—components that aren't easy to make bad. It is a measure of the power of Moore's Law in action that when a malfunctioning video game cartridge or calculator or watch is returned to the manufacturer, rather than being repaired it is usually junked and replaced. It would be many times more expensive to repair a chip than to simply provide a new one.

What saves the electronics industry (particularly in consumer products) from selling itself right out of business, or putting manufacturers

and consumers on a roller coaster ride of tumbling, then sharply increasing, prices, is the second lesson of Moore's Law. Manufacturing
costs certainly continue to fall, but innovation also races forward. For
the price one paid for a single-function LED watch in 1974 that sucked
dry a battery every two months, one can now own a hyperthin LCD
watch that is also an eight-function calculator, plays Pac-Man, can
clock two races at the same time and tootle out a musical selection of
four popular tunes.

For a few thousand bills you can carry in your briefcase a computer
more powerful than the gas station–sized ENIAC. Sure the old Pong
games still work, but who wants to play one when for the same quarter
you can get ZAXXON, or next month another game ten times more
realistic and entertaining than that? As long as the rate of innovation
remains steady, and Moore's Law holds true, novelty will save the electronics industry in its strange battle with its own effectiveness.

But Moore's Law does more than define the industry's relationship
with the marketplace, it also relates it to itself. The extraordinary, unrelenting pace (it should be noted that Moore's Law accurately describes
integrated circuits but is less precise for other electronics markets) creates a unique business environment that might be best described as
controlled frenzy. If you aren't innovating or cutting prices or both, you
can bet your competitors are—and they are going to blow you right out
of the water. To keep up with the leaders requires more than just hard
work and eternal vigilance, it means sixty-hour weeks that only get
worse when the economy is booming or going bust, and betting the
company over and over again every time there's a new market to attack.
On top of this is the most frightening specter of all, the one nobody likes
to contemplate: the technological breakthrough, like the microprocessor, that not only sweeps other players from the board but introduces a
whole new game. When this happens, even the best-run, most energetic
company can find itself in a slowly stagnating side pool without any
hope of ever regaining the mainstream.

At a single company, this riverboat life-style can be pretty heady
stuff, enough to stamp a firm with a well-earned maverick image among
older, more staid neighbors. But in a geographical region, notably
Silicon Valley, where the most common business enterprise is precisely
of this type, you have what constitutes a new way of life.

The impact of the integrated circuit has not only sent shock waves
radiating outward through society, it has had a similar effect within the
electronics industry. Numerous multibillion-dollar industries, hereto-

fore nonexistent, have been created by the IC—at the front end to get the chips built and at the back to put them to use in products for the industrial, military and consumer markets.

The result is a vast, crazy floating crap game in which the chips are silicon and the bets are made in careers.

* * *

In describing how an integrated circuit is manufactured, one must keep in mind its magnitude: that great companies have grown from just supplying the equipment for one tiny corner of that manufacturing process—and at least one of each firm of this type is represented in Silicon Valley. Only then can the full multiplier effect be imagined.

For example, consider the process of etching the surface of a chip with acid. There are firms that supply the different powerful acids used, others that make the plastic bottles in which they come, others that make the tanks in which they are stored and still others that drive the trucks on which they are delivered. Other companies make the carts on which the acid bottles are transported through the manufacturer's building. And there are firms that make the vats in which the silicon wafers are dipped as well as trays used for the dipping.

There are companies making protective clothes for the workers, too, and chain-pull showers and eye fountains for when there is a spill, and hoods to draw the acid fumes away from the baths, and scrubbers on the roof to keep those fumes from leaking into the outside air—and electronic "sniffers" in case they do.

In the early days of Silicon Valley one could almost start a semiconductor firm in a garage. But with modern chip fabrication facilities costing more than $100 million, every time one of those babies goes up, it's money in the pocket for the semiconductor equipment makers, an industry so big it has its own conventions every year, drawing a total of more than a hundred thousand visitors.

A fabrication facility is a surprisingly small operation—probably smaller than the employee locker room at its only comparable antecedent, the River Rouge automobile plant. Given its cost to construct, fab facilities have the most expensive square footage this side of the cargo area in the space shuttle. Yet despite this compactness, within these walls, under the glowing yellow lights, in pressurized laminar-flow rooms that exhale the tiniest specks of dust, and performed by men and women dressed like a surgical team operating equipment as precise as anything found in genetics or physics, the signal event of the second half of the twentieth century is duplicated thousands of times each day: the creation of an integrated circuit.

The process usually begins with a silicon crystal (or some other substrate) that has been grown by a firm that specializes in that task. Ironically, in light of the fact that the entire point of semiconductor technology is the tainting of silicon with impurities, the silicon when it starts out must be pure to 1/100 of 1 percent (99.99 percent)—purer than most "perfect" diamonds.

The crystals are grown in forges that keep the silicon molten at 4,000 degrees F. As in junior high school chemistry, a seed crystal is used to start the accretionary process. The growing ingot is then drawn outward through a tube and cooled. The diameter of the tube has traditionally depended upon the development of the equipment that works with the resulting wafers. In the late 1960s, it was two or three inches, now it's four or five.

The resulting ingot looks a lot like an artillery shell or like holiday bread baked in a coffee can: a cylinder a foot or more tall with a rounded, pointed top. But the silicon ingot is a rich, glassy blue. And, as one might expect, quite heavy.

Next, the ingot is placed under a diamond saw and sliced, like bologna, into ultrathin (several hundredths of an inch) "wafers" about the diameter of beer coasters. They are not, despite being "glass," particularly transparent.

Next, the wafers are transported to the fabrication laboratory. The first step is cleaning. This is not done with soap and water. Rather a few dozen wafers at a time are loaded into a rack and dipped into a bath of nitric or sulfuric acid (kept hot to increase corrosiveness) to remove any grease or other alien substance.

The wafer is then washed off with cold, then boiling, ultrapure water. "Ultrapure" is not an exaggeration, it is almost inadequate. The water used in fab facilities is cleaner than that used to wash human organs during major surgery.

Next, the wafer is placed in an oven and baked at 1,100 degrees C. This produces an oxidation on the wafer's surface, a rust, resulting in a thin layer of silicon oxide. It is then removed from the oven and painted with a photosensitive chemical (like that on a roll of film). To set the new veneer, the wafer is again baked, this time at about the boiling temperature of water.

At this point the process begins to look a lot like the printing of a photograph. A photographic mask has been prepared, like the stencil of a silk screen, that contains the designs of the circuitry. These masks begin as drafting table–sized blueprints bearing the fine latticework of the thousands of lines and circuits that make up a modern IC. This drawing is then photographed and reduced hundreds of times until it is the size of a real circuit. The image is replicated a couple of hundred times into a larger mosaic that will be printed on the wafer.

The actual printing process is called alignment, and in it, the mask negative is placed over the wafer, and the unmasked areas of the wafer are exposed to ultraviolet light.

The wafer now has the integrated-circuit patterns on it, but they are negative and of the wrong material. The next few steps then are to replace the photoactive chemicals with the actual materials—dopants and metals—to create the circuitry.

The first step is to remove the unexposed chemicals—that is, the lines where the circuitry will be. This is done by dipping the wafer into a bath of hot, concentrated hydrochloric acid (to remove the chemicals) and one of hydrofluoric acid (to etch the glass). The wafer is again rinsed with ultrapure water.

Next the wafer is placed into an airtight, tube-shaped furnace containing a dopant gas and baked at 1,000 degrees C. The dopant gas chemically reacts with the surface of the wafer, altering the latter's electrical characteristics—and creating a semiconductor.

This mask-etch-diffusion cycle is repeated a number of times in a modern integrated circuit as layer upon layer of circuitry is built up to produce the complex structures now required. The final result is not far from what British scientist G. W. A. Dummar described prophetically in 1952: "It seems now possible to envisage electronic equipment in a solid block with no connecting wires. The block may consist of layers of insulating, conducting, rectifying and amplifying materials, the electrical junctions connected directly by cutting out areas of the various layers."

With the stacking of silicon layers complete, the chips must then be made ready to communicate with the outside world—another round of photomasking and etching. This time, however, instead of a diffusion furnace the wafer is placed in the dome of a vacuum chamber and sputtered with the molecules of an evaporated metal, usually aluminum. The resulting hyper-thin regions of metal serve as electrical connections into the IC. The wafer is then placed in an oven to evaporate any unwanted metal, washed in ultrapure water and then coated with a surface layer of glass (at 420 degrees C.) in a process called passivation.

The integrated-circuit chip is now complete.

This process only *seems* straightforward. In reality, the entire operation has about as much built-in voodoo and superstition as a major league baseball team. No one is even quite sure why "yield rates" (the percentage of good chips) are what they are. Thus, when they suddenly fall, there is general panic. When they rise, fab managers scurry about trying to find the magic key. Short of a scientific solution, the managers revert to an almost primitive faith in retaining every vestige of status quo. One of the women wore a silk blouse that day? Then she'll wear it every day. Someone else used his left hand rather than his right to dip the wafer in acid? Then from now on he's a southpaw.

These examples are a bit extreme, but every fab lab in the Valley can come up with a similar example. In the old days, before clean rooms and laminar-flow ventilation, making chips was even more unpredictable. Yield rates would plummet for no apparent reason. For example, one company found its yield dips corresponded to phases of the moon: it seemed that high tides also raised groundwater levels and thereby increased the moisture in the lab. Another lab found that during their menstrual periods female lab workers secreted extra oil in their hands, ruining wafers.

The lab at Signetics nearly shut down in the spring of 1965—until it was discovered that the crop-dusting taking place at the farm next door was wrecking chip surfaces.

But perhaps the most unusual cause of early low yields was discovered by a local firm faced with a disconcerting and destructive appearance of organic crystals on wafers. Thorough chemical analysis finally came up with an answer: the crystals were formed by droplets of urine left on male workers' hands after they used the rest room.

One obvious result of all these early problems is the now mandatory use in labs of plastic gloves or fingertip protectors (nicknamed "rubbers for midgets" by workers)—and, of course, the growing use of automation and specialized robots.

To return to the manufacturing process: the complete chip must now be separated from its hundreds of identical siblings on the wafer and be packaged. Before this is done, imperfectly formed ICs are located by microscope and marked for later culling out. Remarkably, the separation is usually accomplished, as with a pane of glass, by scribing and breaking.

The 1/16-inch-square integrated circuit may have enormous potential, but in its present form it is less useful than a chip of wood. The chip is glued with epoxy resins (or brazed) into the recessed top of the familiar tiny-table-with-many-legs, ceramic frame.

The ubiquitous "lead frame," as this package is called, is often confused with the actual circuit, which in reality lies underneath the square cover atop the frame. After the circuit ("die") is glued into the recessed area, incredibly thin wires—a fraction of the diameter of a human hair —are welded to it at the points where the metal contacts were formed. The other ends of these wires are attached to the top of the frame, where buried wires radiate outward and attach to the legs (the "leads"). To protect the circuit and the even more vulnerable wires, a plastic or ceramic cap is glued over the top of the recessed area.

That's the traditional way to make an integrated circuit. But it isn't the only way. For example, there are two primary semiconductor technologies: bipolar and metal oxide (MOS). Among other features, bipolar uses two types of semiconductor carriers, MOS only one (hence it is unipolar). Each has certain advantages in specific circuits (for example, MOS uses less power, bipolar is faster and more radiation-resistant). MOS is increasingly becoming the technology of choice, with almost 60 percent of the total semiconductor market, but it is a difficult technique to learn (some firms have failed many times over the last decade) and it is not expected to ever fully supplant bipolar.

The endless progress of technology is also changing the way IC's are made. Packaging has changed from almost wholly ceramic to predominantly plastic frames. The almost microscopic lead wires, once welded by hand, are now attached by machine in an amazing staccato burst.

In the wafer fab laboratory itself, as the tiny lines on the chips narrow to less than one micron (1/271,000 of an inch) width, the traditional photolithographic techniques described above lose their crispness as it stretches for a precision smaller than the wavelength of visible light. In response, new masking methods have been developed using electron beams, X rays or deep ultraviolet light.

In the future, the entire masking and aligning step itself may be bypassed for direct "writing" of the circuitry on the chip using electron or focused ion beams. Direct beam writing is expected to be common practice by the end of the 1980s; the timing is important because these systems will be critical for the next step in integrated circuitry, very large scale integration (VLSI), the true "computer on a chip."

One common item of manufacturing equipment that will become increasingly rare in the fab area by the late eighties is the human being. Even when you dress them top to toe in plastic gowns, slippers and hairnets, people are just too dirty for the submicron world. They are dusty and wet and produce or wear all sorts of chemicals that can ruin the pristine chip surface. They're slow too. And besides, they sometimes get hurt by all the dangerous chemicals and end up on the evening news talking about lawsuits and unions.

Already, some large systems companies, with their own in-house semiconductor operations, are moving rapidly toward a fully automated fab lab in which wafers are moved from station to station by robots and conveyor belts and aligned by little puffs of air. IBM is doing it. So are a number of Japanese firms. Each new semiconductor facility being opened these days seems a little closer to every manufacturing manager's dream of a fully automated factory in which one needs only to shovel in sand at one end and out will pop finished ICs, in their plastic shipping tubes, already addressed, at the other.

For now though, once the IC is finished, it is tested by computer to assure that it performs all of the duties for which it was designed and, especially in military applications, tested in hot environmental tanks ("burn-in") to simulate extended time and check their durability. This burn-in stage of production, having no visible effect on the finished product, is easy to fake—as the National Semiconductor case in 1984 proved. (See Chapter 4.)

The reader also might have noticed in the preceding description of how integrated circuits are made that the process has very little to do with electronics, and a whole lot to do with chemicals, and that a semiconductor laboratory at, say, Signetics, has more in common with Dow Chemical than with Atari. Many residents of Silicon Valley noticed the same thing in the late seventies in the wake of Times Beach and Love Canal.

Returning to the newly built IC. It is important to know that not every IC built by a fabrication laboratory works. On the contrary, it is only with the most mature (and often obsolete) lines that a *majority* of the finished chips are operational. On a brand-new prototype product line, a 10 percent yield rate can be cause for a party and pay bonuses. Integrated Circuit Engineering Corp., a consulting firm, estimates that the yield rate for a small, comparatively simple logic-type IC is about 60 percent. On the other hand, average yield for a complex microprocessor chip with a large die size is well under 5 percent. Broken down by process step, actual wafer-processing ruins 5 percent to 25 percent of the total production; probing the wafer for flaws after processing finds, depending upon the chip type, 5 percent to 90 percent of the remainder bad. Assembly takes out 5 percent to 20 percent of that, and final testing fails 5 percent to 40 percent of the remainder.

Only in a high-volume, low-unit-cost operation like semiconductors can one throw away 95 percent of production and still earn what is among the greatest profits in American business.

The failed wafers and ICs are scrapped and sold to dealers who extract the precious metals, such as the gold, from the leads. Scrap metal is a particularly lucrative business, particularly when run crookedly—but that story belongs elsewhere.

So the finished, *working* chip sits at the end of the testing gauntlet. The next step, which will occur elsewhere, is to build a structure to do something with it. Just as different types of tubes were needed to build an old-fashioned radio, different chips must be interconnected in various combinations to produce the wide range of modern electronic equipment.

As discussed, there are three basic kinds of semiconductor devices: discrete devices, linear and digital ICs, and hybrids. Digital ICs and microwave hybrids are centerpieces for entire systems industries. Discrete devices and linear ICs are the Rosencrantz and Guildenstern of the business; the lesser-known secondary players who hold the cloak or back up the hero in a fight. Discretes and linears make sure that the power and the information get into the digital circuit (the distinction isn't so great with microwaves) to be processed and then make sure that the results are properly conveyed back out to the operator. Rip out the guts of, say, a Commodore personal computer, and one will find dozens of linear circuits of all shapes and sizes serving, like drones and workers to a queen bee, a handful of digital chips.

The discrete and linear markets are by far the most stable of the IC businesses. Demand grows little from year to year. Prices have been driven down as low as possible, so any profits come with volume (hence the sobriquet "jelly beans").

Nevertheless, despite its apparent placidity, discretes and linears offer the greatest opportunity in the semiconductor industry, perhaps in the entire electronics industry, for the old-fashioned lone-wolf, Edison-type genius to come up with an exciting new design.

If discrete and linear circuits come in a number of different types, the more celebrated digital ICs come in only two: logic and memory. However, as we have only begun to see, an entire universe can be subsumed under those two functions.

Memory chips come in two forms and an almost endless number of sizes. The two forms are ROM (*read only memory*) and RAM (*random access memory*). ROM-type memory is like that found in a video game cartridge. It stores certain items of information—such as how the game is played, what the screen looks like, how the push buttons or joy sticks work—that can be elicited from the chip but not changed.

The RAM is a blank slate. Information can be written on it, then erased to be replaced by something else. The memory key on a calculator is connected to a RAM, while the function keys address a ROM. The information on the screen of a personal computer is stored in RAM until it is transferred to a more permanent storage medium such as a disk.

Two decades of research have led to several new types of ROMs and RAMs. For example, the electrically programmable ROM (EPROM) enables the once permanently stored information to be altered. This is particularly useful in fast moving markets like games, where the products must be perpetually updated—making EPROMs the staple of black marketeers everywhere. CMOS, a special kind of MOS semiconductor technology, has made it possible for RAMs to continue to hold data for extended periods using only a fraction of the power. For that reason, many modern calculators and portable computers can be ostensibly turned off (there is still a small power drain from the batteries) and be turned back on months later with the data still intact.

Memory size has changed drastically over the years. In the early days of Fairchild, it was considered a major breakthrough to surpass 100 stored bits of data on a single chip. But Moore's Law (for which it was first proposed) has held truer for memory than for any other sector of electronics. Expansion in memory size, as Moore's Law dictates, has been nearly logarithmic: there was the 1K RAM (1,024 bits of data storable), then the 4K, and the 16K. Next the 64K RAM, first introduced by the Japanese in 1982, was king of the hill. Now it is the 256K RAM. The next step after that is the 1-million-bit (1 megabit) memory chip. It's expected about 1990, unless unforeseen obstacles arise from circuit geometries that small. When operating in a world smaller than a micron, the landscape begins to become bumpy with atoms and one begins to enter the surreal world of quantum physics.

Because of their comparatively homogenous layout and because they so accurately track Moore's Law, RAMs have traditionally been the trend setters for the rest of the industry, setting the precedent for each new increment of density. Memory has also traditionally been the most volatile of all chip markets, the easiest to enter, the most difficult in which to maintain the pace, the most profitable when demand is high, the most price-bombed when it is not. Its extreme profits have financed the rest of the semiconductor revolution, yet its sudden collapses have caused Silicon Valley considerable grief. The memory chip business was insane enough when it was just American firms fighting and disemboweling one another over market share. But in the late 1970s, the Japanese electronics firms, backed to the hilt by their banks and government, targeted the memory market and went after it with every legal and illegal trick they knew. The rest has been near-chaos—and the Japanese for now seem to have taken the lead.

The logic business—and its participants thank their lucky stars for this fact—is not as manic as the memory business, though that probably will change. The future of electronics is the computer on the chip, no matter which way the revolution turns or down which new path it heads. The Americans know this. So do the Japanese and the Common Market, the Soviets and the Red Chinese, and the leaders of every country that has crawled even close to the twentieth century. If you can't build them, then buy them; and if you can't buy them, then steal them. Without the microprocessor you can't compete for your place in the modern world, you can't think fast enough, communicate with enough lucidity, manage your people or your resources, get your missiles and bombs to land on target.

Like memory chips, the history of logic chips has been one of ever increasing complexity. At their core is the transistor, now grown by the thousands on each chip in the two-dimension form of the gate. But unlike memory, which has a storage function, logic chips are the site of processing. So, beyond the *hardware* of the silicon chip there must now be the *software* of programming, the instructions telling the logic chip how to manipulate a piece of information. In the most basic form, the program is permanently placed in the logic chip, enabling it to run through a predetermined series of functions. This is how a calculator or a digital watch operates. You can't order the credit card calculator in your vest to do the income tax, but it will accurately complete a square root to fourteen places.

A far more sophisticated logic chip sits in an automobile engine and continuously (that is, in "real time") adjusts the air-fuel mixture, injectors and distributor advance to assure maximum performance with minimum air pollution. Finally, and most advanced, is the logic circuit that is programmed to be programmable—in other words, it has certain basic built-in functions as well as a language (an operating system) that enables the user to compose programs to take on a specific task. These circuits are the heart of a computer.

Over the years, logic chips have not only increased in power but, by incorporating additional functions, spread out horizontally into other markets. The traditional logic chip is precisely that: it performs logical operations. It is like the cerebral cortex without the rest of the brain beneath it. It can't do anything alone but must be surrounded by numerous support circuits, including memory, input/output (another logic chip) and a host of linear circuits. But by the late 1960s, as circuit geometries grew smaller and mask-making more sophisticated, it became feasible to put more than one type of circuit on a single chip. In 1972, Ted Hoff and his team at Intel did just that—logic and a little bit of memory on a single chip—and the microprocessor was born. In the last decade, further refinements have increased the complexity of this microprocessor. With the addition of a built-in controller for power and for input/output, the result is the microcomputer with all of the functions of a computer on a single chip.

With no other standard for comparison, microcomputers have related to the systems to which their processing power was supposedly equivalent. Thus the microprocessor was a watch or a calculator on a chip, a microcomputer the simplest form of computer on a chip, a microminicomputer (not yet achieved), a minicomputer on a chip and the much anticipated (1990–95) micromainframe, one of those big, number-crunching IBM computers on a chip. Such comparisons, however, are spurious. For one thing, in application, a room-sized computer and a chip are quite a bit different in use. But more importantly, the targets of such comparisons, the computers, are perpetually receding targets. For a number of years they have been stuffed with the latest logic and memory chips. Thus, the mainframe described today is about as far from the giant computer of 1995 as the home computer is to a contemporary monster machine.

*   *   *

So that is the semiconductor chip; the money sandwich, made from one of the world's most common elements, some scratches, rust, muddied by a rare chemical gas, then plated and framed. A work of engineering art that is the most prosaic and most sublime creation imaginable.

But chips don't work by themselves. The newly fabricated microcomputer perched in one's hand is incapable of eliciting new data from the world or of returning finished information. It has to be combined with other circuits and devices into a *system,* tethered by wires and other connections to supporting structures, much as the circulatory and nervous systems tie together diverse organs into a single living organism. No circuit stands alone. Even the most independent discrete device, performing like a variable resistor, still must have wires running in and out and a surrounding mechanism (rheostat) in order to become a light dimmer switch. With an advanced integrated circuit such as a microcomputer the need for support becomes even greater.

Now, one could tie together one of these chip constellations strictly with wires, but the result would be a ball of chips and wire that might be aesthetically pleasing but the antithesis of the engineering mind. A more practical, more organized method is one little removed from the "breadboards" in Edison's lab. This is the printed-circuit board. PC boards are the most primitive link in the electronics chain. Basically, they are rigid sheets of hard plastic, plated with a network of flat wires and perforated by orderly array of drill holes—like the boards used to hold tubes in old TV sets.

The reason integrated circuits are packaged in little cases with numerous legs is that those legs are wires that can be stuck into the holes in a PC board. On the underside of the board, where the plated wiring is, the tips of the legs are soldered down to make a connection. From a clock-radio to a supercomputer, almost every digital electronic product can be described as merely a box around one or more printed-circuit boards loaded with chips.

It sounds easy because it is. It may take an engineer with a Ph.D. in electronic engineering to come up with the right chips in the right array on the right board, but once the first prototype is built and proven workable, making copies is just a matter of stuffing chips on a board— the kind of thing that can be done by teenage village girls in Malaysia, poor people in Puerto Rico and illegal aliens and boat people in cramped Silicon Valley apartments.

As the most retrograde, labor-oriented sector in the electronics industry, board-stuffing is also one of the most savage and, with precious-metal recycling, the one most likely to cut a few illegal corners.

With the stuffed PC boards, one enters the systems universe, which multifurcates out in every direction, including new products resulting from the semiconductor revolution (personal computers) and old products given a new life by microprocessors ("smart" instruments).

There are a lot of ways to carve up the systems world. Perhaps the easiest (though it is not all-encompassing and suffers badly from overlap) is to see systems as composed of data processing devices, test and measurement instruments, communications equipment and consumer products. With the rise of such hybrid markets as personal computers, the electronic office and robots, the lines between the markets grow fuzzier by the year. But for an initial pass, these divisions will do.

The instrument business, as the opening chapters of this book describe, is the oldest and most revivified of the industry sectors. Modern-day oscilloscopes, voltmeters and the like are chock-full of ICs, making them more accurate, smaller and cheaper than their ancestors. Some, armed with microprocessors, now can both gather the data unaided and process it according to the needs of the operator. This processing power has made possible some amazing new products, such as the gas chromatograph/mass spectrometer, which "sniffs" a vaporized test sample (polluted air, a sample of a murder victim's hair) and precisely measures the chemical components; and the patient-monitoring systems which can keep track of vital signs and warn of threatening changes (medical electronics has been one of the biggest beneficiaries of the semiconductor revolution).

Of course, chips themselves need to be tested, and the business of boxes of chips testing other chips before they go off into boxes of chips has become a big-time business.

Microwave chips, understandably, have been the cornerstone of the telecommunications industry. But there is more to communications than just transmitting and receiving: you need "front end" equipment, and here digital ICs have made deep inroads. Digital chips are now found in telephone company switching centers, in computer-based PBX exchanges and tucked into "smart" telephone consoles that remember phone numbers or play tunes.

In the computer business, semiconductors have expanded the industry vertically and horizontally. First, chips have replaced traditional wired memory in the largest computers, making them faster, less expensive and more modular (thus more expandable). This in turn has verticalized the market by making possible smaller and less expensive models with comparatively the same power. Thus the mainframe computer of the 1950s, the minicomputer of the 1960s, the personal computer of the 1970s and the portable computer of the 1980s all have roughly the same power. This process is expected to continue almost indefinitely.

Because of semiconductors, the computer market has grown horizontally as well. Data entry into the early computers required punched cards or magnetic tape; output was punched cards or numbers on a display. But computers changed and so did the needs of users. Input became a terminal or keyboard, which at first required chips in the computer to make the communications link. Later, these "peripheral" devices gained chip intelligence of their own.

There were also new ways of storing information away from the central processor of the computer: hard metal disks, soft plastic floppy disks and banks of memory chips. Each of these too became a huge new market and began to "verticalize" (expand within the market) and "horizontalize" (expand into other markets) on its own. For example, rigid disks, originally 14-inch-in-diameter platters in washing machine–sized boxes capable of storing a few hundred thousand bits of data, in one market (for mainframes) retained the 14-inch size and race upward to several billion bits of memory storage, but in another market shot downward (in pursuit of the ever smaller computer) to 8-inch diameters, then 5.25 inches, then 3.5 inches. There are now hard-disk drives on the market for $1,500 that can store 20 million bits of information (the entire works of Shakespeare) in a package the size of an automobile tape deck.

Printing followed the same bidirectional expansion. Within a few years after the development of the modern computer there were several different printer technologies in use—line, print wheel, thermal, ink-jet, etc. Each has verticalized to cover the market spectrum from the high-cost, high-speed screamers for the supercomputer market to the poky, cut-rate models for use at home tapping out correspondence. At the same time, within each of those markets, the available products have consistently improved in speed and reliability.

Printing characters isn't the only modern way to (as engineers would say) "output" computer data. If the data is in the form of a chart or graph, there is also a plotter, which will draw the image. Sometimes the computer-screen image itself is the output, as in computer art and graphics, and that requires high-resolution color screens.

The title for all these products, *peripherals,* may once have accurately described their position in a computer room, but in terms of sales nothing could be further from the truth. For the past few years—and undoubtedly for many to come—computer peripherals have been the hottest electronics market. Every year, literally hundreds of new firms pop up to take advantage of some new printhead or servomotor or disk surface technology. And every once in a while one of these firms will come up with an entirely new product, as Shugart Associates did with the floppy disk, and dozens of other companies will pop up overnight in hot pursuit. In 1982 alone, more than thirty new peripheral-equipment companies appeared just to compete for a share of the hot new 5.25-inch rigid-disk market.

The consumer electronics market too, of course, is no stranger to thrills and spills, great fortunes and tragic falls from fiscal grace that light up the business night.

This consumer business is usually split between the more sober industrial market and the everything-goes toy market.

The industrial-consumer market is almost invisible to the end user. It's what's called an "OEM" (*o*riginal *e*quipment *m*anufacturer) business—that is, electronics manufacturers sell subsystems to other manufacturers who include them in their products for sale to the public. For example, the controls on a microwave oven, the electronic heart of an office copier, the engine computer in a Cadillac and the talking dashboard in a Toyota. This is big contract work, often requiring custom work, even custom chips.

The industrial market is of mixed value for electronics, particularly chip, firms. Certainly an order from Westinghouse or General Motors is a big-ticket deal, but the custom chip business is a tricky one, often leaving a semiconductor firm stuck down a blind alley of technology and out of the race. Even the biggest contract is never a permanent deal. Eventually, when the OEM costs to the contracting firm reach a certain unacceptable level, the giant manufacturer begins to look at the cost savings of having an in-house chip operation to do the same job. With the astronomical costs of starting a new chip house and the general shortage of qualified engineers, a buy-out of the old supplier—be it friendly or unfriendly—becomes strategically sound. So the big manufacturer goes cherry-picking, and the chip firms that want to retain their independence cower, while those needing a savior (or at least a sugar daddy) primp and preen and try not to look too anxious.

All of the electronics business is slightly mad, but the toy side of the consumer business is an asylum run by the patients, who dance an endless, exhausting, often fatal tarantella twitching this way and that according to the latest fad. This is component television and high-tech stereo and credit card calculators and electronic keyboards and video games and arcade games and video disks and audiodisks—and all the other Next Big Things that help people burn off excess hormones while rotting their brains, make a handful of businessmen and businesswomen brain-numbingly wealthy and then end up in the closet with the white disco suit and the mood rings. The consumer electronics market is a lot like drug-dealing, with similar profit margins, excitement and prospect of utter disaster. The only difference is that in the consumer electronics business, the users don't get addicted *enough*. Just ask someone who used to work for Bowmar calculator or Microma watch or GRT cartridge tapes or . . .

On the other hand, just ask Nolan Bushnell (Atari, Pizza Time, Catalyst) how much money can be made if one knows when to cash in one's chips and get the hell out of the casino.

That's the markets of electronics, or at least how they stood in the mid-1970s. Balkanized and, except for a dependence upon the semiconductor business for components, pretty much self-contained. But by the end of the decade, the situation had changed drastically. As each industry expanded it found itself overrunning neighboring fiefdoms. Microcomputers heading upward in power ran into computers heading downward in price. Video game firms, watching their market dwindle, lauched into personal computers. Digital equipment makers went after large sections of the microwave market. The microwave business in turn (even after the fiasco of CB in the early seventies) went after the consumer electronics market with portable telephones.

But extramarket migrations were only part of the change. Dr. Hiroe Osafune, dean of Japanese electronics, explained the situation best in 1980 when he predicted that the giant electronics firms that would emerge from the 1980s as victors would be those which had expanded their operations to achieve a triune of semiconductors, computers and telecommunications. Only when a firm could display such a triple threat encompassing the three major electronics markets could it have the flexibility, muscle and range needed for the all-or-nothing battle anticipated for the late eighties. Some have suggested that the big story of the decade will be a battle between an unleashed AT&T and IBM for the entire electronics world. But no one is counting out the Japanese giants, like NEC, either. Skirmishes have already occurred and, if the recent IBM-Hitachi Japanscam sting by the FBI is any indication, the fight will be vicious and probably to the corporate equivalent of death.

Forcing this pressure toward expansion and multidisciplined product lines is the prospect of the so-called office of the future, a multibillion-dollar market whose arrival is trumpeted every year but always remains just around the corner. This is the paperless office of a word processor at every desk wired to every other electronic device in the building, including printers, big payroll computers, copiers, the mailroom; as well as linked via satellite to similarly wired offices around the country. It is a splendid image and daily it fills the minds of high-tech executives with dreams of robber baron glory. But each realizes that until certain interconnection standards are agreed upon (which competitors seem to have little interest in doing), the office of the future is going to be a win-lose proposition. Either a customer is going to buy a manufacturer's entire package or he isn't. Patchwork networks won't do.

So for now, the office of the future receives a lot of sustained and a bit too enthusiastic applause from firms that are still nervously dipping just a toe into the waters. The most successful entries made so far have been by the little companies who have sacrificed the grand, all-encompassing scheme for the tiny, office-sized network built around a few personal computers, a rigid disk and perhaps a large computer or two. In the next few years, these little firms may be trampled as the giants finally crash in and stomp about. But then again, like insects, they may have the last laugh.

The joker in what might otherwise be a deck stacked for big electronics conglomerates in the 1980s is *software*. Once the province of programmers stuffing stacks of punched cards into gigantic computers, software has become one of the most ubiquitous—and still among the most nebulous—terms in our culture.

When you build a toaster capable of thinking, you have to teach it how to think and what to think about. In the computer world, the former (how to think) is called "operating software," the latter (what to think about) "applications software."

On one's DEC personal computer, the operating system (such as MS-DOS) gives the computer its language. It tells the computer what it means to think, what the alphabet is, what code words mean, how to run the printer, video screen and disk drives. It usually comes with the machine (or is an unseen portion of a high-power applications program).

Applications software "dedicates" the computer to a desired use. It can turn the computer screen into graph paper for developing tables and charts, or a video game, or an adding machine or a word processor.

The relationship between operating software and applications software is symbiotic. Each is useless without the other. Operating systems are the engines around which the automobile of applications software is built. Not surprisingly, there are a few dozen operating systems, while application programs just for personal computers alone number in the tens of thousands.

Writing sophisticated software is difficult, as much an art as a science —which explains why English majors have often made the best software engineers. It takes very special individuals to write best-selling games or word-processing programs—and most seem to be as much born as made. This means that good software engineers operate in a sellers' market, able to write their own tickets. The top designers, the ones who write the most popular games for Mattel or Atari, or operating systems and word-processing programs for Apple and IBM, are the Prousts of their disciplines. Their value is immeasurable (but you can be sure their employers try), because their work defines the future of the industry. CP/M and VisiCalc are as much landmarks in the creation of the huge personal computer industry as are the Apple II and the Radio Shack TRS-80. As we know people as much by their personalities as by their appearance, we come to know our computers as much by their software as by their packaging.

Software can't be built like an integrated circuit or an oscilloscope. It has to be conceptualized, plotted, written and edited. An analogy to writing a novel is not far off. You can't compose a symphony using dozens of people at numerous stations on an assembly line. Neither can you write an innovative new software program with a committee. It is a solitary act of creation, done as well on a kitchen table or on the porch of a mountain cabin as in a fancy office with a couch and credenza. As it happens, those two unusual locations were the sites of the creation of two of the best-known applications software packages ever developed, MANMAN for HP minicomputers by Sandra Kurtzig and Apple's Word Processing by Paul Lutus.

Market-analysis firm Dataquest Corp. has developed its own rule for software development akin to Moore's Law. It is that for any important new product, the development cost of a reasonable library of software to support it is ten times that of developing the hardware.

It is a stunning idea: some nonphysical "product," no more than numbers on a piece of paper or magnetic blips on a sheet of plastic, could have more intrinsic value than a roomful of flashing steel and plastic boxes and hundreds of miles of wire. But the average person has begun to experience this topsy-turvy situation when he or she finds the software needed to make a five-hundred-dollar computer do anything important costs nearly as much as the machine itself.

As one might imagine, the result is very much a case of the tail wagging the dog. This has certainly become the rule among large mainframe computers. IBM's greatest competitor has long been the computers it already has sold. The IBM 360 computer family introduced in the 1960s was comparatively the greatest computer success of all time. But in the subsequent decade, the amount of software developed by users for these machines amounted to ten times the value of IBM's 360 sales.

So IBM was trapped. If it introduced a new family incorporating all of the newest technological innovations, IBM would lose those old customers, who couldn't afford to develop all-new software for a new computer. Finally IBM did what it could: developed a new family (the 370 series) that incorporated as many of these new improvements as possible, yet still remained compatible with software designed for the old family. IBM has been caught in that lucrative, but frustrating, velvet trap ever since.

A similar pressure for continuity and compatibility has moved down through the market. Now HP, DEC and Data General (as well as IBM) minicomputers are forced to conform to those which preceded them. Similar signs are cropping up in the personal computer and even the microcomputer businesses.

One might ask if this demand for compatibility will slow the rate of technological progress. Perhaps, but mainly in hardware, which is increasingly the less important half of the duo. In software, continuity is a boon. It allows for creativity and refinement, it means that every few years the wheel doesn't have to be reinvented. Instead, software writers can take advantage of past efforts and launch from a raised platform, adding still more to the vast software superstructure atop a given product.

With hardware of necessity holding rather steady, the onus of innovation is on the software designer. After everything, the arcane technology, the complex manufacturing process, it all comes back to the brain matter of a handful of men and women. In the race for the world's technological leadership, it is increasingly coming down—as it should—to the solitary individual and his or her imagination.

PROFILE

The Dark King

CHARLES E. SPORCK

Floyd Kvamme vividly remembers the first time he met Charlie Sporck, the man at whose right hand he would serve for the next fifteen years:

> Cloyd Marvin and I were having a cup of coffee in the middle of the Fairchild cafeteria. Now eight or ten people can sit down along a normal cafeteria table and there was just the two of us sitting at one end and like four other guys sitting at the other end, with an open space between us.
>
> So we're calmly having our cups of coffee and suddenly the bloody table almost jumps off the floor, and here's this enormous guy sitting down at the far end of the table, and he's going *blam! blam!* and slamming his fists down on the table and screaming at this guy across from him: "When you tell me those *blankety-blank* things are shipped, I want them shipped, not still on the dock!"
>
> I leaned over and asked Cloyd, "Who in the heck is that?"
>
> "That's Charlie Sporck," Cloyd replied.

Charlie Sporck's dark silhouette stands tall over Silicon Valley. No man incites such a complex series of emotions—from awe to fear to hatred—among workers, the press, even among his peers. In a industry filled with likable saints and even more likable sinners, decent church-goers and flamboyant rogues, Sporck is none of those things. He is neither nice nor particularly friendly; what charm Charlie has is deeply buried in that brooding, taciturn giant, who stands six feet five and smokes an imposing cigar. Even the Zapata mustache, which looks charmingly insouciant on Jerry Sanders, turns mean-looking on Sporck's upper lip, drawing the corners of his mouth down into a look of perpetual anger.

The table-pounding Kvamme saw in the early 1960s was not the mark of youthful inexperience, an early example of the Attila the Sporck management style. In a Valley full of managers raised on Theory Y and the nurturing, supportive school of management, Sporck is a character out of Theodore Dreiser. He yells, intimidates and pounds on tables, and this style of management has spread from the top to the bottom of his company, making it the closest thing in Silicon Valley to an old-line, pressure-cooker East Coast corporation. It is also notorious in the Valley for having one of the harshest work environments.

Yet National Semiconductor is one of the Valley's success stories. It became only the second firm in the Valley, after HP, to reach a billion dollars in sales—and it did it in half the time. And despite perennial claims that he is in well above his head, that a corporate collapse is imminent, National Semiconductor and Charlie Sporck continue to thrive.

More than any other company and its president, National Semiconductor *is* Charlie Sporck, its strengths and weaknesses are his—and thus National's great success would seem to indicate that Sporck is more than just a brooding king driving on his minions with curses and blows.

In fact, Sporck is charming despite himself. Even as one struggles to get more than one-syllable answers out of the man, even as he accuses the press of being disreputable, you sense that in reality he is a likable man who simply does not share the charisma or the lucidity of most of his more popular peers.

Part of this no doubt comes from his upbringing, which differs from that of the other founders of Silicon Valley in both its orientation and its apparently singular lack of ambition.

Charlie Sporck was born in 1927 in upstate New York—Saranac Lake to be precise. Most people are surprised to find that Sporck is fifty-seven, closer in age to Hogan than to Sanders, because he looks much younger. Apparently that is genetic: his father is still alive in his nineties.

Unlike most of the Valley's pioneers, who came from middle-class, Midwestern upbringings, Sporck's father owned a taxi and was a taxidermist on the side. He has an older brother, a doctor of physical chemistry, and a younger sister who is a librarian.

Attending high school during the Second World War, Sporck decided that his life's goal was to be a professional soldier, a West Point grad. "It wasn't until after I was in the service that I found that it really wasn't my cup of tea." (It should be noted here that to fully appreciate the style of Charlie Sporck, all quotes should be interspersed with long pauses and scores of "Uhs," as though he were having a painful confession wrung out of him.)

As soon as he could get out of the infantry, in 1947, Sporck jumped, landing at Cornell University. He graduated in 1951 with a degree in chemical engineering, sharing with most of his peers an education in a field other than electronics. He married his high school sweetheart in 1949.

During his college years Sporck had supported his education with a work program at various places, the most notable being General Electric. And it was General Electric that offered him work after graduation.

His first job was in the company's manufacturing training program— "a three-year session where they moved you around to different jobs in different locations." That completed, Sporck went to work at the G.E. capacitor operation in Hudson Falls, New York, building power fab capacitors.

He loved the work. "I went to work for $320 a month—and that was a hell of a lot of money. I had pictures of myself really rolling in the lap of luxury. I really planned on doing it indefinitely."

And he almost did, spending six years as a foreman in charge of shop operations, the equivalent of manufacturing engineering. This was where Sporck learned the day-to-day skills of making products that would serve him well later.

The jump to executive row would never have happened if outside forces hadn't soured Sporck on his GE job:

> About 1959 I found that for the first time I was experiencing a level of disappointment at G.E. It had to do with a method, a new process that I had been involved in establishing for the assembly of the capacitors. But this was a union shop, a very strong union shop, and when I had the process developed and was in the midst of instituting it I suddenly ran into a lot of resistance on the part of the union.

It was a very strong East Coast union, and by and large they were opposed to whatever you wanted to change.

Anyway, the company ended up deciding that they weren't really going to go through the hassle of instituting it. They didn't want to make waves . . . Well, that was a real disappointment to me because I had put a lot of work into that project. It convinced me that I had better look for a work environment where making waves was attractive.

. . . I looked into the New York *Times* and saw an ad for Fairchild Semiconductor, a division of Fairchild Camera and Instrument.

It turned out that Fairchild was looking for a production manager, so I wrote them and they arranged to interview me in New York.

So I went down there in August 1959, eleven o'clock in the morning. I remember it to this day. I rapped on the door and these two guys let me in and they were already in their cups. They were under the influence, deeply under the influence. They had obviously had an early morning exercise or a late night.

They proceeded to offer me a drink and started interviewing. Then, after a couple of hours, they offered me a job. At the time I was making eight thousand a year. They offered me a job at thirteen thousand, which to me was whew! *spectacular.* I thought, "I'll take it, work a couple of years and then come back East."

Sporck went home, packed up his young family and headed West. A month later he was standing in the lobby of Fairchild Semiconductor in Mountain View. He was stunned to find that no one had heard of him, and no one had expected his arrival. "Which was kind of frightening since I had cut all my bridges. It took me some time to find one of those two guys who had offered me the job. As it turned out, they had hired two people for the same position."

So young Charlie Sporck, fresh to Silicon Valley, found himself sharing an office with another man holding the same job, both of them directing a sole general foreman between them. "It was typical of that period because the company—the whole area for that matter—was growing like crazy. There was very little maturity, very little control."

But in a short time life at the company settled down to the semicontrolled chaos that was Fairchild in the early sixties. The other production manager soon disappeared, and Sporck, alone among all these young men in having hard experience in getting stuff built, began to rise to the top. It wasn't easy. The wild life of Fairchild played hell on personal lives, but Sporck was nearly unique in staying married, in time becoming the father of three sons.

After only a year and a half, Sporck was made division operations manager. And just three years after that, when Noyce moved upstairs to run all of Fairchild, Sporck was made head man (division general manager) of Fairchild Semiconductor—a job equivalent to company president.

During these years Fairchild thrived, much of it due to Sporck's extraordinary manufacturing skill. But, bumped up to the general manager's job, Sporck found himself bogged down with the same problems Noyce had faced—notably the corporate bureaucracy and the continuing loss of talent.

Throughout Sporck's tenure as general manager, he found himself trying to convince employees not to leave but having no carrot, like stocks, to wave before them. By 1966, Sporck was infected by the same bug, and two years later he too left Fairchild to try his hand at saving National Semiconductor.

Why National? Because it was going belly-up—"which is obviously the only kind of company you can make a deal with." How did he find it? "I just went down the list of semiconductor companies. There weren't many of them."

Stock options or not, few executives have ever left the reins of one of America's most successful companies to take over a tiny wreck of a firm sliding into bankruptcy and unsure where the next payroll would come from. But Sporck had no doubts: "It never occurred to me that we would fail. I look at the situation quite straightforwardly. We had a lot of harrowing experiences for the next few months, but I never had any doubt."

Now, after eighteen years of struggling, National Semiconductor has become one of the largest companies in electronics, ten times as large as the Fairchild Sporck left in 1968. Yet the way seems no easier. National still seems assaulted on every side. There were the drug abuse and chemical leak exposés involving National in the local press. There was the scandal over the improperly tested military chips that cost National its military sales qualification and the reputation for quality it had tried to build. Then there was the IBM civil suit over the trade secrets stolen by the Japanese involving a subsidiary of National as a way station.

Most of all, there is the Japanese threat, which often seems targeted directly at National, with its full-product line and production orientation. National, almost alone, has been fighting the Japanese at their own game—volume manufacturing and competitive pricing—an extremely dangerous course given the size of Japanese companies, their government support and their occasional breaches of ethics. But hardball, playing a little loose with the rules, has been Charlie Sporck's talent from the beginning. Nevertheless, in this particular match, Sporck appears to believe that he's at a huge disadvantage. That's why the mention of Japanese competition seems to send him into paroxyms of rage. In the middle of what was a careful interview in which he has tried his best to restrain his famous anger and strong opinions, the Japanese threat can still draw out the dark clouds and make Sporck loquacious for the only time (edited for coherence):

> I became interested in the [Japanese problem] about eight years ago. I talked about it for the first time at an analysts meeting in Los Angeles—long before it was a popular issue. And at that time I said I thought the Japanese were a real threat to the semiconductor business, because it is a natural for them with their organized industrial policy approach. That they were going to make a lot of headway. Meanwhile our government's approach was to sue IBM in court [under antitrust]. The point I was trying to make was that the U.S. Government's approach was just the opposite of Japan's. What we do is to go after and destroy our most successful companies, while the Japanese help build up theirs. Can you imagine Japan suing IBM if IBM was a Japanese company? (By the way, IBM asked me to testify for them after that speech.)
>
> I think the same thing is true now that was true then. The problem is not the Japanese per se. I mean obviously if the Japanese changed their policies and made them the same as ours our economic problems would go away. But there's no reason to assume that they would do that. And why should they? They decided how they wanted to do things and they were right to do it. None of us can knock that. Our problem is that the U.S. Government has never responded to that problem—and it must . . .

I don't propose tariffs. What I propose, number one, is that we must have an industrial policy. We must understand what is important to us from the standpoint of the future. [We have to recognize that] shoes may not be as important as computers. We've got to have the ability to define where we want our economy to go. Once we have that, and a bipartisan consensus can be reached, then we can start doing something. And boy, that's long overdue. If we don't get that we're in deep sauce, I believe.

So, now, let's say the industrial policy says that the semiconductor industry is important to us in the future of the computer industry, then what has to be established is the financial environment that assures success. *Whatever that takes.* And, you know, we can be as creative as anybody else in the world coming up with the solutions.

. . . A foreign industrial base now can attack a U.S. industry, financing it in such a way as to drive down the profit margins such that the U.S. industry cannot maintain research and development and not attract investment money. That way they can drive the domestic industry into a weaker and weaker position. That's why we have to decide what the hell's important and do something about it.

What's frightening to me is that if we don't do something about the long-term plight of the high-technology industry we aren't going to have any. And if we don't have any, we will not have a strong industrial base. You can't have one without the other. If we don't have a strong industrial base our society is going to change because we will become an underdeveloped country. It's difficult to get that message across because everybody seems to feel that, hell, what's wrong with buying our computers in Japan? They're cheaper. What they forget that means is we're not producing anything. All we're going to have left to sell the Japanese is soybeans.

I'm not proposing to stop trading with the Japanese. I just want an equivalent environment, all barriers down, 100 percent, both sides. Then if we can't compete, so be it.

That said, Charlie Sporck returns to his usual taciturn self. It is not that he is an unfriendly man, as many outsiders might think. Rather, he is genuinely uncomfortable talking with strangers, and the strain shows as grumpiness. Sporck is not blind to this weakness. In the early years it worked to his advantage.

Unfortunately a reputation like that is all but impossible to shake. The situation was aggravated by the fact that, as Sporck freely admits, "I never felt comfortable with the press. Basically I felt it was like, when a quarterback throws a football up in the air, he knows there's three things that can happen—and two of them are bad. It's kind of the same thing when you talk to the press—only the odds may be worse."

Charlie Sporck has made other mistakes. Many of them. But he has had at least as many victories. National may not be the first choice for work (sometimes it's the last) of people in the semiconductor industry, but on the other hand it has endured, made many wealthy and emerged —despite all the doubters—at the front of the semiconductor parade. It hasn't the glory of Intel or the style of AMD, but neither is it an also-ran like Intersil or a burned-out shell like Fairchild. Actually, it's come out on top of them all.

One suspects that's entirely what Charlie Sporck expected all along. Where the other Valley pioneers moved into elegant offices or drove magnificent cars, Sporck's office is just a messy corner on a busy executive floor. One nearly trips over boxes to get there.

Sporck's personal life is no different. He still dresses much of the time as though he shopped at clothing clearance stores, with the loud ties and short-sleeved shirts. And though he lives in a fine house in Los Altos Hills, Sporck's taste in transportation runs to the pickup he drives to work every day.

In the end, as much as he denies it, National Semiconductor *is* Charlie Sporck, as much as Advanced Micro Devices *is* Jerry Sanders, the other remaining lone wolf among the founders of the Silicon Valley semiconductor industry. There is simply no better explanation for the congruence between the personalities of these two companies and their chief executives. Both National and Charlie Sporck are uncommunicative, aggressive, tough, indifferent to creature comforts, and perhaps a little hurt by the lack of respect that should accrue with success.

But the semiconductor world is changing; the day of the independent semiconductor company may be at an end. Even mighty Intel has sold some of its soul to IBM. National has long been tossed out as a leading possibility for a merger—a fact the company has disputed for years. Sporck has threatened, should there be an unfriendly takeover, to disembowel the firm of its people and products in a sort of corporate hara-kiri. Says Sporck, "It isn't in the interests of the stockholders or the country itself for the independent semiconductor companies to be absorbed by conglomerates. It's a fact that there hasn't been one conglomerate that's been successful in penetrating this business except through acquisition, and invariably the acquisition reduces the effectiveness of the particular company."

If that is the case, and National can survive the rigors of the eighties and nineties, one must then question the rite of succession at National. Kvamme, the heir apparent, left for greener pastures at Apple. The only other name that surfaces is Jon Finch, general manager of the company's chip division, but he doesn't appear groomed for the top spot.

Sporck claims to be unconcerned. He may be right. The fact that National has lost many people who've turned out to be effective company presidents elsewhere may be indicative that the firm has enough native talent to get by after he retires. But it also shows how many people have left National knowing the path to the top is all but closed.

Sporck says he never thinks about retiring but when pressed says he'd probably move to Hawaii and enjoy his hobbies of swimming and scuba-diving. He adds that his real hobby is to work in his yard in Los Altos Hills, "physical stuff, seat-of-the-ass-type labor."

That also describes Charlie Sporck's way of doing business. The young man who would have been content being a shop foreman the rest of his life has become a powerful businessman. Yet in many ways he has never left that GE power fab capacitor plant. In many ways he is still that foreman, son of a taxi driver, with a workingman's tastes and attitudes. In the same light, the hard-charging, frill-free megacompany he built becomes comprehensible if seen as an enormous shop floor, with tens of thousands of employees and millions of square feet. Of course now he must deal with national politics and stockholders and the media and enormous personal wealth, but at bottom one senses that Sporck has so richly succeeded because he always returned to the basics, what was tried and found true at the Hudson Falls manufacturing plant. He has been counted out many times, and always come back with a vengeance.

Now, like his Silicon Valley peers, Sporck has to compete with time, and against that opponent he must lose. Already he begins to sense it. His age and his traditional attitude have conspired to leave him out of touch with the revolutions that have swept the Valley in recent years. He may sell these new firms the chips they need to survive, but he doesn't pretend to comprehend their management styles. In fact, though Silicon Valley is often described as a tight, incestuous family,

Sporck knows very few of the presidents of the hot new computer, video game and peripheral companies.

Walking with a visitor across the lawn at the center of the company compound, Sporck asks about these young whiz kids, what they're like. It is a week after Apple cofounder Steve Wozniak's latest rock concert. Sporck says he doesn't know any of these people, having only met Steve Jobs at some political event for Jerry Brown which Sporck found idiotic and walked out of.

As the visitor describes some of the antics of these young tycoons, Sporck shakes his head. "You know," he says, "us guys who started out at Fairchild and built all of these semiconductor companies, you know, when you get right down to it, we're a pretty conservative, old-fashioned bunch. This new generation is beyond me. I just don't understand them . . ."

6

The Technology Sieve

On Tuesday, June 22, 1982, two executives of Japan's Hitachi were in the offices of Glenmar Associates of Santa Clara gleefully tearing off labels as souvenirs from what they believed were stolen IBM computer documents when their Glenmar "partners" in crime suddenly announced themselves as FBI agents.

"Oh? Okay," was all one of the Japanese could muster in response.

In all, twenty-one Japanese and American defendants were charged in the Glenmar-FBI sting—know as Japscam to all but a few nervous newspaper and television news editors—as well as two giant Japanese electronics corporations, Hitachi Ltd. and Mitsubishi Electric Co.

The initial hearings, held in the cramped and ramshackle temporary federal court building in San Jose, quickly became a media event on both sides of the Pacific. On hearing days, dozens of American reporters would gather on the lawn before the tiny redwood building: photographers, courtroom artists, sleepy reporters, local TV crews excited by the big chance at a network feed. Even more in evidence were the Japanese media: reporters looking shell-shocked and wrinkled from a hurried plane flight or weeks spent in a motel room with one change of clothing, tiny cameramen straining under comparatively huge videotape cameras. And there were unusual hangers-on, such as a private detective hired by the Japanese press to locate any secret witnesses and a young attorney on retainer to explain to Japanese television the eccentricities of American jurisprudence.

Before and after each hearing, all hell would break loose as reporters swarmed around prospective interview subjects. A common sight after each session was the federal attorney, trapped in a tight knot of forty or fifty reporters with cassette recorders and cameramen adjusting lenses, being bombarded over and over by the same handful of questions from inquirers who didn't quite understand the language. On one occasion, the crush became so great that a Japanese cameraman stepped backward for a better shot, tripped over some feet and nearly toppled half the crowd.

No one was exempt from being a subject for Tokyo's curiosity. The local New York *Times* stringer was standing on the sidewalk chatting with the judge about a good restaurant when he turned to discover that he was being filmed for Japanese network news.

On one of these hearing days, after the mob had disappeared, the cameramen had packed their equipment and the reporters had filed their stories, there was another, equally remarkable case on the docket. This time the defendant was a lone black man with one cloudy, dead eye: John Henry "One-Eyed Jack" Jackson. The charges were grand larceny, conspiracy and buying, receiving and possessing stolen and altered property.

One-Eyed Jack was no newcomer to courtrooms; he had been convicted four times in the past for passing bad checks, forgery and burglary. And the pretrial hearings on this case had stretched on for a year. But even with his well-attested complacency about legal proceedings, Jackson probably wasn't in enough of a philosophical mood to enjoy the significant coincidence of his own hearing with the more celebrated one that morning. Here, in a single day, the little courtroom had seen the gamut of the Silicon Valley black market underground—from a dignified, well-financed corporate business trying to illegally obtain trade secrets from a competitor to a run-of-the-mill street thief whose cache of stolen chips had ended up in Europe and perhaps behind the Iron Curtain.

Thievery has always been good business in Silicon Valley. One reason is the fine line between taking what's in someone's head—the legitimate employee raiding which helped build the Valley—and taking what's in his or her desk or notebook or file case—which is grounds for a lawsuit or even arrest.

Silicon Valley firms are forever suing one another for what they believe to be different types of thievery. One reason is patent violation. Sometimes a company will find that paying royalties as the "second source" for a product to the original manufacturer is an expensive nuisance and will refuse to do it. Call in the lawyers. Just as often, a pioneering manufacturer will look upon every new product even remotely related to its own as a damnable case of patent infringement. This sort of thing has been going on in electronics for most of this century. Fairchild and Texas Instruments slugged it out for years over who actually invented the integrated circuit.

Another type of suit common to Silicon Valley is the one aimed at spin-offs; new firms created by former employees in the same product areas. The Valley didn't catch on to this weapon until late, but in the last few years it has embraced it like an old friend. Fairchild under Noyce in the sixties didn't sue any of the dozen or more firms that spun off from it—even though most of them were in the exact same business and, agreements to the contrary, raided Fairchild with absolute abandon.

But times had changed in 1981 when ten employees in 1981 quit Noyce's Intel to form a semiconductor company. This time Intel went after the spin-off, Seeq Inc., with hammer and tongs, suing it for $25 million, demanding access to the materials taken from Intel and enjoining the firm from competing with Intel for years. The case, like most, was settled out of court, the details forever secret.

The Seeq suit served two purposes, as it was intended to do: ensure that the parent firm was not being stolen blind by employees who had taken advantage of the training and experience received from their former employer, and, just as important, put the living fear of God into remaining employees about attempting a similar escapade.

The scent of hypocrisy hung around all of these proceedings, of course. The fact that most of the executives who made these sanctimonious pronouncements had done their own share of company-jumping and idea-thieving was not lost on either the résumé-passing employees or the rest of the Valley.

Nevertheless, with a few exceptions the threats worked. The sword of a massive lawsuit, with the attendant hassles and monstrous legal costs, frightened budding entrepreneurs. It was mainly a matter of modifying some rules of business to cover one's ass more completely. For example, in late 1982, when sixteen Intel employees in Portland made plans to split off and start their own firm, they held private meetings and made sure that no prospective product for the new company was ever discussed. Afterward, the group claimed that it also had never talked to an investor before the break with Intel (a good story for Intel consumption, but insiders in the venture business claim a fix was already in). And, to make sure they had done everything right, the group hired the lawyer who had defended the Seeq suit.

So, with all their ducks in a row, on a single morning all sixteen (there was an additional Intel employee in Santa Clara) quit within an hour of one another. At the time of this writing Intel has still not brought suit. It has, however, made a lot of pronouncements about employee loyalty and the dangers of having *too much* venture capital flying around.

The most entertaining of suit types is the one filed by one established firm against another for employee-raiding—and, by extension, the theft of trade secrets. These are wonderful little business passion plays displaying all the baser human emotions. When in any electronic discipline there are only a handful of imaginative, brilliant individuals, the loss of even one of them to a competitor can arouse greed, envy, viciousness and fear.

A colorful case that brings together all of these hues occurred in 1979 when $800-million-a-year National Semiconductor sued $80-million-a-year (and unprofitable) Zilog Corp. for stealing trade secrets. In particular, National claimed that six former employees, notably Bill Sweet, had taken with them price analyses and product specifications about a new National microprocessor and that Zilog was using those trade secrets to competitive advantage. National asked for $5 million in damages and a ruling that Zilog be enjoined from any such activities in the future.

Whether or not Sweet and his team actually had those papers will never be known, because, as usual, the two companies settled out of court. The only information available seemed to erase any Zilog culpability: a court-assigned arbitrator found that Zilog did not use any National secrets in its new microprocessor.

It seems, according to depositions and other court papers, that within National the development of the microprocessor in question, code-named the 16000, had been a difficult and acrimonious one for everybody involved. Arguments over design had created two opposing camps, one led by Howard Raphael, National's director of microprocessor operations, and the other by Bill Sweet, then marketing manager of National's minicomputer group.

"Both sides put together an army of consultants, industry experts, Cal Tech scientists, whoever they could find. You have to allow for that kind of controversy, but in this case it got personal," according to a National insider.

Sweet lost the battle, and within a short time he and five members of his team quit National and joined Zilog across the Valley in Cupertino. There was a considerable amount of bad blood between Raphael and Sweet.

The situation might have remained calm (this was 1979; by 1983 the situation was much more hysterical) but by unlucky coincidence Raphael happened to run into Ken McKenzie, an old friend from their Intel days together, who now was marketing manager for microprocessors at Zilog.

They each had a few moments, so McKenzie and Raphael sat down to talk. Since they were direct rivals, the conversation between the two men quickly turned to their respective companies' products. McKenzie teased Raphael about National's delay in getting the 16000 out the door. Raphael started to defend his position when McKenzie calmly informed him that he had already seen at Zilog a copy of National's design plans for the chip.

Stunned, Raphael returned to National and voiced his concerns. Only then, National later claimed, did it realize that anything had been stolen. McKenzie claimed that he had just been baiting Raphael, who, he said, "is a very proud man and becomes extremely defensive when anyone challenges him."

In the end National came out looking foolish, an instrument for a personal vendetta between a present employee and a former one. Nevertheless, the truth of the case might not have been so straightforward: under court order, Zilog produced six cartons of material that the National employees had taken with them to Zilog. There were no design specifications, but there was an insider overview report on the National microprocessor. Zilog denied that the employee had taken this particular document illegally, and besides (in typical legal doublethink), it was *illegible*.

In the years since that landmark case the suits have grown larger and more bizarre. Now litigation is no longer just the province of the older semiconductor companies. Systems houses nowadays are big enough to get into the act. (Hewlett-Packard was the first—on the receiving end of one of the craziest cases in electronics history. HP salesmen, with police, visited a Midwestern customer to reclaim a computer for delinquent payments. The customer, who weighed in excess of four hundred pounds, attacked the men [and they had all they could handle subduing him], then promptly expired. HP settled out of court.)

In March 1980, Pizza Time Theaters sued its largest franchiser for

$250 million for fraud, unfair competition and breach of contract—in essence claiming that the franchiser, according to the Pizza Time president, "picked our brains" for technical information to build its own pizza restaurant. Byte Shops personal computer retail store chain sued Apple for dropping it from the licensed distributor list.

The most remarkable suit to date came in May 1983 when a former vice-president of Advanced Micro Devices sued that firm for $31 million, claiming that AMD had defrauded him by purposefully causing the subsidiary he helped run to fail. The individual, James Grabner, who had been chief financial officer of Advanced Micro Computers, charged that he was promised a stock-option package that should have made him about eight hundred thousand dollars. Instead, in October 1981, AMC crashed and burned—ruined, Grabner said, by the board of AMD. The shattered subsidiary eventually was folded back into the parent corporation as a division. Grabner was offered his original investment back. He refused, and instead sued. (At the time of this writing, the suit has not been settled.)

The Grabner case had many Silicon Valley veterans scratching their heads. AMD president Jerry Sanders had been accused of many things —flamboyance, arrogance, insensitivity—but no one had ever suggested that he would purposefully destroy a piece of his own company. Instead, the suit raised in the minds of many of these veterans the disturbing thought that overnight riches had become so commonplace in Silicon Valley that they were now *expected* by entrepreneurs. It seemed that becoming a millionaire to the new generation of Silicon Valley executives no longer required a terrifying risk but rather a guarantee— and when the Big Score was not fulfilled someone else must be held accountable.

The Grabner case documents the belief held by thousands of Silicon Valley workers that success and wealth will be automatically ensured by the inherent strength of the industry. The overnight-success dream is part of the American personality, but one would have to look back to the Klondike or the Comstock Lode to find such a high percentage of a population taking such rewards for granted as a by-product of a normal amount of work and skill.

When this dream collides with the other great underlying force of Silicon Valley—the self-centered drive of the entrepreneur that creates a sense of lawlessness, or at least of making one's own rules—the result is One-Eyed Jack Jackson, Japanese businessmen buying trade secrets from the FBI and tens of millions of dollars in stolen parts and chips.

The magnitude of crime in Silicon Valley is impossible to estimate accurately. During boom times there is so much money flying around that there is no way of telling how much winds up in the wrong hands. Estimates just for gold and other precious metals stolen from Silicon Valley each year range up to $20 million. For years semiconductor companies didn't keep track of how many chips they scrapped, only worrying about the smaller number that actually worked. These bad chips, sold to scrap dealers, often ended up resold as quality parts to unsuspecting customers.

Thievery is as old as Silicon Valley and is the darker underside of the Valley's entrepreneurial splendor. Just as the local industry has grown from a single chip maker to hundreds of firms offering a bewildering array of products, the criminal underground of Silicon Valley has expanded from a few opportunistic thefts to a sophisticated, international business with a similar drive toward growth and market expansion. As the revolution wrought by Silicon Valley offers the prospect of improving the world through innovation, the Valley's black market threatens to tear apart American society, fatally weakening it, by feeding these innovations to America's competitors and enemies.

The underground in Silicon Valley appears to be no more organized than its legitimate twin. The only true organized-crime representation in the County appears to be the Bonnano family, which has lived up to its image in Breslin's *The Gang That Couldn't Shoot Straight.* Patriarch Joseph Bonnano may have been a tough cookie in his day, but he moved to San Jose and got his sons into the cheese business and the boys haven't seemed to get anything right since. What other mob connections there are to Silicon Valley seem to be with warehouse-type operations in New Jersey that serve as distribution centers for hot goods.

The apparent absence, for now, of the Cosa Nostra in the Valley does not mean that the area is free of high-powered criminal elements. Certain unreported elements of the Jackson case suggest the frightening prospect that the Black Guerilla Family, a half-terrorist, half-organized-crime group based in California prisons, may have a hand in the black market for stolen chips.

Further, whether or not they actually have agents stationed there, the Valley is an important target for foreign intelligence operations, both friend and foe. The KGB has chip-thief contacts in Silicon Valley. So does the People's Republic of China. The Japanese are here, as are intelligence agents from Israel, France and Korea.

But the idea, promoted by the national press in the early 1980s, of a foreign agent behind every lamppost in Silicon Valley is highly dubious. The reality is that foreign countries, including those declared off limits to American high technology by the U.S. Commerce Department, have no trouble finding suppliers willing, even anxious, to sell to them anything they desire. This is because the Silicon Valley underground, like the Silicon Valley aboveground, is composed of numerous small businessmen, each carving out a market niche, competing for key customers and dreaming of the Big Score.

A case in point is the celebrated story of James Durward Harper, Jr. If ever a man epitomized the cost of chasing the Big Score it is Harper.

Just another anonymous Silicon Valley engineer, Harper lived in a condominium in Mountain View with his new wife, Ruby Louise Schuler. Harper, forty-nine, had married Schuler, thirty-four, in 1979 after the breakup of his twenty-four-year marriage. She was a ten-year executive secretary and bookkeeper at Systems Control Inc. in Palo Alto, a defense contractor. He was a semiretired engineer who'd once owned his own company, Harper Time and Electronics Inc. (which made stopwatches), and now took on thousand-dollar-a-week consulting jobs. The most recent of these was an eighteen-month contract with Solectron Corp. of San Jose, where he'd made a hundred thousand dollars finding out what kind of power supplies customers needed in Solectron transformers.

But to neighbors, Harper's family and to friends, there was something odd about the marriage. Schuler was a serious alcoholic on her last pass at this world. Harper seemed to have little faith or interest in her from the start: when arrested for drunk driving, he asked that his first wife be notified. In fact, the indifference seemed mutual. Schuler told a close friend, "There was a reason Jim and I got married that only he and I know. I can't tell you or anyone else and never will."

Eighteen days later, she was dead of alcoholism. Harper asked a neighbor to help carry her body out to his car. Three months later, on October 19, 1983, James Harper was arrested by the FBI for espionage for the sale of top-secret Minuteman missile secrets to Polish agents.

"We were all taken by surprise," said the Solectron president. "He didn't seem like the type. He seemed like an engineer who was a nice guy. He always seemed to be smiling."

The source, of course, was Schuler, who had used her security clearance at Systems Control to steal critical documents. She had in turn passed them on to Harper, who, through a middleman, got them to the

Polish agents. How important these documents were will never be publicly known, but there are indications they were of extraordinary significance. For one thing, the notoriously tightfisted Polish agents offered to pay a reported $1 million for the materials—an almost unprecedentedly high figure (Harper had received $250,000 at the time of his arrest). Further, according to the San Jose *Mercury-News*, "The Soviets were so excited about obtaining the documents that in 1980 Soviet President Yuri Andropov, then head of the KGB, signed commendations for two Polish intelligence agents who initially procured the secrets, according to the FBI. Investigators said they learned of the commendations from an American spy who was highly placed in Polish political circles."

The FBI, in its affidavit, wrote:

> The communication of these documents to the Polish People's Republic and the Soviet Union would cause serious damage to our national defense and would provide Warsaw Pact analysts with a windfall of intelligence information about the capabilities of our strategic forces and our present and future plans to defend them.
>
> . . . The documents describe extremely sensitive research and development efforts undertaken by the Department of Defense which would enable the Minuteman missile and other strategic forces of the United States to survive a pre-emptive nuclear attack by the Soviet Union.

Harper had turned himself in to the feds in hopes of obtaining immunity. But the government didn't bite. Said prosecutor John Gibbons, "[He] came to the government with the cunning of a jackal. He wanted immunity . . . it was refused, and rightly so." Facing a potential death penalty, Harper began to name names—and one in particular, "the Big Man": William Hugle. Hugle, as this is written, has not been indicted, but according to the FBI affidavit, it was Hugle who introduced Harper to Polish spies in 1979.

Hugle is a far more interesting character than Harper, the latter being another good argument for the banality of evil. Hugle is a different case. One of the founders of Silicon Valley, he helped form Siliconix back in 1962. Throughout the sixties, Hugle was a respected Valley executive, often giving speeches before Valley groups. But for all of his fame, he was one of those men in the world of Silicon Valley who never quite make it, always falling short of the riches that fell into the hands of his peers. He was wealthy, of course, but by Valley standards, Hugle was a failure.

In the seventies, Hugle all but dropped from sight, involved with a series of companies (some of them his own, like Hugle Industries) and occasionally spotted by Valley veterans drinking at his favorite bar in downtown Los Altos. He seemed like just another Valley pioneer fallen by the wayside.

But in reality, Hugle had merely switched to a more dangerous game to make his killing. Hugle Industries went bankrupt in the mid-seventies amid suspicions about a $638,000 shipment of semiconductor processing equipment to Poland. Another firm in which he was involved was investigated for illegal shipments of similar equipment into Communist China, via Japan. When this writer submerged into the Silicon Valley underground pursuing a story in 1981, Hugle's name was constantly mentioned as a key figure in the gray market.

Did Hugle mastermind the Harper espionage? The FBI sure thinks so. But their controlled leaks to the press implicating the man smacked of desperation, a program to socially lynch a man they could not legally capture. Perhaps one day Hugle will be indicted. But he never has been before—and when last seen, he was back drinking at his favorite Los Altos restaurant.

Big-time espionage is only part of the dark side of Silicon Valley life. There are employees who steal chips or parts, guards who are paid to look the other way when crates are left overnight on the shipping dock, salesmen who sell samples rather than return them to the company. The Hell's Angels sell drugs brewed in amphetamine laboratories in houses and caves in the Santa Cruz Mountains. There are parts distributors who fence stolen goods or make illegal shipments to embargoed nations, scrappers and refiners who skim part of the gold they reclaim or resell junked parts as good. And there are manufacturers who ship high-tech equipment to Finland or Austria or Monaco with full knowledge it is destined to disappear into Eastern Europe.

With the Silicon Valley money machine cranking out riches twenty-four hours a day, who's going to notice a few million dollars missing? Nobody. At least not until the Soviets casually mention that they have the latest U.S.-developed computer or defective chips turn up in malfunctioning pacemakers or American ICBMs.

One-Eyed Jack's world touched more corners of the Silicon Valley underground. He was found guilty of leading a crime ring that stole ten thousand $100 memory chips from Intel and remarketed as many as a hundred thousand other similar devices, many of them stolen. These chips, 32K EPROMs, are used in everything from video games to guidance systems aboard fighter aircraft.

The Intel chips were stolen from a fenced storage room protected by alarms, twenty-four-hour security guards, an employee badge system, after-hours sign-in logs, security audits, spot checks and closed-circuit television. According to police, Jackson circumvented all of this security by having an Intel security guard as an accomplice—Albert Williams, who also was convicted. Williams carried the chips out of the storeroom in the lining of his leather jacket and, cheekily, in plastic garbage bags.

According to Williams, he and Jackson were helped in the heist by an Intel executive who prepared the paper work to get ten thousand memory chips produced so they could be stolen—and later destroyed the paper work. But as is often the case in the Valley, no such executive was ever named or prosecuted.

The use of inside agents was the most effective technique available to Jackson. When that was not possible in other thefts, he had different methods. In a secretly taped interview with a private investigator, one Jackson employee described how his boss would sometimes use a pretty woman in hot pants to distract workers at the loading dock while someone else carted off goods. According to Jackson, 90 percent of all thefts occurred during the shipping and storing of chips.

The stolen Intel chips, which were fresh off the assembly line and as yet unmarked and unculled for rejects, were then taken to a Sunnyvale apartment and stamped with Intel logos. From there, Jackson's independent distribution company, Dyno Electronics in Santa Clara, sold the chips to Space Age Metals, a metal reclaimer in the Southern California community of Gardena. (Space Age denied this but admitted it had bought parts from Jackson on other occasions.)

According to Jackson, Space Age sold the parts to neighboring Mormac Technology Inc. of Tarzana, California (Jackson also sold some of the hot parts directly to Mormac), and to Republic Electronics of Arlington, Virginia. The two chip-brokerage companies, "shlockers," as they are known in the trade, sold the parts to the same customer, E.D.V. Elektronik, an electronics distributor in Munich, West Germany, which in turn sold them to A. G. Siemens, the West German electronics giant.

Siemens, it seems, had not been satisfied with its one-thousand-chips-per-month allotment from Intel, so it had asked E.D.V. to locate more. E.D.V. had then put word of the order out on the gray market of shlockers and part-time thieves. The theft only came to light when Siemens, which had unwittingly mixed Jackson's parts with the usual Intel allotment, complained to Intel about the unusually high failure rate of the chips.

But that was only one path the stolen chips took. Another was even more ominous. Charged with Jackson was Patrick Ketchum of Mormac. According to Jackson, Ketchum took some of the stolen chips and sold them to Anatoli Maluta, a Russian-born naturalized American, and Werner Bruchhausen, a West German. Both men have been indicted for illegally exporting semiconductor manufacturing equipment to the Soviet Union. However, charges were dropped against Ketchum (who was convicted in 1979 of selling counterfeit chips to the U.S. military) because the federal government could not prove that he knew the Jackson chips were stolen.

In this way, a small-time thief, and a relatively patriotic one at that, dropped his cache into the source of the great underground river of stolen parts flowing out of Silicon Valley, and after considerable journeys and intermediaries, some of those chips may very well have ended up in the nose cone of a Soviet intercontinental ballistic missile targeted right back at Silicon Valley.

There is no way to estimate how many One-Eyed Jacks are at work in Silicon Valley. The number seems to vary with lead time—the average amount of time it takes an average semiconductor firm to fill an order for a specific part. Normally, this is three or four weeks. But when end users are selling equipment as fast as they can build it, chip houses become strapped for manufacturing capacity and lead times for specific products reach extreme levels. In the late seventies, the demand for certain memory chips, notably EPROMs, was so great that lead times slipped to as high as forty-eight weeks.

For a video game manufacturer who must constantly modify the product to remain competitive, the idea of having to wait a year for a crucial component is terrifying. Procurement officers, under pressure to get those parts before entire assembly lines have to be shut down, begin to shift from primary sources (chip manufacturers and distributors) to secondary ones (shlockers) and sometimes even to criminal elements for the necessary goods. (They also double- and triple-order at different manufacturers, creating a synthetic demand that, when it rapidly disintegrates, is a key cause of the Valley's periodic recessions.) The end users, in their desperation, are willing to pay these more sordid suppliers many times the retail price for the chips they need just to keep the lines moving. The higher the price, the greater the number of people willing to commit a crime to earn it.

Of course even in bad times there are always junkies and part-time thieves on the loading dock or assembly line who'll pocket some chips or gold or tools with the prospect of making a few bucks. But it's during periods of shortage and inflated prices that more professional networks form and normally legitimate middlemen slide over into the nether side of the law.

In April 1980, Michael Moe, a maintenance supervisor at Intel, carried thousands of dollars in memory chips out of a storage area in the false bottom of a box. He was caught and charged with grand larceny in May of that year. Convicted for buying those chips was Glen Johnson, owner of Glen Manufacturing Inc., an electronics company in Stockton, California. During the trial, Johnson contended that the eight months' lead time for receiving Intel chips pushed him into doing business with Moe.

In September 1984, a "sting" set up by the Sunnyvale police and Signetics Corp. arrested two men, one of whom, Shiri Chawla, owner of a local chip brokerage firm called Microcomponents International, bragged to authorities that he earned $40 million per year reselling stolen computer parts throughout the world. On the same day, a brilliant former Hewlett-Packard engineer was arrested by Palo Alto police on suspicion of stealing three HP computer tapes that, according to the police, were worth "millions of dollars" on the black market.

Sometimes the offers are too great to be refused by even the most honest shlocker. During the 1979 EPROM boom, representatives from Far East video game makers were arriving at the San Francisco International Airport with suitcases literally stuffed with millions of dollars in cash and orders to buy the chips at whatever price they were offered. Some deals took place right at the Airport Hilton, at the door between adjoining rooms. (This led to one episode in which buyer and seller both had one hand on the chips and the other on the money, trying to hide their faces, and neither party willing to let go.)

Periods of high lead times are when foreign agents also make their biggest scores. The Soviet Union may not have any KGB agents in Silicon Valley, but certainly the Soviet consulate in San Francisco, with its diplomats well versed in electronics and its roof bristling with microwave eavesdropping equipment, exists to spy on Silicon Valley. As noted, there is really no reason for foreign agents or competitors to risk capture in the Valley when they need only wait for the perennial stream of stolen parts to turn into a swollen flood and simply dip in their buckets at one of the river's many mouths. In fact, sometimes the thieves will come to them. For example, it is reported that at certain European trade shows there are booths that offer only a blank wall with a door. When one walks in, there are just two chairs—one containing a broker who can get products into the Eastern bloc.

It is also reported that gray marketeers take advantage of a loophole in international law. Flights from the Far East to Europe stop over in Moscow, and as long as the passengers do not leave a specific area they are considered to be in international territory and their passports are not stamped for the Soviet Union. The area is supposed to be secure, but it seems that the KGB has found a means of spiriting individuals in and out.

The irony of all of this is Silicon Valley and the rest of the electronics industry needs the gray market to exist. For as long as these shlockers and middlemen stay legitimate—and even after they go bad—they play a necessary role in getting products out to every corner of the market, to tiny firms that have no pull with manufacturers and might therefore go hungry yet, in a few years, if allowed to survive, could turn into major customers. Thus the gray market is a critical step in the chip distribution process.

The fact that Silicon Valley needs the gray market to smooth over the rough spots in distribution is one reason why the underground continues to exist. But there is another reason, which explains why destructive activities, such as robberies and espionage, are allowed to occur.

Until recently, Silicon Valley refused to cooperate with the local police in apprehending criminals. In keeping with the insular, incestuous nature of the industry, it was felt that crime (as well as drug abuse) was an "in-house" problem, best handled by the companies themselves rather than inviting in the cops. Some security directors have said they have been ordered not to call in the police, even on major crimes, by higher-ups. At one leading Valley semiconductor firm, an executive even sat in on a stakeout of a major drug deal in the parking lot—then told the detective to forget what he saw.

"When I'd ask, 'Do you want to bring in law enforcement?' they'd say, 'No, no, it's bad business if the public knows the company has a leak of products,' " said one company security director.

"[Companies] never prosecute," said another. "It's bad publicity.

And they don't want people to know they have so much valuable stuff lying around."

Only one company, Intel Corporation, seemed to actively pursue thieves and to aid in their prosecution. More cynical Valley observers have suggested that the reason local firms were so reluctant to invite the police in (forcing them instead to make their busts at stolen-parts fences or in nearby parks) is that there is too much white-collar crime going on, much of it sanctioned by the firm, to take the risk of letting the cops inside.

However, even if this were indeed the reason, it seems doubtful the police would have spotted a sophisticated high-tech crime even if they had been part of it. As late as 1980, only one Valley city, Sunnyvale, had an officer devoted to electronics—and he only worked on it half time. Only the County Sheriffs seemed to show any appreciation of the magnitude of the problem by adding an electronics specialist to its organized-crime unit.

Said a security chief at the time: "Our biggest bottleneck in security is the police. They are more concerned with arresting the prostitute on the corner than with millions of dollars in burglaries at local firms. They don't understand what we have, so they're scared of it."

Thus the thievery goes on. Those denizens of the underground who are brought to the surface are usually captured in the months right after a boom, when the market is shrinking but ambitions continue to expand.

In 1981 alone, police in Silicon Valley caught a Shugart Associates employee with two hundred of the company's disk drives in his possession, three young men in a Milpitas hotel with 2,000 of 68,000 chips stolen from Signetics Corp., twenty employees of Calma dealing in stolen chips and drugs, and two employees of Advanced Micro Devices who tried to bribe a guard to look the other way as they stole twenty-seven thousand dollars' worth of chips.

The biggest haul came in November 1981 when $3.2 million in chips were taken from Monolithic Memories Inc. in Sunnyvale, one of the Valley's smallest semiconductor firms. It took six months for the crime ring, which included a security guard on duty at the time, to be broken, and a couple of months more for the cache (which also included Apple computers and other popular high-tech goods) to be found in a rented storage locker at South Lake Tahoe.

Besides being the largest reported theft of its kind in Silicon Valley to date, the Monolithic Memories burglary had other, more disturbing implications. Among the thieves apprehended by police in the case, one was driving a white Lincoln Continental owned by a certain Larry Lowery. Another suspect was driving a van owned by a Nevada electronics company run by one of Lowery's business associates.

Lowery at the time of the heist was free pending sentencing for a conviction involving the April 1980 theft of eleven thousand computer chips, valued at $275,000, from Synertek, Inc. of Santa Clara. During the course of the case, one of the prosecution witnesses against Lowery was brutally beaten. Two months after the MMI theft, Lowery was sentenced to two years in state prison.

Beyond the circumstanial evidence of the vehicles, no direct connection was ever made between Lowery and the Monolithic Memories rip-off. A search of his company, Brut Electronics, found nothing.

This wasn't the first time Lowery's name cropped up on the periphery of a serious crime. A former associate, David Roberts, a likable but shady young man with a growing heroin addiction, had been scheduled to testify at the Lowery-Synertek trial. He was found in September 1981, murdered gangland style, in a shallow grave in the Santa Cruz Mountains. He had been stabbed seven times and his skull was broken, apparently by a pistol butt. His murder has yet to be solved.

It is this series of "coincidences" that has led Santa Clara County deputy district attorney Doug Southard to claim that the Lowery ring "represents the clearest case of consistent, habitual, organized criminal activity aimed at Silicon Valley as yet uncovered."

The image of an organized-crime ring operating behind a legitimate front that can intimidate or silence witnesses, that can conduct sophisticated robberies of millions of dollars in goods, and that might have links to national organized crime groups (the mob, the Black Guerilla Family) and the Eastern bloc is a terrifying thought that has only begun to sink into the consciousness of Silicon Valley, long one of the safest industrial regions in the country.

The world has changed. The lowliest janitor, the most isolated farmer, the youngest schoolchild now knows that those little chips are worth more than their weight in gold. Said William Marshall of Elmar Electronics in Mountain View, who was approached to steal chips but instead alerted the police: "It's easy to go crooked and make so much money it's unbelievable . . . I could go to a company, and I could make an easy hundred thousand dollars in six months' stealing—and probably never get caught.

"All of a sudden, the whole world said, 'Goddamn, [the] revolution is here, baby; these things are priceless!' "

But, fittingly, the last word on the gray market belongs to Larry Lowery, who, in a letter to the Court, wrote that the buying and selling of chips is "a very loose business . . . there are a lot of irresponsible people in it."

* * *

And then there are the Japanese. The relationship between Silicon Valley and its Japanese competitors is complex and elusive, the villain changing with the storyteller—much as in *Rashomon,* the famous Akutagawa P yūnosuke story.

One fact is without question, though. It is that the Japanese stole much of their electronics technology from America. Most of it was legal, of course, a clever, much-deserved conning of arrogant Yankees; but when the victim refused to be suckered the Japanese—as in the IBM secrets case—were more than willing to sink to slimier means to get what they wanted.

It all began so quietly and amicably . . .

From the turn of the century Japan had modeled much of its industry on the United States (it is no coincidence that the names of some Japanese giants like Nippon Telephone and Telegraph sound familiar. After V-J Day, the occupying forces under MacArthur set about rebuilding the Japanese economy even more along American lines. It was a slow and painful process, and the Japanese had to suffer the humiliation of becoming synonymous with shoddy, cheap products.

But, like most underdogs, the Japanese were avid learners. Their social structure was superbly suited for large manufacturing companies (if not to lone genius) and so they focused on production over marketing or breakthrough-type innovation. Japan might never come up with an invention on the order of the integrated circuit, but it was intent upon building them better, faster and cheaper than any other nation. As a country with little national resources, a confined and aging population and a dependence upon imported energy, Japan naturally gravitated toward electronics, with its high profits and low labor and materials requirements.

All Japan lacked was the technology itself. "We have no Dr. Noyces or Dr. Shockleys," said a Japanese journalist. That was true, but Japan knew where to get the knowledge: America, the most open society in the world, a nation of innovative loners that would be easy pickings for an organized society of master builders. It was a process that developing nations had undertaken for millennia. The Romans, of course, plundered Greece for its culture, even its gods.

At first it seemed harmless enough. The tiny Japanese electronics industry couldn't service its own nation, much less threaten U.S. giants like Texas Instruments, General Electric and Fairchild. So the Japanese visitors were welcomed, if not with open arms then at least with an amused condescension, like poor relatives at the family reunion.

Recalls James Cunningham, author and vice-president of Advanced Micro Devices:

> Back in the 1960s we used to laugh at the Japanese.
>
> In those days, I was a process engineer working for Texas Instruments and I traveled quite regularly to professional society meetings such as the annual Electrochemical Society meeting or the Institute of Electrical and Electronic Engineers' Electron Device Conference. Even then those events were grand and prestigious affairs held in posh downtown hotels, and had as many as 500 or 600 engineers and scientists in attendance, with all the electronics companies there—and as the years passed, a growing number of them were Japanese.
>
> Usually several hundred technical papers were delivered at these meetings. Of these, Japanese electronics companies might contribute only one or two, and even these were invariably of minimal importance. Not only was the technical content of these papers of little significance, but the limited English of the presenters made them all but unintelligible. It really didn't matter, as the papers said little of value anyway.
>
> It wasn't until years later, when our smugness gave way to fear and awe, that we realized that the Japanese hadn't come to talk; they came to listen, and to photograph. Every time a slide would go up all of the Japanese cameras in the room would go off at once. We supercilious Americans even had a joke about it: You know what that sound is every time a new slide goes up? It's the Japanese cameras going *crick, crick.*
>
> That was more than a decade ago. We don't laugh anymore.

From this unsophisticated start, within a decade the Japanese electronics firms, backed by Japan's Ministry of International Trade and Industry and a monopolistic arrangement with banks that would be illegal in the United States, turned information thievery into a science. Nothing, it seemed, escaped their notice. Conferences and trade shows were blanketed, trade magazines and speeches carefully perused. New U.S. patents were quickly translated and used. In 1978, 40,000 Japanese citizens made technology-related visits to the United States, compared to 5,000 American businesspeople traveling the other way.

Information-gathering was only a small part of the all-out Japanese assault on U.S. innovation. Far more important was licensing. If a Japanese company couldn't develop the technology itself, it would look to its prospective American competitor for a deal to license the right to second-source that company's technology or product—thus obtaining the knowledge for a fee or royalties on future sales. This had two advantages: first, because the Japanese had superior manufacturing, once they got the product they could often outrun the originator. Second, down the line the license could be terminated, leaving the Japanese firm with the technology.

At U.S. universities, Japanese students learned the latest American breakthroughs, as one did in low-threshold semiconductor lasers at Cal Tech, then took it home. Said Cal Tech computer science professor Carver Mead afterward, "I don't think that one should be able to obtain a whole technology for the cost of only one man's work for a year."

In all, the Japanese looting of America's technological secrets was brilliant—so successful in fact that other countries have used it for a template. The latest reports show agents of Israel, France, Germany, Taiwan, the Philippines, China, Libya and, of course, the Soviet Union, all collecting technological data in Silicon Valley. But no one has done it as well as the Japanese. That's how—despite a Japanese study that showed that between 1960 and 1980 it produced only 26 technical innovations, only two of them "momentous," while the United States produced 237, of which 65 were "momentous"—Japan carved off huge chunks of the U.S. electronics business, including 30 percent of state-of-the-art computer memory chips.

As one Japanese writer put it: "Today, one tantalizing question still remains. Why on earth were American and European firms willing to aid the Japanese competitive efforts to close this technological gap?"

Why indeed? But the story doesn't end there. When American firms refused to help, the Japanese decided to help themselves.

One technique was listening posts. Some were sales offices of Japanese firms, others small storefront Japanese retail companies, and some, the most shameful, were "market-research" companies owned by

Americans but little more than fronts for large Japanese corporations. Whatever their appearance, the listening posts had one job, to gather key technical information for their employees. The posts owned by Americans would buy reports unavailable to the Japanese. At others, new American products were bought and sent home for "reverse engineering." Some posts even hired employees of a targeted U.S. competitor as "consultants," ostensibly to prepare a report, then sucked that individual dry of his or her proprietary knowledge.

A case of the last occurred in 1973 when a Celanese Corp. manager, hired by a Mitsubishi front firm in Los Angeles, was caught passing the Japanese giant 12,000 drawings and 9,000 documents for $130,000. The American went to jail for four years. Mitsubishi, presaging the FBI sting, pleaded no contest and paid $300,000 in fines.

By the mid-seventies, most of the listening posts were beginning to close down. One reason was that the Japanese had obtained most of the knowledge they needed. Another was that, fearing U.S. protectionism (a matter they feared greatly knowing how effectively similar Japanese protectionism had worked against the United States), the biggest Japanese firms began to move onshore. Toshiba Semiconductor, Toyo Electronics, Fujitsu (through Amdahl investment initially, then sales offices), Hitachi, Mitsubishi and Oki all opened or acquired operations in the United States. NEC went the furthest, first acquiring Mountain Views Electronic Arrays, then building a $100-million chip facility near Sacramento. From now on, the listening posts would be in-house.

The Japanese, through brilliance and deceit, skill and fraud, had punched a very nasty hole into the once-thought-invulnerable wall of U.S. high technology. It has been a lesson in hubris for American electronics companies.

Now the Japanese could gloat, as they did at their most frighteningly revealing, in a remark made by Toshio Soejima, deputy director of engineering at Nippon Telephone and Telegraph, to *The Wall Street Journal:* "The Japanese are a people that can manufacture a product of uniformity and superior quality because the Japanese are a race of completely pure blood, not a mongrelized race as in the United States."

* * *

A subindustry of the gray market is precious-metals recovery. Even though it is used primarily only for plating electrical connections (because it is a top-quality conductor), in terms of value gold is one of the largest contributors to the cost of an integrated circuit. It has been established that Silicon Valley alone uses six hundred thousand ounces of gold—about $240 million in current prices—each year. As noted, as much as 5 percent of this may be stolen; some companies lose a million dollars in gold annually.

The difference between a scrap dealer–gold thief and a shlocker–chip thief is often simply one of supply and demand. The scrap dealer who buys faulty chips from a manufacturer, crushes those chips and dips them in a cyanide tank to retrieve the gold may decide, when the lead times for those chips extend, to cull through the lot instead and try to resell the least defective pieces. Once some wealthy customers are found it is a short step to hiring an inside person at a chip maker to salt the bad chips with some good ones.

When demand for chips drops again, or the price of gold rises, the scrappers return to the precious-metal business.

The Silicon Valley electronics industry itself must bear part of the responsibility for the magnitude of the problem. During the 1950s and 1960s, chip firms seemed almost indifferent to the value of the materials they were throwing out. Scrap was scrap. All that mattered was the almighty *Yield.* If production levels met quotas nothing else mattered. Some companies didn't even keep accurate records of how many failed chips they threw away. Worst of all, some companies were so naïve—or indifferent—that they actually paid scrap dealers to *take* the junk away. Hewlett-Packard, for example, paid a penny a pound to scrappers they quickly made rich.

It was truly the Golden Age for scrap dealers. One dealer, nicknamed "Mr. Slick," recalls that Signetics Corp. in Sunnyvale periodically called in scrappers and reclaimers to inspect and sample the company's scrap and bid on the lot. Shrewd scrap dealers would simply help themselves to a fifty-pound "sample" and then bid high enough not to get the contract.

"We used to get four thousand to five thousand dollars per year in samples from those guys," Mr. Slick says, laughing.

Another trick to which Valley firms fell victim for years—and the smaller firms still do—is to depend upon the scrappers and reclaimers to determine the amount of gold in a given lot—something akin to giving a store clerk one's wallet and telling him or her to take out however much money is needed to buy an unmarked item. But manufacturers are trapped: they haven't the time, skill or equipment to properly assay their scrap. About all they can do is try to find a refiner who seems honest. Or they accept bids (but all the bidders may be crooked) and take the lowest one (though that scrapper may have some shlocking up his sleeve).

Said one executive, "You can agree with them on weight and the value of your scrap, but then after that it becomes a three-ring circus . . . You are ultimately at their mercy."

Scrappers aren't the only vultures eyeing the Valley's corporate gold. Refiners (both reputable and disreputable) themselves must be equally concerned about thefts by their own employees.

Gold is stored at factories as industrial powders, liquid solutions and wire, at refineries as bars and salts—and employees have discovered some inventive techniques for stealing it in each of these forms. Certainly the incentive is there: a piece of gold the size of a matchbook will buy a car. It is so valuable that when thieves stole three barrels of gold solution (valued at eighty thousand dollars) and spilled some on the ground, the wet *dirt* was assayed at seven dollars per pound.

Workers dip their bubble gum in gold dust and then chew on the evidence as they walk out the door. Gold wire is turned into quick rings or other jewelry. Hollow rings are slid across gold bars, curling up a sliver of gold inside.

A popular target is the acid-gold solution in the plating tank. One need only attach a piece of metal to an electrode clamp and throw it into the tank and walk away. Then, when the coast is clear, one can return and pocket a now gold-plated item. Until security officers caught on, it was not unusual for workers during lunch to take the aluminum foil wrapped around a sandwich, gold-plate it and slip it out in a lunchbox. One worker at a printed-circuit-board company was caught gold-plating a Harley-Davidson motorcycle engine. On his first tour of the Fairchild plating shop in the mid-sixties, company executive Marshall Cox out of curiosity pulled on a wire leading into a tank—and found a gold-plated .38 revolver dangling on the end.

A gold-plater from a printed-circuit-board company said he scraped gold from the plate clamps themselves, sold the gold to jewelry stores for eighty thousand dollars and gambled his take at Lake Tahoe. A minimum-wage worker at the same place stole enough gold to buy a retirement home in Florida and a Lincoln Continental. One gold thief even claimed that half the expensive homes in ritzy Almadén Valley south of San Jose were bought with stolen gold money.

Some workers dispense even with plating. Instead, they go directly at the plating solution itself, letting the gold salts precipitate out later. A quick dip in the tank is all that's needed and any container—a thermos, a Coke bottle—will do.

Well, almost any container. One worker tried to sneak a pint of acid-gold solution out in a plastic bag stuffed down the front of his pants. Unfortunately, as the man climbed into the car the bag broke, squirting acid all over his groin. Pretty soon, the man had to roll down all the car windows to try to cool the rising heat in his crotch. By the time he reached the hospital, the thief had second-degree burns and a brush with emasculation.

Refiners also face a thievery problem, except that with millions of dollars in gold around the shop the temptation is all the greater.

"I've been ripped off big and I've been ripped off small," says one refiner. One employee bored a hole in the men's room wall. On subsequent trips he hid small gold bars. Another escaped searches by hiding gold in his socks. Still another tried to hide gold in cigarette packs.

Part of the problem, manufacturers and refiners both claim, is the recent federal laws allowing private ownership of both raw and processed gold.

"When there was licensing for gold dealing that kept out the thieves," says Mr. Slick, "but when the government opened things up, it wasn't long before the Yellow Pages listings for gold refiners and dealers tripled and quadrupled.

"And then, when the price of gold jumped, it spawned even more amateurs. That's made it tough on us professionals. It's forced us to steal on a daily basis."

Mr. Slick is only slightly exaggerating. In reality, many of the stolen goods are delivered to him without solicitation by Silicon Valley workers looking for a buyer who'll keep secrets. The author was at Slick's refinery one day in late 1980 when a visitor—a stereotypical Valley junior executive with short hair, horn-rimmed glasses, dress pants and a sport shirt—arrived nervously clutching a pair of shoeboxes.

Mr. Slick took the man off to the side, had a brief, whispered conversation, then shook the man's hand. The visitor quickly disappeared. Mr. Slick then brought over the boxes and opened one. Inside, dozens of electronic parts gleamed warmly as only 24-karat gold can.

"That right there is about two hundred dollars' worth of hot parts," said Mr. Slick.

Gold thievery poses other risks to Silicon Valley beyond increased operating costs. At the very bottom of the pyramid, the equivalent of the junkie chip thieves, are the home strippers. These are folks with a basin or tank of heated cyanide stripping solution in a garage or rented industrial space. Into these caldrons go anything these home strippers can get their hands on: chips, printed-circuit boards, jewelry. The process is continued until the solution is exhausted or greed takes over. Then the vats are dumped and the gold precipitate scraped off.

It's the dumping part that causes trouble. Cyanide is not only incredibly poisonous but also a very durable organic compound. Dumped into a sink or down a storm drain the poison slowly makes its way to the San Francisco Bay. Dumped out of a fifty-gallon drum in a local dump (after the manager has been bribed to look the other way) it leeches into the soil and groundwater.

A terrifying, but perhaps apocryphal, story told by gold thieves has it that in the late 1970s, a private gold stripper was operating a large tank out of a rented space on Evelyn Avenue, the road that separates the industrial from the residential sides of Sunnyvale. Dissatisfied with the slow rate of the process, the stripper and his assistants decided to hurry things up by putting a large gas burner under the vat. The solution was quickly boiling furiously. Pleased with their inventiveness, the stripper and his confederates left for dinner.

They returned several hours later—and discovered to their horror that the burner had worked all too well. The liquid had boiled off, leaving the gold and cyanide salts—the latter burning and producing billows of deadly white smoke. All that kept most of Sunnyvale from looking like the Battle of the Somme, with scores of people killed instantly in a nearby trailer park, was that the wind happened to be blowing in the other direction, sending the ever dissipating smoke out over empty fields and a few darkened factories toward the Bay.

Big-time scrapper or part-time home stripper, each shares the ubiquitous Silicon Valley dream of the overnight riches, of the Big Score. And just as Silicon Valley executives idolize success stories like those of David Packard and Robert Noyce, gold thieves have their own dark hero, whose career has been an archetype of inverse success. The man's name is well known, as is the company he victimized, but because no charges were ever filed, both will remain anonymous here.

According to the story, the individual was a scrap dealer who had a contract to process the reject-chip lots from a major Valley semiconductor company. He, of course, skimmed some of the gold refined from these lots and did a little reselling of marginally rejected chips.

But he had an even better trick up his sleeve—a scam that has been copied (no one knows how many times) ever since. The scrapper placed one of his own people inside the chip firm as the company's own liaison to him. By controlling both ends of the transaction, the King of Scrappers could then run just about any operation he desired. The one that proved most lucrative was salting the reject piles with good chips. This was a very difficult crime to spot, not only because the firm did not keep precise production records but because even if it had, a continuous and constant rip-off becomes permanently absorbed into the yield rate. Theoretically, such a skim operation might be going on at a Silicon Valley firm right now that has endured for two decades without being discovered—having become an invisible addition to the cost of doing business.

To make sure that his actions were well covered, the Scrap King found himself a silent partner—one of the company's vice-presidents. He then proceeded to loot the firm of at least $2 million, according to a gold thief who claims to have been on the periphery of the crime.

In time, the Scrap King was caught, and that's when the payoffs to his angel on executive row paid off. The Scrap King was hauled into the office of the president of the company . . . and reemerged less than an hour later scot-free, his loot his own.

The gold thief grows wistful when he talks about this caper. He claims that the Scrap King used his money to buy an estate in Scotland. He is also a common fixture at rare wine and antique car auctions throughout the world. And recently, the Scrap King's name even turned up in the black book of one of San Francisco's biggest cocaine dealers. The Scrap King's continuing good life is testament to the fact that in Silicon Valley, for the criminal entrepreneur, crime can be very lucrative.

But at what cost? On May 14, 1984, as he sentenced James Harper to life imprisonment for conspiracy to commit espionage, U.S. District Judge Samuel Conti (whose earlier ruling that the death penalty could be applied was overturned) told the defendant: "This crime is beyond comprehension. You are a traitor. You did it for greed and money. You exposed everyone in this country to danger into the twenty-first century. There is no crime more serious than selling your country's defense secrets."

The bloody, needle-tracked, half-buried body of David Roberts suggests that belowground, just as above, the Silicon Valley Big Score comes only to a select few.

7

The Ghost in the Machine

"Systems," assemblages of components that create a complex whole, have been around since the early hominids. Fire contained in a pit for warmth or cooking is a system; so is strapping a sharpened blade onto a stick to create an ax. In time this concept became synonymous with "machines," increasingly intricate and powerful mechanical devices designed to perform specific tasks.

With the rise of civilization, machines became increasingly sophisticated: some Roman weapons and medieval mining and manufacturing equipment are remarkable in their complexity. And throughout that evolution, the advance of machinery has always been intimately tied with manufacturing technology: metallurgy, machining, assembly, testing, etc.

The same processes continue today: blacksmithing and lathe-turning are now replaced by the arcane chemical and physical processes required to produce a modern integrated circuit and by the circuitous logic of programming. But still, the evolution of modern-day computers and instruments remains deeply dependent upon the latest developments in component design.

The transition between "machines" and "systems" was a slow one. A clock is a sophisticated machine, but it is also a rudimentary system, its many components converting external power into an abstract function for use by its operator. By the seventeenth century, clockmakers were building remarkable mechanical "toys" in the shapes of human beings or other animals whose behavior was so lifelike that they drew gasps from admiring crowds—so lifelike in fact that the greatest mind of the age, René Descartes, found in them an allusion to human life. Sitting in a sauna, he envisioned man as a ghost or spirit trapped in the machine of physical body—and the mind-body dualism paradox has haunted great thinkers ever since.

The inventions of Bell and Edison and others at the end of the nineteenth century are systems—electromechanical systems. Electricity is used to power, through magnetics and heating coils, mechanical devices like switches and gauges. Electromechanical devices are still part of modern life, even in high technology. The first computers, with their banks of clicking switches, were electromechanical; so were phone systems until the 1970s. Computer disk drives, printers, tape and record players and automobile engines are electromechanical devices; the movement of the actuator arms across the disk or the print head across the paper is created by the flow of electrical current defining the actions of a mechanical device.

By the turn of the twentieth century, a new world was opening up, the technology of Fleming's diode and De Forest's triode. These were not electromechanical devices, there was nothing mechanical about them. They had no moving parts. Instead, they took electricity and broke it up into electrons and then manipulated this electron stream to their needs. This was electronics, and the business of measuring and manipulating these electron streams as they shot down Klystron tubes, across circuits or through vacuum tubes, was called instruments. In Silicon Valley pioneering firms like Hewlett-Packard and Sylvania took these emergent technologies and created such products as audio oscillators, voltmeters and oscilloscopes.

With the transition from switches to tubes and then to circuitry between the Second World War and the 1960s, computers also became an electronic business.

Then, of course, came integrated circuits and microprocessors, and electronics became the preeminent industry in the world, and "system" suddenly became a buzz word for everything from computer to software to the interaction between human beings. (Descartes would have been shocked; the machines it seems had exorcised their ghosts. Now people interfaced and inputted, downloaded their problems and upgraded their lives. *Computo ergo sum.*)

The penetration of electronics into the fabric of society and commerce has been so rapid and complete that even in the tiniest corner of daily life or the remotest market niche there is bound to be an electronic system. Radios, televisions, toasters, ovens, thermostats, telephones, cars, drill presses, mill saws and streetlights are now in some way electronic systems. Even light bulbs are coming equipped with a little integrated circuit strapped on the bottom to conserve power consumption.

So pervasive is this electronic interpenetration that it is almost rendered invisible by its ubiquity. Invisible, that is, except in Silicon Valley. If one had read articles about the Valley up until the late 1970s and the rise of Apple and Atari, one could have come away thinking that the primary product of that industrial center was integrated circuits. Nothing could be further from the truth. In reality, silicon is the least common material in most of the manufactured goods of Silicon Valley, usually found in less quantity than the gold that plates connectors and the copper that fills the wires, and certainly an infinitesimal amount compared with all the plastic and steel and glass that surround the few tiny silicon chips.

The same is true for the Valley itself. Out of the more than two thousand electronics companies in Silicon Valley (the number is never precise because at any time no one knows how many start-ups are beginning in garages and living rooms) perhaps at most forty of them are in the business of making silicon integrated-circuit chips, perhaps an equal number again making the parts or materials used in those chips and perhaps a hundred more assembling those chips or distributing them. That still leaves nearly two thousand Valley firms in some way involved in the systems business. And what makes it even more amazing is that most of these firms were founded less than ten years ago.

Like some furiously alive plant, the Silicon Valley systems business has interwoven its branches so tightly there are few openings, but it still shoots tendrils outward toward greater light or finer soil. That is how, in just two years' time, such an apparently precise market niche as the personal computer 5.25-inch-diameter Winchester hard-disk-drive industry can suddenly sprout 120 competing firms, one third of them in Silicon Valley, all of them struggling to find the angle that will distinguish them from all the rest: more memory, higher information-access speed, lower price, greater reliability, smaller packaging, superior product service and support, higher volume discounts . . .

The vitality of all this is breathtaking. Talented scientists and businesspeople hopping back and forth between companies, one day at a big corporation like Rolm, the next in some closet-sized concrete tilt-up with the company name, decided upon that morning, written on a sheet of paper and taped to the window.

*   *   *

Probably the only way to get a handle on the systems industry is to divide its history (and its companies up) into technological eras.

The first systems industry was instruments. This industry enjoyed two great growth periods: from World War II until about 1960, and then again during the seventies. The first period featured analogue devices for the simple test and measurement of distinct functions, like the voltmeter or the audio oscillator, or, a more sophisticated product, the oscilloscope. The big Valley companies in this business were Hewlett-Packard, Varian and Sylvania.

The second jump in the instrument business, in the seventies, came with the rise of microprocessors. Now the instruments of the past could not only be made digital, which increased accuracy and the ability to manipulate the data, but they could also be given semiconductor intelligence to make operations more flexible and adjustable to changing needs. In addition, this "smart instrument" era was propelled by vast improvements in sensor technology, which led to an explosion in the analytical instrument business, with products such as gas analyzers, medical patient monitoring systems, ultrasound devices, X-ray tomography and industrial pollution "sniffers." The big Valley companies in these fields were: medicine—HP, Diasonics, Xonics; gas analyzers—HP; and process control—Acurex, Measurex. All of these businesses were hot markets in the 1970s and early 1980s . . . except at the end, when pollution control suffered the vagaries of the economy. It seems customers only worry about pollution when they are making money.

Computers had their first great era a decade before, in the 1960s. In the Valley, the chief participants were IBM's memory division in San Jose; Ampex and Memorex, with computer tape and disastrous forays into computing; HP with minicomputers; and Tymshare, which pioneered the concept of selling computer time to subscribers. Waiting in the wings at the end of the decade was the business of building large computers to run on IBM software, the attack to be led by Amdahl Corp.

(As you may have noticed, IBM has its hands over every corner of Valley life, to its victims seeming like some evil genius, a corporate Dr. Mabuse.)

It was in the 1970s that the local systems business, particularly the consumer wing, really took off. It began with the pocket calculator in 1973, followed quickly by the digital watch. At the time it seemed as though everyone and his brother was making one or both of these products: computer companies (HP), chip houses (Intel, Fairchild, National Semiconductor) and new start-ups (Litronix). But within two years it was all but over, the price-bombing marketing policies driving out or destroying every competitor in the business, before itself succumbing to Japanese competition. The Valley was littered with ruined consumer electronics companies and suddenly cash-poor chip houses. Only a bloodied HP remained in the business.

The consumer electronics crash came at the same time as the recession of 1974–75, putting a double whammy on the Valley. This was Silicon Valley's first great bust, but it hit the semiconductor houses the worst. The next one would belong to the systems companies.

Like all good high-tech recessions, the 1974–75 downturn was a time of great entrepreneurial activity. The conditions were right for new companies to be formed and get a running start in time for the next upturn. It was during this period that many of the firms for which Silicon Valley is now known got their start, either being founded or coming together as serious firms: Rolm (entering the telephone market), Apple, Amdahl (introducing its first product), Atari, Commodore (as a computer company), Shugart (in its second incarnation) and Tandem. It was these firms that would lead the resurgence of the late seventies in Silicon Valley, filling in the orchards and making the systems business the primary manufacturing activity there.

It started off slowly, with scores of little companies hidden away in rented rooms in industrial parks working out their product ideas, building prototypes, finding investment money. By 1978 and 1979, thanks to changes in capital gains taxes, the boom was on again, and these firms suddenly stepped into public view with fancy new offices and extensive ad campaigns. For the experienced Valley watcher, the hints had come a year or two before, with sudden departures of executives at established firms for parts unknown: they would appear a year or two later in some hot new start-up. Signs also came in the growing number of personnel advertisements in the back of the San Jose *Mercury-News,* a Valley economic barometer, followed by new product announcements in *Electronic News* by companies never heard of before, then product advertisements and technical articles in *Datamation* and *Electronics*—then *pow!* The Silicon Valley entrepreneurial boom was back on.

The development of the microprocessor and the general expansion of the semiconductor technology made this boom possible. It seemed (as it still does today) that the number of applications for this new microtechnology was unlimited, so new firms branched off in every direction where they could, with luck, create a demand large enough to support them. One way was personal computers, which drew several dozen Valley companies. Another was in the peripheral devices for computing products, such as rigid disk, tape and flexible-disk memory, printers, telephone modems, terminals (color, graphics, intelligent work stations, etc.) and interconnection networks. Other companies developed equipment for use by the semiconductor industry to build chips, notably computer-aided design systems. And, of course, there were the consumer products: video games and home computers.

This third generation of Silicon Valley (instruments begat chips begat systems) quickly led to a fourth: software. This was the cheapest business of all to get into—and the most profitable. The new smart systems needed to be told what to do in languages they understood. And the more unsophisticated the operator the more ingenious the software required—as in personal computers. The companies that rose up to meet this demand, most of them between 1980 and 1984 (ASK, Digital Research, Visicorp), were like publishing houses with success often the result of a single best seller.

With all of this entrepreneurial activity going on in the late seventies, something in the Valley had to give under the strain, and it was employment. There simply weren't enough talented people around to fill all of these companies—and serve the needs of the rapidly growing older firms as well. That meant somebody had to go—and it certainly wasn't the little new companies who needed the Valley safety net. Instead, the late seventies saw the migration of entire divisions of some of the larger systems and chip companies to places like Idaho, Oregon, Arizona and North Carolina.

It wasn't enough. There still weren't enough warm bodies in the area to meet demand. So companies went to extreme measures: three-twelve-hour-day workweeks, promises of extended holidays, biplanes towing employment ads over Stanford football games, bonuses to employees who brought in friends, open houses in which job offers were made on the spot (often workers, in delicious revenge for what the Valley had done to them, would spend lunch hours going from open house to open house jacking up the offers), even prizes for becoming an employee—as if the companies were savings and loans looking for depositors. When hard-bitten National Semiconductor installed a recreational par course, it was obvious the employment situation was desperate.

Then came the 1982 recession. The promises and prizes quickly disappeared and once again employers had a buyers' market and the upper hand. By then, the game had changed. Silicon Valley was now the home of hundreds of new systems companies. The following is a sampling of some of the more interesting case histories.

* * *

When Dr. Gene M. Amdahl walked out of IBM for the second time in 1970, he informed Big Blue that this time he planned to start a company to compete with the computer giant. They were brave words —and they also sounded insane. After all, in the previous twenty years, IBM had taken on the biggest firms in America and beaten them to their knees—and now this, entrepreneurial upstart, with little prior management experience and no business experience, proposed to succeed where those heavyweights had failed.

But Amdahl had something very special going for him. And back at IBM headquarters in Armonk, New York, amid the amusement and anger, there must have been a few moments of meditation on just what this man might do. After all, Gene Amdahl wasn't just any backlab prole with a fancy degree. He was Dr. 360, chief architect of the IBM 360 Series computers, the most popular computer family of its day, and, in the upgraded form of its direct descendant, the 370 Series, the most popular family of computers in history.

This was the Gene Amdahl who promised to come back as a competitor. And equally disturbing was how he intended to do it: by building computers that would run IBM software. "Compatibility" at that time was still a relatively new word in the computer-industry lexicon. Up until a few years before, almost every computer on the market had its own way of doing things, its own operating system. Quite often, computers in the same company product line couldn't talk to one another. Customer frustration was slowly pushing computer companies toward a certain degree of compatibility between the computer models of a single company for a single product generation.

But that was it. The big competitors in the business—Burroughs, Univac, IBM and others—felt no compulsion to agree on any hardware or software standards. After all, that might mean that one company's disk drive might be hung on another's computer, which also used the printer of a third, and then where would you be? No, if a customer wanted to buy an NCR computer, he had to buy the whole package or nothing. And if he later wanted to move up to a more powerful model, he still had to sell the whole kit and kaboodle and start over.

The Series 360 changed all of that. For one thing, all of the family members were relatively compatible. But even more important was the 360's incredible success. It ran over the top of the computer market, becoming a de facto industry standard and sending the competition into years of twilight. In the mid-sixties, before the introduction of the 360 Series, 34 percent of all computing was performed on IBM machines. In 1970, this number jumped to 56 percent.

Yet IBM soon found itself wondering if the 360 family had been too much of a success. The problem was software. The installed base of 360s was so great, with an estimated $200 billion spent on software (ten times that of the hardware) by owners of these systems, that they simply represented too much of an investment to be quickly replaced.

Thus, by the time IBM was ready to replace the 360 with the next generation of machines, it found the market unreceptive, even hostile to the prospect of making enormous capital outlays for an entirely different computer system requiring completely new software. IBM, which had planned a technically more advanced computer family as a follow-up to the 360, had to backstep and, for the first time, contemplate intergenerational compatibility between computers. The result was the 370 family, which for the most part could run all of the software designed for the 360. IBM would have to come to terms with competing with its greatest competitor—its own past success—but at least now when one bought an IBM 360 computer, one joined the IBM "family" forever.

Amdahl had seen what the success of his 360 had wrought. More than anyone else he knew what the new customer commitment to computer vendors meant. His experiences charging around the inside of Big Blue had taught Amdahl something else about the big computer companies and their product pricing strategies. As *Fortune* explains:

> To maximize total revenues, . . . IBM priced its machines so that their price–performance ratios would be similar and the customer would always have to pay more for higher performance. If IBM had priced a high-performance computer low enough to get the volume . . . its price/performance would have been better than ratios for other parts of the line. Customers using middle-of-the-line computers would have migrated to the high end, either by replacing a number of

smaller computers with one big one, banding together to share a big machine, or accepting overcapacity for a period of time.

With a markedly superior price/performance ratio available, in other words, a lot of customers would spend less than they otherwise would; overall, IBM would forego more revenue than it would gain. And it would forego even more profit than revenue, since the margins on an advanced machine with a relatively lower price would probably be thinner than on middle-of-the-line systems.

What this meant was that not only was IBM trapped by its past, but each individual machine in the IBM line was locked into position by those around it.

This was where Amdahl believed he saw a weakness in the IBM strategy. He knew he couldn't assault multibillion-dollar IBM head on, but with a little company he thought he could buzz around the computer giant, chewing off pieces of market big enough to be exciting but small enough not to annoy IBM into a murderous slap.

Central to this strategy was the Amdahl computer itself, fully compatible with the IBM 360 Series (capable of using all of its peripherals as well), yet featuring the latest in semiconductor circuitry. Further, this machine, to be called the 470 V/6, would be aimed right at the heart of the HP line (the Model 168 central processor, a $2-million machine raking in a half billion dollars a year), yet offer a superior price–performance ratio.

It was a brilliant strategy, the result of a Gene Amdahl philosophy that most resembled, according to Amdahl vice-president David Morgenthaler in 1979, the aggressive, adventurous "IBM of the '50s." However, in execution the plan was fraught with pitfalls. Chief among them was trying to sell investors on the idea of tackling the most feared competitor in all of business. As Amdahl said, "Everyone who has competed head on with IBM has been crushed under its iron heel, so our strategy is hard for people to accept."

Equally hard for prospective investors to accept was the idea of this scientist with no real business experience in the daily grind of payroll and inventories and accounts receivable trying to organize the kind of large and tightly organized business structure needed to produce a big-ticket item like a mainframe computer. Just as difficult to accept was the thought of investing a venture bankroll of $50 million (compared with, for example, $2 million for Rolm) on an unproven firm that did not expect to ship its first product for a half decade.

So, hat in hand, Amdahl tried every corner of the investment market, looking for anyone willing to back him—and that's exactly what he found, to his regret. By 1972, two years after the founding of his company, Amdahl had raised the $27.5-million first round he needed to get his company under way.

The money came from two investors: Heizer Corp., a Chicago-based venture firm, and Fujitsu Ltd., the billion-dollar Japanese electronics giant. From the beginning the forty-nine-year old Amdahl harbored doubts about both of his investors. A naturally suspicious and defensive man anyway, Amdahl didn't need much help in spotting problems with both firms right away: Heizer, particularly its "brash" founder Ned Heizer, had put a lot of money into Amdahl—more than in any other firm—and it was acutely and perpetually concerned about getting its return on investment. Fujitsu's motives seemed far more sinister: it didn't seem to care about profits; rather it seemed to see Amdahl Corp. as its larder of technology for a planned assault on the U.S. computer market.

The whole setup had the makings of a complete disaster, which seemed imminent when IBM announced the 370 Series and sent Amdahl Corp. back to the drawing boards to redesign its half-finished first product. By 1974, the company seemed on the brink of failure. Some of the company's executives weren't panning out and Gene Amdahl, never a top-flight businessman, tried to fill in for them. Meanwhile, Fujitsu was demanding that Amdahl lay off several hundred employees—most of the staff—and Heizer was complaining that the company was being run into the ground. When a public stock offering failed miserably, Amdahl even offered to resign.

Finally, an exasperated Gene Amdahl allowed Heizer to bring in Eugene White, formerly of GE computers, as the new company president. Despite Amdahl's initial suspicions that White was a Heizer front man, the new president worked out extremely well. He was everything Gene Amdahl was not: practical, businesslike and happiest working out administrative details. As one company employee told *Fortune:* "Gene White has added as much to Amdahl Corp. as Gene Amdahl has. They are exact opposites and the best pair of men I have ever seen teamed up."

White was just what Amdahl Corp. needed to turn itself into a professional firm. White fired 250 of the company's 580 employees (just as

Fujitsu had wanted) and built up the company's marketing and sales operations. He also convinced the two investors to come up with another $16 million to help the company finish getting the first product to market.

Still, that wasn't enough. When Amdahl Corp. finally introduced its first machine, the 470 V/6 in the spring of 1975, the company was still $30 million in the hole—and as a measure of the market's doubts about the firm's viability, a private sale of stock had to be canceled because not enough buyers could be found.

But the 470 V/6 was an engineering marvel, one of the great electronic inventions of the 1970s. It was one third the size of its IBM counterpart, the Model 168, half as heavy, about one and one half times as powerful and cost at least 10 percent less.

Inside, the Amdahl computer was equally a marvel. Amdahl's use of integrated circuits instead of the IBM-type wiring made the new computer not only fast but also the most reliable data processing system of its time.

At first there was some question if even those advantages would be enough. Amdahl Corp. didn't take any chances. Customers were provided with the most complete support system in the industry, from built-in telephone diagnostics to a full-time service representative to repair any flaws in the system—including the IBM software—and a chance to shake hands and have lunch with the legendary Gene Amdahl. Fujitsu even publicly announced that it would guarantee to maintain all Amdahl computers if the Sunnyvale company went out of business.

It worked. In its first full year, 1976, Amdahl Corp. enjoyed $93 million in sales and an amazing $24 million in profits. The next year sales jumped to nearly $200 million, with more than $50 million profits. In 1978, sales were $321 million.

As Amdahl himself had predicted, IBM initially reacted to the new company with relative indifference. After all, as Amdahl vice-president Morgenthaler noted, as late as 1979 Amdahl's sales were probably less than the interest IBM made just from its cash on hand. But IBM was giving subtle hints it didn't like this company run by an ex-employee yipping at its heels, particularly when that pipsqueak began to steal away prime clients like NASA, General Motors and the Bell System. It wasn't long before IBM sales people were reportedly hinting to customers that Amdahl Corp. was on the ropes and threatening voided guarantees or reduced service if an Amdahl computer was hooked up to IBM peripherals.

But Amdahl Corp. continued to grow. Like all successful entrepreneurial ventures pioneering new markets, it was soon followed by a host of imitators, notably the giant leasing company Itel Corp. of San Francisco, Control Data Corp. of Minnesota, and nearby start-ups Two Pi and Magnuson, the latter boasting a chief designer named Carlton Amdahl, Gene's son. Each of these firms staked out a different market. CDC and Itel sold replacement memory systems for IBM computers; Two Pi and Magnuson were like Amdahl in offering replacement processors.

By far the most memorable of these "plug-compatible" (that is they would hook up perfectly with IBM equipment) firms was Itel Corp. Itel had made a huge name for itself in the leasing business, lining up investors to acquire freighters and boxcars that Itel would in turn lease to corporate customers. So successful was this program that Itel seemed on its way to becoming the youngest billion-dollar firm in U.S. history. In fact, by the end of the decade that goal seemed to be almost Itel's raison d'être; everything else—consistency, a solid financial foundation, an industry reputation—was subordinated to cranking the company up to a gigabuck in annual sales.

Only with hindsight did it become apparent that Itel was the rock star of American business. No company, at least no legitimate company, ever lived so high, with so much flash, on so little, as Itel. At the corporate offices in San Francisco, in one of the city's tallest buildings (in the Embarcadero Center), visitors nearly drowned in the thick-pile white wool. Tapestries covered the walls. A beautiful receptionist sat at an antique desk that was dwarfed by the large foyer.

Itel lived a lot the way it looked. It wasn't unusual for a company salesman (most of them made in the six figures) to charter a jet to pick up a key client in Chicago and fly him someplace for dinner, like gumbo at Antoine's in New Orleans. The high-water mark of this business bacchanalia came in January 1979, when, to celebrate a $50 million profit in "plug-compatibles" for the previous year, Itel spent $3 million to fly 1,300 employees to Acapulco. In truth, the whole company seemed to be living like pimps, as if there were no tomorrow.

And there wasn't.

IBM had been lying low for some time, appearing to ignore the plug-compatibles. Then on Wednesday, January 31, 1979, just days after the Itel Acapulco trip, IBM dropped its bomb. It was called the 4300, the

E-Series that had been rumored for a year before, and it was the apparent successor to the low end of the 370 Series. Suddenly everything Itel (and Two Pi) offered was obsolete. IBM had changed the rules.

At that point Itel began to die. In 1974, Itel had revenues of $144 million, with profits of about $10 million. In 1978 (as originally reported), the firm had revenues of $689 million and profits of about $50 million. In 1979, Itel's revenues were flat at $643 million, but the firm had now lost *$444 million* in a single year. By then the company was in Chapter 11 bankruptcy (which would last for three years). At the end of 1980 the company had a net worth of a negative $260 million. It had laid off six thousand of its seven thousand employees.

Itel's collapse had also come very close to sinking the venerable Lloyd's of London. In the words of computer journalist Hesh Wiener:

. . . Lloyd's made what could be the most interesting and tragic bet in its history: Lloyd's set odds on the rate of technological progress. Specifically, Lloyd's set a price on its assuming the key risk in computer equipment leasing: the chance that some machinery would bring in rents greater than the cost of buying, financing and placing the gear in the hands of users. It was an enormous bet; Lloyd's accepted millions in premiums against a chance that hundreds of millions might be paid out. Lloyd's lost.

The total payments Lloyd's had to make was estimated at $400 million, half of it Itel's policy alone. The Lutine bell at Lloyd's rang once that day to signal the man-made disaster. When it was over, National Semiconductor, which, with Hitachi, had built the Itel products, took over the computer wing of the expiring company, and renamed it National Advanced Systems. The first thing National Advanced Systems did at Itel's exquisite Palo Alto plant was to take down all the tapestries, remove the statues and pull up the oriental rugs. The new company did well.

In fact, after the initial disaster, everybody but Itel did well—except, ironically, Amdahl Corp. It seems that even IBM hadn't realized what sort of monster it had created by being so competitive with the 4300. Lead times stretched out to twenty months or more, and fifty thousand potential customers experienced the humiliation of participating in a lottery for delivery dates.

All of this was good news for the plug-compatible folks. Most already had new competitive models on the drawing board. So the plug-compatibles charged ahead, sacrificing some profit margin for a chance at chipping off IBM customers unwilling to wait almost two years for the 4300.

Amdahl Corp. faced a different sort of problem. Its product line in no way competed with the 4300, yet its sales slumped immediately. It seems prospective buyers sat down with the 4300's price–performance ratio and charted the resulting curve up into the large-computer market. The upcoming product they saw, the so-called H-Series, made their eyebrows jump off their faces: here was a computer that made everything IBM and Amdahl had to offer seem a rip-off by comparison.

With the H-Series rumored to be introduced any week, prospective customers of both the Amdahl and the IBM computers held off. After all, why buy one of these machines now when a helluva lot better and cheaper computer will be available any day now? So, instead of buying, the customers decided to lease instead, so they could quickly jump to the H-Series when it came.

The effect on both Amdahl and, fittingly, IBM, was devastating. Suddenly, instead of immediately recording in the books $3 million or $4 million for each computer sold, the two competitors could book only $80,000 to $100,000 in lease payments. Amdahl, which had been running at a profit of $10 million to $15 million per quarter, saw its margins drop to $1.2 million and $1.8 million. IBM lost $99 million in profits over the same period—over a product it wouldn't even admit existed. (And when introduced a year later, it was merely competitive.)

Amdahl Corp. had barely gotten over the shock of the 4300 introduction and the H-Series speculation when it decided to make the boldest move of its brief career. In August, it announced its intention to acquire Memorex Corp. down the road in Santa Clara for about $260 million. If it seemed presumptuous for a company in rough straits to be looking at conglomeration, one had only to add up the assets and inventory. A combined Amdahl and Memorex would have more than $1 billion in annual sales and fourteen thousand employees. It would have become the second largest company (after HP) in Silicon Valley. The combination of Memorex's expertise in computer memory and Amdahl's in computer processors would have made a formidable firm.

Memorex, the company Amdahl proposed to buy, had a checkered career. At one time it was the star firm of Silicon Valley. Founded in 1961, the firm had ridden the crest of the boom in computer and consumer recording tape. By the late 1960s it was easily the best known company in the Valley, eclipsing the rising Fairchild and the falling Ampex. Memorex stock, initially offered at $2 per share, had jumped to

$170 by 1969. The company's magnificent and award-winning head-quarters, with its hanging gardens and sculptured lawns, sat almost in the middle of nowhere near the San Jose Airport and was a local landmark, for a decade defining the southern terminus of the Valley and acting as the magnet for the South Bay high-tech buildup.

But the company made the nearly fatal mistake of entering into the mainframe-computer business in the early seventies—and was crippled for its efforts. By 1973, the company suffered losses of $90 million and had been kicked off the New York Stock Exchange. Just as bad, the firm had misled the press and stock analysts about the magnitude of its problem—and they subsequently refused to trust the company, much less cover it.

Bank of America, the big loser in a Memorex bankruptcy, had stepped in to reorganize the firm. The man they hired to do it was Robert C. Wilson, a legendary business turnaround expert. Wilson indeed got Memorex back on its feet, but, as rumors had it, the firm was a paper tiger. Nevertheless, Wilson must have done something right, because by 1978 the company's profits were up to nearly $60 million, revenues climbing to $633 million. The company's stock had climbed to a high of $60. Memorex was ripe for selling.

Amdahl was the first suitor, despite the fact that it was a smaller company. The Amdahl bid was for $280 million, or $34 per share (by then Memorex stock had fallen again to under $30). But within a few weeks, a second suitor appeared: Storage Technology of Louisville, Colorado, Memorex's biggest foe, a company half the size of Memorex but probably twice the firm under the volcanic leadership of Jesse Aweida. Storage Tech's offer was even lower than Amdahl's, but it offered the prospect of combining the world's leading computer-tape company (Storage Tech) with the world's greatest computer-disk maker (Memorex).

Obviously something was going on here. Why were two smaller companies offering to buy Memorex for a fraction of its value, and Memorex taking the offers seriously? Obviously they knew something outsiders didn't about Memorex—and Robert Wilson knew they knew.

In the end, Amdahl broke off its offer for Memorex. Scuttlebutt at the time was that Amdahl investor Fujitsu had nixed the deal, but according to Gene Amdahl the real reason was that Amdahl Corp. realized what it saw at Memorex was a false front hiding a shattered company. Recalls Amdahl, "I was opposed to the Memorex deal because I had gone through and looked at the technology Memorex was supposed to have, and it wasn't there. In the laboratories the equipment was so new they hadn't even taken off the labels. They just bought the equipment to make a good impression."

Meanwhile, on the street there was even talk of a STC-Amdahl-Memorex merger, but that soon disappeared, as did the Storage Tech offer for Memorex, which the latter had resisted from the beginning. Finally, to complete the circle, Amdahl Corp. made an offer for Storage Tech, to create a conglomerate similar to the one it had tried with Memorex. But this time, Fujitsu really did veto the deal, according to insiders, because it knew it couldn't manipulate a Jesse Aweida the way it did the Amdahl staff.

So it was all a tempest in a teapot. Everybody went home. Memorex quickly exhibited why its suitors had suffered second thoughts about buying it. By the end of the year, Wilson had retired, saying that 1979 had been "the most difficult year in our recent history" as the company suffered from high interest rates, shortages in the chips it needed for its products, a drop in profits from $11.8 million in the first quarter to $2.2 million in the last, and a collapse in the company stock from $30.25 per share at the beginning of the year to $17.88 at the end. Worst of all, Wilson said, as he prepared to move back East, the judge's verdict against Memorex in its antitrust suit against IBM the year before had "unleased IBM's predatory actions." Since then, he said, IBM "prices have been slashed, new technologies and products announced and rumors circulated with respect to other products. It has been, by far, the most active IBM in my memory."

The new president of Memorex, Clarence "Clancy" Spangle, brought in from Honeywell, spent the early eighties trying to turn Memorex around. He cut the workforce by almost 10 percent, reorganized the company's management structure, dumped unprofitable products and tried to promote a new honesty in the company. But the company was leaking talent faster than Spangle could plug the holes, and it found itself struggling to get products out the door. The company staggered under enormous debt—$240 million in 1981—and perpetual quarterly losses (for example, earnings plunged 91 percent between the second quarter of 1979 and the same quarter of 1980). One wag was led to say, in parody of the company's long running audio-tape advertisements, "If it's alive, it isn't Memorex."

Finally, in 1981, the medicine Memorex needed for its ills finally arrived: the firm was acquired by Burroughs.

For Amdahl Corp., the path after the merger crossroads has been nearly as rocky. The final straw in the miserable year of 1979 came at the end, when founder Gene Amdahl walked away from the firm that bore his name. He claimed at the time that he was tired of corporate bureaucracies, but later he would admit he had given up hope he would ever wrestle his firm away from the tightening grip of the Japanese.

Amdahl Corp. continued into the eighties as the key name in the IBM-compatible computer business. Leases finally turned back into sales and the company began to regain its lost profits, but Amdahl Corp. would never be the same again. Its wild growth had been slowed in the bloody battle with IBM. The firm would never again be a young David fighting the IBM Goliath; rather it had become another mature computer company, facing economic upturns and downturns (the company had a sizable layoff in 1983), no longer the brash kid of the computer industry, its thunder stolen by the Japanese.

Among the other plug-compatible companies, Two Pi was bought by Philips, the same folks who owned semiconductor maker Signetics. Magnuson, after coming out of the 4300 introduction strong, seemed to come apart. Carlton Amdahl quit to join his father. Founder Paul H. Magnuson, now a millionaire, quit to found a competing company, Prodigy. His departure was particularly ugly, as Magnuson Computer, now in bankruptcy, charged him with grand theft of computer secrets worth hundreds of thousands of dollars. Paul Magnuson was eventually cleared of all charges, but not before his name had been dragged through the press and county prosecutors had described him as representative of the increasingly ugly nature of Silicon Valley business.

National Advanced Systems, formerly Itel's computer group, slowly wound down. As the years passed, the operation, though successful, became less and less a manufacturing arm for National Semiconductor and more a marketing arm for Hitachi computer products. The subsidiary was unexpectedly cast into the spotlight in 1982 during the IBM Japanscam case.

Of all the participants in the plug-compatible wars of the 1970s, only Gene Amdahl remained in the public eye afterward. After he quit Amdahl Corp. he disappeared—only to be found working in a tiny office in the back of a trucking company. He talked about building another company, this one not controlled by outside parties, to again take on IBM.

If anyone else had said this, he would have been considered a lunatic. But this was Gene Amdahl. Three years later he had been joined by his son, had raised an astonishing $100 million in venture money and had moved into a magnificent new building that was not only the most beautiful industrial building in the Valley but also the most advanced circuit-design facility in the world. The new company was called Trilogy, and Amdahl confidently expected to sell the first $4 million machine by 1985, and to have sales of $1 billion by 1987. At the time few doubted that he'd make it.

So, it seemed, the IBM-compatible business had come full circle, from boom days to broken decline. And now the man who started it all was about to send the wheel spinning around once more. Once again, it looked to be a wild ride.

Meanwhile, IBM as it had done once before, seemed to be biding its time . . .

*   *   *

Now is the time to talk about the entrepreneur.

Founding a successful new high-technology firm is one of the most complex and demanding—and rewarding—jobs in all of American business. The entrepreneur must play all of the roles normally distributed among a dozen executives in an established company: president, publicist, facilities manager, manufacturing manager, personnel director, research and development scientist, treasurer and, quite often, janitor.

Such an individual must also be able to cope with a staggering rate of change. The company may grow 10,000 percent in the first two years, grow in employment from a handful of founders in a living room to several hundred workers, and move offices several times. Within months the company's product may evolve from a quick sketch on the back of a napkin to a fully developed (even obsolete) device rolling off the assembly line by the hundreds each day. In less than a half decade, as in the case of Atari, the firm can grow from an amusing little newcomer to the best known company in the country.

Throughout this dizzying process, the entrepreneur must keep a cool head and a well-developed sense of perspective. He or she must hire the middle management that will carry the firm through its first $100 million in sales; fire those who can't maintain the pace; court prospective investors and customers; and survive the fourteen-hour workdays, the seven-day workweeks, the marriage that's crumbling under stress, the feuds between partners that often end with the breakup of old friendships, and most important, the wild financial swings that threaten the firm's future at any moment.

So, who is this elusive creature called an entrepreneur? Academics delight in trying to pick apart the minds of such individuals. Unfortunately, these researchers tend to study small, less successful business-people—because, says Steven Brandt, a Stanford lecturer and author of *Entrepreneuring*, high-powered entrepreneurs "are usually moving too fast to be analyzed." Those few researchers who have spent consider-able time with high-tech entrepreneurs have come up with some basic shared traits. Brandt lists a big ego, an abrasive personality in social settings, a high level of energy and a tendency to be very competitive even outside of work. Monetary success, he adds, seems to be second-ary: "Many of them see that the fun is in the game, not in the end of the game—in flying the ship, not just the landing."

Albert Shapero, of the University of Texas School of Management, has noted that "most entrepreneurs are D.P.s, displaced persons, who have been dislodged from some nice, familiar niche and tilted off course." This displacement can occur in many ways, he notes—in child-hood, by being fired from a comfortable job or even from becoming a political refugee—thus the high degree of entrepreneurship among Cubans and Indochinese.

Entrepreneurs themselves, as might be expected, have their own quirky lists. B. J. Moore, founder of Biomation Corp. in Santa Clara, suggests that a good entrepreneur must have an average intelligence ("If you're smart enough to be able to think of all the things that can go wrong, why would you ever want to get into this business?"), a strong sense of urgency, a high pain threshold and energy level and a slight sense of insecurity.

Moore also developed a second list, this one of traits entrepreneurs don't exhibit: an intense desire to be wealthy, a prima donna attitude, a chaotic personal life (at least when they start) or an introverted person-ality (an entrepreneur cannot dwell on failure).

Where else does a personality profile similar to that of the entrepre-neur appear? Mercenaries? Mafia torpedoes? United States senators? No, according to Robert Schwarz, educator of entrepreneurs and founder of Tarrytown House Executive Conference Center, such a per-sonality mix is only found elsewhere among Peace Corps volunteers.

This would seem to indicate that entrepreneurs, despite their unusual collection of traits, are as much made as born, that certain environmen-tal factors had to be in place for the Silicon Valley new start-up boom to explode. Industry observers seem to agree that these ingredients include a source of venture capital, a ready market for new technology and the unusual respect Americans have for entrepreneurship unmatched anywhere in the world.

In the United States electronics industry, and particularly in Silicon Valley, each of these pieces fell into place during the 1950s and 1960s with the success of such entrepreneurial ventures as Hewlett-Packard Co. and such Fairchild spin-offs as National Semiconductor and Intel. The venture capital companies that invested in these new semiconductor and computer firms not only earned fortunes but in the process all but perfected the incubation of new high-technology companies. Silicon Valley could now provide new start-ups with a strong support structure as well as a pool of ready customers. Finally, as the stories of these individuals and their all but overnight wealth became known, entrepreneurship gained a legitimacy it had never before enjoyed—as the last bastion of rugged individualism, and the only legitimate work for grown-up flower children.

By the early 1980s, this brew was boiling. In 1981, $3 billion in venture capital was poured into young companies, according to *Venture Capital Journal,* fueled by a 1978 cut in the maximum capital gains tax (from 49 percent to 28 percent for corporations). New markets opened for entrepreneurial prospecting: software, computer peripherals, genetic engineering, portable computers . . . By the end of 1982, $6 billion in capital was waiting to be poured into start-up companies—much of it from sources unheard-of a decade before: one third from pension funds, 14 percent from insurance companies, 13 percent from foreign investors. Successful entrepreneurs, such as Nolan Bushnell (Atari, Pizza Time Theaters) became venture capitalists for their own private stables of new companies.

Still, a fertile soil for entrepreneurship is not enough. The other ingredient Silicon Valley added to the mix was a new kind of legitimacy to starting one's own company. Hewlett and Packard started it, the Shockley Traitorous Eight set the rules, the semiconductor founders like Sporck and Sanders made it legitimate and the T-shirt tycoons like Bushnell and Jobs made entrepreneuring the highest goal of any young businessman. It was a long way from the days when the dream of the business school graduate was to put forty years in at a corporation in hopes of one day earning a directorship.

It takes guts to start a new company. Even when studies, such as those conducted by Dr. Albert Bruno of Santa Clara University, show that high-technology start-ups are as close to a sure bet as anything in the history of American business (even the fraction that go bankrupt usually make money selling equipment and patents), it still requires considerable courage to start one's company. The commitment is enormous, the stress and long work hours and fear can rob you of your youth, the riches, when they at last arrive, may have lost much of their meaning when you are exhausted and prematurely aged and your family has disintegrated. But even for those for whom entrepreneuring is a tonic, an adrenaline rush, and even for those companies started by teams, there is one common characteristic to entrepreneuring: loneliness. You are out there on the wire, trying to keep your balance in wild gales, fighting off a headlong fall into oblivion. There is never, particularly during the first few years, a hint of safety. The wire is endless, so unless you enjoy heights and perpetually being a breath away from corporate death, you'd best not venture out in the first place.

This image of the loner appears throughout most of the research on entrepreneurs. Robert Lorenzini, founder of a silicon refinery, Siltec Corp. of Menlo Park, California, described a successful entrepreneur as "a pragmatic dreamer, a loner, a person willing to take full responsibility for his or her actions."

But one shouldn't get the impression that entrepreneurs are some kind of devil-may-care business barnstormers. On the contrary the man or woman out on that wire is purposeful, sure of what he or she is doing. One of the greatest myths about entrepreneurs is that they are latter-day riverboat gamblers, betting all their chips on a single roll of the dice. Observers disagree. According to William G. Ouchi, author of the best seller *Theory Z* and professor at the UCLA Graduate School of Management, entrepreneurs see themselves as risk-aversive. "The popular conception to the contrary, the average entrepreneur sees himself as extremely cautious, careful. He knows that, for example, if he orders too much inventory he may be out of business.

"Very few believe they are taking a risk going out on their own. Many enter into an existing business, or prospective customers asked them, or they spun out of existing firms."

Entrepreneuring author and Stanford lecturer Steven Brandt agrees: "I don't know anybody who ever started a deal who didn't think the odds were with him. They aren't gamblers, they don't take the cards and hope for the best. Entrepreneurs don't go around looking for risky deals, they look for opportunities."

This attitude has led some psychologists to question whether entrepreneurs view risk and their own ability to control it differently than the average person. One would suspect however that this self-assurance is rarely innate, but instead the result of experience and a growing sense of competence. Certainly the aggressive, confident style must be there from the start, but it also must be combined with the technical experience needed to come up with a new product idea (or appreciate that of someone else) and the business maturity to know how to raise money from venture capital, rent buildings, hire employees and set up production schedules.

But still, why do it? Money—or, more accurately, *equity*. Equity, in the form of stock options, is the mother's milk of high technology. In a fast-growing industry like electronics, stock far outweighs salary. Why else would someone put up with the endless hours and the vein-bursting stress of working for a new start-up company without the prospect of getting a ten-to-one, perhaps even a hundred-to-one return on investment after a few years? It is estimated that when Apple Computer went public it created as many as a hundred millionaires. Silicon Valley has semimillionaire secretaries and technicians and clerks who got on board a company early enough to get stock at bargain-basement prices.

But equity is more than just money; in fact, it is sometimes never money, just paper. Equity is power, the ability to direct your own life, to be your own boss, to never have to take shit off of anyone ever again (though, with bankers and venture capitalists and stockholders in the world, that's not strictly true).

Power and equity are only as great as last quarter's earnings statement. In order for one to reach the top rung of Silicon Valley entrepreneur-tycoonship, one's company has to survive long enough and grow strong enough to have its first public sale of stock. Though founding an enduring company in Silicon Valley has pretty good odds, building one successful enough to go public is a different story. Out of the perhaps two thousand electronics companies in Silicon Valley, fewer than one hundred are publicly traded.

Experienced entrepreneurs agree the most important job at any new start-up company is keeping a tight rein on cash flow. Too many firms with strong management teams, a brilliant product and a hungry market have been left crippled or dying because they ran out of money somewhere between the time the checks went out for payroll and the checks came in from customers.

Says Charles Askansas, founder and former chairman of microfiche maker Quantor Corp. of Mountain View, California, "In a small company, it can be a disaster if you slip behind your schedule or let inventory or receivables get out of hand. Cash flow is absolutely the first priority."

Stanford's Brandt compares this process to driving with the police right behind you: "You just keep looking at that speedometer, in this case the one labelled 'cash flow'."

But entrepreneur Alan Shugart put it most succinctly in the most famous of Al's Laws for Start-ups: "Cash is more important than your mother."

(Another important lesson is learned too late by some entrepreneurs: Never give away controlling interest of your firm. It was an experience shared by many first time entrepreneurs. Ouchi suggests this is the main reason why there are second-time entrepreneurs.)

Despite their shared traits, those individuals who do take the giant step into entrepreneurship come from a wide range of backgrounds. Some, like Dr. Eugene Amdahl, are soft-spoken, research geniuses. Others are flamboyant and gregarious sales types, like Jerry Sanders. There are kids (Steven Jobs, Bill Gates at Microsoft) and college professors (Dr. William Shockley). Sandra Kurtzig, the best-known woman entrepreneur in the electronics industry, designed the computer software that was the basis for her company, $20 million ASK Corp., in one bedroom of her small apartment while her young children squawked in the other.

Some entrepreneurs are slick con men, wearing Wilkes Bashford suits and adept at selecting fine wines. Others are mumbling engineers in the proverbial Hush Puppies, wearing taped glasses and plastic pocket savers for pens. One venture capitalist was overheard recently plotting a tour for one of his entrepreneurs of East Coast stock analysts. Critical to the plan was the exclusion of dinner meetings, because the young founder "barely knows how to use a fork, for chrissakes."

The question remains, are these goal-oriented, opportunistic individuals an advantage or a weakness in our society? The easy answer is that they are useful, forever creating new inventions that generally improve society, tilt the balance of trade in our direction, create new jobs and counter the effects of economic downturns.

But there is another side to entrepreneurs. When they quit an established firm, they often take the best and brightest with them—crippling the firm that spent considerable time and money training those employees. And, of course, some entrepreneurs also leave with trade secrets.

Further, despite their innovativeness and vitality, new start-up firms lack one thing larger firms have: economies of scale. Big firms, by building in volume, can build cheaper. That's how the Japanese, with their skill at large organizations, have taken over nearly half of the computer memory chip market. In the ever changing modern world innovation is crucial, but so is the ability to form huge multinational companies that can tap large, distant markets. The same American spirit that gives rise to entrepreneurs also chips away at the foundations of our largest firms. Will the jobs lost at the latter be balanced by those created by the former? Perhaps, but will it be the same workers?

Finally, few new start-ups perform original research. Rather most take the ideas from large research institutions or corporate laboratories and convert them into mass-producible, mass-marketable items—so-called value-added products. Certainly this is a boon for the consumer, but at what cost to basic research in this country when most of the reward and much of the talent goes to the new start-ups?

One thing seems certain. The Age of the Entrepreneur is with us, and will be for a long time. Though subject to the swings of the venture capital market, the trend is upward. Each year more and more men and women with dreams flood venture capitalists with business proposals.

Says Brandt of Stanford, "In 1965, only 5000 MBAs graduated. Last year [1982] it was 600,000. That means that there are a lot of people walking around now who know how to do basic business . . . Used to be you had to be old and gray to start a company, now you can do it after two years of school. You don't have to be a Commodore Vanderbilt learning from 40 years of hard knocks."

With their achievements now coming with comparative youth, what will happen to today's entrepreneurs as they grow old and gray? It's hard to say, because there is so little precedent. They can't go on starting new companies forever, the stress is too great. If people like Packard are any indication, the next logical step after entrepreneurship is philanthropy and politics.

One can only wonder what type of political punch this present crop of young entrepreneurs will have when it awakens to politics in a decade or so . . .

*   *   *

Despite the fact that a new company is considered to be a new start for its founders, its future can often be predicted by which established firm it chooses to emulate. While companies copy the hard-charging style of Intel or National Semiconductor, it can be argued that the most successful and admired firms in Silicon Valley are those which have either spunoff from (Tandem, Apple) or modeled themselves after (Rolm) Hewlett-Packard Co.

Rolm Corp. (for years, the company tried to convince the press to print it ROLM, as in AT&T) was founded in 1969 by four alumni of Rice University: Gene *R*icheson, Ken *O*shman, Walter *L*oewenstern, Jr., and Robert *M*axfield. The young men weren't close friends during their Rice years; in fact for the most part they hardly knew one another. Only when they all ended up in Silicon Valley were the connections made.

As Loewenstern told the Rice alumni newsletter:

> The whole thing really got started when I quit at Sylvania. The reason I left was that I was interested in a business opportunity that Sylvania had turned down. My supervisor said either to stop looking at the idea or quit, so I quit. I started doing some consulting and thinking about starting a company. Ken approached me and said, "Let's do something together." I said "Okay, but let's make it something interesting." We made business plans and were thinking of going into lots of areas. The product was Gene's idea.

> *Oshman:* When we started the company, Gene, who was working on military systems, told us that many people were in the minicomputer area but not many were making minicomputers that could be used by the Defense Department in the field. Our logic was that if we could make our minicomputers more cheaply and of good quality, we would be successful . . .

The result, said Oshman, was "a general-purpose digital computer, with software and peripherals—very reliable for offshore and military uses." The computer, based around the Data General Eclipse, was designed out of standard parts but constructed in such a way as to be able to withstand wide variations in temperature and humidity, as well as be resistant to shock and dust—the kind of computer that could be taken ashore on a landing craft and then carried into battle aboard a jeep or tank.

Obviously Rolm's idea was a good one, because the computer shortly became the standard for the German, South Korean and Taiwanese navies as well as the de facto standard of the U.S. Navy. But in the beginning, the young company had good reason to doubt if it would even survive. For one thing, the Vietnam War was winding down, and as usual the U.S. military was cutting itself back to the bone. Secondly, the company had one hell of a time trying to raise money from venture capitalists who could see only a bunch of inexperienced businessmen, a fraternity of ex-college kids, trying to bust into an untested market populated at the time by only a few giants like IBM.

In the end, Rolm was founded in June 1969 with just seventy-five thousand dollars—and, in a nearly mythical beginning for a Santa Clara County firm, Rolm's first building was an abandoned prune-drying shed. Oshman assumed the presidency. The founders worked feverishly, and by November the company had more than a dozen employees and its first working prototype. At twenty thousand dollars the new Rolm "mil-spec" computer was less than half the price of its nearest competitor. Still, it took several years for the company to break into the club of military contractors.

By 1974, Rolm had reached $6 million in annual sales. Like most firms, it could have stuck with the product line it knew and enjoyed a nice, comfortable growth for many years, riding out periodic cutbacks and slowly growing to $100 million in sales before selling out to a larger defense contractor.

Instead, in a breathtaking move, the company completely changed direction. Like Amdahl, Rolm decided to take on a giant, in this case AT&T. And, just like Amdahl, Rolm decided to hit its opponent in its weak spot, at the "central processors" of its system, its switchboards (PBXs), by using the latest technology to improve performance yet drive down costs.

The strategy not only worked, it turned into one of the success stories of the electronics industry. In its first year selling PBXs, Rolm made $6 million from those products, but by 1983 these products and their descendants made up more than 90 percent of the company's sales. So popular were these systems that by the end of the seventies they could be found at nearly every one of the nation's top one hundred companies. In mid-1983, Rolm had installed more than eleven thousand of these systems. Not surprisingly, in these years Rolm was the fastest growing public corporation in Silicon Valley.

But for that kind of growth, having good products isn't enough. It also requires extraordinary management, talented and prescient enough to anticipate the "walls" blocking growth at $10 million and $100 million in sales and be ready to meet them. A number of firms in Silicon Valley have had superb products but stalled at one of these two breaking points.

Credit for this remarkable achievement goes to the top management of the firm, notably Oshman. As a Merrill Lynch analyst told *Business Week* in 1981, "They have done as good a job managing the company as they have in designing and building their products." Stanford business professor Steven C. Wheelwright would add, "Rolm has always been more systematic [than other companies]. Time and again, [it] has managed to anticipate the problems that come with growth."

One important reason why Rolm was so successful was that it treated its people well. As Oshman wrote: "The humanity and challenge of the Rolm work environment is predicated on a dual responsibility. Rolm Corporation acts to provide equal opportunity to grow and be promoted; fair treatment for each individual; respect for personal privacy; encouragement to succeed; opportunity for creativity; evaluation based on job performance in the context of the Rolm philosophy."

This is pretty gutsy stuff, particularly the part about respect for personal privacy. And Oshman wasn't all talk. The facility Rolm built for itself in Santa Clara became, thanks to wire service photographs, famous throughout the world. And with good reason. Some grimy steelworker sauntering out of a belching northeast steel mill in the freezing rain would open up the evening paper and read about this California company whose buildings looked more like botanical gardens than a factory. He would read about the tree-lined creeks gurgling between airy, wood-beamed offices and manufacturing buildings and splashing down little waterfalls as employees walked over wooden bridges on their way to the gym.

The gym! This was the photograph that made the winter cold all the more bitter. Here were handsome men and beautiful women sitting in a hot tub or swimming in a pool or lifting weights or playing racket ball or shooting baskets in the full-sized gymnasium. These weren't executives either, but workers just like him who happened to be lucky enough to work for a company out West called Rolm.

The Rolm gymnasium was easily the most conspicuous part of Rolm's employee-support program. But in many ways it was the least important. The key to Rolm lay in its daily treatment of the employees —not in the big grandstand play but in the tiny details.

One need only walk around Rolm to see that philosophy was in practice. The gym, an employee cafeteria that was more of a restaurant, the carefully tended office and manufacturing areas, the friendliness of the employees matched by an equal reserve that indicated that Rolm people felt as though they were part of a team, and, most of all, an intense loyalty. These were the things that made Rolm another shining example of how a company can be both successful and oriented toward its employees.

In the early eighties, Rolm again began to change course, building on its existing expertise in telecommunications to jump into the office automation business. It was a clever strategy.

The company is still in the midst of that transition, which will take most of the eighties. The firm is also showing signs of maturity. The new, unbridled AT&T is not going to play with kid gloves anymore. Rolm got a taste of that in the first quarter of 1984, when a phone company employees strike kept Rolm's systems from going on line for three weeks—resulting in only a 7 percent increase in sales over the year before and a 64 percent drop in net income. Even perfect Rolm, it seemed, could be hurt by a changing market.

Still, there was ample evidence that the rest of the world saw Rolm's downturn as only a temporary setback in a long, ever climbing path. After all, in less than fifteen years the company had grown from seventy-five thousand dollars and a prune-drying shed to more than $500 million in sales and more than seven thousand employees scattered around the world. The stock market showed its faith in Rolm by giving its stock, even during the downturn, an extraordinary forty-three-to-one price–earnings ratio—which gave Rolm a market value of $1.6 billion.

But the best confirmation of Rolm's true value came in mid-1983, when IBM agreed to purchase nearly 4 million new shares of Rolm stock for about $230 million. IBM had done this once before, a few months earlier, with Intel—and it was considered an indication that America's largest technology company had anointed these two firms as the best in their fields, as future partners in the combined computer/ chip/telecom market of the future, and was guaranteeing to back them. Just what IBM had in mind was a matter of considerable speculation— but by the end of the year, two IBM executives had been nominated to the Rolm board of directors.

That, it turned out, was only IBM's opening gambit. With AT&T newly trimmed and unleashed on the open market, Big Blue wanted more than just friendly telecommunications equipment. It wanted Rolm, lock, stock and volleyball net. So, in mid-1984, Rolm stopped being a Silicon Valley firm and became merely another brick in the monolith of IBM.

In retrospect, if one complaint could have been leveled at Rolm it was that it was rather dull. A good place to play basketball maybe, but a little too straight. The only quirkiness in the company had been Richeson, who'd taken riches and retired to do volunteer work with Creative Initiatives, a religious and philosophical organization that advocated world peace and fellowship. This cult for professionals was a big hit among engineers in the mid-1970s and rainbow-colored "Bless Man" and "We are One" bumpers were sported all over the Valley. Now that was kinky, but once Richeson left, Rolm went back to button-down sobriety. Oshman just wasn't a hoot-and-holler type, and the company was so damn organized it seemed to have worked out all the interesting creases.

No wonder IBM bought it.

But across the valley, in Cupertino, the other Hewlett-Packard imitator had enough wrinkles for both firms. This was Tandem Computer, founded in 1974 by James Treybig, two technical people (James Katzman and Michael Green) and financial whiz John Loustanou—all of them from HP. There probably never was a more eccentric crew that ever started a Fortune 500 company. Cowboy Jimmy Treybig, with his easygoing manner and country drawl, seemed like a hayseed from Clarendon, Texas, come to Silicon Valley to teach them city slickers a lesson. Loustanou, on the other hand, was a figure out of Noël Coward drawing room comedy, the George Sanders of high tech.

Eccentricities aside, these guys were pros, and they built themselves a monster company. Treybig in particular was often underestimated. As one vice-president said, "a lot of people when they meet Jim for the first time think he's a bullshitter, just shuckin' and jivin'." That attitude was easy to understand when Treybig created his own version of the HP corporate philosophy:

—All people are good.

—People, workers, management and company are all the same thing.

—Every single person in a company must understand the essence of the business.

—Every company must benefit from the company's success.

—You must create an environment where all of the above can happen.

To read this blue-sky philosophy and then to meet Treybig, with his drawl and shirttails hanging out, was to find yourself questioning how Tandem could have been successful. A New York *Times* reporter was stunned when, after years of interviewing stiff company presidents, Treybig showed him some snapshots taken on a recent trip of a shirtless Jimmy T. (as Treybig is called), beer belly hanging out and swigging from a bottle of beer, and asked, "How about this one for the employee newsletter?"

But Treybig was dumb like a fox. Behind the country-boy persona was a driven, aggressive and extremely competent businessman with a Stanford M.B.A. and years of experience at TI and HP and in venture capital. So sharp was he, in fact, that the prediction he made in his 1974 business plan for Tandem's sales in 1979 was off by only $1 million. In other words he had, before the company was born, planned for sales to double every year to $56 million in 1979. This wasn't good planning, it was divination.

Treybig had first gotten the idea for Tandem after he left Hewlett-Packard in 1973 to join venture capital firm Kleiner, Perkins, Caufield, Byers in San Francisco. At HP, says Treybig, he first ran into customers, such as banks, that needed a computer that would never break down. "What I saw was that to get a system that wouldn't fail, customers were spending large amounts of money to modify the computers themselves."

With $1 million in Kleiner Perkins money, Treybig and his three partners founded Tandem in November 1974. Six years later the company broke $100 million in sales. That was just about as fast as a company could go.

The key was the product: a computer system that theoretically never broke down.

The solution Tandem found was a skillful combination of hardware and software. Two central processors operated redundantly and were linked through special software that switched control back and forth in the event that one of the processors broke down and needed to be repaired. As most computers were relatively reliable anyway, the chance of both processors breaking down at the same time was minute.

At least that's the way Tandem told it. Others, like industry analyst David Gold, suggested that the main reason people bought the Tandem computers was their fine software. "Fail-safe is just a great marketing and advertising ploy."

Either way, for its first six years in business, Tandem appeared to operate in a market with no rivals—and the company seemed to grow like a monopoly. Between 1974 and 1982, the company just about doubled its sales every year, breaking $300 million in 1982.

Again, as with Rolm, it took an extraordinary corporate environment to maintain the kind of explosive growth that would have blown most companies apart. As with Rolm, the key for Tandem was a modified HP Way. Tandem became famous for its swimming pool and its Friday afternoon beer busts. Other HP programs Tandem adopted included flexible hours, pushing responsibility down through the ranks, promoting from within. Tandem also took ideas from elsewhere: it shared with Rolm the Intel concept of a sabbatical after several years of service.

But Tandem carried the process one step further—one step too far, according to some detractors. Treybig sometimes seemed almost obsessed with forming a new corporate gestalt at Tandem, creating a mandatory two-day course on the company philosophy and even a book called *Understanding Our Philosophy.* He dreamed aloud about building a Tandem University where employees could live their whole lives around the sense of community created by working at Tandem. In reaction to what he felt was too many meetings and too much paper work at HP, Treybig created at Tandem an atmosphere so casual that no formal meetings ever occurred.

Yet it worked. Tandem grew like crazy. Its turnover was one of the lowest in Silicon Valley. The press was entranced by the whole crazy mess, the Executive Hunk contests and the beer busts and all the twists in a company that seemed so disorganized but yet roared toward a billion dollars in annual sales. Only *Fortune* hit a negative note when it suggested that Treybig's people-oriented style was a little more cynical than it looked on the surface—a Californicated version of

> the so-called Hawthorne effect, an increase in productivity that appears to result from *any* new attention paid to employees' working conditions or amenities. Even the beer bust, in terms of the current fashion for fostering unstructured communication across an institution's vertical and horizontal boundaries, is arguably a productivity ploy.
>
> Also hardly novel is soaking employees in an endless stream of company-boosting propaganda urging loyalty, hard work, self-esteem, and respect for co-workers . . .

Undoubtedly, much of that was true. But so was the counterargument that Tandem's well-educated employees could see through any overt attempts to manipulate them and would vote with their feet—which they hadn't done. Further, it was apparent that Treybig and his staff seemed to believe their own platitudes and lived them—so that if anyone was being manipulated it was the manipulators themselves.

There was a lot of talk about the efficacy of the Tandem corporate philosophy during the days when the firm was flying high. After all, one of the great Silicon Valley truths is that success covers up mistakes that failure throws into sharp relief.

That acid test came in 1982 and 1983. Suddenly Tandem, which had operated almost unmolested in its market, found itself under attack from every direction. Big guns like IBM and Digital Equipment announced high reliability computers. And the same time Tandem was attacked from below by a host of new start-ups, including two Valley firms, Tolerant Systems and Synapse, and most notably Stratus Inc. of Massachusetts, composed of ex-Tandem employees. Then Tandem suffered the embarrassment of having to restate and downgrade its 1982 results because it had improperly tallied orders that had not yet been shipped. The company's grow rate fell to "just" 50 percent. The slump continued into 1983. Tandem's stock at one point fell 45 percent and industry watchers questioned whether the company had finally grown beyond the control of its management style. Said David Gold, "That gunslinging management style doesn't seem to be working as well as it used to."

Treybig appeared to wonder about the same thing as he began to tighten the company's internal controls and turn the place into a more mainline firm. Observers waited to see if the funky Tandem style would survive.

* * *

In the beautiful Mark Hopkins Hotel, atop San Francisco's Nob Hill, the Western Association of Venture Capitalists—"the California Mafia"—meets monthly to talk shop and to hear presentations from politicians or the presidents of Silicon Valley firms the members control.

The setting is elegant, the conversation convivial. Nothing could be more at odds with the fiercely competitive and engineer-ascetic life-style of Silicon Valley, forty miles to the south. Yet this is the other, hidden, half of a symbiotic relationship that makes the Valley possible. Perhaps no tighter relationship exists in American industry than this one between electronic entrepreneurs and those crapshoot investors who not only give them money and eventually take them public but hold their hands during the years in between.

Ever since the 1960s, West Coast venture capital firms have been closely tied with Silicon Valley firms, the success of each dependent upon the other. In those early days, only a few investors in the nation had the risk-taking attitude and the technological expertise needed to back a state-of-the-art electronics firm. Some were East Coasters who migrated west. Others were homegrown Valley executives who crossed over. These individuals cut their teeth in the early Silicon Valley wars.

Some individuals, such as Arthur Rock, Fred Adler and William "Pitch" Johnson, and such firms as Hambrecht & Quist and Kleiner, Perkins, Caufield & Byers, have become well known for their ability to spot young winners. But for the most part, it is an anonymous industry. Like all good bankers, venture capitalists tend to seek a low profile, keeping their names out of the newspapers, except of course for the tombstone ads announcing a company going public and on the 10K forms listing major company shareholders. It is also very democratic. The opinions of some venture capitalists are more highly respected than others, "But," says David L. Anderson, general partner of Sutter Hill Ventures, "I don't believe that because Kleiner-Perkins or the Mayfield Fund turns down somebody that everybody else will too."

It is this strange-bedfellows arrangement that has made Silicon Valley work. The frantic competition and wild-eyed self-aggrandizement of the electronics industry is countered by the collusive, genteel and invisible venture capital industry supporting it. But the nature of each industry makes those characteristics necessary. Silicon Valley must be competitive to survive, coming up with new innovative products and companies that can only be built by the aggressive, paranoid, maverick minds of entrepreneurs.

The members of the venture industry, on the other hand, need one another. Few can (or would) put up all the venture money or have all the technical expertise needed for a new start-up. So they create consortiums among themselves, swapping information at the monthly WAVC meetings or in the Sun Deck cafeteria at 3000 Sand Hill Road in Menlo Park, the home of more than a dozen venture capital firms and the center of the business on the West Coast.

Nevertheless, "you can't really call us a cabal because sometimes we work together and sometimes we compete," says Thomas Perkins, Kleiner-Perkins's general partner.

In the eighties, the venture capital industry has changed, a victim of its own success. Though the old fraternal feelings survive on Sand Hill Road, the venture capital "family" of a decade ago is becoming a memory. There were a number of reasons for this change, among them the new investment laws adopted after the 1974 recession, which made venture capital more appealing to outsiders. But just as important, by helping turn the Valley into an investment paradise, the local venture firms caught the eye of East Coast and European investors, such as Citicorp, Fireman's Fund, Allstate Insurance, the Hillman Co., and Burr Eagan Deleague.

The result was that by 1978 Silicon Valley was awash with money. A lot of capital flowed into electronics—$681 million committed to private venture firms in 1980, $1.4 billion in 1982, according to *Venture Capital Journal.* A third of that went to Silicon Valley alone. The total venture capital funding (including invested and uninvested funds from banks and corporations) jumped from $5.8 billion in 1981 to $7.5 billion a year later.

"One reason for the increasing interest," wrote the *Peninsula Times Tribune,* "is that few other investments can match venture capital returns on an annually compounded basis. Apple Computer Inc., one of venture capital's best known success stories, reportedly returned some $240 to its venture capitalists for every $1 invested." The first Hambrecht & Quist investment fund, operating during the 1970s, returned on investment an average of 29.8 percent per year, compounded. The next one, begun in 1979, returned an amazing 59.9 percent per year during its first two years.

Added Michael Child of TA Associates in Palo Alto, "You don't need to invest in very many Tandons [a company in Southern California] or Tandems to do very well for yourself or your investors."

But this new money changed the complexion of the venture business. The days of the old clique were clearly numbered, and though the established firms still worked with one another and formed consortiums, there was a new, almost unseemly competitiveness in the venture industry. Outside investors, though still shying away from the chancier first-round investments, were driving down the requirements and pushing up the dollar amounts of second-round infusions, forcing the oldline local venture firms to match.

This was not a positive thing. Though the new recipient start-ups clearly enjoyed this unexpected bonanza, it wasn't good for them. Competition in the venture capital business is not as salutary as in electronics. For one thing, according to Don Cvietusa, a vice-president of Bank of America, this flush of money "makes entrepreneurs a little less cautious than they ought to be. They know it's no problem to get money now and they've gotten sloppy . . . Too much money is toxic to the entrepreneurial environment."

Then about this time the 1981 recession hit.

For entrepreneurs, recessions are traditionally fertile times. Boom periods give budding entrepreneurs an incentive to start a new company —an idea that reaches the end of its gestation period about the time the economy slumps. In other cases, newly laid-off engineers and managers find themselves with a lot of time to plot and plan. Finally, there is an element of self-fulfilling prophecy, in which entrepreneurs believe that recessions are good times to start firms because they provide a respite to get manufacturing up to speed.

Unfortunately, prior to 1981 there was often one ingredient missing from the recipe: capital. Usually, as in 1974, recessions see a precipitous drop in investment money. But 1981 was different: Valley business slumped, yet there was an unexpected glut of venture capital.

Thus all of the elements were in place, and the resulting explosion in new start-ups pushed the venture capital firms—old and new—into near-panic. Venture firms, when they should have been training new employees, began carrying their usual load of new firms and, pressured by the largesse of the parvenu venture firms, began making rushed investment decisions. The result was a lot of money chasing a few good firms, overcapitalization of some less than needy firms and, worst, unwise investments. Outside consultants, like David Gold, normally giving well-considered judgments on new technologies, increasingly found themselves hired over the phone to race over, check out a new firm and call back with a snap judgment.

Needless to say, on the reverse side, it was probably the most hospitable time in history to start a new company in Silicon Valley. New Valley companies sprouted like mushrooms, stuffing the rent-a-room industrial parks thrown up to hold them.

"There were a lot of deals made that shouldn't have been done," Gold recalls. That fact became apparent in 1982 when the recession continued. Gold, speaking at the time, said, "I can think off the top of my head of maybe a half dozen new firms that are in trouble right now." In the rush to invest, even experienced firms like Kleiner-Perkins missed recognizing instances in which the entrepreneurs misrepresented, often unconsciously, information on their business plan.

It is too soon to estimate the number of weak or dying firms that were born in the venture capital boom of the early eighties. Some may take years to succumb. Dr. Albert Bruno at Santa Clara University notes a growing number of venture capitalists "yanking" top executives at new firms—indicative of a growing dissatisfaction with performance.

According to Kenneth W. Rind, venture capitalists spend about 70 percent of their time providing their start-ups with additional assistance. But with the added case load of 1980–81 those firms got a smaller share. Worse, this reduced aid came at a critical time, because, if only from sheer numbers, the quality of entrepreneurs declined. These weren't the company presidents branching out on their own, as in the sixties, but engineers and software designers and salesmen hoping for the Big Score. Says Stan Pratt, publisher of *Venture Capital Journal,* "Venture capitalists were spoiled from '74 to '79 because they were financing only exceptional entrepreneurs, and because there weren't too many out there."

But these new start-ups and their investors won't be the only ones hurt by that frenzied period. Many of these firms became cash holes, with good investment money chasing after bad to keep them afloat. Even good new companies required extra injections of capital to get through the enduring recession. Says Pratt, "You can start up a company in a recession, but you hope like hell when you're ready to ship that your customer will be ready to buy."

In 1982 and most of 1983, the customer wasn't. New issues slipped to $620 million from $2.7 billion the year before, as venture firms found themselves with less money to spare for new companies.

Venture capital, like Silicon Valley, is a cyclical business, with the venture people usually a half cycle out of synch with the manufacturers. As 1983 closed with the economy booming, the venture business began to dig itself out. There's nothing like a good economic upturn to cover the weaknesses of even the lousiest company. And, of course, there was more work to do. "The number of new start-up proposals is accelerating," said Perkins. Added Anderson of Sutter Hill, "There are a lot of people out there who deserve backing. I don't see any limit in the number of good business proposals."

As for making money, that has never been a problem in the venture capital business. Arguably it is the most successful high-tech business of them all, with a continuous record of success for twenty years. Even the problems of the early eighties only meant enormous profits rather than spectacular ones.

That fact alone caused some grumbling in Silicon Valley. No one, of course, wanted the funds to dry up. But many observers, even some recipients, began to ask if Gordon Moore's phrase "vulture capital" might be correct. They suggested that the venture capital industry was less interested in creating new businesses than in raiding established companies, building "me too" products and propping up their new start-ups only long enough to take them public and cash out. "How many successful companies more than eight years old do you see in Silicon Valley?" asked one new start-up executive. "Not many. That's because the venture boys are not interested in building companies that last. Everyone points at the Japanese for stealing America's intellectual wealth—but most of these venture capitalists are just as bad. They're selling out American business over the long term for their own short-term gains . . . and yet they end up in the press looking like heroes."

When asked if that was indeed true, and why he had accepted $5 million in venture money, the executive argued that his particular case was different. His firm, he said, was going to last.

Meanwhile, the venture capital industry hurtles forward, as it will for many years to come, the "hiccup" of 1980–82 becoming a memory, one about which these tycoons can happily reminisce at the monthly meeting at the Mark Hopkins—their closest brush with competitive business, Silicon Valley style.

* * *

Tracking the growth of the small computer industry is like attempting to chart the path of every atomic particle in a nuclear chain reaction. At best, only general trends can be discerned, and even then most detail is lost in the heat and light.

The small computer revolution can be said to have begun with the first IBM, HP and Digital Equipment minicomputers in the late 1960s, or with the HP and Texas Instruments programmable pocket calculators in the early seventies, or with the first hobby computers (such as Altair) in the mid-1970s or with the Apple I in 1975 or the Apple II in 1977. Some might even argue that history will recall only one event: IBM's introduction of the PC personal computer in 1982, which coalesced the industry and made the personal computer legitimate in the public's mind.

It is difficult to figure out not only when the industry began but even what happened. First there was the minicomputer industry, which struggled for acceptance of its products in the mainframe world. And there were supplemental companies like Four-Phase Systems, Inc. (the only major early Fairchild spin-off company not in chips) and Tymshare, with innovative ideas in networking.

Then, about the time that the minicomputer industry finally became settled into some kind of coherence, with $50,000 to $100,000 machines capable of running an office or department, along came personal computers and muddied the scene all over again. Only this time, instead of a dozen minicomputer companies, there were perhaps two hundred personal computer companies building products ranging from tiny introductory computers priced under a hundred dollars which hooked up to a television to twenty-five-thousand-dollar "supermicros" which infringed on the territory once exclusively owned by minicomputers. Not only that, but there were perhaps twice as many companies building peripheral memory and output devices for these computers and several score more beyond that making the platters and films used in these disk drives, tape drives and printers.

There were also dozens of companies specializing in perishable supplies, like paper and ribbon, used by these computers, and thousands of personal computer retail stores. To these were added thousands of companies, large and small, designing software for these computers, and hundreds more making hardware, such as plug-in memory boards or telephone modems. And this didn't even count the people writing and publishing computer magazines and books or building desk furniture to hold personal computers, or printing Apple logo decals or computer-screen covers to reduce eyestrain or running computer summer camps or giving seminars on how to do one's income tax on a home computer or giving speeches on how personal computers would be the savior/ death of mankind.

The only way to give some glimmering of what all of this energy was about is to profile some of the Silicon Valley companies and characters involved in the small-computer boom. It is also important to realize that by the end of 1983, as was apparent to every one of the seventy-five thousand people at the Las Vegas Comdex computer show, the crazy game was all but over. Now the New Order was to line up behind IBM —that is, become compatible with IBM software—and try to stay alive.

Nevertheless, it was fun while it lasted.

William Stevens was middle-aged and unemployed when he founded Triad Systems in 1972. "I had a wife, three children, a little stock and was within one month of turning 40," he later told *Forbes.* "I got fired on Thursday, cleaned out my desk on Friday and on Saturday I rented office space and started working on a business plan." It was Burton McMurtry, the man who brought together the Rolm team and by then a venture capitalist, who lent Stevens and two partners $250,000 to get the company started. And even McMurtry didn't think Stevens's idea was viable—to sell low-priced (twenty-five-thousand-dollar) inventory-control computers to auto parts wholesalers. Admitted McMurtry later, "I didn't think it could be done, but I figured Stevens would find something better to do."

But Stevens stuck to his plan, shipping the first Triad computers in July 1973 to a nearby U-Haul parts wholesaler. One of the partners delivered the machine by hand. Ten years later Triad had sales of $56 million.

Fast growth was hardly what made Triad unique in Silicon Valley. It was unusual, however, that in generally nonreligious Silicon Valley, nearly every employee in the company belonged to the same church in Redwood City. At breaks and lunchtime, numerous employees could be seen in the cafeteria reading the Bible.

Faith—in his own competence—also was key to Stevens's success. When Triad went public in 1980, he instantly became worth more than $10 million. The naysayers proven wrong, Stevens could then say, "We've done a simple thing. In some ways it was very low risk."

Ken Eldred was a second-generation Silicon Valley success story—probably the first of many. His father, Noel, spent thirty years helping Bill Hewlett and Dave Packard build their company, eventually becoming a vice-president. Initially, Ken's career took him as far as possible from high technology, into plumbing equipment. But in 1975, Eldred decided it was high time to start his own company. While at Stanford business school he had developed a list of seventeen things that made a firm successful and he wanted to put them to a test.

So, in November 1975, Eldred and Jim Willemborg, a salesman at Data General, started Inmac Inc. with five-thousand dollars in start-up money. Willemborg wanted to stay employed at Data General, so the two men met every morning from 7:30 to 9:30 to decide on products and write catalog copy for their new company, which, they decided, would sell computer and office equipment. By 1980 the firm had 250 employees and forty thousand customers, including every Fortune 500 firm. Eldred, his father's son, also put into practice many of the management techniques he had seen as a boy at HP—the most visible being the famous HP morning doughnuts and fruit in every office.

Sandra Kurtzig was a Ph.D. in chemical engineering when she found herself a bored mother of two stuck in a little apartment in Silicon Valley. Out of frustration she decided to try her hand at writing software. The result, called MANMAN, was designed to help owners of HP 3000 minicomputers handle many of the resource management activities in a medium-sized firm, such as scheduling and inventory control.

HP loved MANMAN and with its help, Kurtzig built ASK Inc., probably the most successful software firm in Silicon Valley. When ASK went public in 1982, now multimillionaire Kurtzig became not only one of the first women in American history to take a company public but also the first woman president of a large Silicon Valley firm.

Englishman John Peers had an idea that what the world needed was a business computer priced under twenty-thousand-dollars that spoke in English commands. The result was Adam. But Peers made his fortune, and in the process seemed to be having a wonderful time. For example, the cover of the brochure for the Adam computer showed a very naked and very blond Eve sitting before the computer and taking a bite out of an apple. During this period, Peers also wrote a book of mottos and one-liners that included such worthy aphorisms as "A Smith & Wesson beats four aces." The book was even reviewed favorably in *Fortune* and *The Wall Street Journal,* which was more than could be said for the company. When last seen, Peers was walking a robot down a Silicon Valley sidewalk before excited television camera crews.

Dan Fylstra was twenty-six years old and fresh out of Harvard Business School when he founded Personal Software Inc., now called Visicorp. He was armed with a business plan he developed in grad school for a company that would market personal computer software in the same way a publisher did books, acquiring the rights from the author and adding sophisticated marketing and distribution.

With the help of his wife, whose family founded Grove Press, and a handful of computer games, Fylstra launched Personal Software in February 1978. Publicity came from ads in *Byte* magazine, the personal computer programmer's bible, which Fylstra helped found.

The games were a moderate success, but the business plan was brilliant. All the company needed was to find the right software program out there on some programmer's kitchen table. As it turned out the answer was much closer at hand: two of Fylstra's acquaintances from his days at MIT and Harvard had designed a program intended to be the equivalent of graph paper on the screen of a personal computer. With it, the user could quickly develop tables and graphs and modify the entries.

The software program was called VisiCalc, and Fylstra believed in it so much he took the firm's entire sales to date—one hundred thousand dollars—and spent it marketing Visicalc. He wasn't the only person who believed in Visicalc; a few months later, Arthur Rock, the king of venture capitalists, teamed up with the Rockefeller venture fund (Venrock) and invested five hundred thousand more in Fylstra's company, later renamed Visicorp.

Rock is rarely wrong. Visicalc went on to become the best-selling personal computer software in history, the software that legitimized personal computers in the office and earned for itself the software industry's first "gold cassette," the computer equivalent of a gold record.

From its beginning, Commodore was easily the most mysterious company in Silicon Valley. Any company registered in the Bahamas, Canadian-incorporated but based in Santa Clara, California, then Norristown, Pennsylvania has got to be the subject of suspicion. Then there was the firm's pudgy, bald-headed president, Jack Tramiel, famous for statements like "Business is war" and "Real business is sex. It's one on one." Obviously a sweet guy. Tramiel had been involved in the 1965 bankruptcy of Atlantic Acceptance, one of the nastiest business scandals in Canadian history. Atlantic's president, Powell Morgan, had also been chairman of Commodore and no doubt would have gone to jail for defrauding investors of millions had he not died. The final report of the Ontario Supreme Court on the matter had concluded that Tramiel and Commodore were implicated in the mess.

Tramiel and Commodore, then just a small typewriter and adding machine company, were never prosecuted. Instead, the company moved to California and kept growing. As for Tramiel, he remained the tough competitor he had been since he had walked out alive from Auschwitz and started a little typewriter repair shop in the Bronx.

With the help of Canadian investor (later chairman) Irving Gould, Tramiel began building Commodore into a powerhouse adding machine company. But a trip to Japan to find a manufacturer for his designs convinced Tramiel that electronic calculators were the wave of the future. He quickly signed up some Japanese calculator makers to let him sell their products in America under the Commodore name. By 1969, Commodore was building its own calculators and making a reputation for itself with low-priced (and somewhat flimsy) models featuring an incredible array of mathematical functions.

Caught in the crunch of 1974 with an unusable inventory of chips, Tramiel swore never to let that happen again. So he bought his own chip house, the failing MOS Technology, in 1976. The luck that had enveloped Tramiel his whole life held, because MOS had the rights to the 6502 microprocessor, the seminal chip of the personal computer era. Two months later Tramiel had a prototype. It was called the Commodore Pet and it was the first personal computer to be priced under a thousand dollars. It was a primitive machine, but in 1977 when it was introduced the Pet was a revelation, particularly in Europe, where it swept the market.

Commodore followed in 1982 with the VIC 20, priced under three hundred dollars and hawked on television first by Captain Kirk himself, William Shatner, and then with a brilliant series of ads comparing Atari games with Commodore educational programs that drilled right into the naked nerve of guilt in every American parent. The VIC 20 was one of the most popular personal computers ever made and it propelled Commodore over the $1 billion mark by 1984, making it the largest seller of personal computers.

In early 1984, never one to lose its edge, Commodore introduced the 444, a personal computer system featuring built-in software and priced below five hundred dollars targeted to compete with the Coleco Adam and the IBM PC*jr*. Once again response was enthusiastic.

But if Commodore was a successful company, it was hardly the place one went to work with long-term career plans. It often seemed that the only person happy at the company was Tramiel himself, whose autocratic, top-down style inflicted on Commodore one of the fastest executive turnover rates in the Valley. The company was also notorious for dragging out its bill-paying, particularly to smaller, more vulnerable vendors. Even *Forbes* publicly mused about whether Tramiel had really changed from the Atlantic Acceptance days.

If it wasn't a nice place to work, no one could argue that Commodore wasn't a success. As the shadow of IBM fell over the small computer business from one end to the other, forcing companies to either join its team or die, Commodore always seemed one step ahead. That was

Tramiel's doing, and many wondered how much longer he could keep it up.

Not much longer, in fact. In March 1984, he mysteriously resigned, citing Commodore's need for a "professional executive." The likely reason was a battle for control between chairman Gould and Tramiel.

True to form, Tramiel, the Valley's great Underground Man, disappeared. On the still surface of the Valley, competitors, enemies and allies waited anxiously for three months for the man to again burst into the open.

It occurred at the unlikely spot of Adac Laboratories in Sunnyvale, a little-known and financially ailing ($6.9 million lost on $12 million sales for the quarter ended December 31, 1983) maker of X-ray imaging systems. Tramiel, with two family members (including the stockbroker son who introduced him to the firm), quickly controlled 7 percent of the firm and demanded a position on the board of directors.

The timing of this earthshaking reappearance of Tramiel was too perfect: two days before the Valley had been hit by its largest earthquake in twenty-five years. The quake beat up Adac's new San Jose facility sufficiently to delay the company's move there by two weeks.

Still, Adac seemed a small-ticket game for a high roller like Tramiel. Many longtime Valley watchers predicted that the move was merely a penny-ante play to keep Tramiel's hand in until he found a more worthy high-stakes bet.

They were right. On July 2, 1984, Tramiel bought the shattered shell of Atari, one of the Valley's most famous firms and one of Commodore's biggest competitors. Tramiel acquired Atari for $240 million in ten-year and twelve-year notes—in other words, almost nothing up front—an indication of how anxious Warner's was to distance itself from its debacle.

Now, with no chairman or stockholders to hold him back, Jack Tramiel, fifty-five, Nazi death camp survivor and former typewriter repairman, had the proper vehicle to pursue his secret, but apparently infinite, ambition.

Probably the best thing that ever happened to computer color graphic display maker Ramtek Corp. of Santa Clara was that its $7 million manufacturing facility burned up in 1976. And not because the company received insurance money, either: it had let the insurance policy lapse the month before.

The company had been founded in 1971 by five aerospace engineers to build computer terminals featuring color imaging and crisp graphics. The company grew by "bootstrapping"—plowing profits back into manufacturing—and borrowing money, according to president Chuck McEwen, from "aunts, uncles and little old ladies in tennis shoes."

By 1974, Ramtek had $6 million in sales. The market was ready for Ramtek's new line color systems and the company estimated it needed another $1.4 million to get under way. For two years McEwen and his crew searched for that money. Then, on the November night before McEwen was to go back East to close the deal for the money, the manufacturing facility burned down. "Obviously," said McEwen, "the debenture didn't close."

Instead of a disaster, the fire was a turning point for the company. A rush meeting with Ramtek's bankers raised enough money to get the firm back on its feet. More important, the company seemed to change its attitude. The fire had created a sense of community rare in Silicon Valley. Two years later the firm went public, with 250 employees, $15 million in sales and full insurance coverage on its new Santa Clara facility.

Not everybody could fit into Silicon Valley proper. Some new companies chose to dig in on the periphery, either in East Bay cities like Hayward, or just north of San Francisco in the Marin County city of San Rafael. Two who chose the latter were George Morrow of Morrow Designs and Charles Grant of North Star Computers.

Morrow was a true character, a bald-headed man with a taste for rolled-up shirt sleeves and a natural bent toward theatrics. His company, founded in 1976, initially marketed floppy- and rigid-disk drives and eventually added small computers. The products were good but it is doubtful the company would have earned a tenth of the publicity it did without George Morrow's genius for self-promotion. He printed up file cards showing him looking dour and headlined ANOTHER MEMORABLE MESSAGE FROM MORROW . . . , followed by some motto like:

> Successful products are simple products.

or, bits of wisdom like:

> Programmers are like rock stars. But with rock stars, at least you get to hear the song before you buy the record. A programmer spends six months tuning his instrument and, whether it works or not, you're paying the whole time.

Morrow also sent out a Christmas card showing him in an old-fashioned toy store holding one of his products. The caption read: "May All Your Morrows Be Merry."

But Morrow was best known for the stunts he loved to pull with suppliers, particularly if they were Japanese. He'd sit in negotiation with one of these businessmen and ask what he would charge for a particular order. When the price was given, Morrow would gasp, clutch his chest, flail about the room as though experiencing a massive cerebral hemorrhage, then collapse to the floor, his eyeballs only showing whites. It would take several minutes for employees and the stunned suppliers to "revive" him.

Charles Grant came to computers out of Berkeley, and he looked the part. In 1975, he and partner Mark Greenberg, both with Ph.D.s in computer science from Cal Berkeley, were codirectors of a project to build a computer for the university's School of Business. Impressed by their ability to work together, they decided to start a small software company out of Grant's kitchen. They quickly decided that more money could be made selling complete computers. Almost by accident they became dealers of another company's products and the experience taught them what they needed to know about making their own machines.

Unfortunately, said Grant, "We chose a whimsical name, which we will regret to our dying day—Kentucky Fried Computers." It was hip, but it was also a disaster. "I think it was a name which consistently embarrassed us. It just detracted from the professionalism of the company that we were trying to put together. It was fun for a while; that's all I can say for it."

The new name chosen was North Star and by 1981, the two Berkeley hippies had built a company with $25 million in sales, 20,000 installed systems and 170 employees.

*   *   *

For a time in the mid-1970s Adam Osborne was the most famous "civilian" in the personal computer industry. With equal parts brilliance and arrogance he first chastised the industry for its shortcomings; then, when no one listened, he set out to build his own computer.

Osborne came to America from England in 1961 and by 1970, had founded Osborne and Associates, a technical writing and consulting firm. Soon he was off writing books on the computer industry.

With perfect timing, Osborne jumped onto the personal computer bandwagon almost before the industry began. But even more than timeliness, Osborne had style. At a time when the computer industry bathed in the warm glow of embarrassing trade press propaganda, Osborne had the guts to call things as he saw them. In his famous column, called, with typical megalomania, "From the Fountainhead," Osborne took on all the icons of the personal computer business.

But Adam Osborne had bigger plans. Not content to be the gadfly of the personal computer industry, he now wanted to be part of it, a Valley tycoon, and to vindicate himself to those who doubted the genius of his logic. In September 1980, he set about to build his own computer company—to be named, of course, Osborne Computer.

In truth, Osborne really was a genius, not at technology or business, but at self-promotion, as captured in quotes:

> I told everybody what they should build and nobody did. So I built it.

> Quite frankly, I was amazed afterward when anyone said it was innovative or a mark of brilliance. It seemed utterly obvious.

> I understand the press. Certainly I used the press. But then, the press wanted to be used. Every journalist is interested in creating stories that sell. There's no question about that. So whether I'm using the press, that's a question of definition. I'm helping them create a product that will sell . . . and symbolically sell my own.

The amazing thing was that for two years Osborne proved his exorbitant claims valid. Osborne had two good ideas: first, to take advantage of ongoing miniaturization of circuitry to produce a personal computer that was small enough, light enough and rugged enough to be portable; second, to take the most popular software programs, until then only sold independently and at great cost, and "bundle" them in with the upfront cost of the personal computer.

Like a good entrepreneur, he got to the market first. The result, the Osborne 1, was a sensation. Introduced in July 1981, the product offered the market a computer that could be carried to and from the office and stored under airline seats—at the remarkable price of just $1,795. It wasn't long before Osborne was running at a $100-million-a-year pace, and Adam Osborne, in typical style, was predicting that his company would reach $250 million in annual sales in its first fiscal year (HP took twenty years to reach that mark, Intel ten, Apple four).

All of this hoopla and hype hid the numerous shortcomings of Osborne Computer. For one thing, the machine was rather shoddily constructed and suffered from a screen far too small. In the words of *California* magazine, the Osborne 1 was an innovative product but also "a sloppily designed gimmick."

That wasn't all that was wrong. The company itself was teetering. Osborne was rarely around, leaving the company in the hands of inexperienced young managers, most of them in their twenties. The first Osborne 1 delivery to the nation's largest computer retailer, Computerland, was dead on arrival.

Still, Adam Osborne played the press like a violin, and they danced along. "60 Minutes" came calling. The national news magazines embraced him as the new high-tech guru. The industry hung on every word of this "quasi-religious figure."

By the middle of its second year, Osborne Computer began making serious mistakes in judgment. First, stuck with more than eleven thousand soon-to-be-obsolete units, the company initiated a program to make those machines more desirable by bundling in a very popular software package. The strategy was too successful: the sudden surge of demand further squeezed the company's already strained manufacturing operations, resulting in delays and slips in quality.

Adam Osborne knew the key to success in a new company was the follow-up product, followed hard after by the first public sale of stock. He had two new models up his sleeve, a low-cost replacement for the Osborne 1 and a new business model called the Executive. Realizing that the company was on weak financial footing, he brought in a pro, Robert Jaunich of Consolidated Foods of Chicago, who turned down eight hundred thousand dollars a year and $1 million in stock for a shot at making ten times that when Osborne went public.

Jaunich was dismayed by what he found at Osborne: the disorganization, the immaturity, the incoherence. He quickly started firing top managers, ruining the one thing Osborne Computer had going for it: morale. Even worse, as he looked over the books Jaunich quickly realized he'd made a big mistake taking the job. Somewhere, probably through neglect, Osborne Computer was missing $10 million.

Jaunich realized that with the bad debt and some additional worthless inventory written off, Osborne could lose $1.5 million for the quarter ending February 1983—a long way from Adam Osborne's prediction of a $1-million profit—and the company could lose as much as $4 million for the year. So, in a move that probably cost him $10 million personally, Jaunich canceled Osborne Computer's first public sale of stock.

Osborne Computer now faced devastating competition from some new firms, like Kaypro and Compaq. The only hope for Osborne Computer was the Executive (the replacement model had been dropped). Adam Osborne, told by Jaunich of the company's problems, returned to lead the introduction. The fate of the company now depended upon the sizable publicity skills of the King of Hype.

Osborne, in his proper milieu, came through beautifully. The Executive's introduction was a roaring success. But the arrogance that had made him finally brought him down. There was a change in the personal computer marketplace by the time of the Executive's introduction in April 1983. IBM was now in the market with the PC and compatibility with IBM software was rapidly becoming the rule of survival. The Osborne Executive was not IBM-compatible.

Still that might not have been fatal, except that Adam Osborne apparently could not live with the idea that the industry he had smugly drubbed over the years was whispering he had made a mistake. So, a week after the introduction of the Executive, the company's last chance of survival, Adam Osborne made it obsolete by announcing he was at work on a new IBM-compatible model. Sales instantly fell off.

By August, Osborne Computer had fired 203 people, half its employment. On September 13, 1983, the company went into Chapter 11 bankruptcy, owing $45 million to six hundred creditors. Soon afterward, the ever interviewable Adam Osborne was photographed for *People* magazine coming out his company's now abandoned building holding his briefcase in front of his face like an indicted Mafioso.

He was unrepentant. As he told *The Wall Street Journal,* "I don't feel any personal embarrassment. You cannot be the kind of person who takes failure hard and be an entrepreneur."

Then, returning to the profession that had always served him best— self-promotion—Osborne sat down and wrote himself (with help from computer columnist John Dvorak) a nasty little book. In it, Osborne "suggested" that Jaunich had purposely destroyed Osborne Computer so that he, Jaunich, could obtain control over what was left.

Not unexpectedly, Adam Osborne portrayed himself as an innocent

·victim of unfortunate circumstances, misplaced trust and his own managerial inexperience.

The book had limited sales.

*   *   *

Qwyx, Qume, Xebex, Epid. The jabberwocky of Silicon Valley corporate names reads like a list of new third world nations or entries in a thesaurus written by Ogden Nash. The signs that line the avenues of the Valley's industrial parks read as if the sign painter were on hallucinogens.

Each new Silicon Valley company seems to come up with a more abstruse title for itself—the more unintelligible the name, the more the company's founders feel they've captured the firm's business essence.

It's hard to say just how the Silicon Valley name game started. In fact, when the local electronics industry was young, company names were almost too dull, almost indistinguishable from the neighborhood roofing company. Most often the titles came from the names of the founders, such as Hewlett-Packard Co., Varian Corp. and Fairchild Camera and Instrument. These were good solid names, like Smith Brothers or United States Steel.

Even as late as 1959, with National Semiconductor, old-fashioned naming remained the rule (though few outsiders had the slightest idea what a semiconductor was).

But by 1961, whether as a result of the New Frontier or the Mercury space flights or just an unnatural local perversion, Silicon Valley began to go a little nutty with names. In subsequent years it has only gotten worse. The first was Signetics Corp., whose name is an acronym for "Signal Network Electronics"—a name which in a few years had nothing whatsoever to do with its product line. The name was created in five minutes at an executive meeting and has haunted the Valley ever since. Perhaps the Signetics executives should have taken a little longer.

With Signetics the horses were out of the corral. The next year saw the incorporation of Molectro Corp., whose name was reminiscent of a robot in a 1950s science fiction film. Also that year, Siliconix Corp. of Santa Clara opened, and between it and Signetics, they created a precedent for the endless number of "icks" firms—Litronix, Exonix, Chromatrix, Econics, Hematex, Heuristics, Liconix, Macronetics, Mardix, Onyx, Plantronics, Quantronics, Flextronics, Versatronex, Waltronic, Xynetics, Xltronix and Mnemonics, which has to be pronounced twice in your head before you dare to say it out loud. Finally, there was Alltronics.

Puns on "electronics" weren't the only word games companies played with their names. "High technology" increasingly became a favorite term and each year brought more and more "techs," "tecks" and "eks," usually among firms involved in making electronic systems, such as instruments and computers: Adtek, Avantek, Antekna, Caltex (a pun on the school), Disotec, Dionex, Envirotech, Holex, Intech, Intectra, Kylex, Measurex, the arrogant Mytex, Nortec, Omex, the all inclusive Omnitek, Pebex, Ramtek, Rectec, Solitec, Synertek, Versatec, Xebec, Xidex, Zentec, and ultimately, Supertex, then topping even that, Ultratech.

Silicon'x also initiated the incorporation of variations on the name of the basic substance used in making semiconductors, silicon, like Siltec and Intersil.

Other companies just cut their own paths, following corporate compasses into the wilderness of stranger and stranger names. The first, Intel, was a variation on "integrated electronics." Electronic warfare simulation firm Antekna was named after a three-hour argument between the founders, who finally found it in the Swedish section of an unabridged Funk & Wagnalls dictionary. By their description:

> . . . the name Antekna was arrived at under the following logic: Founder Bibbens liked it because it started with an A (and would be at the beginning of customers' lists). Founder Digiovanni liked it because it had the "tek" part of technical, and that's how Italians spell it anyway. Founder Murphy acquiesed because he got tired of arguing his point. (It means "to write down" in Swedish.)

Acurex found its name in true Valley style. It set down its requirements—that the name begin with an A, be technical-sounding and be six letters alternating vowels and consonants—and plugged them into a computer. Out of the dozens of words the computer spat back out, many of them obscene (Asahola), Acurex was the clear winner.

Obviously when it got to the point that a computer had to be called in to help find a company name things were getting seriously out of hand. A brief respite was offered by the seventies, which took the luster off space-age names and opened up a whole new market of "mellow" titles that were dedicated to truth, health and Marvel Comics.

Hence, Apple Computer, Byte, Bits and Bytes, Care, Centurion, Cognition, Coherent, Commodore, Computerland, Cronus, Force, Gemini, Halcyon, Ithaca, Odin, Phenix, Pyramid, Sartorius (a Faulkner fan?), Snook (???), Stellar Systems, Time and Space Processing, Thor, Trilogy, Triad, Priam, Diablo, Ec-Lec-Tic Engineering, Quest, Stag, Verbatim, Epic, Epyx and the perfect California name, Aquari Components—a sort of high-fiber Conan-*cum*-Star Wars collection of names. (The founder of one disk drive firm named it Priam because that mythical figure as a youth was a champion discus thrower. He hadn't heard of the fate of the same Priam, much older, as King of Troy—and what it might imply for the future of his firm. Luckily, nobody else in the industry read mythology either.)

Some firms, faced with the apparent impossibility of coming up with a new name, gave up. One company, in fact, found its name by doing precisely that: the notorious Solfan (an acronym for "sick of looking for a name").

Perhaps the worst offenders were the two industrial giants Xerox and Exxon, which seemed to take almost perverse pleasure in giving their Valley subsidiaries bizarre names.

Exxon subsidiary Zilog Corp. achieved its name through a thought process as circuitous as some of its microprocessors: "*Z* stands for the last word. *I* represents integrated, and *LOG* is for logic. In other words Zilog is the last word in integrated logic." Obviously, you had to be there.

But Zilog was just a warm-up. Later Exxon would inflict on the Valley names like Kylex, Epid, Magnex and Vydec. Xerox came up with Qwyx. ITT, not to be outdone by its rivals, entered with Qume.

The company names of the eighties also seem to reflect the world in which they were created. There are the M.B.A. terms: Synergistics, Forward Technology, Perceptive, Cogito, Leading Technology, Catalyst, Grid and the pragmatic Failure Analysis. And there is more alphabet-soup confusion, like Msmasks, Jakbak—the worst case being Ixys, which looks Greek, but actually stands for Integrated X-Y Systems. And, of course, there are still the disturbing oddballs, like work station maker Daisy Systems, which sounds like a feminine hygiene product. And, of course, there was still the fern-bar funky: Diablo, Durango, Digital Deli, Brut. Some took advantage of the local connection: there were a Silicon Valley Associates, a Silicon Valley Marketing, a Silicon Valley Sales and a Silicon Valley Travel.

Inevitably given the demand and the entrepreneurial environment, at last in 1980, someone set up a business just to give Valley high-tech

companies their names. Ira Bachrach, a retired Valley advertising executive with a love of language, started Namelab as a hobby. Three years
later he had a full-time business with two staff linguists and a backlog of
orders so great that he could pick and choose clients he wanted to work
with. Like any good entrepreneur, Bachrach has learned to price what
the market will bear—in his case, twenty-five thousand dollars for labor, two thousand or more for expenses, and 20 percent to 30 percent of
the labor cost as ownership fee.

So, as usual, the tiny new start-ups are forced to come up with their
own names—and they grow stranger by the year. Perhaps there is some
solace in the name of a new Sunnyvale firm that seems to have opted
out of the Valley name game, but with a delicious sense of humor.

Acme Electronics.

PROFILE

The Angry Genius

GENE AMDAHL

Silicon Valley has often been compared to Hollywood. But in reality, the story of the Valley, if left to its own collective voice, would most resemble—in its inaccuracy, solipsism and amnesia—a Soviet encyclopedia. Only, in Silicon Valley, one does not become a nonperson through a purge but through business failure; and no government censor orders readers to glue a new picture of a wheat harvest over a some bemedaled but now fallen Beria. Instead, in Silicon Valley, the name of last year's hero simply drops from conversation in boardrooms and restaurants and gyms by unspoken but universal agreement. Or, worse, the name is only uttered accompanied with the chuckle reserved for fools and pathetic losers. Hell comes in different forms for different people; for the entrepreneur it is the laugh of pity. Just ask Gene Amdahl: he's been there twice.

* * *

Dr. Eugene Amdahl looks on paper and in photographs a lot slicker than he really is. With his thick wavy gray hair and cleft chin, Rolls-Royce and sterling résumé as an entrepreneur, one might expect a hearty backslapper with a booming voice and a quick line for everything.

Thus it is a shock to meet the man for the first time. The key to Gene Amdahl is in the eyes. If one looks again at the photographs, past the other features, and focuses upon his eyes, the man's essential gentleness shows through. In person, Amdahl is a surprisingly frail-looking man, with a voice to match, and most painfully shy and reticent.

To understand Amdahl one must have a conversation with him. It is then that the man's formidable intelligence shows through. Amdahl's speech is slow, almost halting, a reenactment of the old Bob and Ray routine with the president of the Slow Talkers' Club: one finds oneself filling in the missing words just to get the sentence through. Only after a few minutes of this does one come to the shocking realization that Amdahl's brilliance is so surpassing, like the computers he has designed, it may be performing hundreds of calculations between the words it tosses out. For all one knows, in the course of a simple conversation about the weather, Gene Amdahl may have worked out a design problem that has haunted computer scientists for decades.

It is this powerful intelligence, with its private demands superseding involvement in the outside world, that has been the source of Gene Amdahl's greatest triumphs and his most painful tragedy.

Of all of the Valley's leaders, Amdahl's roots are most deeply in the bedrock of American life. He was born in November 1922, in Flandreau, South Dakota. Two years later, his family moved outside of town to a farm that had been homesteaded by his grandfather. Amdahl stayed at that farm until he became an adult.

"It was a dirt farm. It wasn't gentleman farming. We raised small grain, corn, and fed a lot of cattle, sheep, pigs and chickens. When I first began working in the fields we didn't have a tractor yet, just horses. This was before the Depression hit. We generally started working the fields, a little bit, about the time we started preschool."

As a result, Amdahl and his older brother Al attended school year-round in order to make up for time lost in plantings and harvests. Flandreau was a close-knit farming community, with sober traditional values and a strong work ethic. Young Gene used whatever free time he had to indulge his deep love of tinkering. By the time he was twelve, he had built a model of a complicated counterrotating rotor for a helicopter. His only brush with electronics was when he built himself a cat's-whisker crystal radio—only to discover that there were no stations within range.

Graduating from high school, Amdahl went off to war, then returned to get married (one of the Valley's enduring marriages) and attended college at South Dakota State, earning a bachelor's degree in engineering and physics. He then went on to earn a Ph.D. in theoretical physics at the University of Wisconsin (where transistor coinventor John Bardeen was also based). Theoretical physics was a big jump for a farm boy like Gene Amdahl. "I was in high school before we first got rural electrification and they brought electricity to the farm. So when I thought of technology it was mechanical, like a tractor or other farm equipment." Now Amdahl found himself working in the world of sub-atomic particles and quantum mechanics and even a little bit of a new discipline called solid state physics. He also learned of an even newer invention called a transistor.

Amdahl earned his doctorate, after a hitch in the Navy, in 1952, but by then its usefulness was already moot. In the process of working toward the degree, Amdahl had chanced upon a new field that would turn out to be his life's work. It began with an assignment with two other students to determine whether or not "a proposed force between nuclear particles could describe the bound state of the simplest three-body nucleus (tritium).

"For thirty days the three of us used the combination of a mechanical desk-top calculator and a slide rule to hold twelve-digit figures" (the calculator held only ten: "and the round-off error was killing us"). They disproved the hypothesis, but the experience was so frustrating for Amdahl that "I decided that there had to be a better way of doing that."

So, a few months later, with only two years' electronics experience in the Navy as a technician during the war and a summer of programming, young Gene Amdahl had designed and helped build one of the first computers. "At the time there was no real idea what computers were other than ENIAC, and even that was a military secret. Since I had no access to anything confidential or secret I of course didn't know anything about them.

"The first machine I designed was a digital differential analyzer. We never actually built that, but it was designed to use vacuum tubes."

The second design was for a digital computer. With the help of some professors at the school, who taught him what constituted a true computer (as opposed to a high-powered calculator), Amdahl not only designed the machine, he actually had the honor of seeing it built by the University of Washington. It was called, fittingly, WISC (Wisconsin Integrally Synchronized Computer). Not only was the WISC one of the first privately owned computers but, though comparatively slow, it was also the world's first "floating-point" (now a standard feature) computer—beating even mighty IBM to the market.

Not surprisingly, IBM suddenly became quite interested in this bright young man who had outsmarted even its large and famous design staff. So, soon after the unveiling of WISC, Amdahl was visited by the local branch manager of IBM and was offered a job with Big Blue. He joined the firm in June 1952, though even then, as he now admits, "What I really had in mind was starting my own company. But in those days it was just in the back of mind."

He went to work in Poughkeepsie, New York, where the development laboratories were located for all of IBM's high-end commercial computers. Amdahl's first project was the modeling of neural networks of the human brain, trying to determine whether or not existing theories of how the brain worked were accurate—and discovered that it was not complete. This attempt by Amdahl to use computers to duplicate the brain was one of the first experiments in what would become the fields of artificial intelligence and robotics.

Amdahl worked on that project for close to a year, and, after determining the theory was inadequate, decided that "I really didn't want to spend the time trying to polish up that theory, and so I decided to get on with the field of computers." Nevertheless, he didn't quite hit the discipline squarely, ending up in a tangential research project, this one into computer-based character recognition. Here too, Amdahl's work was one of the pioneering projects in the field.

In fact, much of Amdahl's career at IBM can be seen as groundbreaking work in one technological sector after another. Part of this has to do with the fact that Amdahl was timely; he was there at the birth of the computer industry. But there was more to it than that. Amdahl was a computer genius. There were a lot of other scientists at IBM at the same time who didn't have a fraction of his success. The fact was that this South Dakota farm boy, who hadn't even had an electric light in his home until he was a teenager, was rapidly becoming known as one of the leading computer scientists of his time.

The record stands by itself. Amdahl's work in character recognition led to a system that could read the three leading typefaces with more than 97 percent accuracy—not yet good enough for commercial sale, but still the best of its time.

Next, Amdahl was assigned the task of improving the IBM scientific computer of the era, the 701. Which he did—splendidly, of course. The resulting machine, the 704, which incorporated many of the features of future computers (floating point, indexing), was one of the most successful vacuum-tube computers in IBM history. Compared with the 701, which sold 18 computers, the 704 sold 160 at several million dollars apiece—a big success in those days. After that, Amdahl proposed a packet of additions to the 704, which became the 709. By the time (late 1955) that machine was under way, Amdahl was already at work designing STRETCH, the Model 7030, the first transistor computer. Only the basic part of Amdahl's design was used here—and as a result, Amdahl says, "The final machine got too complicated . . . it wasn't economical enough to be a success; so IBM ended up cutting back and made only seven or eight of them."

By then Amdahl wasn't around to be part of IBM's mistake. In the first of his celebrated walkouts, Amdahl left to take a job at Ramo Wooldridge, now TRW, in north Los Angeles.

The Ramo Wooldridge job was primarily government contract work. "I was hoping I could interest them in some commercial computer work. But it became very clear that they weren't interested." So, seven months later, Amdahl quit, joining a new start-up called Aeroneutronic not far away in the San Fernando Valley. Aeroneutronic was a subsidiary of Ford Motor Company (it now has an operation in Silicon Valley) and was also heavily into government contract work. "But I thought their connection to Ford Motor Company might make them interested in commercial electronics. I also got them interested, but after about four years it was clear that that wasn't going to happen."

Aeroneutronic was a frustrating experience for Amdahl. "At least I was in on the ground floor of that company, so even the government contracting work was more interesting," he said. He also had a little equity in the firm—a lesson he should have learned better for later years. In September 1960, IBM hired Amdahl back.

All of this job-hopping didn't quite jibe with the fifties work philosophy, and it was especially difficult for Amdahl and his wife, now that they were towing along three young children (including Carlton). But now Amdahl was back in the warm bosom of IBM—and the company realized what a treasure they had let slip out of their hands. This time IBM was going to take care of Gene Amdahl, and in return he would make the company billions of dollars.

He returned to take over Project X. "Well, I didn't really want to go back East, I wanted to stay out in California. They told me I had to go back there for at least five months, but not more than seven. Well, I got there and was there for four *years.*"

Project X turned out to be the Model 91, a monster computer designed to counter the new big scientific computers introduced by Control Data. After sixteen months on that research, IBM talked Amdahl into heading up the design activities for the Series 360.

> Bob Evans, who was president of the division, called me
> down to Poughkeepsie to talk me into taking the job. He said
> he had to attend a budget meeting at a place called Fox Hill.

So he asked me to meet him there and he'd talk to me between budget presentations. Then when I got there he made me sit in and listen to find out what was going on. I didn't realize until afterwards what he had done: he'd given me the best sales talk he possibly could have by having me listen to presentations in which there would be about five or six projects of each kind [tape drives, new software packages, etc.] to be undertaken for each member of each family of computers that had been developed in the division . . . What I saw there was the multiplication that all of those different lines had in terms of their demands on the company's resources. One thing was clear: even IBM didn't have the resources to do all of those things.

Thus, by the time Amdahl did sit down with Evans, Amdahl already had a good idea of what the proposal would be: a compatible line of IBM computers that would enable the same software and peripheral hardware to be used with every member of the family.

It was a revolutionary concept. And Gene Amdahl knew from the moment it was suggested to him how he wanted to do it. "I was convinced that we could meet all the economic and performance requirements. I knew it would be tough, but I thought it was possible."

The 360 design program was directed by Fred Brooks. Of the four groups reporting to him, Amdahl was responsible for three: architecture, engineering (in the initial stages) and the operating system (which in the end was done differently from Amdahl's original plan). The fourth operation, product requirements, was handled by the marketing group. Brooks's primary job was to run interference and keep upper management out of Amdahl's way.

All told, the 360 project took three years, from 1961 to 1964. The finished machine was unveiled in late 1964. "It hadn't been planned to be introduced that soon, so some of the stuff was marginally ready."

The company needn't have hurried. After the 360 there wasn't much competition. It was the most successful computer ever introduced up to its time, and with its direct (and compatible) descendant, the 370 Series, it became the largest-selling computer family in history. It can be argued that the 360 Series changed the world. With it the computer age arrived. Computers now had a future. Now a company could acquire, say, the low-end Model 20 and, as it grew, graduate to increasingly powerful models, right up to the 360 Model 91, which was five hundred times as powerful as the Model 20—yet the firm could still hang the same printers and tape drives on its newest 360 Model and run the same software.

What this did was to simultaneously break open the computer market and close it up. Computer owners now felt less need to hang on to old machines because of the enormous sums they had spent in software development and peripherals. Now they could carry those things forward onto the latest model. But in a short time the sheer volume of software and hardware they had developed meant that they had to stay with their computer family, *forever.*

Needless to say, this was a win-win situation for IBM. The 360 Series, Gene Amdahl's present to IBM, blew up the computer industry, turning it into a collection of fiefdoms and leaving IBM all but guaranteed perpetual preeminence. It is difficult to think of another single inventor who has ever done so much for an employer.

At the end of 1964, after Amdahl had set IBM on a course it would follow for at least the next two decades, the company finally let him come back to California. Not long after he arrived, IBM named him an IBM fellow, the highest research position in the company (a clever management technique to keep the top talent around). With the move to California, Gene Amdahl at last arrived in Silicon Valley, stationed at IBM's research lab in Los Gatos.

Still in the back of his mind was the thought of one day starting his own company. It was not that Amdahl was being treated badly, but "one thing I was really deciding was that management by and large screwed a lot of things up."

> I had been out here a relatively short time when IBM decided they were going to an advanced computer systems laboratory and they decided to set it up here because I was out here. Well, I worked there for about four years. But I had only been there seven or eight months when it suddenly occurred to me that the machine I was working on would be better off compatible with the 360. I was just about thrown out of the project by the others because they didn't want to make it compatible with the 360 Series—because they were absolutely convinced that you couldn't make a fast 360-compatible machine. So I proceeded for the next year to prove that in fact you could . . . and demonstrated it to the satisfaction of management.
>
> Well, we went on for one year more and we discovered after doing our cost analysis that we would have to have three machines in the series in order to have enough machines to amortize the cost of a semiconductor start-up [these computers would contain chips] to make it profitable. IBM didn't

want to do that because it would upset the carefully managed price–performance ratios.

In other words, nearly all of the computers in the IBM family, no matter what their power or their price, were arrayed along a single curve representing a certain performance for a particular price. An IBM computer that had twice the performance of the next closest model would cost twice as much. The new chip-based 360-compatible computers that Amdahl proposed, with their higher performance for the same cost, would send a devastating ripple effect through the entire IBM family; the seamless joints between each model that formed a single impenetrable line from the tiniest computer to the biggest "fighting machine" would suddenly pull apart.

So IBM, faced with the terrifying prospect of having two machines competing for the same spot, throwing the whole family out of kilter, and operating under the dark cloud of an antitrust suit that wouldn't look kindly on such a competitive product, gutted Amdahl's plan.

"Well, I didn't want to be involved with bringing out a loss leader, because that would only make me a bum," says Amdahl, so he returned to being an IBM fellow and did analytical work, primarily cost analysis. It was this work, combined with some of IBM's own sales statistics, that led him to the conclusion that no one else had yet reached: that there was an equation that accurately predicted which IBM computers would be profitable and which would not. This in turn led to Amdahl's breakthrough discovery: there was a fundamental flaw in the IBM strategy. By creating that seamless curve and relating the price of its high-end machines to that of its low-end ones, IBM had left itself vulnerable. A competitor could exploit that weakness by building a computer not unlike the one he had just seen turned down, a plug-compatible computer that could use both IBM software and peripheral hardware.

That was all Gene Amdahl needed. He still dreamed of starting his own company. And he had grown embittered by what he felt was cavalier treatment by IBM. The Norwegian farm boy had a very precise sense of what was proper and due him, and when he felt that line had been crossed, this shy, soft-spoken man suddenly started playing for keeps. *Fortune* magazine caught him well in the mid-seventies:

> He is a wily negotiator and a consummate gamesman expert at foreseeing his opponent's moves—whether in combat against IBM, across the bargaining table from one of his backers, or in games of liar's dice or bridge. He sometimes hustles guests into games of billiards, where his superb feel for the

angles makes him an almost sure winner. He has a touchy ego, easily bruised by real and imagined slights, and a profound suspicion of the bureaucratic mind. Under pressure he reveals a stubborn, even rigid adherence to principle.

It was these traits—and his hole card of knowing IBM's secret weakness—that led Gene Amdahl to quit IBM, for the second time, in 1970. He had been asked to sit on the board of his brother's company, which by coincidence had a name similar to an IBM competitor. IBM, without looking closely into the matter, accused Gene Amdahl of working for a competitor. Amdahl fumed, particularly when IBM apologized for the error but still demanded that he quit the board position anyway.

That cut it. If IBM wanted a competitor it would get one. With probably the nerviest fuck-you-I-quit letter ever written, the quiet, shy Gene Amdahl informed the world's largest electronics company that he intended to start a company to take it on, and not only endure but win.

IBM tried to talk Amdahl into not leaving. They took him back East and had heavyweights like chairman Frank Carey and president John Opel talk to him. But they couldn't change his mind. Neither could his own division president back in Los Gatos. Amdahl was adamant, and the president, realizing this, said to him sincerely that he hoped Gene wasn't planning on going into the large-computer business; after all, there just wasn't any money to be made there.

Eight years later, Amdahl Corp. was a $330-million firm precisely because Gene Amdahl had ignored that advice. Pursuing his discovery of IBM's Achilles' heel, he had built the chip-based large computers he had first thought of at Big Blue, and now he was tearing away big chunks of the market.

It wasn't easy getting there. Nineteen-seventy saw a recession; three other large computer firms went bankrupt within two months after Amdahl started his firm and Gene found that being the Father of the 360 wasn't enough credentials to make investors consider him an astute businessman. After meeting closed doors from most of the U.S. venture capital industry, Amdahl found himself embracing Fujitsu because only the Japanese firm offered enough money to get the company going.

The watershed year was 1979. IBM was striking back at the plug-compatible market and was hurting both itself and Amdahl Corp. with rumors of an as yet unannounced computer called the H-Series. Dwindling sales weren't the only problem Amdahl faced at his eponymous firm. He had long since given over the presidency to a man handpicked by one of his investors. And the company had grown so large that the bureaucracy he so disliked was once again enveloping him.

Amdahl, reduced to only 3 percent ownership of the company that bore his name after giving away 97 percent to investors, found that what little control he had left was quickly being taken away from him. "I could never persuade the U.S. investor [Heizer, with 24 percent] that it wasn't necessarily in his interest to keep Fujitsu [27 percent] totally happy. One should treat Fujitsu fairly, but one must retain enough independence so that you could determine your own costs and your own projects."

> Fujitsu kept making it such an attractive thing for the rest of the company management to let [Fujitsu] do the things that were hard to do. Finally they let Fujitsu do all of the hard things, and then [Amdahl Corp.] found it couldn't do anything for itself. For example, the complex back-panel wiring . . . Amdahl Corp. could never quite master that, so after a couple of tries it quit. Fujitsu made them an offer they couldn't refuse—namely they'd do it for a price that clearly precluded [Amdahl Corp.] from doing it itself. Fujitsu did the same thing with multilayer boards and with chips.

Thus, according to Gene Amdahl, by the late seventies every time the going got tough at Amdahl Corp. the firm would look to Fujitsu for help. And Amdahl stood by helplessly as he watched what he believed was a slow, subtle Japanese takeover of the firm that bore his name. "It was all done so smoothly by Fujitsu that you almost felt like you were complaining about motherhood when you'd point out what was happening. It was like saying that you must make a child do things that are difficult and disagreeable to do because it has to learn to stand on its own two feet. The trouble was that we [Amdahl and senior vice-president Clifford Madden] were trying to explain that to the child."

So it was time to leave. This time the departure was more difficult. Gene Amdahl had fulfilled his dream of building his own firm. Every day for nine years when he drove up to the growing complex of company buildings, he saw his name emblazoned on a sign out front. And, of course, he had stood toe-to-toe with his old employer and, though bloody, was still on his feet. Nevertheless, in late 1979, Amdahl quit Amdahl. (He admits it still feels odd to drive by a company wearing his name.)

Then Amdahl dropped from sight. He went to Europe to pick up a Mercedes for himself, but the tension of the final days at Amdahl had wrenched his back so badly he had to be taken off a plane on a stretcher and spent six weeks in a London hospital.

When at last he was found working out of the back of the trucking and contractor company in San Jose, Amdahl spoke of great plans to start another company to take on IBM again. It sounded like the pipe-dream of a beaten man.

Once the back pain went away and his brains unscrambled, Amdahl came up with a new strategy to take on IBM. He'd built one helluva company in Amdahl Corp., and though it hadn't worked out, he knew now he could do it again. Certainly the success of that firm had given Amdahl the business credentials he'd been lacking the last time around. This time though, he was going to hang on to stock for dear life.

On the brink of perhaps his greatest triumph, Gene Amdahl's life hit its lowest mark. In late 1981, while driving home in his Rolls late one night, Gene Amdahl ran over a motorcyclist momentarily stopped at a stop sign. The motorcyclist was dragged for a considerable distance and died of injuries. Amdahl, accompanied by his lawyer, turned himself in the next day.

Amdahl claimed he never even knew he hit the man, which raised a lot of eyebrows and led to cynical remarks that despite the famous advertisements, even Rolls-Royces weren't silent enough to keep out that kind of noise. And then there was the matter of Amdahl turning himself in the next day.

On the other hand, the intersection, on a wooded street in the hills, was notorious for its lack of lights. When Amdahl, who had once fallen down a flight of stairs while thinking about a problem, claimed he was lost in thought at the time of the accident, it was difficult to refute.

Just what really happened will never be known. Men like Gene Amdahl don't often go to trial, and apparently the memory is so painful he simply will not discuss it.

Amdahl pressed on despite the tragedy. His new firm is called Trilogy and it was founded in March 1980 with Cliff Madden of Amdahl Corp. and his own son, Carlton, formerly the tech whiz of another plug-compatible firm, Magnuson.

To beat IBM this time, Amdahl pushed against the boundaries not only of computer technology but of semiconductor technology as well. When the chip industry could not provide him with the incredibly complex circuits he needed, Amdahl decided to make his own—and so he built the cleanest and probably the most advanced semiconductor-fabrication laboratory in the world.

That takes a lot of bucks, but this time Amdahl got them. Unlike the last time around, when he had gone out looking for venture backers for

Amdahl Corp., they now came to him—in droves. By the end of 1983, Trilogy had raised a mind-boggling quarter billion dollars in stock sales and research and development partnership money and was on its way to the 1985 introduction of its first product, one of the most powerful computers in the world.

Trilogy had taken on a daunting task. A single Trilogy chip produced as much heat as a 900-watt bulb—an awesome cooling job. When prototypes burned themselves up in 1984, delivery dates were set back to 1986. Then, a few months later, Amdahl's son Carlton suddenly resigned, saying he couldn't handle the pressure and blaming himself for the delays.

Rumors grew that Trilogy, the Valley's dream firm, its greatest hope for a future as thrilling as its past, was stumbling badly.

The bad news came in early June 1984. Gene Amdahl publicly announced that Trilogy had abandoned its plans to build its new supercomputer to take on IBM. Gene Amdahl would not beat the giant twice.

Trilogy would continue to develop the incredible chip that was to be at the heart of the planned computer. But not the computer; the development delays already guaranteed that Trilogy would not beat IBM to market.

Now would come the acts of a defeated firm. Within days, Trilogy laid off 120 people, 20 percent of its workforce. Investors, who had hung on with almost religious fervor to their belief in the boundless genius of Gene Amdahl, would now begin to disappear. Trilogy would fall from the public eye as just another glorious Silicon Valley failure.

Trilogy still had a wondrous chip, though, if it could get it to work. Perhaps it could still be built in acceptable volume—maybe even sold to IBM. Some investors still believed in Amdahl, often only for what he represented. Valley veteran Don Valentine, now a successful venture capitalist, was reported to have said, upon hearing the sad Trilogy announcement, "This is my only chance to kick the big guy, IBM, in the ass and I'm staying with it."

Nevertheless, as he sat there at the Trilogy annual meeting, letting someone else deliver the bad news, refusing all interviews, the magnitude of the disaster was unmistakable in Gene Amdahl's tragic, fallen face and downcast eyes.

Perhaps, as he listened to the death of his dream, poised again on the brink of oblivion, Amdahl remembered the words of his old boss at IBM that there was no money to be made in computers.

8

Moving Uptown

On the morning of Wednesday, June 8, 1983, Dennis Barnhart, forty, became a millionaire. In Silicon Valley, the date one becomes a tycoon can often be so precisely reckoned: it is the day the company you founded goes public.

Barnhart's firm, Eagle Computer of Los Gatos, made personal computers, and in the heady period before that industry's shake-out, Eagle was one of the rising stars. So hot was the market—and Eagle's product —that the firm, which had been founded just in November 1981 as a division of another company, had grown to a sales pace of $40 million a year. The number of employees had jumped from sixty to two hundred in a matter of months.

Barnhart had worked hard to get to this point, and throughout the day, as he watched his millions rise, he was satisfied. A confident, professional and often difficult person, Barnhart had climbed up through the ranks of the electronics industry to achieve this reward. He had run the business side of Rockwell International's microelectronic device division in Anaheim. Then he had spent a year as a free-lance microcomputer consultant with the Hayden Book Co. and Victor Business Machines. Next he was vice-president of marketing and sales at Commodore Business Machines.

Finally, Barnhart's chance came with an offer from Audio Visual Labs. He at first turned the offer down, but when AV Labs offered him the chance to start a new business systems division, he jumped. Soon Eagle had bought its way out of the parent company, and Barnhart was president of a hot new firm doubling its sales every quarter. Befitting this new success, Eagle moved into new offices in Los Gatos that quickly became famous for the huge (eleven-foot-wide) mahogany eagle that hung in the lobby.

Not unexpectedly, the climb to the top had fattened Barnhart's pocketbook. He already owned an expensive home in Los Gatos and he was often seen tooling around the Valley in his new Ferrari 308 GTSi with personalized license plates that read: EAGLE B.

That June day was the capper. As the hours passed, Barnhart quietly watched and occasionally answered calls from the press as the offered shares were snapped up by investors and the price per share rose. By lunchtime, Barnhart knew that Eagle had raised $37 million in new capital in its first day as a public corporation. He also knew that his personal wealth had, in just eight hours, jumped by $9 million.

What does a person do on a day like that? Barnhart jumped into his Ferrari and went out and got drunk with a yacht salesman in typical Silicon Valley style.

There have been a lot of going-public days in Silicon Valley, more than a hundred at last count, and each has had its little stories of instant wealth for an executive or a brilliant scientist and, sometimes, even for the rare secretary or low-level worker who got in on stock options early.

Occasionally the riches rain on only a single individual, the founder who struggled to lift the company up by its bootstraps. Usually it's a small group that hits it big: the founders, who took the risk of trying to start a company from scratch, the venture capitalists who backed them, and a small group of specially talented managers and technical types who were wooed away from their already lucrative jobs by founder's stock at ground-floor prices and the promise of a distant going-public day.

The payoffs can be stunning. At the height of the bull market of 1983, David Packard was worth $2.115 billion, his partner Bill Hewlett $1.05 billion. Down the road at Apple Computer, chairman Steve Jobs's wealth jumped to $362 million, while cofounder Mike Markkula saw his net worth jump to $283 million. Across the Valley at Intel, soft-spoken Gordon Moore was up to $327 million. They were leading examples of the several thousand millionaires (at least on paper) created by Silicon Valley.

Of course there are the miracle stories. Like that of K. Philip Hwang, who emigrated from South Korea. Hwang worked his way through Utah State sweeping floors at Lake Tahoe casinos. When he started his company, Televideo, in 1976, his résumé was so weak that he couldn't find a venture capitalist willing to back him. So he mortgaged everything he owned to raise the start-up money. Televideo went public in 1983—and within weeks Hwang was worth $755 million.

Porter Hurt, a beefy middle-aged businessman with a penchant for gold jewelry and Cadillac limousines, started his career in Silicon Valley pounding four thousand nails a day into Sheetrock and ended up owning three electronics companies, including personal computer maker Actrix Inc., with combined 1984 sales estimated at $300 million.

So far we've just been talking about electronics types and their bankers. There are also the hundreds, if not thousands, of other people who have been made rich by supplying Silicon Valley with expert information, or food, or housing or entertainment. A visit to the Marriott Hotel in Santa Clara or Ferrari of Los Gatos (where Barnhart bought his car) underscores the realization that many a buck can be made feeding the desires of that entrepreneurial engine of the Valley.

Dataquest Corp. began as a tiny consulting firm researching markets for semiconductor companies. By the early eighties it was the preeminent market-research firm in electronics, with three hundred employees, quoted almost weekly in the national news magazines.

In 1973, long-haired political science major Rory Fuerst drove a half-demolished old VW Bug down from San Francisco State looking for a career. He found it renovating the Valley's seemingly endless supply of worn running shoes. With thirty-seven dollars and the use of his mother's oven, Fuerst built a $15 million company by the time he was twenty-eight.

Where does all of this money go? Where do the billionaires, and decamillionaires, and even the puny millionaires and demimillionaires, spend their cash?

First, one must realize that in the business world, particularly in new start-ups, there is a sizable difference between total personal value and disposable income. As Steve Jobs said, "All of those millions don't really mean anything because I can't use them. In reality I only have access to a million or so." Getting rich is not the only reason entrepreneurs build companies. In fact, according to psychologists, it is one of the least important reasons. Control is far more important—and control is measured in percentage ownership of the company's outstanding shares of stock. Thus, every sale of stock signals a commensurate erosion in control.

This conservation of equity, combined with a native, almost Calvinistic reluctance toward ostentation, made Silicon Valley a pretty egalitarian place in its early days. Men like Packard and Hewlett, Moore, Grove and Sporck were not exactly high-living, flashy types. Hewlett and Packard could be seen on weekends shopping for tools in paint-spattered clothes. Sporck drives a pickup. Moore has lived in the same modest house in Santa Clara for two decades.

In the early 1960s, with no slums to speak of in the Valley, it was hard for outsiders to tell who were the success stories and who were not. The average-looking guy beside you in a bar might be a legendary inventor, a cherry picker, a tycoon or a janitor. In fact, one could generally assume that the neighbor with the most expensive sports car or the tailored suits was probably not a tycoon at all but a middle manager with dreams of glory, probably a salesman. The lone exception to this, of course, was Jerry Sanders, who might be considered a forerunner of things to come, and whose vilification by his peers for relatively tame eccentricities is a measure of how conservative the Valley was.

Much of this charming humility, or at least self-effacement, could be laid at the feet of the engineering sensibility. The prototypical engineer of the first half of the century, the image these pioneers modeled themselves after, was the man in the hard hat and rolled-up shirt sleeves who built the bridges and the skyscrapers. This man had little truck with the effete glitter and flash of wealth. This model was combined with that of the research scientist, a man immersed in improving the lot of humanity with little time for the trappings of society.

But there has always been that insanity factor in the society of electrical engineers, a structural weakness that, given the right external pressure, can crack and send the individual crashing down into perdition, or at least a good time. Lee De Forest was an early case in point, with his run-ins with courts and his infatuation with movie stars. Shockley is another case, with his racial theories and genius sperm banks. The latter-day case, of course, is Steve Wozniak, with his rock festivals and Datsun commercials.

For the most part, these occasional bouts with pixilation in the ranks were overwhelmed by the predominating soberness of the profession as a whole. This changed, however, with the rise of the modern entrepreneur, the man or woman who was just as much a businessperson as a scientist, who not only had to design the product but had to sell it to a skeptical market. In truth, entrepreneurs weren't just engineers turned executives, but just as often the other way around. This odd cross-fertilization between two species rarely found together in the same environment produced an odd sort of hybrid that is Silicon Valley's most famous creature.

By the mid-seventies, the Valley was seemingly filled with such people. These were the new trend setters, the best known being Nolan Bushnell and Steve Jobs. Not only were these folks unrepentant about their wealth and nonconformity, they positively reveled in it. Nolan Bushnell's rise at Atari serves as a kind of watershed. Before that, to flaunt one's wealth or position was considered all but taboo; after that it was a mark of personal repression not to. Not long after Bushnell came the next generation: Jobs on his motorcycle or spouting counterculture clichés, Jimmy Treybig swigging beer and acting down-home. And since these individuals and others like them were the role models for thousands of Silicon Valley up-and-comers, it wasn't long before every wateringhole in the area was overrun by hip Bushnell clones and arrogant Jobs junkies, many of them in hock up to their blow-dried hair.

There was another element in all of this. It was that many of the men who had made it big in the Valley's early years were beginning to grow tired of the rat race and were pulling back from the day-to-day operation of their firms. Many decided that, God damn it, I've earned the right to enjoy myself, to be extravagant. Others, in typical Valley form, had gotten divorced, and like all divorced men on the hunt, began to spend considerable time and money on getting the packaging just right for public presentation.

Whatever the cause, by the mid-seventies, Silicon Valley's freeways were jammed with the world's most expensive and exotic automobiles and the hills were pockmarked with the latest California mansions. The days of remaining "among the people" in some tract house in Cupertino became history. Being worth $100 million and still living like some car salesman fresh out from Des Moines remained admirable, but also a bit suspicious. It was too forced, too recherché. Now, one's status in the Valley began to be measured in terms of one's topographical elevation. To still live in one of the Cities of the Plain was to somehow not have made the Big Score. Far preferable was to have an address in one of the towns that ran along the base of the Coast Range overlooking the Valley. Places like Woodside and Los Altos Hills and Monte Vista and Saratoga and Los Gatos.

Los Gatos had long been a funky little village, a haven for artists, bohemians and rich vacationers down from San Francisco or up from Hollywood. By the sixties it had become a counterculture haven from the sterility of the rest of Santa Clara County, its eccentric style fueled by hippie back-to-the-earth folk who'd come down from the mountains for supplies. Los Gatos was a small town in which everyone seemed to know everyone, from the mayor down to the strange little man who voluntarily cleaned the streets. Los Gatos had the Valley's best bars and funkiest stores, and it became a Mecca for Valleyites looking for such a respite.

Sometime around 1970, Silicon Valley discovered Los Gatos, and within a decade the town had changed forever. Woodside and Saratoga simply absorbed their few wildly affluent newcomers, forced them to adapt to old ways. Los Altos and Monte Vista became more inhabited. But Los Gatos was too fragile for such an onslaught. Within a decade it had become an utterly different town. Rents, which had been the lowest in the Valley, were now the highest—and it goes without saying that the older citizen was quickly driven out. Now the typical Los Gatoan was a young executive at an electronics firm, making one hundred grand a year, driving a Porsche, married, but probably without kids. The commerce of the city changed to meet this new crowd. At one time the unofficial town meeting place was a Laundromat, now it was Mountain Charlie's or C. B. Hannegan's saloons, where on Friday and Saturday nights the smart set jammed together like herrings. The streets, particularly the main drag of University Avenue, became parking lots. The town's artistic side changed too. Los Gatos was no longer the place to buy fine crafts; rather it was the place to buy an exotic car (as Barnhart did, at Ferrari of Los Gatos).

For those who didn't or couldn't take to the hills there were a handful of enclaves in the flatlands. Tucked away in neighborhoods in Los Altos, Santa Clara and even Mountain View, Sunnyvale and San Jose were a few exclusive homes, many of them former estates, or formidable and towering Victorians and Edwardians left over from another time. Perhaps the most appealing of these areas was in Palo Alto, next to the downtown. Here were several hundred blocks of magnificent old manors on arbored lanes. Even better, the best stores in the Valley were just a walking distance away: revival theaters, fine-art galleries, specialty stores, the Stanford Shopping Center—perhaps the world's only famous shopping mall—and beyond, the University. Here, in Palo Alto, one's neighbor didn't always have to be the CEO of a disk drive company. He or she might well be a successful writer or a Stanford philosophy professor, or even Dave Packard. Only here was the roaring river of high tech refreshed, if only a little, by a spring of nonscientific thought.

Driving through these exclusive neighborhoods, especially the newest ones, the visitor would be amazed at the diversity of housing styles. Here was a French Tudor next to a French Provincial, there an ersatz Victorian just down the hill from what could only be described as a traditional suburban California ranch-style home inflated to forty rooms. A drive up Freeway 280 along the spine of the mountains to San Francisco was a lesson in architecture, ranging from the sublime (the award-winning Foothill College with its wooden walls and exquisite hill-hugging layout) to the absurd (a house with stained-glass windows of prancing unicorns). High on a hilltop aerie could be seen a house that looked like a modern Gothic church, while just below it was another house in the shape of a pyramid. Farther up were imitation English country homes that had an uncanny resemblance to some local bars, the ancient and magnificent country mansion of the Spreckels family (sugar refining) and even a cluster of cement huts that looked exactly like a mud village in Central Africa.

For all of their outrageousness, at least these few houses offered a modicum of novelty and entertainment. For the most part the other homes had a disconcerting sameness. For all of their cost, the majority resembled nothing more than glorified tract homes; the owner, despite his wealth, unable to shake off his Valley roots. The interiors of many of these homes were the same, the decor right out of a Breuners showroom. It was often quite shocking to walk into an enormous home, with Mercedeses and Porsches parked out front, and find a living room full of knickknacks and old reclining chairs, or garish leather-and-wood furniture and mirrored wallpaper.

There was also something disarming about this apparent innocence. A visitor at a party at Steve Wozniak's enormous English turreted mansion high in the Santa Cruz Mountains was amazed to find the house furnished in such a way "that it looked like they had just walked into Sears and ordered everything they saw."

Like the fabled Texas oil tycoons, the Brahmins of Silicon Valley recognized their own stylelessness and went to great pains to overcome it. Many were Beverly Hillbillies, high-tech style—the brilliant young computer scientist whose only dream in life was to design the perfect program, and his wife, a former lab assistant or receptionist, who suddenly found themselves worth $5 million and told by their tax accountant to buy a big house—fast.

Of course, there were exceptions to all this, folks who used their fortunes to build a well-stocked library or wine cellar. One local corporate attorney had rare modern paintings on his wall, but on the whole the median life-style among the Valley's wealthy was skewed toward a sort of overblown middle-classedness.

So where did all the money go? A large share, of course, went into homes. In Silicon Valley, where a three-bedroom home near a freeway went for $150,000 and a half-demolished shack in Palo Alto for the same amount, a ritzy chateau in the hills cost a hunk of change. Then, of course, there were the cars. With the possible exception of a few other nouveau riche high-rent districts (Newport Beach, Dallas), Silicon Valley probably had the highest-quality road gear per capita in the world. On a given day, one could see every car spotlighted in this month's edition of *Road and Track*. This being California and Silicon Valley, every sporty or expensive new car introduced in the United States usually arrived here first. The day the $140,000 Rolls-Royce Corniche was introduced in the local paper it could be seen tooling down Bayshore Freeway. Mercedes limousines, the new gull-winged BMW M1 and the old gull-winged Mercedes 300 SL, Bentleys, Lamborghini Countachs, an endless stream of Porsche Turbos, all were there. Cars that weren't even supposed to be in the United States could be seen. Al Oliverio, vice-president of sales at Hewlett-Packard, who wanted a new Ferrari but discovered it wasn't allowed in this country because it hadn't been crash-tested and certified, joined a consortium of prospective buyers to pay a little more in order to buy one of the model to be demolished for the test.

In cars, as with everything else, the engineering mind was at work in the purchase of new cars. Maseratis and Aston Martins were nice, but when the time came to plunk down the cash, most Valley tycoons opted for a big BMW or a Porsche or a Mercedes. They may have been staid, even ugly, but by God those Germans knew how to engineer a car! This attitude, not unexpectedly, filtered down to the vast middle population hankering to make the big money. So, as a result, spurred on by well-used leasing programs at local dealerships, probably the two most ubiquitous cars found in the parking lots of Silicon Valley were the lowest-priced models of these three German companies.

Of course, not everyone who can afford a Porsche ought to be driving one. Too often sitting behind the wheel was a mousy engineer or secretary with little understanding of the car's capabilities—"Porsche Twinkies" they came to be called—and they accounted for the high number of accidents in Santa Clara County involving Porsche 924s.

After houses and cars, the next most likely acquisition by a new

Silicon Valley tycoon was electronics. It shouldn't surprise anyone that Silicon Valley was one of its own biggest customers. The man who spent his day designing a new computer wanted to come home to the very best stereo system, projection television, the hottest video game and the latest electronic gadget of any kind. Many a Valley mansion was indistinguishable from a toy store or video game arcade. Life imitated work in Silicon Valley.

It was hard not to notice that much of this money was spent not just on material things but on practical, physical, *mechanical* things—another manifestation of the engineering mind, a triumph of function as form, a late victory for the Modernist school.

People everywhere, when they come into great wealth, soon find themselves disenchanted with their own Babbittry. This didn't happen to the nouveau riche in Silicon Valley with such immediate force as it might on Long Island or even the computer enclave along Route 128 outside Boston. After all, Silicon Valley was a fairly remote setting, remarkably homogeneous in its composition and for many years quite insulated from the rest of the world. When the rich man up the road wears the same Penney's short-sleeved shirts as you, there is hardly the pressure for upward mobility one might find in more cosmopolitan regions.

But the outside world in time found its way into Silicon Valley, and where it didn't, Silicon Valley rushed out to embrace it. Just an hour's drive to the north, in San Francisco, one of the world's most sophisticated cities, lay an unforgettable lesson in how to live rich properly. On pre-"going public" tours of stock analysts in New York, these Westerners got a chance to go one-on-one with the Wall Street boys in their pinstripes and Ivy League ways. Then, as the company grew, and as marketing breadth expanded, these same executives found themselves in London and Berlin cutting deals with the cream of the European business community and staying in the world's most elegant hotels. After that it was "How you gonna keep 'em in Hush Puppies after they've seen Paree?"

Now, they wanted class.

But where to find that class is a different story, and the Valley is still in searching. Some have gone the route of increasingly extravagant toys, like Lear Jets. For others it is to mingle with the jetsetters in Malibu or Aspen or Manhattan. For some executives it is simply getting the right table at the Lion & Compass, Nolan "Pong" Bushnell's restaurant for Silicon Valley's executive elite. Others have settled for more elegant, and thus more elusive things. Like an appreciation of art: the better Valley homes are now lined with lithographs acquired from the local gallery chain, which presents them to prospective customers in a darkened room illuminated by a single spotlight. Late Picasso and Miró, Kasimir, Dalí and Neiman seem the artists of choice as this book is being written—a couple of grand a pop, about all one ought to have to pay for art, and they are supposed to appreciate as fast as Atari stock. (Some, it should be noted, have advanced beyond this art-to-match-the-couch stage, notably Steve Jobs, who has become a fanatic collector of rare Japanese prints.)

Another source of great pride from those who've made the Big Score is a knowledge of wines. Here alone (except maybe in cars) the wealthy of Silicoᵢ. Valley have an average depth of knowledge that surpasses that of any other comparable society. With America's greatest wine regions ninety miles to the north and fifty miles to the south, Valleyites had a unique opportunity to specialize in viticulture, with particular emphasis upon spotting some remarkable pressing from the tiniest and most obscure winery.

The role of two shopping centers can never be overestimated when discussing the education of the Valley's elite. The Stanford Shopping Center in Palo Alto and Valco Fashion Park in Cupertino were the finishing school for all of the Valley's electronics debutants and debutantes. Here, specialty stores displayed for them the latest in fashions from around the world, taught them to eat pasta and espresso, showed them how to use a French coffee press and a gelato machine, wear Harris tweed, rep ties and Italian shoes. Here, women could buy the dresses they saw in *Vogue,* men the suits and sweaters their wives spotted for them in *GQ.* Even more, as one of the Valley's leading social centers, it provided them the opportunity to show off these clothes before their peers. On nights and weekends, these two malls took on the look of a vast cocktail party in which children were invited, with several thousand guests all milling counterclockwise in a great whirlpool.

None of this should be seen as condescending; rather it is part of the evolutionary process found in all boomtowns—only here, like the pace of technology, simply accelerated. What counterbalanced this often amusing race toward respectability was a fundamental decency among the wealthy. After all, these were not dissolute fourth-generation heirs spending their fortunes on decadent self-gratification, but the people who had earned the money. Among Silicon Valley's tycoons, almost everyone was a self-made person. Through brilliance and terribly hard work, not the death of some ancestor, they had made it. And like most pioneers who had come through the fire to the Promised Land, few seemed ready to rest out their days in noblesse oblige.

In fact, what the Valley lacked in sophistication it more than made up in energy. Perpetual, bottomless, infinite energy. After a seventy-hour week it was not uncommon for the young and affluent to jam into a singles bar like T.G.I. Friday's or, some morning at the start of fourteen-hour workday, to squeeze in an hour of intense racket ball. This emphasis on physical health, taken to its peculiarly California level of hysteria, was behind the success of such places as the Good Earth, a chain of three all but vegetarian natural food restaurants in Silicon Valley that were jammed every night for years after they opened. Exercise clubs replaced the East Coast eating clubs as the places outside of work where deals were made, companies founded.

The great secular temple to the worship of health and eternal youth was the Decathlon Club, a fitness center turned way of life. Complete with tennis and racket ball courts, an indoor stream and a French restaurant, the Decathlon Club seemed to capture all that Silicon Valley wanted to see as best in itself. Here could be seen the cream of the Valley's executive rows. Multimillion-dollar deals were made on the tennis court or in the carpeted locker room. Here the sun and health and competitive fire combined to create the perfect sweaty, energetic oasis from the passions of daily Valley business life. So accurately did the Decathlon Club fit the style of Silicon Valley that some firms even used its meeting rooms for press conferences. That introducing new products in a glorified gym surprised no one only proves that nothing could have been more apt.

The health orientation in Silicon Valley found other outlets as well. Mornings and evenings residential streets seemed jammed with joggers in their designer togs. For the serious runners there were numerous weekend ten-kilometer races, the San Francisco Bay to Breakers (with tens of thousands of participants) and marathons. For the true zealots there were also only-in-California events like hundred-mile cross-country hikes up and down rocky mountainsides in the Sierras. In the summer, local lakes, percolation ponds and inlets of the bay sported wind surfers and Hobee Cats. Winter, of course, was dedicated to skiing at the numerous resorts around Lake Tahoe (and for the very wealthy, Aspen, Sun Valley and Provo). It has been said that only in the Bay Area can one ski in deep powder in the morning and surf ten-foot curls that afternoon, and many rich and single young Valley residents seem to try that each weekend.

All in all, to have made it in Silicon Valley while one was young was just about the best of all possible worlds. The best part was that, contrary to most urban areas, one rarely saw people much less successful than oneself—which happily kept guilt from interfering with one's self-actualization.

* * *

Engineers, computer scientists and executives of electronics companies weren't the only folks to enjoy the largesse of Silicon Valley's success and multiply those revenues out through the local economy. The number of recipients is too great to list, but a partial selection might offer an idea of the many different ways to dip the bucket into the Valley's river of gold.

On the personal side there were department stores, wine shops, automobile dealerships, gourmet kitchen-tool stores, computer and stereo stores, boutiques, boulangeries, hot tub shops, gardeners, ski shops (one of them the largest in the world), Nautilus health clubs, athletic-shoe stores, an endless number of real estate agencies, beauty salons, bicycle shops, volume art galleries, Italian-ice and yogurt shoppes, software stores, divorce attorneys, psychologists, hookers, florists, foreign auto parts joints, saloons, catering trucks ("roach coaches"), restaurants, fast food franchises, drug dealers, laundries, lost-cat-and-dog detectives, horse stables, limousine services, private schools, drug rehabilitation clinics, car-polishing, foreign restaurants, yacht repair, bookstores, record stores, video stores, drugstores, movie theaters . . . in short, everything that makes up the fabric of affluent American life in the late twentieth century was here in Silicon Valley. If this sounds like, say, Manhattan, keep in mind that the Valley had less than a fifth the population and no more than a handful of buildings taller than ten stories. What makes this even more remarkable is that in every one of these businesses at least somebody got very rich by tapping into his or her neighbors' fortunes from electronics.

The same was true of selling to the Valley's business side. It was often joked that the people who really made it rich in Silicon Valley were the ones who sold it those ubiquitous five-foot, carpet-covered office cubicle dividers found in every office in the Valley—that and the folks who sold the potted fiddle-leaf fig and ficus plants that fit into the alcoves of these dividers.

For every way there was of making a fortune from the flow of electrons in Silicon Valley there were probably ten equally effective ways that required absolutely no knowledge of electromagnetic theory at all. Like consulting. Small fortunes were made telling the Valley what precious metals to use, how to keep out unions, what the latest threat was from the Japanese, which were the newest patents, how to increase productivity, how to hire an ad agency, how to train top executives to deal with investigative television reporters, what color to paint the walls, how to keep the workers happy, and on and on—and not an electronics specialist in the lot.

Companies needed office equipment too, putting a lot of money into the pockets of the Herman Miller Co. At one point, Sunnyvale Stationery, originally little more than a pen-and-paper place, became a fast-growing local firm. Its new headquarters, which housed the company's expanded line of office equipment, computer supplies and graphic arts materials, was one of the Valley's more impressive structures.

Another big winner in the Silicon Valley sweepstakes was hostelry. As late as 1975 there were no more than three or four large hotels in all of Santa Clara County. Visitors to Hewlett-Packard in the sixties would stay at places like the Tiki Inn and the Glass Slipper Motel. San Jose's great hotels, the De Anza and the Sainte Claire, had fallen into seedy disrepute. That left the increasingly aged Hyatt in San Jose as the host of everything from Eagle Scout dinners to corporate annual meetings.

The first hotelier to take the plunge in Silicon Valley was Marriott Hotels, which built a hotel in Santa Clara in 1976 as much because of its neighboring Great America amusement park as anything else. But the Mormon firm quickly discovered that it could keep the cash registers ringing selling rooms and firewater to the local gentiles. Pretty soon the calendar of the Marriott was full of events like dinner meetings of the American Electronics Association and the hotel had embarked upon the construction of its second tower.

The success of the Marriott was not lost upon the other great hotel chains and by the seventies the Valley was the home for multihundred-room hotels bearing such names as Hilton, Sheraton (two of them, including a restored Sainte Claire), Red Lion and Holiday Inn (two). On any weekday the odds were better than even that by twilight none would have a vacancy.

Less obvious beneficiaries of Silicon Valley's success were transportation companies, notably airlines and rental car firms. Tiny San Jose Airport, once little more than a municipal runway for a few dozen Piper Cherokees and Bonanzas, became what might best be called a pocket national airport. All the major airlines were represented here, with flights arriving—almost through the spires of downtown San Jose —from every part of the country. At last an equal number of additional Valley visitors (and all Asian visitors) kept San Francisco Airport busy. And these businesspeople needed wheels to get around the extensive freeway system of the peninsula, so rent-a-car businesses made a killing, and everywhere could be seen dull American intermediate cars with their little square yellow bumper stickers. (Travel agents of course enjoyed a continuous booming business, the most aggressive of which, Silicon Valley Travel, became one of the largest in the country.)

It goes without saying that the construction and real estate firms were among the leading recipients of Silicon Valley's growth boom. In construction, a handful of firms vied for leadership in the business of tilting up concrete walls, the best known being Carl Berg and Associates. Because of the extraordinary expansion rate of the Valley in the mid-seventies, these firms employed the latest techniques for slapping four walls up fast, getting the place wired, piped and certified, sod rolled out on the ever present four-foot, sidewalk-free earth berm out front (there are almost no sidewalks in Silicon Valley: one is simply expected to drive, even to the next parking lot, yet it is de rigueur to run five miles in the street during the lunch hour). One technique nearly all the construction companies settled upon during the real runaway growth periods was this concrete tilt-up, now less common as the Valley begins to grow vertically, but still synonymous with the area. In this technique, the walls are created on-site, from concrete poured into forms staked out on the ground (sometimes with a pattern of rocks for design). Dried, the walls are yanked on end by a crane and bolted together. Windows are then glassed and floors poured, and in a couple of weekends the new corporate client has already moved his equipment in, hired a staff, put a sign out front and is busy manufacturing as if he had been in business twenty years.

Although they sound like houses of cards, Silicon Valley tilt-ups are remarkably sturdy structures—as they need to be to meet local earthquake standards—and, when looked at singly, quite attractive. Unfortunately, when massed by the hundreds in a ten-square-mile area, their inescapable common features begin to assert themselves to the point of nausea and they take on the monotony of what they ironically most resemble: integrated-circuit chips stuffed in rows on a printed-circuit board.

Dull or not, these buildings were certainly not ugly, and they played a crucial role in the development of the Valley. So did the developers. In many instances, these firms served as a special type of venture capitalist by backing the construction of buildings for young companies with no track record on the hunch that the investment would one day pan out. It almost always did. Berg, for instance, became one of the Valley's wealthiest men, even owning (with Corvus disk drive president Michael D'Addio) the San Jose Earthquakes professional soccer team.

Commercial and residential real estate took off shortly after the Second World War with the general California construction boom and never looked back. By the sixties, it was enjoying the almost exponential growth of the electronics business and its surrounding support industries. These companies had an insatiable thirst for warm bodies, and these new employees and their families needed homes. Down went the orchards and up went large housing tracts, filling in the gaps between old Mountain View, Sunnyvale and Santa Clara and creating almost new towns out of Cupertino, Campbell and the flatland portions of Los Gatos and Saratoga. In the fifties, the best-known name in housing developers was Mackay, with its embryonic California home of enclosed courtyards and exposed-beam roofs. A few years later the mantle was taken over by Eichler, which peaked or flattened the beam roof, replaced walls with huge windows, veneered entire rooms with mahogany and completely enclosed the courtyard in an atrium. The result was an exquisite (if flammable) house of light, in which one seemed as much outdoors as in. The Eichler home remains, for many, the quintessential northern California home, and more of these homes were found in Santa Clara County than anywhere else.

A simple explanation for why real estate was such a plum opportunity in Silicon Valley comes from a look at the prices. An original four-bedroom Eichler, circa 1965, sold for about fifteen thousand dollars. Fifteen years later, the same home, its slab heating and all-electric kitchen about to go on the fritz, went on the market at two hundred thousand dollars. Not only that, but during the intervening decade and a half that house may have gone through four upwardly mobile owners, each dutifully paying a commission to his or her real estate agent.

This housing boom combined with the inflationary seventies to create a market bubble, with speculators racing around buying up every house in sight and young buyers betting on the permanence of inflation with balloon payments. Real estate agents had a field day. By this time every important national real estate firm (Century 21, Red Carpet, Coldwell Banker) had set up shop in the Valley, providing employment for legions of housewives looking to liberate themselves, and, just as important, a refuge for victims of the nasty aerospace layoffs at Lockheed in the beginning of the decade. But homegrown real estate firms did even better, with operations like Contempo, Merit-McBride, RAM and Taylor Properties having offices in nearly every large town. The biggest winner was probably Cornish & Carey, which was not only a leader in residential but also the preeminent agency for office space. Scott Carey even became mayor of Palo Alto for a time.

* * *

A by-product of the electronics revolution was the rise of a trade press of unequaled wealth and power. By 1980 there were more than *two hundred* trade magazines covering, it would seem, every inch of the electronics industry. There were magazines not just for mainframe computers, minicomputers, and personal computers but for every facet of those businesses: magazines for educational users of personal computers, software magazines, computer retailers, corporate buyers of minicomputers, electronic games hobbyists, computer communications and computer peripherals. There were also magazines for owners of individual products, like the Radio Shack *TRS-80* magazine, and the IBM *PC* magazine—the latter so stuffed with advertisements that it resembled a Sears catalog. This doesn't even count the company-produced magazines, like *Apple* on Apple's or HP's *Measure.* A laboratory scientist at Intel might subscribe to ten trade magazines, an executive five. A personal computer freak might subscribe to about forty others. It wasn't just one magazine per market either. Big publishers like Ziff-Davis, McGraw-Hill, Cahners and Hayden all stood toe-to-toe with magazines in almost each of these markets.

All of this crowding had the expected effect: it flattened out the quality of the journalism in the trade press. There were only a handful of good writers in the business, compared with hundreds of jobs, and so much of the writing in the trade press was little more than rewritten publicity releases or roundup stories offering little insight for the reader. Making matters worse was the fact that with so many magazines vying for such a small population of companies, no one was about to piss off an advertiser. That's why a newspaper reporter looking for the first time into the problem of toxic chemical leaks in the Valley was shocked to hear from a number of trade press peers that they had known about the problem for years. Why didn't you write about it? the reporter asked incredulously. "Well," replied one, "you've got to think of the trade press as being in the business of sort of *publicizing* the industry."

(There were a few exceptions to this general shoddiness. The flagship magazine of McGraw-Hill, *Business Week,* was one. So was a tiny, but expensive, newsletter published for fifteen years by Don Hoeffler, a former reporter for *Electronic News.* Hoeffler's newsletter was gossipy, cruel, petty, occasionally libelous, but he also unflinchingly aired the stories no one else dared to write.)

Keeping track of all of these publications, filling their ravenous need for copy and keeping client companies satisfied were the P.R. agencies, the last piece in the puzzle of moving uptown in Silicon Valley.

The P.R. czar of Silicon Valley was Regis McKenna, and his Valley experience dated back to Noyce's Fairchild. Regis was an average P.R. man when it came to the day-to-day business of pitching the newest memory chip story to the *Electronic Design.* He was also, by most reports, a miserable manager. But he was a visionary, as much an entrepreneur as the men building chip houses around him. One of those chip houses was Intel and Regis quit National and started his own independent agency to handle it.

Regis McKenna Public Relations became the preeminent P.R. agency in Silicon Valley and its chief kingmaker because McKenna had one brilliant insight: in time, he thought, the companies of Silicon Valley would be big enough and important enough that their activities would become a daily concern of the entire world; and the trade press would diminish to lesser importance as the nation's most important publications came to Silicon Valley to cover this most important story of the late twentieth century. And Regis McKenna P.R. would be there waiting for them with a collection of hot companies and executives ready for national acclaim.

By the mid-seventies, McKenna's dream came true. On his platter he had two of the best firms, Intel and Apple, and a host of others. With the revenues of the big two he built the largest P.R. firm in the Valley. For nearly a decade he had cultivated the East Coast press, visiting them, helping them to comprehend high tech. He knew them on a first-name basis. So well trained was the national press that whenever a reporter came to Silicon Valley, his or her first stop was usually Regis McKenna P.R., there to sift through McKenna's clipping library prepared especially for reporters, then off for a tour of McKenna clients, plus a few other notable companies thrown in.

When Silicon Valley exploded into the national consciousness in the late 1970s, as much from McKenna's spadework as from any historic imperative, it was his clients who received the majority of national attention, Apple's Steve Jobs being the subject of two *Time* profiles, McKenna client Visicorp the locus of most software companies, Intel the name most associated with the microprocessor revolution.

In contrast to the anonymous careers of most great P.R. men, McKenna himself became relatively famous. The accolades were well earned. Regis more than anyone had put Silicon Valley on the map and given its leaders the final step uptown to national attention, speeches before Congress, meetings with the President, *legitimacy.* On the other side, McKenna had all but served as the marketing wing of some of his young corporate clients, telling them how to sell their products and where. McKenna was indeed the maker of kings, and he became the confidant of princes, from Steve Jobs to California governor Jerry Brown. His story was even written up in *Fortune* magazine. Once again, a comparison with Hollywood was inevitable: only there and in Silicon Valley could a flack become equal to, if not greater than, his employers.

*　　*　　*

The newly ordained Silicon Valley tycoon followed a path cut by those that had come before, a Move Uptown whose steps were tightly choreographed, just as the process of building a new company from scratch had been refined by venture capitalists. The new tycoon knew where to live, where to go, what to buy and whom to know. He or she also became part of a constant but ever growing myth about Silicon Valley that had been created by reporters and press agents years before, an image that allowed considerable flexibility and improvisation yet still contained a set of key images for outsiders to lean upon. This process of Moving Uptown and becoming a Silicon Valley tycoon usually began with the coming-out party called "going public" with its step up to national glory and perhaps even fame.

Sometimes the Moving Uptown program short-circuited, the well-worked, case-hardened process broke down and sadly revealed its fragility, showed that it too was vulnerable to human folly and to fate.

So it was with Dennis Barnhart, the president of Eagle Computer on his going-public day. That afternoon, with his yacht salesman in the seat beside him, Barnhart rocketed his Ferrari off the freeway, through a railing and down a Los Gatos hillside. He died pinned under the car with the EAGLE B license plates.

"They had to be flying," said a spokesman for the fire department.

9

T-Shirt Tycoons

Now it is time to discuss two of the best-known names in the modern Silicon Valley: Atari and Apple.

By the mid-1970s the Silicon Valley ground was ripe for a new breed of entrepreneurs. The local new start-up support network was now sufficiently in place to support even the least experienced businessperson— as long as that person had the right idea and was willing to work hard. There were in the Valley people just like that, young geniuses who just a few years before would have been, for their youthfulness and eccentricities, relegated to the back lab of some large company.

Now these entrepreneurs in jeans and long hair had enjoyed their own liberation, and out of this revolution would come two of the best-known Silicon Valley companies, Apple and Atari (even their names bespeak a change). Their founders were of the generation of the sixties, and they took on some of the countercultural trappings of that era, yet retained the hard business sense of true corporate builders. In an extraordinarily short time they would revolutionize the way we worked and played—and in the process become the Valley's "T-shirt tycoons."

*　　*　　*

Probably the most famous of all high-technology start-ups is Atari Inc. No other Silicon Valley company had a more unconventional beginning, reached a higher zenith of fame, or grew old and rigid so fast. The quintessential Silicon Valley firm, Atari was the most in every way.

Silicon Valley had never seen a firm so unconventional. Founded and run in a dope smoke haze, it grew faster than veteran businessmen thought possible, stumbled, then was acquired by an entertainment giant; then, in a handful of years, it achieved $1 billion in annual sales and created a consumer revolution in the process. But, entranced by all of this success, convinced of its own invulnerability, Atari spread itself too thin, believed its own press releases, lived its illusions, alienated its personnel—and finally toppled over in a crash that echoed across the world's business community. Atari was a firm that did everything to excess.

Its relatively inauspicious start is evidence for the argument that any one of the hundreds of tiny "garage" start-ups scattered about the Valley at any given moment might one day blossom into a world beater.

The firm was founded in 1972 with five hundred dollars in start-up money in the modest Santa Clara home of a twenty-six-year-old research engineer for Ampex named Nolan K. Bushnell. The title "Atari," though it sounded like another alphabet soup Valley name, was actually the name of the "checkmate" move in the venerable Oriental strategy game go—one of Bushnell's favorite games at the time.

In this house, late into the night, Bushnell worked in a shop converted from one of his two daughters' bedrooms. In a blizzard of diagram-covered papers, Bushnell slowly roughed out an idea he had contemplated since his college days at the University of Utah. It was to be a cross between the space wars game he and his engineering school classmates had played on the university's multimillion-dollar computer and the midway games he had enjoyed during his summers working at a carnival.

One of the Valley's most remarkable idea men, Bushnell was only a mediocre engineer. But that mediocrity gave him the detachment to look in on the industry from the outside and recognize the precise moment when a new technology's time had come. And in 1972, Nolan realized that the inexorable development of the integrated circuit had finally made possible a mass-producible consumer version of his college space wars game. And it was a version of this game, called Computer Space, over which Bushnell spent months laboring.

Computer Space, the first commercial video game, was a technical marvel for its era. Too marvelous; it was ahead of its time, scaring away customers accustomed to a lifetime of pinball. In the end, fewer than two thousand were sold.

But, like a true entrepreneur, Bushnell was only convinced by failure that he was on the right track. As the saying goes, no one ever lost money underestimating the intelligence of the American public. So the next time, Nolan, decided, he would build a game so mindless and self-evident a monkey or its equivalent (a drunk in a saloon) could instantly understand it. Bushnell borrowed fifty thousand dollars from his buddies and a local banker, hired a computer programmer and incorporated Atari Inc.

The resulting game, a simple, electronic form of Ping-Pong, was called Pong. Shopping malls, amusement parks and bars would never be the same.

Gun-shy after the Computer Space debacle, Bushnell decided a more conservative approach was necessary: he would field-test Pong before launching into full-scale production. He chose Andy Capp's Tavern on El Camino in Sunnyvale, a young people's bar housed in one of the Valley's oldest buildings. (It is now called the Country Store and, fittingly, it is across the street from an appliance store and a Radio Shack, two big beneficiaries of the consumer electronics revolution Bushnell was about to initiate.)

This time, Bushnell had found a game simple enough to be approachable by anyone. As the story goes, less than a day later the tavern owner called to complain that the game had already broken down. A quick repair check found the reason: the coin basket (a plastic milk jug) was so full of quarters that it was jamming the machine. The Age of the Video Game, for better or worse, had begun.

Within two years, Bushnell had sold more than ten thousand games (ten times as many counterfeit games were also sold) at about three thousand dollars apiece. The pinball machine, that gaudy electromechanical wonder of flashing lights and cavorting cartoon sirens that had eased the adolescent angst of generations of sweaty-palmed young men, was doomed, its staccato bells and drubbing flippers replaced by electronic beeps and whirs, cubist creatures and bursts of migraine-like flashes.

Pinball machines weren't the only victims, only the first and most obvious. There were also pool tables and board games, Ping-Pong sets and playing cards, all similarly marked for obsolescence. Centuries of human imagination had gone into developing standardized devices to organize the play of cultured people. Now they could be replaced by little engines of pleasure that could reduce excitement to a video screen, a joystick and a couple of push buttons. The entertainment here was not the intellectual stimulation of a chess match, but rather the exhausted exhilaration of a fighter pilot in a dogfight. The brain was assaulted through every sense, hand–eye coordination was all, strategy was worthless to all but the most expert. A good video game was well-crafted, organized hysteria, an electronic fire fight, in which the only goal in the midst of chaos was survival—an increasingly unlikely prospect as the game's built-in metronome slowly accelerated to panic.

In the end, one always lost, was defeated, destroyed, annihilated in a burst of light—truly a game for our time. Victory lay in losing less slowly than others, a fact proven by a point tally, left in the machine's memory with one's initials as a gauntlet thrown down to all comers.

When it was over, as the screen resumed its patented huckster routine in siren call to the next person with two bits in his or her pocket, the spent player was left with little joy, but rather a residue of adrenaline rush. Each generation finds its game—crossword puzzles, Monopoly, Scrabble, touch football—and in the passive age of television, computers, Star Wars and the brief, jolting hit of cocaine, could there be a better instrument of amusement than the video game? Could Silicon Valley have found a more apt metaphor for itself and the new society it was helping to create?

As history repeatedly shows, those responsible for a new cultural force often have little idea at first of the magnitude of their achievement —and sometimes end up not among the beneficiaries. Usually they are just as much caught in the wave of a new fad as everyone else, and are just as likely to end up on the rocks when it crashes. That seems to have been the case with the video game pioneers: none of them, even the extraordinarily prescient Nolan Bushnell, had more than a fragmentary notion of the cultural zeitgeist that would grow out of Pong and its descendants: arcades, movies, clothing, a new subset of the language. Pac-Man itself would make the cover of *Time* and go into the lingo of corporate merger watchers as a term for voraciousness and greed. Certainly firms like Atari and Bally and Mattel were beneficiaries of the video game rage, but even out there on the curl, they had no more idea than anyone else how long the wave would keep going. When, in 1983, Atari lost $300 million, the surprised winners became equally surprised losers.

But in the heady days of the mid-seventies, it seemed as though nothing could stop Bushnell and Atari. Pong ruled every bar and amusement arcade and campus student center in America.

It was hard for anyone with any experience or education in management to figure out just how Atari ever got anything done. This wasn't

Theory X management or Theory Y management; Atari's management style belonged somewhere out beyond the end of the alphabet. Management appeared to play video games all day long, occasionally retiring to Synanon-like retreats to strategize and get high. The manufacturing and design areas looked like a cross between *Modern Times* and Woodstock, with scores of brilliant, ponytailed young men building the latest smash hit game to the sound of rock and roll and in the heady, sweet atmosphere of dope.

That Atari ever got anything out the door is surprising. Less surprising was that during much of the late 1970s, Atari made less money on its games than many counterfeiters and copyright jumpers who worked with more discipline.

What saved Atari during these years was the simple fact that in the high-tech business, a good product usually will make up for any amount of incompetent management, incoherent marketing and lousy cash management—and at times Atari exhibited all of these failings, in spades. The awesome success of Pong smoothed over a lot of gaping cracks and fissures in Atari's corporate structure.

It needed to. The next product was called Gran Track 10, a car-racing game, and it bombed—partly because, in typical Atari style, it was months late and suffered from development cost overruns. So, instead of being another trophy for Bushnell's mantel, Gran Track 10 lost Atari an amount equivalent to the previous year's sales (five hundred thousand dollars). In shock, Bushnell cut the firm nearly in half and wisely, both for himself and for the future of consumer electronics, recognized his own inadequacies as a businessman and pulled back from the day-to-day operation of the firm.

From that moment, the company's revenues began to curve upward. At the same time, the spirit that had made the company so remarkable curved downward.

Besides Bushnell's retreat from everyday decision-making in 1974–75, another big factor in Atari's turnaround success was the entry into home video games. Home video games had been around, in the form of the Magnavox Odyssey 2, since 1972 and had been very popular. Bushnell, looking for a way out of the Gran Track debacle, decided to make a move at this market with a home form of Pong. Sears came up with the capital in exchange for Atari's first-year production of 150,000 units (up from the 75,000 Atari had planned).

It was one of the smartest moves Sears or Atari ever made. Introduced in the fall of 1975 in nearly nine hundred Sears stores, 13 *million* copies of the Atari home version of Pong were sold over the next three years.

Atari now entered into its golden age. In 1976, only four years old, the firm had sales of nearly $100 million. Bushnell, who owned more than half of the joint, embarked on his well-publicized foray into conspicuous consumption. Now divorced, he was photographed for the San Francisco *Chronicle* in a hot tub with a beautiful woman. He also bought a sailboat and christened it *Pong,* held wild parties near the company headquarters in Los Gatos and the division in the Sierra foothills at Grass Valley, and kept himself and his staff amused with activities such as dressing up as gangsters and driving around in Bushnell's Rolls-Royce. New video games were code-named after female employees. *Fortune* quoted Nolan as saying, "I remember Arlette the best. Boy, was she stacked and had the tiniest waist. I think she was 'Super Pong.' "

For the time being at least, it was a scenario right out of a Ritchie Rich comic book: bright postadolescents unconstrained by money worries, propriety or the vagaries of middle age. They were true T-shirt tycoons, the living image of everything Midwesterners and Manhattanites imagined young, hedonistic and high-tech Californians to be. Atari was a men's dorm filled with millionaires.

For Atari, the business strategy was quite simple: every game built equaled one sale. And building a game had become simple too, ever since the semiconductor industry had come up with a programmable chip (the EPROM) that made it possible to reduce the single-game home box into an inexpensive cartridge to be used with a universal, single-purchase, player box. With this breakthrough, production could be accelerated to as fast as a new game design could be programmed onto a chip.

Even that wasn't fast enough, because the chip makers couldn't fabricate sufficient EPROMs and delivery times stretched out to as much as six months. This not only led to the creation of a gray market to fill the demand of desperate domestic and Asian game makers, but it also created a window for new competitive entries, notably in the arcade business, like Bally.

Everybody who could get into video games that year made money. Atari emerged from this period as perhaps the greatest and the least of winners. It came out rich, established, well planted in both sides of the market (home and arcade), and all but a generic term for the industry.

On the other hand, the firm now found itself faced with serious competitors for the first time, discovered its limitations as a manufacturer and marketer and, most importantly, found that the days of being a funky, laid-back hobby shop were over: video games were a big business now, requiring network advertising campaigns, worldwide distribution programs, high-powered lawyers to scare off copyright jumpers, a Big Eight accounting firm to audit the books for the quarterly statements and underwriters to direct the first public offering of stock. This was heavyweight stuff, not the kind of thing accomplished very well with one's brain buzzing from a toke of killer Hawaiian Elephant and the Rolling Stones on the tape deck.

By 1977, anyone with any experience in high technology knew this any-company-with-a-product-gets-rich boom wasn't going to last too much longer. Soon, consumers would become more sophisticated and selective in their purchases—and considerably more cost-conscious.

By late 1976, there was growing doubt whether Atari, though preeminent in the game business, was going to be able to hold its own for long against the big boys. Atari didn't have the capital for a showdown and wasn't turning into a mature company fast enough. It was hanging on to its rebellious adolescence too long. Much of this problem lay at the very top of the company, with the man who set the rhythm for the rest of the firm: Nolan Bushnell. Keeping little Atari a contender through a violent industry shake-out called for the likes of a Charlie Sporck or an Alexander Poniatoff. The proof that Bushnell and his crew were out of their league came in the spring of 1977 when Atari began to sink under the weight of huge, unsold inventories of outdated games that shouldn't have been built and would never be sold.

But in this apparent failure Bushnell found a way to success. After all, he had created, almost alone, a huge new industry, and at the center of this gold rush Bushnell had placed Atari. So what if Atari was a corporation built on financial sand? For the time being it was the best-known company in the world, beloved by the press and the man on the street. After all, it doesn't pollute the environment or rot kids' teeth, it makes *games,* man, it makes people happy. Even Communists contributed to Atari's revenues, one quarter at a time.

So Nolan had done his job. Bushnell, with his other genius in self-promotion, had given Atari the highest profile in the land. The tower was beginning to wobble, but the chances were good that a sugar-daddy company, its eyes shiny with excitement, would come along just in time to catch this little corporate baby before it fell.

Three Fortune 500 sugar daddies were initially in the running: MCA, Disney and Warner Communications. MCA bowed out (and probably kicked itself for years afterward); Disney, where if every wish made on a star came true Atari rightly belonged, followed the pattern of executive incompetence it had exhibited since Walt's death and also declined.

Warners, however, was just as anxious for a bailout as Atari, having come off a rotten movie season, watched yet another year in the seventies-long collapse of the record business, and was still pouring cash into a cable television business that had yet to come alive. Warner executive vice-president Emanuel "Manny" Gerard, the man in charge of new business development, wanted Atari. It took four months of hard negotiations, made tougher by a lawsuit brought by Bushnell's ex-wife for some of his shares. It all ended in 1977, when Warners acquired Atari for approximately $30 million.

Of this amount, half went to Bushnell. Nolan Bushnell, the lapsed Mormon boy with dreams of glory, had pulled off the perfect Silicon Valley coup. In four years he had built a company whose name was worth more than its physical plant, had sold it off to a rich white knight and now could walk away a multimillionaire: *Après moi le déluge.*

With this, Bushnell put into place the last brick in the creation of the modern high-tech entrepreneur: the big cash-in. Until Bushnell, entrepreneurs had for the most part followed the pattern set by heavyweights of earlier generations—the Henry Fords and J. P. Morgans, even the Bill Hewletts and Dave Packards—who had built companies and then stuck with them, winter and summer, garage company to multinational, angry young men to distinguished elder statesmen, impoverished backyard tinkerers to hoary amateur philosophers in a mansion at the Breakers. For these men, their own existence, the sole purpose of their tenure on this earth, was intimately bound up with their companies. It was impossible to imagine Ford Motor without Henry, or Standard Oil without John D., Sr., or Kaiser Industries without Henry J., or for that matter National Semiconductor without Charlie Sporck.

It seemed that way with Atari and Nolan Bushnell. The company's hyperkinetic yet casual style was an extension of the founder himself. But Bushnell short-circuited the whole process by cashing out early. It just wasn't done that way, not voluntarily at least, and certainly not with such obvious relish. When it turned out that Bushnell had left Atari in worse shape than the public had previously thought, with several million dollars in unsold inventory, it only added to the man's fame: funky Nolan Bushnell, the ex-carnival con man and backwater

California engineer, had snookered one of America's biggest and best-known corporations and then laughed all the way to the bank.

Atari under Warner was a much different place from Atari under Bushnell. One might think Warner, with subsidiaries in records, movies and *Mad* magazine, would be a relatively loose, creative establishment. (And it was, particularly with the books, as several criminal convictions and SEC investigations would show in later years.) But the man Warner picked for the job, Raymond Kassar, privately and publicly was from a different world.

Kassar, once an Egyptian underwear manufacturer, had most recently been at Burlington Mills. He was an impeccable dresser and a tough businessman. Needless to say, he scared the hell out of Atari with his arrival.* Kassar let it be known right out of the gate that Atari's era of hot tub management was over. If Atari was going to be a big-time company—and that was the way Warner wanted and needed it—then it was going to have to look and act like one. The firm moved its headquarters to new facilities near Lockheed, staffed executive row with Harvard grads and other Ivy League types, hired J. Walter Thompson to do its advertising—and in the process drove away most of the survivors from Atari's Republic period. Kassar had come to build the Atari Empire.

And Kassar quickly exhibited his imperial—and imperious—style. He was a man who knew how to make the most out of perquisites, particularly when they were tacked on to several million dollars each year in salary and bonuses. He lived alone in a splendid penthouse in San Francisco, was a pillar of the social scene there and each day was chauffeured the fifty miles to work in a Rolls-Royce. In Sunnyvale, Kassar ate lunch in Atari's new executive dining room—the only one in Silicon Valley—choosing from among seven daily entrees.

Even in aristocratic Manhattan, such a baroque life-style might have seemed a trifle ostentatious. In Silicon Valley, where Packard, Sporck and Grove ate in employee cafeterias, Kassar's manner was outrageous. Add to this the man's autocratic management style, a widespread resentment among employees about having an East Coast upper manage-

---

* And it probably scared the hell out of him. According to one Atari insider, the day Kassar arrived he called a meeting of top management. One executive showed up in a bunny suit. When Kassar asked what the costume was all about, he was informed that it was Halloween. When, incredulous, Kassar inquired what kind of fool would come as a bunny to an executive meeting, he was informed that it was the vice-president of engineering.

ment nailed atop a traditional Silicon Valley firm and a general bewilderment at the remarkable number of gay top executives, and all the pieces were in place for a general collapse of company morale.

What kept that breakdown from occurring for many years was success. After all, business is business, and Atari for the first four years under Kassar was among the most successful companies of all time. In that period, from 1978 to 1982, the firm grew from a few million to more than $1 billion (the latter figure is inexact because Warner purposely didn't break out Atari's sales figures). Atari succeeded where Itel had failed: it reached a "gigabuck" in sales.

Of course, it can be argued that Atari, riding on the crest of the video game mania, the biggest consumer electronics boom to date, almost could not help but be wildly successful. Riding a business boom is like surfing: you have to see the next wave coming in on the horizon, get out and be turned around to meet it, and then as the swell "feels" the bottom and rises, you have to paddle like hell to get up to speed to be caught in the arching crest. Whenever an electronics boom comes rolling in, there are usually dozens of firms out paddling around looking for an opportunity, and scores more on the beach. Few firms are ready, paddling forward as fast as they can in research, marketing, manufacturing and distribution. The rest miss the wave and kick out in hopes of catching the next one, or ride for a while until they are wiped out.

To Kassar's credit, he kept Atari atop the wave. Thanks to his skill and that of his team (notably people like computer wizard Allan Kay), Atari was able to go as far as it did in such a short time. A $1-billion run-up, particularly when the firm is doubling and tripling in sales and population annually, is a nearly impossible task. Itel and Osborne tried and disintegrated. Apple and Intel got a few hundred million and stumbled, forced to pause and catch their breaths. It seems that even when the market is willing the company spirit often is not. Exponential growth allows none of the mistakes that can be made by other, slower business. New products must precisely meet introduction dates, there can be no slippage in development, manufacturing or selling targets. New plants under construction must come on line at the precise time, with no bottlenecks. The capital must be there to pay for the new buildings and equipment, the cash to pay off suppliers. When a key employee quits or burns out someone else must be ready and able to step into the breach. Most of all, the new products must be good—really good—because there can be no growth without sales.

Atari had the right products. By the time of a secret banquet in late

1982 to celebrate crossing $1 billion, Atari looked unstoppable. It had
the goods, the people and the market share. Kassar and his staff had
every right to gloat: they had coordinated their attack upon the video
game market perfectly.

Warner gloated too. Never a particularly dignified or restrained corporation (as the Securities and Exchange Commission would eventually
notice), Warner burned every ounce of its new Atari-produced riches.
On their regular visits to Sunnyvale, the corporate executives wouldn't
deign to stay in any Silicon Valley hotels. Rather they would use the
corporate jet to fly into San Francisco Airport, then take a helicopter at
Fisherman's Wharf. There, the executives would be met by a limousine
to take them up to the elegant Stanford Court Hotel atop Nob Hill. The
next morning the limousine would take them back to the heliport for
the chopper flight to the parking lot next door to Atari's Sunnyvale
headquarters.

The decadence did not even end there. One Atari manager incredulously remembers seeing Warner chairman Steve Ross step out of the
helicopter into another limousine for the two-hundred-foot trip to the
side door of the Atari building.

If the Silicon Valley story shows anything it is that in the world of
high-technology business any bozo can build a $10-million company,
and even a moderately capable businessman with the right product or
market can take a firm to $100 million annual sales. But to top $1 billion and manage the requisite twenty-five thousand or so employees
needed to do so, you have to be a world-class executive. Ray Kassar, for
all of his flaws, was that. With his team, he took an almost moribund
company and conquered the consumer electronics world.

Like all great conquests, it was at great cost.

In 1978, the Japanese hit the market with an arcade game called
Space Invaders, which had ranks and files of strange creatures descending from the sky to attack the operator and his or her lone weapon. The
game swept the field, becoming the newest best seller, stealing quarters
away from Atari machines across the country, taking floor space from
Atari's own three-thousand-dollar arcade games.

Backed with enough money and still armed with some of its finest
creative minds, Atari counterattacked with the video computer system.
The VCS represented a major breakthrough in the home market because it shifted the integrated circuitry from the dedicated game box to
the general-purpose player. With the VCS, the circuitry common to all
the old games need only be acquired once, for about $150, and the

newest games loaded into it via cartridges containing preprogrammed ROM chips. The new cartridges retailed for only $39.95, and since they cost less than ten bucks to make, Atari had a lot of room in between to spend on advertising, research, price-bombing if the competition heated up and, certainly not least, for enormous—almost obscene—profits.

The challenge in arcade games was met with equal authority. Here, Atari took advantage of the new affordability of high-powered microprocessors to come up with Asteroids. Asteroids was one of the first "cult" games to attract those odd adolescent boys found in each generation who devote their entire young lives to some futile, puerile obsession. With Asteroids, as with Space Invaders before it, and Pac-Man (which attracted girls) and Zaxxon after, these boys spent literally hundreds of dollars apiece—two bits at a time—and thousands of hours trying to rack up a suitable number of millions of points to become the school or city or state or national or world champion. It was a strange quest these teens and preteens undertook, in dark rooms staring intently at hypnotic glowing screens, one hand flicking a joy stick back and forth and two fingers on the other hand tapping frantically on the "fire" buttons—but it certainly was an influential one.

Certainly it scared the hell out of parents, educators and community leaders, who saw their children turning into cathode-ray tuboids. But for video game manufacturers these boys were worth their weight in gold. Any true fad needs its core of fanatics as well as a large population of curious participants. It is the fanatics, with their metronomelike steady click of quarters, who pay the overhead, set the standards and serve as examples for others to follow into the wonderful world of consumerism. The game makers and the gypsies were ready for these entranced youngsters. The small-time hustlers took the games out of stores and bars and put them in arcades. Now the kids could pick and choose the games they wanted, and watch the real star players at work.

Atari did its part, too. The truly virtuous and faithful could buy Atari T-shirts and hats and socks and wristlets and decals and frisbees (for the occasional respite in sunlight). Hot-doggers could compete in local citywide competitions for trophies and prizes. Ultrahigh scorers even earned the height of absurdity with sober-faced press releases listing their astronomical scores and highlighting the great moments of their twelve-year-old lives. These releases, of course, were mailed by Atari to the national and local press, who, equally straight-faced, reported them as news.

All the game makers participated to some degree in this collateral material sideshow, but none with Atari's enthusiasm or élan. Atari alone had a double play in the video game business, with a foot in both arcade and home games. This gave Atari an immediate advantage over its competitors that was greater than the sum of its parts. Kids could play an Atari arcade (or "coin-op") game like Asteroids, then go home and play a $39.95 home cartridge version of the same game. Atari had it all: Tinkers to Evers to Chance, arcade games to home cartridges to the Atari balance sheet.

The most important part of a well-turned double play is to be on the ball at the beginning. Here Atari got mixed reviews. Game designers, as Kassar himself once said, had become the nearest equivalent to a rock star. "Hired guns" might be a more accurate description. During the Bushnell era, these individuals were paid huge sums, buried in praise and their idiosyncrasies pampered and stroked, even when they were at odds with corporate life. If these game stars wanted to wear ponytails and Grateful Dead American Beauty T-shirts and show up at the office only a few minutes a week, that was just peachy—as long as they came up with the next Asteroids. After all, these people were *artists,* weren't they? Creative folks. They aren't like you or I, said the men on executive row. In the hyperbole of the era, video game designers were called —with a straight face—the poets and painters of their generation, the pioneers of the next cultural wave combining art and technology. To read the literature of that time, one might have thought if Titian or Tintoretto had been alive in the late 1970s they would have abandoned their easels to design Turbo or Frogger. No one seemed to notice that behind the flashing lights these were really three-dimensional board games for *children,* a three-minute Monopoly without the allegory at a quarter a throw.

The reality was that video game designers were really the Walt Disneys and Windsor McKays of their time, clever commercial artists who had brilliantly tailored the technology of the day to the needs of the consumer. The best of these games seemed to capture the essence of what it must be like to be an adolescent in America in the last quarter of the twentieth century: a chaos of bursting, shocking, fleeting images; a paranoid hell of continuous, relentless, yet ever changing threats coming from every direction; an existential nightmare in which oblivion is inevitable even for the best. The world of video games, like the bigger world around it, was a hedonistic one, in which the eye seemed to short-circuit the brain and deal directly with the hands and the adrenal gland (wham, bam, thank you, Ms. Pac-Man) . . .

Sadly, that's about all video games were. The comparison to Disney is apt, but only if the animator had stopped developing his craft after *Steamboat Willy.* Video games grew visually more impressive, but never progressed beyond a handful of plot templates: the attack game, the defense game, the pilot game, etc. On the rare occasion when a certain originality popped up, young consumers didn't respond. Atari introduced the Red Baron and Battle Zone arcades, which used "vector imagery" (isometric line drawings) to create extraordinary images of exotic tanks in alien landscapes of geometric figures or a Sopwith Camel doing double Immelmanns in pursuit of a Fokker DR-3—and the machines sat unused in arcades except when discovered by curious adults. (In fact, t'ie only party that found Battle Zone interesting was the United States Army, which contracted Atari to reconfigure the game into a combat simulator for tank crews—confirming the suspicions of conspiracy nuts that video games were a secret plot to train America's youth for the next war.)

The sad truth is that, despite occasional flashes of inspiration, video games were basically unimaginative, even puerile, forms of entertainment. Within a few years it was obvious that there would never be a video game with the depth or human complexity of a game of checkers, *Krazy Kat* or even a Road Runner cartoon. Instead, as Nolan Bushnell himself said in late 1983, there "was just the 154th version of shooting down attacking Martians." Once a kid reached the level of proficiency required to put his initials in the machine's memory, the game was mastered. There was no place to go but the next game, until all the interesting games had been beaten. Then one left the arcade forever.

So, from 1977 to 1982, the arcade and home game business enjoyed a sizable net annual increase in customers. The boom was on, and Atari was king. Kassar may have depended on his game designers to keep Atari's success going, but he also called them towel designers and over-emotional prima donnas and proceeded to scare the bejesus out of them by trying to insert some order into their previously undisciplined lives (some employees took to wearing "I'm just another high-strung prima donna from Atari" T-shirts). Afraid of corporate espionage, Kassar imposed tight security on the R&D areas. The inventors now had to use magnetic ID cards and pass a phalanx of guards. *All* employees now were supposed to be at work at 8 A.M. and properly dressed for success.

Even worse, so deep was Kassar's fear of security breaches that he kept secret the names of Atari's top designers, lest they be stolen by the competition. This may have been the biggest mistake in Kassar's business career. Like true stars, game designers had star-sized egos that needed to be publicly massaged. Respect from one's peers had its place, but adoration by millions of children, now that would be something! The nerve of that Lebanese rug merchant Kassar, they thought, why, he knew so little about electronics that he kept an old issue of *Scientific American* on the subject in his desk so he wouldn't look like a buffoon by asking what an "eye-see" was.

Needless to say, Atari lost a lot of its creative talent during this period, many of them going just a few blocks down the road to the rented offices of a recent start-up named Activision. Here James Levy was doing to Atari what Amdahl was doing to IBM—building plug-compatible products to take advantage of a huge installed base of hardware. In particular, Activision was making its own video game cartridges that fit the Atari player. Even worse, most of Activision's games were better than Atari's comparable products.

Levy did something else at Activision: he carried the rock star issue to its ultimate conclusion. Rather than hide the names of his staffers, Levy extolled them. He listed the game designers' names on the cartridges, he announced them on television ads. The expected happened: certain top designers actually gained a following, a steady, loyal cadre of fans who could be relied upon to buy each new offering by that "author." What's more, despite their vulnerability to headhunters, these ego-satiated designers remained loyal to Activision.

Atari, for its part, in keeping with the rules of Silicon Valley, tried to sue Activision into the ground. It failed. For the home market, Atari found itself locked into a battle with Mattel, while being sniped underneath by Activision.

In late 1981, Atari and Mattel went after one another in what was billed as a shoot-out for the home video game market (Magnavox had already dropped out, Coleco was just beginning to raise its head). Calling it a "Hilarious Punch 'n Judy Battle," *Home Video* magazine described the war this way:

> In an attempt to assert its superiority, Mattel enlisted George Plimpton, the aristocrat as everyman, as spokesman for Intellivision. Backed by a $6 million advertising campaign, Plimpton hit the airwaves last November with a commercial demonstrating that Atari's sports games don't measure up to the Intellivision team. Atari quickly retaliated with a commercial featuring an equally pedantic teenager who complained

that although he'd like to compare Atari's Space Invaders and Asteroids with the competition, the competition didn't make them—only to have Mattel stage an end run by introducing a new campaign in which Plimpton proved to another equally obnoxious kid that whatever their names, Intellivision's space games just couldn't be beat. By that point, both Atari and Mattel were complaining to the networks that the other's commercials were misleading and unfair, and the slugfest petered out.

In the end, the competition between Mattel and Atari seemed both comical and absurd, because by Christmas neither firm could keep up with the insatiable demand for their products. Retailers sold out weeks before Christmas, creating legions of wild-eyed parents racing from one consumer electronics store to the next in the vain hope of finding the last available Asteroids cartridge that Junior just had to have waiting under the tree.

Christmas 1981 was the zenith of the video game business. The industry enjoyed every manufacturer's dream (and nightmare): demand that utterly outdistanced supply. As the nation teetered on the brink of another recession, arcades were still jammed to capacity. Even the lowliest, least imaginative home game cartridge sold out. The race now became not who could design the most exciting new game, but who could manufacture the cartridges and players and get them on the shelves the fastest. Now that was something businessmen like Kassar could understand—none of that artistic mumbo jumbo, just flat-out production. Here Atari had become consummate performer, and it made a killing.

But Atari was not the cause of this boom. Rather credit went to a tiny yellow creature with a voracious appetite for little energy squares: 1981 was the year of Pac-Man.

Pac-Man did the job. It had all the right ingredients. In the theater of cruelty that was video games, Pac-Man exhibited only a charming gluttony. In the slam-bam world of video graphics, Pac-Man was a set piece, a cross between a checkerboard and a maze, in which its characters tootled along. Pac-Man was *cute,* even its violence less threatening than amusing. It was a game girls liked to play as much as boys; and what that meant was profound: among all the forms of recreation that appealed to boys and boy-men, from motocross bikes to pornography, few had ever turned the corner to become universal entertainment, capturing as well the other half of the population. Pac-Man did it and the little yellow gobbler landed itself on the cover of *Time* before any of Silicon Valley's humans did.

Pac-Man was not an Atari creation. Rather the arcade version belonged to Bally, and it quickly made that MidWay Manufacturing Co. subsidiary as big in the coin-op business as Atari ($220 million in 1981). Once again, Atari's business acumen came to the rescue of its fading creativity. Atari obtained the home game rights to Pac-Man from Japanese designer Taito Ltd., which also developed Space Invaders (who said the Japanese weren't innovative?) and within a short time and with a lot of advertising, the name Pac-Man had become synonymous with Atari in the public's mind. It was to be Atari's most clever coup under the Kassar regime. Atari guarded this golden goose tightly. At consumer electronics trade shows, Atari employees could be seen taking down the names of Pac-Man imitations for future suits by company lawyers.

Nineteen eighty-two dawned with industry experts and market analysts predicting the best year yet for the video game business. That's how things started out. The Pac-Man craze continued well into the year. Activision predicted for itself $50 million in sales for the year, ten times that of the year before. And imitators spawned imitators; in this case, Imagic, another Atari-compatible software firm. Disney made *Tron,* a movie that was in essence a giant video game. Nineteen eighty-two was also the year of the big corporate mergers, and fittingly, these became known as Pac-Man mergers. A group of liberal congressmen with rather blue-sky ideas about revitalizing the American economy became known as Atari Democrats.

At Atari, things had never seemed rosier. The company raced to $2 billion in sales and $320 million in profits. The company's third wing of attack, home computers, after a shaky start, moved out strongly by placing a great emphasis in their design on game-playing. It seemed a reasonable strategy: integrate all three wings of the company to create a continuous development path for the consumer from arcade games to home games to the added features available with a home computer.

But Atari was on quicksand; at the very foundation of the firm was an incorrect assumption, a commitment to a mistaken marketing path.

This belief postulated that the video game constituted the birth of a whole new form of entertainment, just like television, radio or motion pictures. People would always want video games with a demand as unfailing and perpetually growing as TV had enjoyed since the days of

Uncle Miltie. Once this view was accepted as gospel, firms like Atari could ignore it as the invisible ground of all of their endeavors, just as the semiconductor industry had long since assumed axiomatically that there would always be a market for integrated-circuit chips.

However, there was another terrifying possibility—one almost absurd to contemplate in a time of jammed video arcades and 100 percent annual revenue growth. It was that perhaps the video game wasn't the next television but the new Hula-Hoop—a Hula-Hoop of sufficient novelty and diversity to capture the interest of a generation not for the usual six months but for several years, but a Hula-Hoop nonetheless. If that was the case, then video games might suffer the same rapid growth, high-arching sales curves, national infatuation, cons, scams, overnight tycoons . . . and the same instant market exhaustion, with dozens of companies and thousands of investors and speculators left holding the bag of unsellable merchandise and lost savings.

At the tail end of 1982, certain subtle clues showed the latter scenario to be the more likely one, tiny cracks at the base of what had appeared to be a monolithic new industry. In November, right in the middle of what was expected to be the biggest Christmas season in video games' short but boisterous history, sales suddenly stalled. Retailers around the country suddenly canceled orders. E.T., an Atari video game based on the most popular movie in history, a natural if ever there was one, all but died in the marketplace, despite a huge send-off.

When business is good anything goes. Employees can be malcontents and drug addicts, middle managers can be drunks, boneheads and psychotics, and executives can be embezzlers or pathological liars. As long as the books are black, price–earnings multiples are high and stockholders of the parent firm get their return on investment, then these individuals will not only endure but be rewarded with promotions, bonuses and praise. But let the bottom line turn a little pink and the walls are quickly splattered with blood, fingers are pointed in every direction, stockholders' suits are filed, managers are canned, workers dumped en masse and executives indicted.

Thus, the unusual life-style of many members of executive row was overlooked or genially derided until 1982 when Atari suddenly announced it was contemplating moving its headquarters to San Francisco —an alien, ugly, dangerous world to Silicon Valleyites. Atari claimed that as a world-class company it needed an equivalent setting for its corporate offices; employees suggested privately that the real reason was the proximity of the homosexual enclaves of Polk and Castro streets.

The increasing San Francisco orientation of the company was just one more annoyance to workers. At times, Atari seemed to have more loyalty to the city, where only the president and a handful of others lived, than to Sunnyvale and the rest of Silicon Valley, where the company was headquartered and thousands of employees lived. The Sunnyvale Historical Society couldn't afford to move out of its little museum; meanwhile the city's biggest resident company donated $1 million to the San Francisco Cable Car Fund. Kassar made frequent appearances in the society pages of the San Francisco *Chronicle* and was often mentioned in Herb Caen's column (perhaps to return the favor, Atari employed Caen's son as a summer intern).

The great tragedy of it all was that if any firm had the opportunity to inaugurate the home computer revolution it was Atari. The home market is the fata morgana of the electronics business—a beautiful vision when approached dissipates and leaves only disaster on the rocks. Nevertheless, Atari, if anyone, could still have burst open the door to the family market, making a computer the latest home appliance—and, for that matter, could have made for itself a magnificent alternate business as games fell away.

Instead, Atari frittered away its opportunity.

There is evidence to indicate that Atari executives saw the end coming months before it became public knowledge. As early as September 1982, when to all appearances the game market was still pretty healthy, Atari began making plans for a massive employee layoff to reduce domestic employment in lieu of cheaper, and thus more competitive, overseas manufacturing.

Even at that early date, the company planned for a swift, surgical strike on its employment rolls. Almost the entire bottom of the corporate pyramid in Silicon Valley would be amputated, dumped on the street so fast that there would barely be enough time for protest. It was a watershed moment in Atari's corporate history, where the good, or at least roguishly charming, old Atari was secretly murdered by the cynical new rulers.

Meanwhile, to the outside world, the game business might be down a tad, but Atari seemed to be enjoying business as usual. Stock prices were holding pretty steady, with only a slight loss. In 1982 Kassar had made $3 million in salary and bonuses—and you didn't give that kind of megabucks to a guy for screwing up. Besides, this was 1983, and even hard cases like National Semi had gone to reduced hours and unpaid holidays and hiring freezes rather than a layoff. People were just too damn precious to be cast adrift every time the economic seas got a little choppy.

But Atari, that weird hybrid of fourth-generation Silicon Valley entrepreneurship and East Coast button-down aristocracy, had long since stopped looking around at its neighbors for experience and was blindly following its own falling star.

In January 1983, Atari (Warner, to be precise) suspended trading on the floor of the New York Stock Exchange. It seems that in December, just before Warner stock had started downward, Kassar and executive vice-president David Groth had sold some of their holdings—this after Atari had hyped its fourth-quarter prospects to analysts, then turned around and announced reduced profits. This did not please the Securities and Exchange Commission, which investigated and eventually fined Kassar eighty-one thousand dollars in an out-of-court settlement.

That was just the opening salvo. Over the next five months Atari would systematically destroy most of the goodwill it had unconsciously gained over the previous decade, and it would do so in the most callous and ultimately self-defeating series of management moves the Valley had seen since the heyday of Wilf Corrigan at Fairchild.

In February 1983, Atari announced that it would lay off 1,700 employees within the next two weeks. A shudder rippled through the entire Valley. It was the largest single layoff in Silicon Valley history, and it seemed to many locals an act more worthy of steel mills or automobile plants than of a high-technology firm. Then disbelief turned to anger. The manner of the Atari layoff seemed to invalidate everything the Valley had learned and tried to put into practice over five decades. One didn't just summarily can hundreds of people like that. It was the kind of thing a company did as a last resort, when the firm itself was on the line—and then one gave employees fair advance warning and supported them through the transition.

Atari did none of this; what company support there was came after the subsequent uproar. In personnel offices and employee relations departments all over Silicon Valley, managers cursed Atari. Said one public relations executive: "I can't believe that they did that. You don't just do that to people . . . Christ, as if we don't already have enough worries about unions—and then Atari goes and pulls this. They don't give a shit. They're going to Malaysia or some goddamn place and they don't care how many pissed-off people they leave behind here. It was stupid, stupid, stupid . . .

Needless to say, all the predictions of a P.R. disaster came true. By the end of the day of the layoff announcement, camera crews and reporters were waiting at the exits of the largest Atari plants. The story made all the networks. And, in the sort of poetic symmetry that appears at such times, as soon as the lights were on and the cameras running, workers, some with no more than an elementary school education, enjoyed moments of profound lucidity. One worker, seen on a local news station, said in broken English something like: "I always treated Atari well, but Atari hasn't treated me well back." With devastating and simple honesty, that line and others like it effectively voided millions of dollars of advertising copy.

The drum roll continued through the spring, with nearly five hundred more layoffs in May and June. By the end of the summer, all of the two thousand blue-collar and one thousand white-collar jobs had disappeared.

It was not only disgusting, but, as the P.R. director of another firm said, a dangerous threat to all other businesses in Silicon Valley. Once the last great bastion of antiunionism in America, Silicon Valley, thanks to Atari, seemed to be throwing its front door open to every shop organizer with enough gas to get to town. Former National Semiconductor personnel vice-president Roy Brandt was sitting at a McDonald's in the middle of Silicon Valley the day after the first big Atari layoff. To his dismay, Brandt, who had spent his career successfully helping keep unions out of the electronics industry, trying to teach his employers that the best way to defend themselves from unionization was through honest communication with employees, found himself surrounded by angry workers openly discussing the possibility of bringing organizers into their plants. "I couldn't believe it," Brandt recalls, "I have never heard anything like that here in my life." Network news showed organizers standing at the entrance driveway of one of Atari's main plants and handing out flyers.

So the Valley spent the summer of 1983, when it should have been enjoying the firstfruits of a new economic boom, still reeling from an ongoing series of dreadful Atari announcements. Kassar, whose head had been on a pike almost from the day of the first bad earnings announcement, endured a standard shotgun resignation in July. He was replaced by James Morgan, a Philip Morris marketing executive who, remarkably given the circumstances, had agreed to take the job after three days of thought from the time it was offered by an executive placement firm. Morgan, who had spent his entire business career selling cigarettes, would now try to bring his skills to hawking video games, a product that did not seem to enjoy the same level of addiction.

The Atari Morgan was inheriting was in deep trouble. By October, the firm had lost more than $500 million—a figure greater than the annual sales of all but a half dozen largest companies in the Valley. Atari had just dumped twenty truckloads of defective inventory into a big pit in New Mexico. IBM had wrecked the personal computer business. And, most humiliating of all, Nolan Bushnell himself, richer than ever from founding Pizza Time Theaters, announced he would be going back into the game business, with games that would bring consumers back into the arcades, as soon as his noncompetition agreement with Atari expired at midnight September 30, 1983.

The delicious irony of having Nolan Bushnell come back to kick the ass of the company he had founded wasn't lost on anyone, especially Atari. The closer the date approached, the more publicity appeared about Bushnell's return to the game, and the more skittish Atari seemed to become. The firm even went so far as to file suit against Bushnell, claiming that he had breached the contract by working on game development before the deadline. It showed how far Atari had fallen: a $2-billion company with a catalog of hundreds of products, running scared from a man who did not have a single announced product, or a company to build it.

Soon thereafter, Atari announced it had reached an out-of-court settlement with Bushnell for exclusive rights to his games in exchange for an undisclosed sum. Bushnell, presumably, again laughed all the way to the bank.

The same couldn't be said for Atari. At the end of October, Atari did the unthinkable: the firm said it would allow a vote to decide if the electrical workers union could organize Atari's Milpitas plant. On the same day, the Los Angeles *Times* announced the fact that Atari's new line of computers—which some thought were the company's last hope —would not be ready for the Christmas season.

So, as 1983 ended, Atari, bloody and bowed, seemed to be limping toward some final reckoning. It announced in January that it didn't expect to show a profit for the year. Parent company Warner was under merger assault by newspaper magnate Rupert Murdoch. The most adored company in American business had in just four years earned the eternal enmity of both employees and peers. Rumors were rife on the streets of Silicon Valley that Warner had Atari up for sale—as though anyone would buy a company that had just lost half a billion dollars in a single year. Perhaps a white knight would come along, or the new computers would turn out world shakers, or perhaps Bushnell's games might revitalize the whole industry.

(They didn't, and Bushnell, reeling from multimillion-dollar losses at Pizza Time Theaters, Inc. [which, like Atari, he left] and the slow development of his dozen other firms, soon pulled out of the business. Apparently this time it was for good. Within a year, his empire collapsed, Nolan Bushnell, King Pong himself, fell into the dark hole of Silicon Valley nonpersonhood.)

By spring 1984 it was obvious that Morgan wasn't going to pull off a turnaround at Atari. So, when Jack Tramiel, the cold-blooded builder of Commodore, came shopping, Warner nearly gave away the once-billion-dollar company for a quarter that amount—and in long-term notes to boot.

Thus ended the long, ugly story of Atari under Warner Communications. As if in keeping with the infamous precedent, within a week Tramiel fired 900 more Valley workers—bringing Atari's local employment down from a high-water mark of 6,000 to fewer than 200.

Tramiel talked of using Atari to capture the ever calling home market. Maybe he will; few businessmen alive have been more successful at accomplishing what they said.

But even if the company is again successful the Atari logo on the door will mean nothing. The firm can never again be the same. Not only has it lost its people, and thereby its innocence, but also Atari has lost its decency. The firm that started out to be the most humane, the most individual of companies, has in the end come to represent the worst clichés of the cruel greedy capitalist megacorporation. Its decline may have been met with cheers, but as the firm collapsed its crash wrecked the lives of many who had been trapped inside, and it threw debris all over Silicon Valley.

The company named after the game of go is gone.

* * *

If Atari burst on the scene like a skyrocket, Apple sort of ambled onstage in threadbare jeans, the spring-loaded, balls-of-the-feet walk of a sixties doper and the hard clear eyes of a computer hacker—the look of a zealot who has found in computers the One and True Faith.

California magazine captured the essence of Apple perfectly in its cover story of July 1982 entitled "Revenge of the Nerds." The cover showed a young man in a white shirt (top button buttoned), horn-rimmed glasses with tape at the bridge, messy hair, a shirt pocket stuffed with pens and an Alfred E. Newman grin. The young man sat at an Apple II computer while two beautiful models looked over his shoulder, tousling his hair and playing with his pens. The caption read: "Remember me? I'm one of those guys everybody laughed at in high school. Well, today I design computers and I'm worth millions. So who's laughing now?"

Who indeed? The advent of Steven Paul Jobs and Stephen Wozniak created a whole new paradigm for Silicon Valley entrepreneurship. But their subsequent careers seemed to have lived up to the oldest and hoariest clichés about the corrupting influence of riches and of the resentful outcast suddenly made a king. Now, when someone speaks of a Silicon Valley entrepreneur and of overnight riches, the image that comes to mind is no longer of graying patriarchs like Hewlett and Packard but of the bearded Peck's-bad-boy face of a mischievous prince of industry named Jobs as he stares out from the cover of *Time* magazine—the first Valley executive ever to earn that honor.

Even Silicon Valley, where the bizarre is a way of life, had trouble accepting Jobs and "Woz" at first. With typical hard-driving, family-second style, the Valley didn't recognize its own children. After all, the two young men were of the first generation of Silicon Valley natives, Jobs born the year Shockley returned to Palo Alto. Wozniak's mother still calls the local papers to complain if "my Steve" hasn't been properly publicized in her ongoing campaign to make sure that her son—and not Jobs—is credited with the invention of the first Apple computer. Jobs spent his childhood in Mountain View—a half mile in one direction from the site of Shockley Transistor, a mile in the other from Fairchild, and just a few blocks from Mayfield Mall—the Valley's first enclosed shopping mall—the construction of which Jobs watched as a child.

If the Valley itself had trouble picturing Wozniak and Jobs as titans of business, to the rest of the commercial world the initial reaction was simply amusement at these unwashed babies and their precocious presumption. Don Cvietusa of the Bank of America remembers with amusement the first time Jobs, in his typical counterculture rags, visited the bank's corporate headquarters in San Francisco. The gray eminences of the stodgy B of A could not have been more shocked if a trained dog had hopped in on its hind legs and calmly asked for a million-dollar line of credit.

That's what Jobs asked for—and he talked the bankers into it. Jobs talked everybody into it. Arguably, Jobs talked the entire world into the personal computer revolution—and that in turn would make Jobs and Woz among the richest and most influential of men.

It is hard to imagine a more unlikely pair of world shakers. But closer inspection seems to argue that the personal computer industry could not have been started by anyone else.

In 1976, when Woz built the first Apple computer, Silicon Valley was entering its golden age. The entire matrix of service and support was in place. Furthermore, the boom was on. The wounds of 1974–75 were all but scarred over. The wounded firms had either succumbed or recovered. Laid-off workers had either been rehired or left the industry forever. It was gold rush time again, time to make a killing, to drive those stocks up and cash out when prices peaked. At such a time, everyone in Silicon Valley is hungry for the fast buck and money is flying loose and free.

Jobs and Wozniak were far out of the mainstream. Teenage friends—though an unusual five years apart—the two were truly like the kid on the cover of *California*. Particularly Wozniak; "Woz from Oz," he's been called. Though his experience as rock impresario seems to have improved things a bit, Wozniak really was the King of the Nerds. Except for the California variations of a beard and long hair, Woz, even when Apple had become a multimillion-dollar company, still had an uncanny resemblance to the famous (at least among college kids) *National Lampoon* poster "What Is a Nerd?" Tucked away in his little office like a gnome, surrounded by piles of dismantled electronics gear, speaking in mumbles and unable to look anyone in the eye, Wozniak was a parody of the eccentric, socially maladjusted genius. It was no wonder that his friend was a half decade younger: in the outside world they'd be equals. Woz was the kid in high school no one knew, the muscleless lump with glasses everyone thought was weird, but who could build damn near anything electronic. At thirteen, at Cupertino Junior High, Woz won first place in the Bay Area Science Fair by building his first computer.

But the focus upon Woz's eccentricities or genius does not do full justice to the man. There is another side to his personality, a child-like innocence, mixed with a disarming honesty Wozniak somehow maintained in the face of executive row power plays, media hype and then abuse, ruthless con men, false prophets and rock and roll. Even Jobs, when asked, shakes his head in wonder at what Wozniak has been through. Seeing Wozniak and talking to him, one feels an urge to protect him. Because, like that of Voltaire's Candide, Woz's innocence, his decency, only seems to lead him to kicks and punches and fleecings by others.

"Decent" is a word rarely used to describe Steve Jobs (though the *Time* cover gave him a halo). It should be said that Jobs also has a genius, not in electronics—by all reports, he doesn't particularly enjoy computers—but for hucksterism. Jobs is P. T. Barnum with cool, Aimee Semple McPherson with a secular product. Jobs is Nolan Bushnell without tongue in cheek, an eighties high-tech version of the yogis he followed in India, but in a tailored suit and tennis shoes. He mixes young-executive patois and the shaman jive of utopianism, poster-caption philosophy and the youthful colloquialism of a self-proclaimed prophet.

Only a mind as brilliant, arrogant and sensitive as Jobs's could have turned the computer revolution into his own apotheosis, charming and manipulating the cynical old American press into his own publicity organ. Jobs is the best and the worst of the seventies generation—a fact even he has come to realize. ("People think I'm an asshole, don't they?" he once plaintively asked this writer.)

So those are the two men, boys really, who made a revolution.

The seeds of the personal computer era extended further back even than Woz's junior high school computer project. As far back as the late 1950s, engineers were taking terminals home from the office and timesharing to big computers over phone lines. By the 1970s there was a healthy underground market in used computer equipment, which were jury-rigged by hobbyists to produce spectacular results. Just like ham radio three quarters of a century before, the computer revolution spawned a healthy, brilliant and ultimately earthshaking hobbyist wing. By 1975, several firms were offering computer processors for several thousand dollars. These were true hobbyist machines, requiring the new owner to write his or her own programming and find his own peripherals. Around the country, groups of hobbyists were meeting and forming clubs to swap programs and technical knowledge. In time, as existing models became inadequate, the brightest (and the poorest) of these cultists began to build their own computers, constructing them around a state-of-the-art microprocessor, like the Intel 8080, supported by various digital (memory, input/output) and linear chips bought or liberated here and there.

The most dynamic (and in the long run, the most influential) of these groups was the Homebrew Computer Club, which met the second Wednesday of each month at the Stanford Linear Accelerator. It had about five hundred regular members, mostly odd young men who dreamed in computer code. Members would work long hours perfecting a new circuit diagram or program to show off before their fellow members. "People at Homebrew openly exchanged [information] that only a few years later would be regarded as company secrets," said one former member. Adam Osborne was there, as were the future founders of Cromemco Computer and the Byte Shop Computer Stores. There were computer professionals as well as kids. And there was twenty-five-year-old Stephen Wozniak.

Besides his already highly regarded technical prowess, Woz had something equally important: the friendship of twenty-year-old Steve Jobs. Jobs, on the other hand, had himself a gold mine. Despite his counterculture style and impenetrable Zen ramblings, Jobs was as much an entrepreneurial capitalist as any pinkie-ringed, blow-dried hustler in a Wilkes-Bashford suit and vanity-licensed Mercedes. Like most true entrepreneurs, Jobs had the ambition and moxie to make himself rich— but he needed a product, a vehicle he could ride to glory. Wozniak may not have looked like Bill Shockley, but he was the best shot Jobs had. It was a stroke of monumental good luck for Steve Jobs that his old buddy Woz turned out to be *the* computer scientist of his generation. The same, of course, was true for Wozniak, who might have labored in backroom-laboratory obscurity forever if he hadn't had as friend perhaps the most remarkable promoter of our time.

The Apple story starts, as do most Silicon Valley firms, with a humble beginning. Apple's, however, is a bit more sordid than most.

Jobs and Wozniak's first foray into electronic manufacturing had taken place when Woz was at UC Berkeley and Jobs still at Homestead High in Sunnyvale. The product was called a "blue box," and was a big fad item among "techies" at the time. It essentially was an electronic device that duplicated the function of telephone switching systems, enabling the user to make long-distance calls anywhere in the world without charge. Needless to say, the combination which blue boxes offered of anti-big business criminality and high technology made them most appealing to whiz kids, enabling them to show off their talents and to experience the thrill of wickedness they missed when their peers were drinking and racing or screwing and protest-marching.

Almost nobody built a better blue box than Stephen Wozniak, and with Jobs directing the program and running publicity, the two became minor celebrities in the techie underground. The two boys even hooked up with the legendary "Captain Crunch," king of the blue boxers.

Neither Ma Bell nor the Federal Bureau of Investigation looked kindly upon smartass kids freeloading on the phone system. So it wasn't long before the federal government came down on blue boxers, nailing a few examples to put the fear of God in the rest.

It apparently worked, because by the mid-1970s blue-boxing had all but disappeared. On the other hand, it may just be that its adherents had shifted their interests by then to the far more thrilling world of digital computing. Certainly that's what Woz and Jobs did, and just in time. On the criminal side of hobby electronics, one bets everything on each roll. If you win, you become famous, if you lose you are (at least for the time being) in very big trouble. Thus, Jobs and Woz became internationally famous and hugely wealthy. Captain Crunch went to jail.

Of course, the extraordinary success of Woz and Jobs has short-circuited this all-or-nothing game a bit. As the only self-confessed (though unconvicted) felons to found and run a Fortune 500 corporation, they have both consciously and unconsciously romanticized the image of the electronics criminal to that of young geniuses unconstrained by the repressive legal system. The new breed of high-tech crook or vandal—the "hacker" as he or she is called—is the object of admiration and respect in movies and television programs. These days, the hacker is just as likely to be hired as a consultant by his or her victim as incarcerated.

In 1975, about the time the Homebrew Computer Club was in full bloom, Wozniak was back in the Valley after having dropped out of UC Berkeley. Jobs was home with his parents, having quit Reed College for financial reasons, spent his apprenticeship working for Nolan Bushnell at Atari and returned from a trip in search of God in India. Woz, who not only didn't care how much money he had in his pockets or what clothes he wore but disliked any kind of competition, suddenly found himself caught up in the thrill of building a better computer than everybody else. And he did.

The computer was in time called the Apple I. Wozniak had little interest in anything but the big technical problems. But Jobs, regular visitor to Homebrew, had dollar signs in his eyes as he watched with awe at how Woz's design was received by the club and calculated the money that could be made selling finished computer central processor boards to hungry buffs who couldn't afford the more expensive systems.

The trick was to get a finished product, and at motivating Woz, Jobs was a past master: "Jobs would pull every trick in the book. He pulled the scorned-lover act, he pulled the enthusiast act, he would bring in people from computer clubs who agreed with him. If he couldn't convince him himself, he'd bring in people to argue with Wozniak en masse."

The finished Apple I was little more than a printed-circuit board stuffed with chips, about the size of a portable typewriter. But in 1976 that was enough, and with Woz's elegant design, and Jobs's salesmanship hawking it on folding tables at computer conventions around the country, the Apple I quickly became a star in the tight world of computer freaks.

Financing for the prototype model was $1,300, raised by the two boys from the sale (the aptness of this remains almost too much to believe) of Jobs's VW microbus and Wozniak's HP-65 programmable calculator. Many of the parts for the first Apple I were lifted by Woz from the stores of his employer, Hewlett-Packard—an unspoken but generally recognized agreement between employers and engineers in Silicon Valley.

The source of the company's name seems to vary with every company profile. Apparently it was Jobs's idea, arising out of happy experiences working in an apple orchard in Oregon, a desire to produce a gentle, nonthreatening corporate image and, as claimed by friends, because Jobs was a fruitarian at the time. Take your pick. Whichever it was, "Apple Computer" was a stroke of genius, an appealingly commonplace name that somehow linked silicon hardware with environmentalism, the back-to-the-earth movement, naturalness, friendliness and just about everything else the baby-boom generation imagined best about itself. It wasn't long before the cute and clever Apple rainbow logo was appearing as a sticker on automobile bumpers and windows around the world. History may record that this was Jobs's most important contribution to Apple: his dead-eye accuracy at understanding precisely what his generation thought of itself and then playing that tune in perfect pitch.

The Apple I was the perfect machine for the moment, but that moment was quickly passing, propelled in part by the Apple I's own success. Apple was a company now, albeit a small one, officially founded in January 1977. The Apple I was Woz's machine, a technological wonder for which Jobs had played the role of salesman. The Apple II would be different. Jobs was president now, and his experiences flogging the first model had given him an unparalleled insight into the changing tastes of the new consumer market in computers. The Apple II would be the one true Woz-and-Jobs computer, a synthesis of each of their skills, the milestone product that would usher in the age of the personal computer.

But the Apple II would not be merely a board stuffed with chips like the Apple I. With the penetrating vision that characterized much of Jobs's work during this period, the young man realized before just about anyone else that what he had was a device that could reach beyond the hobbyists to a market a hundred thousand times that size and turn the toy of a handful of nerdly young men in ponytails and Hush Puppies into a household appliance as common as a refrigerator, a piece of office equipment as pervasive as a typewriter. It sounded like crazy utopianism—and it was. But who would know more about false and real utopias than someone who have lived in a commune and chased gurus all over India? Unlike all of his counterparts at the Homebrew Club (except perhaps for Osborne), Jobs saw personal computers in terms not of their utility but of their utilization. Moore's Law told him that a computer on every desk was inevitable, and he decided to get there first. Of all of the hobbyists who ever played with the newest electronic toy and dreamed of making the Big Score, from Terman on down, only Jobs actually turned the corner—but then, computers never were particularly fun for Steven Jobs.

The machine that Jobs envisaged for his rocket to the top, the computer that he demanded, begged and tricked out of Wozniak, was a departure from anything that had come before it. The Apple II was the first true personal computer. It remains the best-selling (in terms of units) computer of any size ever built, and so much a part of our collective consciousness, so much the model of what a personal computer is *supposed* to look like, that now, less than a decade after its 1977 introduction, it is almost impossible to imagine what an earthshaking impact its introduction had. Here at last was a computer no bigger than a Royal typewriter, with its own keyboard, in a sleek, classy-looking, taupe-colored plastic box. Even for someone who knew exactly nothing about computers (at the time, almost everyone) the Apple II, with its sensuous lines and recognizable IBM-based keyboard and its cute name and logo emblazoned across the top, looked about as intimidating as a Granola bar.

Brilliant as it was, the Apple II would have gone nowhere without the financial backing and the support Silicon Valley provided. Although the Valley was set up to take just about any young entrepreneur, no matter how odd, under its wing, it was not quite ready for Steve Jobs. Silicon Valley could handle strange pale men with hedge-clipper haircuts, ill-fitting suits and an inability to socialize with anything higher than a paramecium; the Valley could deal with these guys, taking their inventions, putting them in new companies surrounded by normal business types, giving them a great title (vice-president of special projects), keeping them away from any positions of authority or responsibility and giving them enough stock to make them rich.

Jobs went only for the best. The first step, not surprisingly, was public relations. That could only mean Regis McKenna, the biggest and most influential agency in the Valley. But McKenna didn't want Steve Jobs; he had a full plate of accounts already—and besides, he had Intel, and in 1977, if you had Intel nothing else mattered.

Jobs was persistent, and eventually McKenna succumbed. It might have been one of Jobs's best moves as a marketing man, because with McKenna came legitimacy. McKenna went back to the early days of the industry. He had dinner with people like Bob Noyce and Andy Grove. If you were accepted into McKenna's select stable of clients, you were suddenly no longer just some asshole kid on a power trip, but an *insider,* a duly dubbed and certified Silicon Valley entrepreneur. Even more, with McKenna you became connected, because, being a good flack, McKenna made it a point to know everybody there was to know in the industry.

The first important heavyweight McKenna took young Jobs to was Jerry Sanders's old nemesis, Don Valentine, now one of the most powerful venture capitalists in the electronics industry. Intrigued, Valentine went to look at the operation—and found Steve Jobs, in sandals, cutoffs, shoulder-length hair and what had been variously described as a Fidel Castro *(Time)* or a Ho Chi Minh *(California)* beard. Valentine's reported comment to McKenna was, "Why did you send me this renegade from the human race?"

But Valentine didn't completely throw up his hands and dismiss the two young men. As a gesture, he recommended that Jobs and Wozniak get themselves some experienced business management. Valentine suggested a guy named A. C. "Mike" Markkula, forty, a marketing manager at Intel who had made his Silicon Valley killing and was looking to get out and enjoy an affluent early retirement.

Markkula knew a marketable product when he saw one and, despite the weird kids that came with the thing, decided to throw his lot in with

Apple. Markkula had made a number of smart moves in his life, but this one was truly the Big Score. He offered to put up $250,000 of his own money, plus his marketing expertise, in exchange for a third of the company. Though history, in the form of P.R. people and magazine reporters, has not recorded it as such, this was the turning point in the story of Apple. Markkula was the critical missing element. He brought the final measure of legitimacy to the firm. It was Markkula who took the boys to the Bank of America to get a credit line, and it was Markkula who enabled Jobs and Wozniak to hook up with the kingmaker himself, venture capitalist Arthur Rock.

Other than that there is little mention of Mike Markkula in most of the official histories. To techies, he represents the first "suit," the first of a growing number of professional businesspeople at Apple who slowly subverted the firm from its initial purity as a commune for brilliant computer artists.

To everybody else, Markkula seems the Rosencrantz to Jobs's Hamlet, the ceremonial president to Jobs's prime minister, always in the shadows, rarely quoted. With his pixie haircut and Atom Ant glasses, he resembles a clerkish John Denver down from the Rockies and lost in Silicon Valley. Sometimes it seems as if the only thing Markkula ever did was introduce Jobs to the bankers and Rock and then get the hell out of the way, to earn an ill-deserved $100 million or so a few years later when Apple went public.

But no one climbs to the upper ranks of Intel without being very good at what he does, and in conversation with Markkula one quickly discovers that here is a mind at least as strong as those of the other two founders—and far more shrewd. Markkula is a two-time winner in Silicon Valley—a mighty rare breed—and he has survived the Valley's battles for more than a decade and a half, ending up at the top of one of the fastest-growing and most successful firms in business history. It is unlikely that credit for all of this can be laid at the feet of serendipity.

So the triumvirate was now in place, each slotted into a role perfectly suited to his personality. (By the way, there was a fourth Apple founder whose existence has been conveniently forgotten. He sold out early and for that clever decision probably deserves oblivion.) Woz was the backroom guy, ensconced in his little cubicle, surrounded by equipment, tinkering an idea into reality. Markkula ran the business side, hiring managerial and manufacturing talent, leasing facilities, negotiating contracts and doing all those other things necessary to create a real company out of what was basically little more than a telephone answering service and mail slot.

Alone, this pair would have composed a stereotypical new start-up team—the businessman and the engineer—to create a solid little establishment.

The joker in the deck was Jobs, whose role was more nebulous. Part of it was to keep an ear to the ground and use his superb marketing talent to determine new trends and changing customer needs. Another role was to be a floater, to move through the company, learning how it operated, giving his two cents at executive meetings, following hunches —the ultimate apprenticeship: infinite power, limited responsibility and infinitesimal blame. It was every boy's dream of tycoonship, *Frank Merriwell and the Billion-Dollar Baby, Tom Swift and the Electronic Fortune 500 Corporate Machine.*

The initial results of this boardroom on-the-job training were mixed. Jobs's youthful pluck and hipness obviously struck a responsive chord not just among hackers and long-haired computer engineers, but also among the millions of young business people who had grown up in the sixties and early seventies, the flower children, the Woodstock Generation, the baby boomers who had sworn themselves to an alternative lifestyle, to the Amerikan revolution, good dope and communality—but who instead cut their hair, put on business suits, grabbed their M.B.A.s and dove into the capitalist world with more selfish greed than the forefathers they had once derided. No matter what they said to each other over quiche and white wine and lines of coke, they knew in their bones that they had sold out in a big way, and they hated themselves for it. As they drove home to their singles apartments or single-parent children in their BMWs and Volvos, these children of the sixties knew that they had become just like their parents—but without the family or the patriotism or religious faith or any of the other "fascist" institutions that made these sacrifices worthwhile.

Jobs reached these people better than anybody else because he seemed to be *one of them.* As they sat in their offices, with the dwindling mementos of their youth and their dreams, they would turn to the full-page ad in *The Wall Street Journal* and see an enormous photo of Jobs in his beard and wicked smirk and think: "That bastard did it. He stuck by his principles and still made so many millions he can tell the establishment to kiss his ass." Then they'd get a little thrill of excitement mixed with envy. The revolution hadn't been lost after all, their lives weren't a sham. The campus guerrillas had just evolved into corporate freedom fighters.

And in their hearts they wished they were Steve Jobs.

In day-to-day activities, Jobs did not perform so well. Voice of a generation was one thing, managing people and selling the corporation to investors was another. Here Jobs's youthfulness got in the way, as did his personality. As a manager, young Steve was appealing and energetic. He was also arrogant, rude, unpredictable and, worst of all, vindictive. Like most amateur businessmen, he took everything personally, treating negotiations as if they were grudge matches, brooking no compromise, ignoring the reality that in business today's enemy may be tomorrow's ally, and vice versa. For Jobs, any sonofabitch who charged him too much for a part or didn't like him personally or who competed with Apple—that is, with Steve Jobs—deserved whatever evil befell him.

This was a dumb strategy when Apple was small, and even dumber when it grew large. Luckily, Jobs's subordinates knew better, and it became standard operating procedure to simply sneak in the back door contracts with his latest set of enemies in order to keep the assembly lines running.

Meanwhile, as Jobs was undergoing the transition to adulthood, Apple continued to grow at a frantic pace. The finished Apple II was a magnificent machine. Inside was Wozniak's masterful design, which required only sixty-two chips (compared with hundreds in other personal computers). This made the Apple II, at twelve pounds, remarkably light—almost too light; the company even considered adding lead weights to make the machine seem more "serious." Outside, the design of the Apple II enclosure was equally splendid. Jobs had turned down several Star Wars designs prepared for him by Atari industrial designers in lieu of a smooth, visually calming, textured plastic box, in gentle earth tones. Jobs knew what his market wanted; the Apple II design wasn't going to turn any heads, but it was a design one could sit before for many years without growing tired of it. It was a 1955 Chevy rather than a 1959 Cadillac Coupe de Ville, a classic design that would grow more admired with time.

As demand for the Apple II skyrocketed, Apple found itself strapped for manufacturing capabilities. As with the rest of the systems business, the biggest drain on overhead was "board-stuffing," the sticking of chips into printed-circuit boards and soldering the attached pins in place. This was mindless work, and at the time robots to do the work were expensive, inaccurate and rare. Thus, one either had to set up a board-stuffing operation in-house or ship it out to firms specializing in that work.

Apple found a third route (though it wasn't alone). While the company propaganda stressed its community, its democracy, its adherence to the ideals of the Howdy Doody generation, each day an unmarked car picked up blank boards and boxes of chips from Apple's back door and delivered them to a roomful of Filipino women and housewives in a Saratoga home, who watched soap operas and stuffed boards at piece rates. That Apple, the epitome of egalitarianism, was resting on the labors of an illegal sweatshop might not jibe well with customers protesting the oppression of workers by not buying Salinas lettuce and Stevens fabric.

But Apple weathered this underpublicized embarrassment with its holistic, Planet Earth reputation intact. Still, the attitude that led to this foray into the ugly nether world of capitalism could not help but arise in other situations and on other occasions. And it did. Perhaps the most distressing of these moments was the so-called Night of the Long Knives, February 25, 1981, when the four-year-old company fired forty of its employees in a single sharp stroke.

So much for corporate conscience. A few miles away, where Ken Oshman, positively a cultural Neanderthal compared to Jobs, had been building equally successful Rolm, there had never been a layoff—despite a complete shift in product strategy. And mind you, Apple's layoff was during a boom, not in the dark hold of a recession; Apple was growing hundreds of percentage points a year. Yet, in one morning, Apple had laid off more people than HP had in the previous thirty years.

Thus it is that reformers and revolutionaries, by eschewing long established and long verified rules of conduct, often slip into behavior far worse than that which they once derided.

Meanwhile, Apple was still growing like a manzanita wildfire. Sales had expanded from $775,000 in the first year (1977) to more than $100 million by 1980 and were continuing to triple every year. The Apple II of course was the key. It had not only started the personal computer boom but now was its greatest beneficiary. The machine that had an original target market of 10,000 was now being shipped at a rate of more than 25,000 per month. At the time this is being written, more than 750,000 Apple IIs (and the souped-up Apple IIe's) have been sold.

By 1980, Apple had a new president, Michael Scott (he of the Long

Knives), an engaging young man who had the only-in-Silicon-Valley practice of giving away shares of Apple stock as Christmas gifts to friends. Scott had two crucial responsibilities at Apple (three if one included getting along with Jobs): first, to build the company up fast enough to keep up with sales; and, second, to create a replacement for the Apple II.

The life-span of the first product can be extended for a while through modifications, peripherals, price cuts and all the other fan dances. But eventually a day of reckoning comes when the company's first product must be supplanted by something else.

As much as the first product, the second product can make or break a firm. Still, inadequacies in each can be overcome with a suitable follow-up. The real acid test comes a few years down the line, after the company has become successful and famous, when the market the company helped create has grown large enough and complex enough to be interesting both to potential new start-up competitors and to giant firms in other industries eyeing the profit of the new market with envy. Then, more than at any other time, is when the pioneering company must get its flagship product ready. Not only must this product be brilliantly targeted and breathtakingly original in technology, but it must also be timely. If a company can indeed hit its target, the great flagship product ready on time, it can effectively seal off the market to all but a handful of weakened competitors for years.

It will "own" the market, as IBM did with the 360 computer, HP with electronic instruments, Tandem with fail-safe computers. Then the only fear is the United State Department of Justice, Antitrust Division.

After brilliantly clearing the obstacle of the first product, Apple Computer had a chance to skip the second step and head to outright ownership of the personal computer industry. By 1980, still with no serious competition, Apple could have sewn up the midrange personal computer business (above Atari) and become so firmly entrenched that no one would have dared to take it on directly. Instead, the company stumbled badly—and in trotted the most fearsome competitor of all.

The follow-up product to the Apple II was designated—remarkably enough—the Apple III. It seemed ill starred from the beginning. Despite a beautiful physical design and some impressive internal advancements, the Apple III at the time of its introduction in November 1980 was a bust; in the words of company employees, a "fiasco," an "abortion," a "camel" (from the old joke about a camel being a horse built by a committee), a "mistake" and a "disaster."

For one thing, the Apple III was nearly a year late—not fatal in the personal computer industry in 1980, but symptomatic. What made this tardiness ironic was that the additional time didn't seem to improve the quality of the Apple III one iota. It was a design nightmare. Apple IIIs started appearing at dealers dead on arrival.

In a frenzy to get the firm on track, Scott declared the company "constipated" and all but took over the production line. The Apple III still failed, becoming an industry laughingstock, and painfully damaged the failproof image Jobs and Regis McKenna had tried so hard to create.

Finally, unable to break the deadlock, Scott, in a fit of frustration, brought out the "long knives." Some observers thought it a good move, pruning the tree to make it stronger, so to speak; getting the company refocused by getting rid of useless people and expensive projects. Strategically proper or not, the layoff ended Apple's adolescence. Apple had driven itself out of Eden. The computer Woodstock Generation had met its Altamont.

Still, in one area, investor relations, the Apple mythmaking machine continued to run at full steam. Apple had scheduled its first public sale of stock at the tail end of 1980. The company, now with more than $300 million in sales and $40 million in profits, was overdue. The market was in pretty good shape so timing wouldn't be a great problem, as long as the traditional October massacre didn't hold over into the Christmas season. Of course, in the critical area of selling oneself to both sophisticated analysts as well as traditional middle-class home-and-hearth common stock investors, Apple had already proven itself a young master.

By this time, the Valley's slickest corporate P.R. guy (Fred Hoar, hired from Fairchild for millions) and the best agency P.R. man (in Regis McKenna), both were devoting their energies to making Apple a desirable stock.

The two men, and their staffs, succeeded beyond anybody's wildest dream. With Hoar sweet-talking investors and Regis landing stories about the coming offering in the national press, the campaign quickly turned into a juggernaut. By Halloween the national fervor for Apple stock had turned into hysteria.

On December 12, 1980, Apple enjoyed what many consider the most successful stock offering in Wall Street history. The offering was fully subscribed within a matter of minutes, primarily by investors such as brokerage houses, insurance funds and pension funds. By the end of the day the stock, initially offered at $12, had jumped to more than $20.

Apple's first public sale of stock created perhaps one hundred paper millionaires among Apple investors, executives, employees and their relatives (within weeks the company parking lot was filled with Porsches, Mercedeses and BMWs). For the three founders, it meant wealth beyond imagination. For Jobs and Markkula, about $150 million apiece. For Wozniak, who had with typical ingenuousness handed out millions in stock to friends and family, about half that.

Those were figures to make outsiders gasp, but in reality, because they were tied up in ownership of the firm, in a sense meaningless. With no plans for cashing in their chips and leaving the table, Markkula and Jobs were in reality just millionaires to some unspecified degree. Only for Woz, now all but out of Apple and dreaming of salvation through heavy metal rock, did those scores of millions constitute disposable income.

The successful stock sale was a godsend for Apple. That extravagant amount of capital ($1 billion) meant that the firm could afford to consolidate its operations into fewer larger facilities, straighten out the Apple III mess and pump however much money was needed into the development of the company's next computer generation.

To Apple's credit, it did all of those things. In fact, so emboldened was the firm by its stock market success that in November 1981, more than a year after the first botched attempt, Apple simply reintroduced the Apple III, almost as if nothing had happened. This time, it had built the computer right, and after some initial market resistance, the Apple III became a major revenue producer (though never a star).

In the year between the false first start and the successful second introduction of the Apple III, Apple lost something far more important than sales: time. The personal computer business had reached that magic $1-billion mark and now big firms like IBM, Digital Equipment and Hewlett-Packard were eyeing it hungrily. So were the Japanese. New little computer firms were springing up everywhere. The big corporations and ambitious entrepreneurs looked over the personal computer landscape and saw a slowing Radio Shack, a disappointing crop of products from Atari and Texas Instruments and, most of all, a confused Apple, and knew the time was right for attack.

The first waves of new and competitive products began hitting in 1980, even before Apple went public. They increased in intensity all through 1981. Most were from smaller firms, like Ohio Scientific, that lacked effective distribution, or from bigger firms, like HP, that were targeted at a higher-rent market like laboratories or large corporations.

In direct competition, such as that from the TI 99/6, Apple usually held its own, thanks to its unmatched software library and the scores of small firms that had sprung up to design and sell specialty hardware and software exclusively for Apple computers. But Apple knew it couldn't maintain the status quo much longer.

Throughout the late seventies and early eighties, three forces propelled the personal computer industry forward. Computer use became ubiquitous, corporate software libraries (that is, at Apple, etc.) expanded to include hundreds, then thousands of custom applications programs, and most important, personal computers continued to follow Moore's Law to lower prices, greater power and smaller size. The last was so important because it increasingly atomized the market. No longer could the Apple II and the TRS-80, as one-size-fits-all computers, effectively monopolize the entire market. By 1980, falling costs for microprocessors and memory chips, keyboards and floppy-disk drives made sure that the center could no longer hold.

Now firms didn't have to compete directly with large veterans like Apple; instead, they could pick out some unique combination of price, power and size and stake out a safe claim. The success of Apple and Radio Shack made the prospect all the more juicy to entrepreneurs and their capital backers, particular with the Big Two looking vulnerable. In short order there were a number of distinct and established markets that hadn't existed two years before, each containing well-established firms: portable computers (Osborne, Compaq), game computers (Atari, Mattel), home computers (Commodore, Texas Instruments), scientific calculator/computers (HP), word processors (Lanier), office computers (Wang), and in time, computers for use with networks (Corvus). The amazing thing was that, at least at first, everyone of these companies made a killing. So did software designers (VisiCorp, Digital Research, Microsoft, etc.), peripheral equipment makers (Qume, Nippon Electric, Shugart, Seagate, Tandon, Hayes), floppy-disk media makers (Dysan, Verbatim) and trade magazine publishers (Hayden, Ziff-Davis, McGraw-Hill). The fact was that for a time it seemed any business connected with the personal computer world in any way had been issued a license to print money. As in every other high-tech boom, some people made an enormous amount of money, many more didn't and everyone confidently predicted that the good times would last forever.

For Apple, having lost a shot at taking the field, this type of competition was more blessing than burden. Since there were few direct competitors and the apparent market was far vaster than all the firms combined could hope to plumb in the near future, all this business activity could only heat up the market and benefit its preeminent firms by raising the public's consciousness. In fact, Apple could confidently predict that after less sophisticated customers tested the waters of programming and word processing with the cheap machines, they would in short order gravitate to the Apple family.

Frankly, Apple needed the grace period the boom brought. Sales were still incredibly strong, but with the Apple III an apparent dog and the Apple II growing old and ripe for dethroning, Apple needed a wild time like this for its new competitors to go through their own growing pains as well as for Apple itself to produce enough profit and capital to straighten out the III problem and start ramping up for the "killer" product it had needed for years, to be code-named "Lisa." Apple's executives knew they would have to hurry, because the ever active industry scuttlebutt was whispering that IBM and several Japanese giants were on their way—and would center their attack upon Apple.

The question for Apple was: in an expanded market, which direction should it go? Should the company launch a new line of expensive, high-powered machines aimed at the business world, or should it shoot downward at the home market and take on the Ataris and the Commodores?

The other possibility, the one Apple chose, was to go up—into the Fortune 1000 market, where customers would pay ten thousand dollars or more for the right computer and would order hundreds of machines at a crack, and where the needs of the market were more explicit: word processing, spreadsheets, charts, electronic mail, networking, scratch pad . . . Profit margins were greater here too. The competition would be mostly over function rather than price. Less obvious was that such a product orientation would give Apple the respect as a serious firm it had long sought, as well as the opportunity to once again show off its technical skill.

So, in 1981, Apple set about building its masterpiece, code-named Lisa for Jobs's out-of-wedlock daughter. The Lisa computer was to include the latest of everything, both hardware and software. The most interesting hardware feature would be the "mouse," a device invented years before at the high-powered Xerox Research Park just up the road in Palo Alto. This mouse, a little rectangle on a wire sporting a button, enabled the user to quickly move the cursor about the screen without even touching the keyboard. Though a useful tool, the mouse required extensive software support. For that reason it was rarely used and, before Lisa, never on a computer priced under fifty thousand dollars.

That was only half the story of Lisa. On the software side, the computer was just as trend-setting. Apple's—or, more properly, Steve Jobs's —goal was to design a computer whose operation could be mastered in twenty minutes rather than the usual twenty hours. The mouse would help, but the key was in the software—software so sophisticated it was simple, "transparent" to the user, who would feel as if the computer were an extension of his or her mind.

With the spectacular sales growth and eventually the successful stock offering, Jobs and Markkula knew they had the bucks to finance the project: an estimated $50 million by 1983. They also thought they had the man for the project—John Couch, thirty. Couch was a hot young manager at HP. But a conversation with Jobs (and a chance to produce a landmark personal computer) and Couch agreed to take a 30 percent pay cut, trade managing an entire department of nearly 150 people for a small design team and, most important, abandon a clear-cut career path to the top ranks at the Valley's preeminent firm.

At first, Jobs and Couch were quite close, free-associating ideas over brandy in Couch's Los Gatos hot tub. But soon, according to insiders, this chumminess chilled when Jobs wanted to take over command of the Lisa project and was told to back off by then-president Scott and, according to *Business Week,* quoting an Apple insider, "Steve was furious and went off and started the Mac [Macintosh computer, the Apple II replacement] project. He was determined to prove that Mac could be a bigger success."

As the Lisa team heroically struggled away in its corporate microcosm, outside the bigger world of personal computing was changing irrevocably. The instigator of this change was the most feared competitor of all: IBM—Big Blue itself, one hundred times the size of Apple, with more loose cash on hand than Apple had sales, the biggest, toughest son of a bitch in electronics. The Armonk Marauder had already demolished its competition in mainframe computers and bloodied minicomputer manufacturers until an antitrust suit made it clean up its act. Throughout the late seventies it had tried to make itself small, pretending to ignore billion-dollar markets like personal computers and acting like it was just some mom-and-pop haberdashery in White Plains. But in 1980 and 1981, IBM stood toe-to-toe with the Department of Justice—and the federal government blinked; actually more like winked, as the Reagan administration was just happy as hell to find a company that could pulverize the Japanese.

IBM Unbound, the resulting two years might be called. In August 1981, as the legions of "IBM watchers" had long predicted, IBM introduced its first personal computer—presumptuously entitled precisely that. The "PC" wasn't an earth-shattering machine technically, but it was more than a match for the aging Apple II, particularly when the software began to appear in abundance. The PC didn't have to be a great machine because what it really had going for it was the three little blue letters on the front. Even an Apple executive stupidly admitted to *Time:* "There's an old adage that you never lose your job buying an IBM."

The IBM PC, like almost all IBM new market entries, looked unprepossessing enough when it was first introduced. Some technical magazines pooh-poohed it for being less than a breakthrough—as if that mattered. Apple bravely, if transparently, ran a full-paged ad in *The Wall Street Journal* that said, "Welcome IBM, Seriously." But it wasn't long before dealers and then computer makers like Apple began to feel IBM's hot breath.

The crowning blow came when IBM hit Apple where the young firm had thought itself strongest—marketing a corporate image. With the award-winning "Little Tramp" ads, IBM brilliantly found a way to make its personal computers more friendly and appealing than Apple's. The bowler and baggy pants magically made a megalithic $50-billion company with a quarter of a million employees in 150 countries seem smaller even than Apple. This was genius.*

Jobs bravely predicted that the PC would be lucky to sell as many machines as the Apple III in 1982. That year, fewer than 50,000 Apple IIIs were sold, compared with 200,000 PCs. By the end of 1982, PCs

---

* And cynicism. *National Lampoon* captured this in a fake IBM ad showing the same square-mustached man first as the Little Tramp ("The IBM Public Icon") and then as Adolf Hitler ("The IBM In-House Icon"), with copy that read in part: "[The Public Icon] incorporates all the honest, integrity and concern for the American buyer that a $36 million advertising campaign exploiting one of the last pure symbols of an era when somebody gave tinker's damn for the underdog can buy . . . [The In-House Icon] represents the propensity for letting brilliant young entrepreneurs establish new markets before we come in and drive them mercilessly into bankruptcy . . ." Cynical or not, the IBM ad campaign was no more manipulative than Jobs's own attempts to coopt the spirit of the sixties. The bottom line was that IBM beat Apple at its own game. Not only that but, feeling unchained by the Justice Department, IBM broke with tradition and priced the PC competitively. Obviously Big Blue was playing for keeps.

were selling at 20,000 per month, approaching the 30,000 per month of that old workhorse, the Apple II. By then, Apple's share of the personal computer market was down from 29 percent to 24 percent and falling. With the Apple III fixed but still less than a star seller, the burden lay on the Apple II, with its enormous installed base of 600,000 machines, unequaled software library and large support network of independent hardware and software suppliers. That was enough to keep Apple growing at a strong rate (1982 sales were $583 million, up from $335 million the year before), but it was apparent that if Lisa was to renew Apple it would have to be a monster product.

Ironically, while Lisa was being developed, the home market, which Apple had perceived as all but closed when it embarked on the project, was suddenly ripe for the picking. At the same time, the high-end market, which Apple had seen as the best shot for sales and profit growth, was rapidly being sealed off by some of the most experienced and successful firms on the New York Stock Exchange.

For Apple, it was too late to change, even if it had wanted to. Couch was driving his little Outward Bound School of Business to an exhausted climax. He had fulfilled his mission perfectly, but industry watchers now questioned whether the market would still want Lisa, no matter how great a breakthrough. Increasingly, these analysts pointed at the Macintosh (sic) computer as Apple's savior. Jobs's little tantrum was swelling to become Apple's Last Great Hope. And, because of the feud, Macintosh and Lisa were not expected to be compatible.

Nevertheless, Lisa, Apple's masterpiece, went forward. As the January introduction day approached, Hoar and McKenna girded themselves. It seemed impossible to top the placement of Jobs's picture on the front of *Time,* but they did. The Lisa introduction was the highwater mark for Silicon Valley flackery. The national press had all but ignored the introduction of the Valley's other great products, the HP-35, the Intel 8080 microprocessor, the Amdahl computer, and seemed to be atoning for past indifference by treating the Lisa introduction as if it were the Salk vaccine. It may have been the most successful new product introduction since the Boeing 707, the Ford Mustang or pull tabs for beer cans.

There could be no adequate follow-up to this act, and though McKenna's agency retained the Apple account, Fred Hoar was fired a few months later. He left a wealthy man.

In March 1983, just a few months before Atari went outside the Valley for a new CEO, Apple announced that it had hired John Sculley, president of Pepsi-Cola, as its new headman. Sculley was known as a marketing star who had brought Pepsi up neck and neck with Coca-Cola in just five years. He had also operated a personal computer for the first time just one month before. Jobs had done the hiring, offering Sculley $1 million up front, another million in first-year salary, a $2-million mansion in Woodside and $10 million in stock.

Sculley professed to love working with Jobs, and indeed they did seem to have a mysterious rapport. At meetings they would begin talking to one another, ignoring everyone else, riffing off each other's thoughts, anticipating the other's ideas before they were said, speaking almost in a private language. Yet there were those Apple managers who looked in Sculley's eyes and saw the shrewdest of businessmen, a chameleon with a color so pure that even Steve Jobs couldn't see past it to the real John Sculley inside.

Apple had at last become a serious company. But it was almost too late. Nineteen eighty-three was a watershed year in the personal computer market. Most of the computer companies on the market recognized the inevitable and offered IBM software-compatible equipment—except Apple. IBM further consolidated its control of the market with the PC and a more powerful version called the PCxt, which as good as obliterated the poor Apple III and stole the lower end of Lisa's market.

IBM also again showed, as it had in larger computers, that it could devastate a market not only with a product it had introduced but with products it *might* introduce. The low-end personal computer market was paralyzed for a year, and firms were driven into the ground as the world waited for the introduction of the mythical IBM "Peanut." When it finally arrived, as the PC*jr.*, in November, it turned out to be nothing fancy, but adequate to be a potential competitor to the Apple IIe.

Equally important, in 1983, Apple, of all places, was slow to realize that the pace of technological innovation had changed. No longer could one build an Apple II and have it command a market for a half decade. Lisa was a magnificent machine (unless you wanted to do word processing, the most common personal computer application), but the day of earthshaking new personal computers had passed.

By the last quarter of 1983, Apple's mistakes finally caught up with it, and sales and profits began to flatten. The Lisa, for all its innovation, just wasn't selling in adequate quantities. It was even rumored that Apple had contemplated a Christmas layoff of several hundred employees and was looking for a big corporate buyer. As a measure of how far it had fallen, at the Las Vegas Comdex computer show in December,

Apple, once the star, was all but invisible. On those increasingly rare days when Apple was discussed, it was to agree that the company's fate seemed to rest upon its long delayed introduction of Macintosh—the low-end computer Apple should have introduced at the beginning.

Nevertheless, while others tolled the company's knell, Apple continued to exhibit its famous elan. An expensive, robot-filled facility in Milpitas almost silently cranked out Macintoshes for the introduction. The firm bought 200 acres in one of the side valleys southeast of San Jose to build its corporate headquarters. Jobs had openly dreamed of building "Appletown," a controlled community, like Disney World, where employees would live, learn, work and play under the benevolent control of Apple Computer. They would (shudder) buy from the company store. Fittingly, groundbreaking was originally planned to take place in 1984. Whether or not Apple employees will ever be blessed with this, the latest of Jobs's visions, remains to be seen.* There is a

* One thing is for certain: in early 1984, just when it seemed that the firm was about to dwindle and die along with the scores of other computer firms caught in the dark shadow of IBM, Apple enjoyed an extraordinary resurgence—thanks to a remarkable combination of a solid product introduction and an all but unprecedented misstep by IBM.

The Macintosh was a terrific piece of technology, but it was overpriced and of comparatively limited practical use. Mac's most important characteristic, though, was that it was the most "approachable" personal computer in history. Its beautiful graphics and mouse, though a handicap in long-term use, made the machine instantly workable to even the rankest computer neophyte. This, combined with an appealing, squat, Volkswagenlike ugliness and a brilliantly incoherent Orwellian television ad, gave the Macintosh one of the best send-offs in consumer electronics industry. The Macintosh was probably the last great example of Steve Jobs's marketing brilliance.

Bolstering the Mac introduction was the unexpected disaster a month before of the IBM PC*jr,* with its unworkable "Chiclet" keyboard. The Junior was a reminder that even IBM could screw up—and, with Mac, a happy lesson in the enduring primacy of a single creative mind over tens of millions of dollars in product development. (So paranoid had the personal computer industry become that some executives secretly suggested that IBM had purposely failed in order to escape antitrust action.)

With Mac and the Apple IIc (a portable version of Wozniak's apparently immortal Apple II design) Apple appeared to have triumphed—or at least earned a stay of execution. The momentum, at least for now, was back.

To celebrate its resurrection and introduce the IIc, in April 1984, Apple rented San Francisco's Moscone Hall, soon to be the site of the Democratic National Convention (where Wozniak was a Hart delegate), and put on a $750,000 party for the press, complete with giant TV screens, a Wozniak stand-up comedy routine and a Herbie Hancock jazz concert. The pièce de résistance of the show was an exact re-creation of the garage in which Jobs and Wozniak built the first Apple. In his megalomania, Jobs now equated himself and Wozniak with Bill Hewlett and Dave Packard—though the two old aristocrats typically have refused all efforts to enshrine their old garage.

sense of foreboding now which even Macintosh cannot dispel. It is a feeling that Apple's days of social tinkering are behind it. And there are many who, out of envy for its success or hatred of its arrogance, will applaud Apple's decline when and if it comes.

Most of this resentment, both inside Apple and out, centers around the ever magnetic personality of Steve Jobs. That Macintosh, a product created basically as a pout, was a roaring success only added to the myth of Jobs as computer genius. This was good for sales but not necessarily for Apple, because in typical style Jobs proceeded to punish the heretics of the Lisa group, driving them out of the corporation.

Playboy interviewed Jobs, François Mitterand went home to France after a visit to Apple and raved about the remarkable young man he'd met. Meanwhile, within Apple, work life often became a matter—if you weren't in the Macintosh group—of bobbing and weaving and staying out of Jobs's line of sight.

Life at Apple now had touches of the bizarre. A $1-billion company now, Apple, in the words of one executive, "would fall apart tomorrow if Steve got run over by a bus or something." Here was a firm, famed around the world for its familylike atmosphere, that in reality was the most top-down, autocratic firm in town. Late one evening, after twenty hours of work, one executive turned to a poster on the wall showing a still from the now-famous Macintosh 1984 commercial and punched it down, yelling, "You want to know where Big Brother really is? It's not at IBM. It's right here."

Meanwhile, Steve Jobs smirked and relaxed by sticking his bare feet in a flushing company toilet.

Yet Apple had become too big even for Steve Jobs to ruin. With Markkula, then Sculley, at the controls, presiding over a growing professional middle management, Apple grew up. Jobs aside, it became a good, solid place to work, with extended career paths and professionalism that instilled employee loyalty. There were no more Nights of the Long Knives and fewer mercurial, unpredictable bosses—except Jobs. Much of the funkiness and flash were gone, but so was the amateurishness and the risky company swings. Apple had finally passed through its childhood. With the arrival of experienced managers like Sculley, it was obvious that whether Apple prospered or failed in the future, it would follow this new style of doing business.

Despite Apple's recent success, there is a new sense of decay about the place, of adolescence held past its prime.

But the past can never be fully escaped—not even when it is sanitized by public relations and personal shrines. No major company had ever mouthed so many platitudes as Apple, or claimed such great moral superiority and so quickly denigrated the tenets of its own philosophy whenever the going got tough.

What goes around comes around. And even the innocent are often victims. For Wozniak, his Apple success has been a mixed blessing. For one thing, there was his airplane crash, which led to Woz's feeling a general dissatisfaction with his life. Quitting Apple, he returned to UC Berkeley to finish his bachelor's degree. While there he fell into a group of sixties survivors and est refugees who became the founders of Unison. Outside of some vacuous philosophizing about world peace, the main goal of Unison seemed to have been to listen to good rock and roll with Woz's money.

Everyone who dealt with Unison in Silicon Valley came away shuddering—everybody, that is, except Woz, who bankrolled two annual US festivals on land he had acquired near Santa Barbara for the purpose. The first year, Bill Graham ran the promotion and Apple exhibited its computers on the grounds as part of Unison's obtuse belief in the relationship between computers, contemporary music and nuclear nonproliferation. The second year, Graham and Apple put as much mileage between themselves and the festival as possible. The final tally was two accidental deaths, Woz out $20 million and a lot of second-rate performances. Obviously the spirit of Woodstock was dead. Soon after, Wozniak was back at his cubicle at Apple. All was quiet until, at the 1984 Olympics, Wozniak's wife was arrested for trying to scalp the free tickets she'd been given by Apple. The King of the Nerds was now becoming an embarrassment. Soon after, Woz, after bad-mouthing personal computers in general and Apple in particular, left for good the company he'd helped found.

"Poor Woz," said Steve Jobs.

10

The Pristine Pit

Fremont Avenue is a distinctively Silicon Valley boulevard. Like an archaeological dig laid on its side, Fremont Avenue, in its short five-mile course, cuts through nearly all of the strata of Valley life. The road is so straight that on a clear day one can almost see from one end to the other, but one might spend a lifetime figuratively making the trip.

It begins in Los Altos, at the base of the hills owned by the Valley's wealthiest. Dave Packard lives up there. So did Bob Noyce. At Mom's ice cream parlor, a Valley landmark at the avenue's source, one can sit in the window eating an ice cream cone and watch the Mercedeses and Porsches whiz past on their way up to estates in the hills.

Almost three miles of Fremont Avenue lie within the boundaries of Los Altos. Here the road is narrow, just two tree-lined lanes divided by a landscaped median, more like a driveway than the major artery it really is. Along this stretch the houses are for the most part smaller, but impressive nevertheless. There is a remnant of another age—a pink stucco mansion with balconies and cement urns that looks as though it were made out of frosting—as well as, in one unforgettable side court, a two-story Colonial mansion right out of Connecticut. There are also tennis courts. Even the Standard Oil gas station that looks like a ranch home and shyly admits its true vocation with a sign showing the chevron insignia but with the name removed.

Farther down, almost at the city limits, if one peeks through the trees at the right moment, there sits, between an elegant older home and the giant new addition behind it, a vintage white Rolls-Royce, parked as if on discrete display, in an open carport.

Then, a quick vault over Stevens Creek and one is in a different world: Sunnyvale. Fittingly, the city greets the new arrival with the cement walls of Freeway 85, the link between uptown Freeway 280 and downtown Bayshore Freeway 101, and nearly a private drive for workers at Lockheed and NASA. After a gauntlet of stoplights, one is in residential Sunnyvale. Fremont Avenue widens to four lanes and, in places, six, all divided by medians filled with gravel and dirt. Here the trees are smaller; in summer, Sunnyvale seems brighter, hotter and newer than Los Altos—and less hospitable to life.

There is a nursing home on the left and, farther along, one on the right, but for the most part the first mile of Fremont in Sunnyvale runs like a luge course between two sets of fences interspersed by adobe walls. Behind these fences and walls can be seen the roofs of homes, hundreds of homes in abutted housing developments. Some are thirty years old, some ten. They are the homes of the Valley's middle class and cost between $125,000 and $250,000. They are three or four bedrooms, usually two bathrooms, a pair of late-model cars in the driveway, usually immaculate yards (except for the standard neighborhood bum), and sit regularly arrayed on lots of about one tenth of an acre. Behind these fences live the Valley's middle executives, product marketing managers, personnel directors, accountants, district sales managers. Ted Hoff, the inventor of the microprocessor, lives here, the only hint of his wealth the hundreds of thousands of dollars of metalworking equipment in his garage.

The intersection formed by Fremont with Mary Avenue is a neighborhood gathering place. On one corner is a large, one-story medical center containing several dozen offices. On another is the Westmoor Shopping Center, containing Petrini's, an upscale supermarket that sells not only groceries but caviar and features a built-in delicatessen, bank and pasta counter. Catty-corner to Westmoor is another shopping center. This one is built around an Alpha Beta supermarket, a main-line market that gets the folks who can't afford Petrini's. This shopping center also sports a Farrell's Ice Cream Parlor, a Velvet Turtle restaurant, a renowned Szechuan restaurant, a video cassette store, and a thriving computer store owned by Apple founder Steve Wozniak's brother. The fourth corner contains a bank and the only two story building around: an office complex that holds, among others, the West

Coast bureau of Hayden publishing *(Popular Computing, Electronic Design)*.

Past Mary, Fremont passes another gas station. Unlike its subdued competitor down the road, this one is a self-serve, with an attached quick-stop market. Here, again hidden behind walls, lie three generations of Eichler homes. P.R. guru Regis McKenna lives behind one of these walls.

This stretch of Fremont is religion row, with Jehovah's Witness, Baptist, Mormon, Presbyterian, Seventh-Day Adventist, Roman Catholic and Christian churches all clustered within a mile. The most imposing is the Presbyterian, a tall, modern A-frame, but the most active are the Jehovah's Witness and Mormon churches. It is in this segment of Fremont that one first detects another change, descending wealth, exemplified by a few tired old homes.

In the next mile, to Sunnyvale–Saratoga Road, the old Highway 9 and once the Valley's most important east–west thoroughfare, Fremont passes on one side several subdivisions of older, smaller homes, fruit stands and a post office, once the city's main branch but now supplanted by a big new station smack in the middle of Sunnyvale's biggest business park.

On the other side, Fremont passes the headquarters of the Fremont Union High School District, and then Fremont High School itself. Built in 1926, Fremont High looks like an old-fashioned high school, with its bell-towered main building, and in old photographs can be seen standing at the intersection of two dirt roads at the center of miles of unbroken orchards. It was at Fremont in 1983 that young Robert Nelson was arrested and accused of sabotaging the school computer.

At this intersection there are two older shopping centers, in one is an old co-op market recently renovated into a Nautilus health club and a small amateur playhouse. There are also an ancient Dairy Queen kept in business by generations of students cutting class, and two gas stations. At one of the stations, the owners supplement their income by building fiber-glass reproductions of Auburn Boat-Tailed Speedsters with modern running gear and selling them at thirty thousand dollars a pop to local tycoons.

Then on Fremont back between the two walls for another mile, with some exceptions, the houses grow smaller and older. Finally, Fremont ends, running first into Wolfe Road, then, a hundred yards farther, into El Camino Real, the Valley's first road, which it has been approaching like a hypotenuse from the beginning. In a small park created by the three roads there can often be seen old people and bums waiting for the country transit buses. There is also an old and seedy shopping center here, with a small supermarket and a pool hall. The parking lot in front of the pool place appears to serve as the site of drug deals. Where Fremont peters out into El Camino, there are a number of small shops selling car stereos, renting tools or repairing upholstery. There is also a takeout Chinese restaurant, a used-car lot, several beat-up saloons and some tired motel-apartments.

Behind these buildings are homes, a large subdivision of postwar "crackerbox" houses with flat roofs and two or three small bedrooms, on surprisingly large lots. This is unincorporated Santa Clara County land: there are no sidewalks, few streetlights and a wait for fire trucks, police cars and ambulances. Originally sold for $7,000 to $10,000, these homes now go for $75,000 to $100,000 and are among the cheapest homes in the center of the Valley.

This is not the bottom rung of the Valley, not by a long shot, but at the same time it is a long way spiritually from the hills of Los Altos. To the urbanite, accustomed to burnt-out slums and bodies littering the sidewalk, even the worst of Silicon Valley looks infinitely better. The sidewalks are immaculate, the houses clean, the cars relatively new, the weather lovely. But this is nevertheless its own form of ghetto. Because here the Big Score is ever present, here Bob Dylan's line: "Twenty years of schooling and they put you on the day shift" rings true; here one can have a doctorate and be making fifty thousand dollars a year and deep inside be torn with a sense of failure, be gasping to stay above water.

From the Freeway 85 overpass to the El Camino bus stop, there is a hidden anger in the homes along Fremont Avenue. Sparks are created when infinite ambition is ground to a frustrating halt, when the sixty-hour weeks don't yield the expected millions, but just more sixty-hour weeks. Fires burn in the guts of people with the requisite skills or education for success but without the traits that make a successful entrepreneur. It burns hotter with the realization that it will never get better, only harder, that there will never be a great leap to economic freedom, just consuming envy for those who have made it.

This frustration and anger remains hidden most of the time, but sometimes it bubbles to the surface, shockingly and in expected places. This happened on Fremont, just in the Sunnyvale city limits, between the two nursing homes, on the beautiful eight-foot adobe brick wall containing Ted Hoff's housing development. It first happened in 1978, soon after the People's Temple mass suicide in Guyana. One morning commuters were stunned to see a spray-painted message that read, with chilling simplicity: "Guyana 600/U.S. 0."

Spray-painted messages were an altogether new occurrence in this part of Sunnyvale. Sure, chicano kids had marked up downtown San Jose with their Gothic lettering and the "N" or "XIV" symbols of the Norte youth gang. But not in Sunnyvale, where the kids were destined for universities and professional careers. The vandalism was bad enough, but the cruel racism was unnerving. The words were quickly painted over with a brown paint, but on the right days, the shiny paint over the offensive words could still be read.

The wall was quiet for four years. Then, again overnight, it was covered with slogans: "Armageddon Time," "Some People Won't Get No Supper Tonight," "Southern Death Cult," and the oddest, "My Ass is on Fire."

Dr. Bruce Abt had heard these voices from the underground before. In his office, in that medical center at Fremont and Mary, the psychologist had encountered the problems shared by many of Silicon Valley's affluent victims, disorders he collected under the overarching name of the Silicon Valley Syndrome: drug and alcohol abuse, workaholism, debt, alienation, divorce and the ultimate frustration of a life based on achievement and not human relationships.

> The Silicon Valley Syndrome is the most common problem I encounter in my practice. I see it every day: the man (and sometimes woman) who's very distant and who's very involved with working.
>
> And when I say working I mean it. I can't believe the fact that someone will go home at twelve noon on a Saturday and be called up at 6 o'clock on a Saturday night to go back to work, stays all night and gets home at 6 on a Sunday morning, sleeps and then goes back to work. That's a pretty steady work diet.
>
> What I often find in these people is not just the dream of the Big Score, but also the fact that they haven't developed too many interpersonal skills. They don't know what to do with themselves. Even their hobbies are work-related. So it's all very incestuous.
>
> Part of the problem is due to the lack of roots, the transient nature of the area. It causes people to turn inward in a sense, to turn toward their own skills—rather than family and

friends—to get them through. Another cause of the frustration comes from the mere fact that these people have packed up and moved out West. They've come out here thinking they'll be more free. It's the psychology of individualism, a psychology of "take care of yourself," of "me first."

In other parts of the country there's roots, there's customs, there are traditions, there's age. Age is not an advantage here. In fact it's a liability. Elsewhere there's something which gives you a framework in which to set your life. That doesn't exist here. You ain't got nothing but you, and you make the most of it. That combines with the myth—and the reality to some extent—that you can do anything with yourself and the result is people in a continual progression, passing through one phase and then on to the next. There's no stopping, but instead a continual search for something that in a sense doesn't exist because they are looking for it in the wrong place, in success and materialism.

His words are echoed by Dr. Eric Cohen, a clinical psychologist at the Palo Alto Center for Stress-Related Disorders. Says Cohen, who grew up in the Valley, "There is no level of success that is adequate here—not when all you can see are Mercedeses and BMWs and three-hundred-thousand-dollar homes. You've got to start a company, take it public and make a lasting contribution to mankind or else you're a failure."

The goal of all of this striving is, of course, the Big Score, the sudden wealth and fame that will make all of this sacrifice worthwhile, that will at last sort out all of the confusion. Says Cohen, "Where success used to mean slowly progressing up a company's ranks until, when you were forty or fifty, you maybe became a vice-president, here the role models are crazy: the Steve Jobses, twenty-eight-year-old CEOs worth $400 million. How can you live up to that?"

Adds Abt, "For many people out there, people like Sandra Kurtzig and Jerry Sanders are superheroes, and the reality of their success is the great temptation. It creates the attitude that if I work hard, if I put enough sweat equity into what I'm doing, I'll succeed."

But success brings little; instead the victory is hollow, as are they. They are the Hollow Men. "Eliot would love it here," says Abt, "the people he wrote about are right here." A Silicon Valley executive said it best: "This valley won't give you anything you can't buy."

It isn't just the Silicon Valley businessperson who suffers. Unfortunately, says Abt, the resulting psychological problems manifest themselves in their families.

> What often happens is that the woman in the picture becomes very anxious because the man is always away. She sometimes reacts by having affairs, but more likely resorts to nagging and complaining about his absence. This, of course, drives the man further into his work because he doesn't want to go home at night. He'll stop off at the Rodeo [the bar at the Sheraton] and have a brew as opposed to going home. So a vicious cycle is created: the lonely wife becomes insufferable and the husband stays at work longer.

When both work, the predicament is amplified. "People don't feel they have time to get together to talk about their relationship," says Jean Hollands, author of *The Silicon Syndrome*. "He's got to go to racket ball and she's got her Junior League meeting. Then he's got to go meet with the board and she's at her women entrepreneurs meeting. They get together around midnight at home and they're both pooped." Says Cohen, "In marriage counseling I see a lot of computer programmer types who've married creative, intuitive women. They complain they can no longer communicate. Good engineers have trouble in relating in human relationships on an emotional level. They just see it as another problem to be analyzed. They want to run their marriages like they run their computers. Well, computers are a lot easier."

A result is one of the highest divorce rates in America. According to a local paper, "If divorce were a war that caused visible wounds, Silicon Valley would look like a M*A*S*H set." Nine thousand divorces occur in Santa Clara County each year, twenty-five a day, more than in all of the other Bay Area counties combined. San Jose ranks ninth among metropolitan areas in the United States in its divorce rate, higher than San Francisco, San Diego or Los Angeles. In 1981 the rate peaked at 7.1 divorces per thousand population, compared to a national average of 5.3.

With divorce come downhill paths for the separated mates. The wife often lands in exactly the same down-spiraling arrangement with another Silicon Valley husband. The husband ends up in working even more hours and coming home to an apartment as sparse and empty as his private life. ("You can't believe some of those places," says Abt.

"It's terrible. There's nothing there. A few chairs. Nothing in the refrigerator. A very bleak place to be.")

A 1985 San Jose *Mercury-News* survey found that half of all respondents said that work stress affected them off the job. It told of one executive who had to take an overworked top engineer to a psychiatric ward one night, and of a successful salesman who'd parked his house trailer in the company parking lot to remain close—and eventually shot himself because of the pressure.

One engineer, whose wife is also an engineer, told the *Mercury-News,* "If my wife and I lived anywhere else we'd probably have normal friends. But we don't have any time. It's a major logistics problem just to get together with people and avoid the traffic jams, the work hours, the projects . . . It puts a lot of stress on things."

For the children there is a worse fate. Silicon Valley kids from middle- and upper-income brackets appear for the most part straight and decent, like Future Engineers of America. But inside many seethe. Says Cohen, "I think a lot of kids around here think it's normal to only see their parents on weekends."

"They may look squeaky clean," says Abt, "but you'd be amazed at the use of drugs and alcohol among these young people. Every school has its stoners, and groups of kids into alcohol. There's a lot of discontent among the young people out there."

Armaggedon time.

So there is *Homo siliconic,* Silicon Valley Man, trapped in a solipsist nightmare in which there is no apparent way out, no family to provide succor, friends that are just business acquaintances, employers that change almost monthly. Just the solitary I, with its psychopathic, unrelenting demands for achievement until that achievement becomes its own end. A self that charges itself with failure even when events lie beyond its control.

In Silicon Valley, the Pristine Pit, with its immaculate buildings and perfect lawns and healthy people, when the walls begin to close in and one screams for help, there is no one there. The old modes of support are no longer there, or have fallen into disarray. Silicon Valley not only has no great art museum (the tiny San Jose Museum of Art almost went broke for lack of support) but it has created no major works of art. It has no opera, its second-rate symphony is backed up by visits from its San Francisco counterpart. Its only important writer, Wallace Stegner, is part of Stanford, not Silicon Valley, and writes of a different world. Even the few bookstores, where one might find wisdom from greater minds than one's own, are slowly converting their shelves to books on Basic Programming Language for the Apple III, and Getting to Know Your Commodore VIC-20. At night, as a sad voyeur, one can drive past the open windows of the Valley's large apartment complex, and in hundreds of living rooms never see a bookshelf, only the blue glow of televisions and personal computer screens.

The horror of it all is that for many, it is a matter not of finding help but of even knowing help exists. Instead, Abt says,

> people get this odd feeling; it's not really stress, but a malaise of getting somewhere and not feeling good about it. And because of the environment we live in, there aren't many doors to open or windows to look out of to see what else is available. There's not a lot of questioning. When you come from a me-oriented society, you blame me, you think you've just got to channel your efforts, you know, work harder, move someplace else, find a new wife . . . you're always looking for that Nirvana.

Adds Cohen, "I see a lot of upper executive types who've made it and are now deeply disillusioned."

One outlet for the frustration is faith. In Silicon Valley, faith comes in many forms. There are the traditional Protestant and Catholic churches and a handful of synagogues, but what is remarkable is all of the other ways religious desire manifests itself in the Valley. One surprise is the number of pentecostal and revival churches. Perhaps when empiricism fails the only solution is to look for miracles. The Mormon Church (the Church of Jesus Christ of Latter-Day Saints) with its strong orientation toward family and community, has had remarkable success finding adherents here.

Equally important are the other forms of mysticism that reach for a different organ than one's soul. This isn't Los Angeles, with its gurus and Herbert Armstrong and cults of the body. The engineering mind balks at such irrational apostasies. Rather, and fittingly, the secular faiths of Silicon Valley target human perfection and try to achieve it, as one would the design of a new integrated circuit, through logic and analysis. Again the Silicon Valley Syndrome. If one just tries hard enough and smart enough and long enough then that empty feeling inside at three in the morning will go away. Hence the success in the Valley of est and Scientology and Marriage Encounter and a host of other "scientific" faiths in search of the Holy Grail of human perfection. Didn't Steve Wozniak spend millions on rock concerts designed to build a perfect world of people and computers?

Along those rectilinear streets and in those precisely laid-out cubicles are thousands of human hearts crying out in loneliness. And no engineering diagram, no equation solved to the ten thousandth decimal place can help them. The lonely I looks for solace wherever it can find it —and always beyond the tight boundaries of the engineering mind.

For many it is drugs. Drugs are everywhere in Silicon Valley. Alcohol is easily the most abused. The number of alcoholics in boardrooms on executive row is shocking. But increasingly just as common, and far more apt given the local life-style, is cocaine. Silicon Valley has become a coke blizzard. The Drug Enforcement Agency has called Silicon Valley one of the biggest cocaine users in the United States.

What could be more perfect for Silicon Valley life? Lasciviously expensive, cocaine is the Queen of Speed, a clean flash of energy for those fourteen hours, for when you need to be up for that next business decision, or that next crucial sale. It also has that air of decadence, of Hollywood, about it. In staid Silicon Valley, a little toot in the face of the law gives an added rush beyond that of the drug itself. Cocaine is new to the Valley, only now making its mark on executive row. Nevertheless, in a few of the big houses in the hills there are some very wealthy young men with dead eyes and crackling synapses in their brains and emaciated bodies and checkbooks filled with daily thousand-dollar entries. They may be a sign of things to come.

Sometimes the yearning soul heads down a different path, and when the buyer has enough money any appetite can be fed. As anywhere else, there is a large and very secret gay underground in Silicon Valley that includes many Valley executives. San Francisco is only fifty miles north, but here in the tight, aggressive male fraternity of Silicon Valley, homosexuality must remain in the closet.

The Valley criminal underground, whose information is always of course suspect, also whispers of other sexual practices. A "little boy" network is occasionally spoken of, as are "whips and chains." Sometimes the name of a top Valley executive or other is appended.

Once in a while, this sordid side of the Valley bubbles up to leave a temporary slick on the bright surface. In one such case, police were called to a small rented tilt-up in Mountain View, just a few blocks from the Valley's birthplace at Shockley Labs. There, a shlocker (a man who speculates on surplus—sometimes stolen—chips) was found dead of a heart attack in the office bathroom. What caused his death can only be surmised, but in the back storage room a Las Vegas hooker was found dead of numerous stab wounds. A large cache of drugs was also found on the scene. In this forgotten corner of Silicon Valley, all of the invisible, dank forces flowing through the Valley seemed to have momentarily converged. Outside, the man's new Jaguar glistened in the moonlight.

Even in the "nurturing environment" of this Brave New World called Silicon Valley, the human condition will out, humanity's natural perversity still burrows through to the darkest places.

But what of the companies? What of their vaunted concern for their employees, of casual management structures and built-in gymnasiums and tattered blue jeans on executive row?

The truth, the great contradiction, is that in this Valley of mavericks and vision, there is stultifying conformity and a narrow point of view. One company's solution to marriage breakups among its managers was to rent apartments for newly single executives. Q.E.D.

With little at home waiting for them and a barren cultural life, many Valley workers turn to their employers to give meaning to their lives.

Says Cohen, "A lot of companies become the personalities and lives of their employees. You see people with company T-shirts, jackets, bumper stickers, tote bags—it's like being on a high school campus during Spirit Week.

"It's dangerous enough when the company is doing good, but it becomes particularly problematic when the company starts to slip. I see people who are in emotional distress because their company isn't doing well."

But even when the firm is flying high, the loyalty and identification is usually misplaced.

"The new breed of companies are stark when it comes to interpersonal relationships," says Abt. "The lack of concern for personal relationships is incredible. The companies have got these beautiful facilities, gyms, swimming pools and everything. But it's all framework. Where's the insides? There aren't any. Maybe that's my sense of the Valley, that the exterior is magnificent but there's nothing inside. It's the hollowness that bothers me the most."

It is the hollowness found in the most severe cases of Silicon Valley Man that is the most frightening. Sometimes a company rises up in the bowels of the Valley that exemplifies all that can go horribly wrong in the pursuit of the Big Score, in the obsessive struggle for achievement.

One of these firms was Solfan Inc. of Mountain View. Founded in 1972 as Sentron Alarm Corp. to make microwave security systems and motion sensors, the company really came into its own the next year when it hired as president Win Emert, a thirty-year old Stanford M.B.A. who had spent the previous eight years working for a competitor. Emert built the company up at an impressive rate. By 1979, Solfan had sales of $7.5 million and doubling each year. It appeared on the brink of going public.

Emert had also made a name for himself and his company through a series of outrageously cocky ads in the San Jose *Mercury-News* and *The Wall Street Journal*. The *Mercury* ad, looking for purchasing managers, offered twenty thousand dollars per year to anyone—trained or not—willing to work seventy hours a week. The *Journal* ad was even wilder: "Help Me Establish a Monopoly," screamed the headline; "We now have 80 percent of the market share . . . in North America and over 50 percent worldwide. I want it all." The ad also warned, "If your family or your lifestyle or your kid's Boy Scout experience is more important to you than your job, then this isn't for you."

It was only when eleven British engineers sued the company for $15 million for breach of contract that it became apparent to everyone that Emert had meant every word he said. He had elevated the Silicon Valley Syndrome to a management style. The suit by the eleven engineers, combined with more than twenty other suits filed in the previous three years by suppliers and employees, painted a picture of Solfan as Upton Sinclair's Packingtown updated for the semiconductor age.

Solfan, according to depositions, was a place where eighty-to-one-hundred-hour workweeks were standard, where workers were continuously and cruelly verbally abused by top management. Female employees were sexually insulted; one even claimed to have been told by an executive to have sex with an angry vendor to shut him up. Employees would work all Saturday night, stagger home at dawn and then have to report back a few hours later for a staff meeting.

Said a former personnel manager, "Some people were so punchy [from overwork] that I'd suggest they'd go home and get some sleep . . . [Solfan] likes green people because they don't know the difference. Mature people don't stay. They want people without previous experience so they don't know what to expect and therefore aren't in a position to evaluate the situation."

None were greener than the British engineers, coming to America for its freedom and prosperity and instead stepping into an inferno, a little business gulag where the president told them as soon as they arrived, without a trace of irony, that "once you pass the Statue of Liberty you engineers cannot be expected to be mollycoddled as you are in the U.K."

One of these engineers was Neil Bradshaw, who had read an ad in the March 1979 issue of the British engineering publication *IEE News.* The ad said: "Solfan Systems Inc. . . . 16,000 pounds per annum and a place in the California sun for career-minded Electronics Engineers . . . Expand your lifestyle! You'll be living in the beautiful, cosmopolitan San Francisco Bay Area . . . As well as a spectacular salary of up to $32,000 per annum, you'll have free life, health and dental insurance, paid holidays and a generous allowance to cover your move to the United States . . ."

The insurance was critical to Bradshaw. His wife was pregnant, and having received assurances from Solfan that it was indeed covered by the Kaiser Medical Plan, Bradshaw took the job.

It was only after he arrived in Mountain View that Bradshaw was told that Solfan had canceled with Kaiser and that he was on his own for medical bills. He also found out for the first time that unless he worked for the firm for two years he would owe the company for a fraction of his moving expenses. If he stayed less than six months he would owe Solfan all $2,600. Worse, Bradshaw was told that if he and his British counterparts didn't sign an agreement to these stipulations they could be fired and deported.

And that wasn't all. The "free" temporary accommodations in Silicon Valley and the "free" legal expenses for immigration were also nonexistent.

What did exist, according to another British engineer, "was like a play. I couldn't actually believe what was happening." According to the suit, the engineers were required to "work unreasonably long hours, including evenings and weekends," were threatened (inaccurately) with deportation should they resign and were forced to perform nonprofessional menial labor.

By August 1979, six engineers were fired, according to testimony, "without just cause, notice or severance pay." A month later, the five others had resigned, some, like Bradshaw, returning to England. In response, Emert "threatened to file a totally meritless and frivolous $10,000 suit" against them if they did so.

Solfan's strategy for dealing with its own suppliers was similarly loathsome. The technique is called financing off your payables and is simple in theory. You order materials or subassemblies from contractors; then when it is delivered you put off paying the debt for as long as possible, turning that money over several times, drawing interest on it and sometimes recouping the debt in the process. Every company does it to some degree, such as paying at the very end of the thirty-day due period. Some firms, like Commodore, are notorious for paying as slowly as possible. But Solfan took the process to the brink of genius.

Vendors, growing increasingly upset as bills weren't paid for thirty days, then sixty days, would call Solfan and be soothingly put off. As payment slipped to 120 days and 180 days, Solfan's purchasing managers—the ones hired by the *Mercury* ads—were instructed to use stronger measures. Said one of those managers: "[Solfan would] leave the ver dors hanging—using delays to finance added growth. When the vendors raise hell, they are told to go fuck themselves. It's taken as an insult—as though [they] should consider themselves lucky to do business with Solfan." Said the former company controller: "When a phone call came in employees were expected to tell a lie or do anything needed to keep [the vendor] hanging on as long as they could—until they were sued."

The effect upon the smaller vendors was devastating. For small machine shops and equipment assemblers the Solfan contract might account for a large share of annual revenues. When the bill wasn't paid, these little firms found themselves out of money but faced with their own raw material and payroll bills accrued doing the Solfan job. Some faced bankruptcy. The only solution was to sue Solfan.

Solfan responded to the smaller of these suits by dragging out the legal proceedings until the vendor, facing mounting legal costs, caved in and accepted cents on the dollar. For bigger suits, Solfan would sometimes respond with a $1-million countersuit claiming defamation and disruption of production. As might be expected, most of the suits were settled on the courthouse steps.

The final abused group was the company's assembly-line workers. Some apparently were illegal aliens, others underage. The personnel manager says he learned not to look too closely at his own personnel records. The company had resorted to these individuals because work conditions were such that the place was experiencing a turnover rate of 1 percent per day—ten times the average even among Silicon Valley's gypsylike population. According to the personnel manager, once a week a group of four or five employees "would just explode and walk off the job."

In the end, Solfan simply died. But even then it got one last lick in. In March 1982, the eleven British engineers were awarded a $7.8 million judgment—only to be informed that Solfan had fired most of its employees and was on the brink of bankruptcy, already owing $1.1 million to a financial lender. The lawyer for the engineers predicted that his clients would never see much of the award.

There aren't many Solfans in Silicon Valley. But there are enough to be a reminder of what happens when the Valley Syndrome is taken to its logical conclusion, when a company not only takes advantage of it but makes it a corporate philosophy.

Win Emert's big mistake was that he didn't recognize the power of the innate drive among Silicon Valley's professional people to succeed. Solfan didn't have to be a chamber of horrors. Rather he could have, like a host of other, more successful Valley companies, installed a gymnasium and a par course, served fresh fruit in the mornings and been a soft-spoken executive in a jogging suit. His employees would *still* have put in eighty-hour weeks, they would have volunteered to come in on Sunday mornings—just as they do without prompting at Intel—and they would have yanked around upset vendors with a self-generated obsession with cost savings. Emert could have had it all, could have achieved the same ends, could have been acclaimed as one of the progressive new breed of young managers.

Says Abt, "People here are mortgaging their families and mortgaging their health in order to succeed." Then, without a trace of irony, Abt adds that he longs to leave the Valley and go to a place where there is diversity and tradition. But he can't; he has a healthy little practice here. Abt, it seems, is also an entrepreneur, selling employee mental health programs. And he's putting in long hours to make it a success.

At the end of a long day, Silicon Valley Man drives his BMW home to his empty condo, dazed, burnt out, a little drunk. He will go to bed soon, as he has a racket ball game at 6 A.M. But in those few minutes of private time, he might decide to relax by reading a few pages of one of the new nonfiction best sellers—the ones that talk about the electronics revolution and the earthly paradise it will bring, of how humanity will meet its true destiny in a magical union with the computer chip.

*   *   *

By the time she got back from lunch, Wendy (name changed) knew she was in trouble. She was working in chip fabrication at Intersil, inspecting the integrated circuits for flaws with a powerful microscope, when slowly she found that she wasn't concentrating. She was just resting her head on the eyepiece, struggling to stay awake.

Finally, unable to take it anymore and afraid of falling off her stool, Wendy went to the ladies' room and lay down on the couch in there. She woke up three hours later. The boss sent her home.

Much the same thing happened the next day, only this time worse. Wendy knew she was running out of sick leave and the supervisor was getting increasingly ticked off. She couldn't help it. She could barely get home at night, and once there fell into a sleep like death until the clock-radio—set at full blast—drove her awake. Then it was off to another day in a zombie-like trance.

It came as a relief when she was fired at the end of the week. Now she could sleep.

In the few times she was fully conscious, Wendy wondered if it was all worth it, this going cold turkey. In her heart she knew it was, and that's what kept her going. Drugs had already cost her her marriage. She now was back with her mother. Her cherished three-year-old son lived across town with his father. That was for the best: her ex was straight and was making good money as a test area supervisor over at Intel. Besides, Wendy need only glance at her checkbook to see that she was spending $75 to $100 every week for "crank" (crystallized methamphetamine snorted like cocaine) at $20 to $25 a quarter tea-spoon. That was $5,000 for the year she had been addicted, more than half her annual income.

Crank was good and clean. Not as clean as coke, but at $30 a quarter teaspoon and only an hour or so of high, cocaine was too damn expensive. Crank was a lot better than Black Beauties, which just messed you up for eight hours or more, or whites, which would give you the shakes. She'd tried acid and PCP on the job, but all they did was mess you up so bad that you spent the entire day trying not to knock anything over. You didn't get any work done, and that would get you canned.

No, crank was just right. That's why everybody called it "go fast." Snort one line at lunch and you'd have a buzz till five. Snort two and you'd stay high through dinner. In the meantime, you'd be working so hard and so fast that the boss would think you were the hardest worker in the office.

Course, crank could be pretty nasty too if you didn't know how to handle it. You could ride that train every day for a five-day week, but then you had to sleep most of the weekend. For the next workweek you'd need a nap a day. By Friday you'd be back feeling like your old self—and ready for another run on Monday. But after a while, a week's rest just didn't do it. Then it was a Monday or a Tuesday off sick until you ran out of vacation and sick leave. After that either you stayed cranked up to keep working or your work slumped off so badly you got fired. With the industry slowing down and everybody talking about layoffs, who could say when you'd get your next job?

Staying cranked up week in and week out was a bad business. After a while you learned to eat on it (a little) and sleep on it (even less), but even then, eventually you'd start flipping out like you'd OD'd. You'd start getting paranoid. That's why that one girl in the lab went nuts that day and tried to kill herself by sticking her head in an acid bath. She was real strung out. Thin as a rail.

Go much longer than that and the stuff would kill you or drive you crazy. That's why it was better to quit.

But Wendy didn't know that Friday, when she went home unemployed, that she wouldn't be looking for work again, hardly even leave the house, for three months. That night she slept for two days, woke up for a while and went to sleep again for a day. She lived in this nether world week after week. Once, after a month, she felt good enough one afternoon to go to the store for groceries. Instead, Wendy fell asleep at the wheel and rear-ended a truck stopped at a light. Her car was totaled. Wendy did not go out again for a long time . . .

When one speaks of Silicon Valley the image is of attractive business parks holding hundreds of companies containing thousands of brilliant and well-appointed white professional men and women. And that is correct, as long as one stays within these business parks, and then only in the office buildings.

Silicon Valley is also 120,000 assembly-line workers, most of them black, Hispanic (like Wendy) or Asian, and perhaps an equal number of similar people in other blue-collar jobs. It was upon these people, and others like them in Phoenix, Malaysia, Puerto Rico and other manufacturing centers around the world, that Silicon Valley rests.

These are the invisible people of the Valley's underground. Invisible because they appear in the news only when something bad happens to them, like a layoff, and also because they live in the Valley's version of ghettos at corners of the area.

One of these enclaves is East Palo Alto, just a rock's throw over Bayshore Freeway from the wealthy homes of Palo Alto proper. This is where a large percentage of the Valley's poor blacks live. Much larger is

East San Jose, at the base of Mount Hamilton. This is home for a quarter of a million Chicanos—making it the second largest barrio in the United States after East Los Angeles. East San Jose is also the home for eighteen thousand Vietnamese and other Asian refugees—many of whom can be seen every day jammed around bus stations in Santa Clara to take them home from trade schools teaching them how to be printed-circuit-board assemblers like Wendy. Some of these Asians never go to work at a company, but instead stuff boards at home or in living room sweatshops, accepting below-minimum-wage piece rates and no social security deductions because no one has told them that it is against the law or that they are being exploited.

During the day and night, this invisible population migrates back and forth from the buildings of Silicon Valley, filling the freeways at the end of each shift, all but faceless. When their spot is empty on the assembly line they are replaced by someone else. The pay is pretty good, though the cost of living eats most of it up, and the companies treat them well except when business is bad. But every day is the same, the same incredibly boring "robot work," the same lack of hope, the same resentment of those who've grown spectacularly wealthy off their hard work.

That's why there are drugs. As one ex-addict said, "Once you knew your job you could do it blindfolded, so you might as well be stoned."

Drugs are everywhere in Silicon Valley. It has been suggested that without alcohol, cocaine and speed in all of its forms, Silicon Valley would cease to function. Certainly that would be the case on the manufacturing lines.

"You start on drugs because the job's so boring, hour after hour, and you don't even know what the board is for," says Marijane Esparza, a former addict teaching at a drug rehabilitation center, "You take crank and you feel a flash of energy—zzt, zzt, zzt—and do you work! You do *twice* as many boards! Then the technician standing behind you says, 'Hurry up, you did a hundred boards last night.' "

"Me and my friends just hate our jobs," a Signetics assembler says. "A lot of people just sit there and say, 'Oh, why? Oh, why am I here?' "

In a four-month period in early 1980, four hundred drug arrests were made in Santa Clara County and one fourth were electronics workers. It is little wonder that Lawrence Lopez, program director of a San Jose rehabilitation house, has called drug use on the Valley's assembly lines "shocking" and "very widespread."

The San Jose *Mercury-News* reported in an investigative story: "Few companies are immune. Users have described cocaine parties in IBM's parking lot; methamphetamine abuse at National Semiconductor Corp.; drying cocaine in microwave ovens at Signetics Corp.; being introduced to methamphetamine on the assembly lines at Intel Corp.; and regular use of the same substance in some departments at Memorex Corp.; taking "angel dust" (PCP) at FMC and similar tales of drug abuse at numerous smaller companies throughout the Valley."

While she was developing her addiction over eight years, Wendy worked in a number of Valley semiconductor firms, including Intersil, National and Signetics. At each of those places she saw extensive proof of heavy drug use. At Intersil her fellow workers would bring amphetamine pills ("whites") to work and chop them up for snorting. Of the ten women she worked with, three were addicted to crank—one of them even shooting up heroin daily in the bathroom. Others smoked "K-J"—amphetamine crystals in a marijuanalike joint. Some workers she saw even took LSD, but "it's hard to work when you're on the stuff, especially wafer-aligning, because your eyes get all messed up."

At National Semiconductor, workers smoked marijuana and snorted crank. The Lawrence Station restaurant a few blocks away, by day one of the area's leading engineer wateringholes and headhunter hangouts, by night became the place to score crank in the parking lot. Even at Signetics, National remained the center of drug activities. A "runner" would go around the assembly line taking drug orders from workers and then drive over to National's parking lot to buy it. At both companies, Wendy says, one could always find in the rest room numerous little finger-sized plastic bags used to hold the speed crystals.

It was at Signetics where she saw marijuana being dried in the maintenance department in wafer ovens there for repair. And the drugs weren't restricted to the manufacturing areas. "You walk into an office where they don't expect you and some guy with white powder all over his nose will look up and yell, "What're you doing here?" Another office worker kept lines ready in her top desk drawer and would take a quick toot when nobody was looking. Another would simply hide under his desk. Most frightening of all, Wendy knew a supervisor at AMD who would methodically before each shift lay two whites at each lab station to assure quota-level production.

The freebase cocaine parties at IBM were also run by a supervisor. Said an IBM employee: "I would sell pounds [of speed] to the supervisor, who would in turn sell ounces to the department employees."

But for the most part, managers in these companies remain blithely ignorant of the problem. To sit in a room at a halfway house and listen to young Silicon Valley drug addicts is to discover a world unknown not only to outsiders but even to company managers. The voices are young men eighteen to thirty, white or Hispanic:

> When I got there [a laser company], it was like a drugstore. Everyone had all kinds of drugs.

> I've worked in the electronics industry since 1971. I'm a gold tipper. The last place I worked the drug use wasn't that bad. There was a lot of whites and lot of weed, and we drank every lunch. But the place I worked at before [a printed-circuit-board company], I was a crank dealer. I dealt speed and I sold anywhere from a quarter ounce to a half ounce a week to the employees at twenty dollars a bag. That's about nine hundred dollars' worth a week of speed. Everybody was strung out. We were working from ten to sixteen hours a day, six days a week. I had to quit . . . I won't go back into plating. There's too much drug use. It's too hard for me to keep away from drugs as it is, but in electronics, it's every place I go . . .

> My supervisor let me go off work for two hours to do a score and covered me when I came back. I'd give him a bag. We used to take chemicals from the chemical room, use it as a cutting agent for the speed . . .

> They have a sump [where I work]. You take off the sump cover and it's twelve feet down. I was looking at the board one day and fell up to my neck in acid. I was wasted [on crank]. I've stayed up twenty-eight days on crank. But usually I'd stay up nine or ten days. Work double shifts. That crank buzzes you out. After a while you start seeing "trails." You get really paranoid. After you stay up nine or ten days, you don't eat. I was shooting crank. Lot of people snort because they're afraid of needles . . .

> I got so high [on PCP] I didn't know where I was, but I still got my work done. I don't know how . . . Every place I went to had drugs. Memorex was a joke. Every person in there that I've seen, except for the supervisors—they had their act together—was using crank every day . . . It seems that from using crank so long, people are expected to work like that . . .

I'll tell you something pretty sick. My wife worked at Shugart Associates. She came from a Christian home and didn't believe in taking drugs. She'd watch me smoke weed and do my crank and stuff, but she wouldn't do it. At Shugart, she got turned on. One of her coworkers started giving her diet pills. She started getting loaded on Dexedrine, coming home and staying up till three o'clock in the morning, then have to get up at six to go back to work and eat some more diet pills. And she never took drugs in her life before . . .

You can find acid, you can find drugs, weed, speed. Inside and out in the parking lots, both. On Fridays, especially. Friday, payday, out in the parking lot, you get fronted the dope and go to the bank and pay for it after work . . . Crank is just like gasoline for people, so they can last ten, twelve hours a day.

"What's sad about it is that if you took all of the drugs out of the electronics industry, it would fall apart."

How many workers on Silicon Valley's manufacturing lines are heavy users of drugs? Companies say no more than a small percentage. Addicts, with a junkie's peculiar world view, claim that in some departments and on some shifts the number may be as high as 90 percent. The truth probably lies somewhere in between.

With drugs come a raft of other problems. For one thing, much of the drugs come from some kind of organized crime. The amphetamine business, for example, it is claimed, is almost exclusively controlled in northern California by the Hell's Angels.

Drug habits, as Wendy's example shows, can be expensive. When wages don't cover it and one's brain cells scream for more, one solution is to steal things. The millions of dollars in equipment, material and product lying around the average assembly line or fabrication laboratory can be tantalizing. Some of it is petty theft: a pocketful of chips, a length of gold wire. One Christmas, Wendy remembers, a fellow employee went around the line handing out as presents coke/crank mirrors made out of silicon wafers.

Often the need for drugs drives addicts to more destructive thefts. The link between drugs and gold and chip thievery and espionage is worth mentioning again. Dave Roberts, the Larry Lowery confederate found murdered in the Santa Cruz Mountains, was a heroin junkie, as was a man reportedly caught trying to sell ballistics missile blueprints from Lockheed. In June 1980 a Signetics employee was charged with grand theft for stealing gold to support her boyfriend's drug habit. And there is the young man, met in a halfway house, who claims he sold HP atomic clock timer secrets to men with foreign accents who said they were teachers. William Harper, the admitted Soviet agent, got his information from his alcoholic wife, who worked at System Control. The gray market, with its connection to organized crime and enemy nations, thrives on Valley drug addicts. Doug Southard, county deputy district attorney, estimates that the Valley loses $20 million in electronics parts and equipment each year. A lot of that haul is going directly into people's bloodstreams.

From the addicts themselves:

> I used to rip off parts, little ICs, and I'd go down here to [name withheld]. So I'd sell them there, and also I'd trade some. A lot of my friends were into electronics, so I'd trade parts for drugs. I figured the way they paid us, what the hell?

> When I worked for [name withheld] they gave me the key to the back door. I went in there and took twenty to thirty thousand dollars' worth of equipment. I set it up like I broke in. They had no alarms or nothing.

Chemicals sold in the workplace present a dangerous enough threat to the people on Silicon Valley's lowest rung. Then in early 1980 this same body of workers discovered that they were also threatened by chemicals in the workplace itself, some of them among the most poisonous known.

*   *   *

Silicon Valley had always prided itself in being a clean, safe industry. This wasn't Gary, Indiana, or some West Virginia coal mining town. There were no smokestacks, just green lawns, no belching, smoky Bessemer furnaces, but high-tech laboratories as clean as a surgical theater. Love Canal was three thousand miles away, and the only concern about pollution had to do with the frightening increase in the number of cars on Santa Clara County roads.

Then, from April 6 to 8, 1980, the San Jose *Mercury-News* ran a series called "The Chemical Handlers," which for the first time looked at the true nature of the processes used in the electronics industry. It discovered, in the words of Hamilton Fairburn, assistant regional director of the Occupational Safety and Health Administration, that: "The electronics industry is misleading. People think of it as wires, soldering and transistors. But when you get to the [semiconductor business] you're really talking about chemical reactions. It's a chemical industry."

The *Mercury* found that the semiconductor industry "uses some of the most hazardous chemicals that exist—including corrosives such as hydrochloric and hydrofluoric acids, toxic solvents such as xylene and dangerous poisons such as arsine gas and cyanide . . ." It also found that the industry has one of the highest incidences of occupationally related illness of any industry in California—1.3 occupationally related illnesses per thousand.

Mere facts and figures don't capture the chilling nature of some of these chemicals or the tragic stories of some of the victims of accidents. For example, in the diffusion step of making chips, semiconductor companies had to use arsine and phosphine gases, chemicals so acutely toxic that the acceptable level stipulated by the National Institute of Occupational Safety and Health amounts to a child's balloon in a football stadium. Though companies went to great lengths to stop leaks, Fairchild alone had seen "eight to ten people who breathed phosphine gas [come down with] bronchitis or pneumonia," according to the company's medical director, as well as "temporary blood count damage from arsine."

Far more common were accidents involving hydrofluoric acid, a clear, colorless chemical used to etch and clean the surface of silicon wafers. Hydrofluoric is particularly insidious because initially it has no effect. Rather it is absorbed through the skin and then, in the frightening words of an SRI scientist, "it seeks for bone," burning down through muscle until it finally neutralizes itself against bone calcium. Adds the scientist, "it gives a horrible pain, like being on fire."

The list of dangerous chemicals used in daily semiconductor manufacturing runs into the hundreds, everything from powerful acids, to hypersensitivity-inducing solvents to dangerous poisons like lead and cyanide—even to some suspected carcinogens.

As the labor report showed, not only were these nameless workers using these chemicals, they were also getting hurt. A May 1979 acid explosion at Fairchild hospitalized three workers and sent fourteen more home after they inhaled fumes. A year before, at the same company, a fifty-four-year-old acid cleaner was pushing a cart bearing bottles of sulfuric acid, when one wheel caught on a broken tile in the floor and the cart tipped over—shattering six one-gallon bottles. The woman slipped and fell in the shattered glass and acid, badly burning her arms, legs and feet. Five employees sued Signetics Corp. claiming that their ongoing exposure to chemical fumes had given them an oversensitivity to everyday chemicals. One woman, Marta Rojas, claimed that she could not walk down the detergent aisle of a supermarket, clean her floors or even read the newspaper without experiencing light-headedness, nausea and burning on her tongue. A twenty-four-year-old AMD employee began losing her hair after an exposure to antimony trioxide. When the fire department found four hundred safety violations at Signetics, the city of Sunnyvale contemplated shutting the company down.

These stories and others shocked the local communities. But the anger quickly faded; after all, these were company problems, involving all those nameless workers. What set the problem of toxic chemicals forever in the public mind came in December 1981 when workmen installing a new water tank at the South San Jose plant of Fairchild discovered that industrial solvents were leaking out of a nearby chemical-storage tank—fourteen thousand gallons of 1,1,1 trichloroethane (TCA), to be precise. A nearby well found TCA levels twenty times that of acceptable levels as defined by the EPA. The legal requirement for making such an announcement was thirty-nine days; Fairchild and the local water company waited fifty.

Then all hell broke loose. Now it wasn't faceless proles on assembly lines getting hurt, it was regular Silicon Valley folks. Neighbors of the plant, like Lorraine Ross, began to remember things. As *Inc.* magazine recounts, "She recalled the times she smelled chlorine or ammonia in the air. But mostly she wondered about the four children with birth defects, the two miscarriages and the one stillbirth on her block within the past three years and the multiple congenital heart defects of her youngest child, then nine months old . . ." In time it was found that hazardous chemicals had leaked from buried tanks belonging to eleven Valley companies. San Jose mayor Janet Gray Hayes told *National Geographic,* "I remember thinking about smokestacks in other industries. I didn't expect this problem in my own backyard."

Even the papers didn't report all of the lesser toxic chemical problems in the Valley—the drums of cyanide tossed in local dumps by gold strippers after paying off owners, tanks of toxic waste to be delivered to hazardous waste dumps that never arrive, used chemicals dumped in vacant lots and railroad tracks behind small companies, poisons and solvents flushed down sewer lines and storm drains into the bay.

A report by the San Francisco Bay Regional Water Quality Control Board, released—fittingly—on Valentine's Day, 1985, listed forty-six chemical pollution sites in Silicon Valley. The list offenders read like a Valley hall of fame: IBM, Fairchild, National Semiconductor, Signetics, Memorex, Hewlett-Packard, AMD, Verbatim, Ampex, Monolithic Memories, Dysan, Intel.

The rise in birth defects—twice as many as normal for a neighborhood near the South San Jose Fairchild plant, according to a January 1984 government study—will probably never be proven to have been caused by Silicon Valley chemical leaks. Nevertheless, the publicity set the scare in people's minds; and ever since local residents have been concerned about the water they drink and the air they breathe.

But what of the workers, who must be in close contact with these chemicals every day? The industry predicts that their problems will disappear in a few years; that is, they'll be replaced by automated laboratories that can work smoothly and rapidly and never grow bored.

So they wait, these forgotten people. Like their middle-management counterparts, they too have an unfocused yearning. Here the Big Score takes on a different meaning. Unions, from the Teamsters to the Young Socialist Workers (in lightning rallies in the National Semiconductor cafeteria), try to organize them but are rebuffed. Perhaps these workers know that as dim as it may seem, Silicon Valley offers them a shot at moving uptown—as long as they stay flexible, moving from one company to another in search of the best deal.

Or perhaps they are too stoned to care. Wendy, straight again, went back to work at another semiconductor company—and took up drugs again. Luckily, she married a sailor and left the Valley forever.

For those who can't leave, sometimes the anger and the frustration grow too great, and it bursts out in spray paint on walls.

Silicon Valley even has the answer for that. Take the graffiti on the adobe wall on Fremont Avenue. Not long ago, the wall was painted again with a new polymer paint that repels graffiti, turning them to atomized droplets that fall to the ground before they can dry. The day it was painted a camera crew came out to record this landmark for posterity.

The graffito, "Armageddon Time," had come and gone. Once again, technology had triumphed.

CONCLUSION
The Big Score

The Silicon Valley of the 1980s was unrecognizable from the vantage point of the Santa Clara County of the 1920s, incomprehensible to the Santa Clara Valley of the 1830s. What was once an uninhabited range land of yellow grass dotted with snarly oak trees and stands of manzanita shrub, then endless ranks of plum, cherry and apricot trees marked out by dirt roads and small burgs, had become a continuous suburban sprawl of two dozen cities, all of them approaching or just beyond populations of a hundred thousand standing shoulder to shoulder, the only intervening boundary the one on a map. Now the roads were paved and expanded to four, even six, lanes and laid in a fine lattice over the landscape.

Even the rivers that once created and defined the Valley were now all but gone, driven underground into conduits or tucked beside freeways —reminding the locals of their existence only in the worst of winters, when they flooded and jumped their banks and roared blindly down residential streets until they were subdued and driven back. The Guadalupe River, which had once been the single most important feature in the South Valley, was now a dirty sluice that meandered through old neighborhoods in San Jose and then slithered, muddy and seemingly embarrassed, past the end of the San Jose Airport runway, past industrial parks and then through the local dump. On its bank, next to the airport, a few blocks from a tired industrial park that was home for many of the Valley's gold thieves, a tiny, rarely visited shrine marked the site of the first Mission Santa Clara. There was a marker to designate the spot, but it was hard to concentrate enough to read it because jet airliners boomed off just a few hundred yards away.

The bay, the great body of water that created the valley, the dominant geographical and meteorological force in this corner of the world, seemed to have shrunk away from the valley's hustling and crowding. Dikes and ponds and levees and landfill had driven it back, the reclaimed land used for dumps and industrial parks. In this way, the San Francisco Bay, the reason the valley was first inhabited, a central part of the lives of generations of local townspeople, was now hidden behind buildings and embankments and dikes, strangely invisible to the modern residents of Silicon Valley.

What had the technological revolution done to Santa Clara County? It had driven off or buried almost every remnant of the old valley and its way of life. Sure there was the occasional Victorian house tucked on the back street or a restored adobe church or an acre or two of cherry trees—but they were just as much of the present as of the past. Like doomed species of animals displayed in zoos, they were less remnants of another time than curiosities of the modern age. Mission Santa Clara might look the same, but it would never again see masses attended by devout old Indians and Mexicans. Now, electrical engineering students would come to hear speeches by Buckminster Fuller or listen to guitarists leading "folk masses."

The modern Silicon Valley was a Klondike boom town adjusted to match the new world of the baby boom and the philosophies of William Levitt. No one really planned to stay in California, except those who had come out to retire or die. For the rest, Silicon Valley was the place you went to make a killing, to take care of business. After that, who knew where? Maybe back home in glory, maybe off the Golden Gate Bridge with a thousand-dollar bill in one's pocket and, always, looking back at San Francisco and the American continent.

Since no one really planned to stay, Silicon Valley was erected with little thought to the future. Companies were built the same way. Entrepreneurs, whether they are home builders or chip makers, rarely think too far into the future, certainly not to ultimate ramifications of their activities. Is there a market for new homes? Then flatten an orchard and get those babies up; curve the streets a little for effect, make 'em a little different—maybe four models instead of two; throw in an elementary school for the kids; but get 'em up fast, decorate the model homes in

California style; offer good VA financing; talk about appreciation; then get the hell out of the way.

Same goes for business. The market needs a new floppy-disk drive? Then round up some experts secretly; crank out a business plan for the venture boys to see; get a line of credit from the bank; rent some space in a tilt-up; rig up a prototype; get the second round of financing; build the product in volume; run the company up to $10 million; then go public and move to easy street. Economic problems? Then fire half the staff; there's always more where they came from.

Those were the three governing strategies of Silicon Valley: fast career development, fast residential development and fast corporate development. Amazingly enough, it worked. Silicon Valley made more millionaires than the Sierras, the Klondike and the Comstock combined. But the result was a crazy quilt of landscape and lives.

Only San Jose was a proper city, with tall buildings downtown. The rest of the towns of Silicon Valley were obvious cases of cities buried in runaway growth. None of them had real centers, unless shopping malls could be called the heart of a community. Yet some of these burgs were the size of some Midwestern capital cities. Certainly other towns in America suffered from the same malady, but almost universally they were in the suburbs of great cities, with their unifying cultural and economic center. Silicon Valley, one of the largest population centers in the country, was a suburb of nowhere—though outsiders, perhaps in an attempt to comprehend this strange new world, insisted that the Valley was a suburb of, philosophically if not geographically, far-off San Francisco; in fact the net flow of commuters was in the other direction, and by the 1980s, San Francisco could more properly be considered a suburb of Silicon Valley.

In business, a similar shortsighted attitude obtained. Firms were founded, built up and let go. In good times recruiting was heated, and companies promised prospective employees the moon and delivered it. When times were bad they tossed these same bonus babies back on the street. The companies lived for today, leveraging themselves to the brink of disaster over and over. But it worked. Executives were taught in business school that the key to success was careful growth, judicious market development and patience—and then these same individuals went out into Silicon Valley and demolished every one of those theories. The books said to precisely define one's product line and stick with it forever. Silicon Valley's businessmen knew that if one was smart enough and fast enough, a company could build up one product line, then overnight jump into another whole new market. Instrument companies could become computer companies, like HP, and computer companies could become telephone companies, like Rolm, and chip companies could become computer companies, like National Semiconductor. The textbooks said to build up by internally generated profits? The Silicon Valley companies found that with a suitably dynamic profit and a little P.R., they could take their case to the stock market and raise millions in a single morning without adding any debt, or losing control, or having to wait for profits. The texts said that to properly function a company needed an established chain of command and rigid lines of communication. Valley firms eschewed offices and who-gets-the-credenza rules and instead held executive meetings in swimming pools and turned Friday afternoon beer busts into a new form of democratic management. And they succeeded—with a vengeance, flaunting their nonconformity—and the academics went back and rewrote the textbooks in their praise.

Finally, the people themselves enjoyed a kind of runaway growth. All had been raised with the idea that one worked a lifetime at a single firm in hopes of one day being rewarded with an important position. But in the Valley they quickly realized they were in a whole new game with a different set of rules. If the companies were out to get everything they could and the future be damned, why shouldn't they feel the same way? Headhunting went from being a service operation to a growth industry, as headhunters stuffed new employees into the front door of Silicon Valley companies while stealing just as many out the back. The workers of Silicon Valley, from the top managers down to the assembly-line workers, migrated like gypsies around the Valley, holding no loyalties, taking the best available jobs, using one promotion to leverage a higher salary at the next company, using the training provided by one firm to get a better job at the next. In their private lives too they roamed, divorced, joined new organizations, followed fads and forever searched for a better relationship, a better car, a better life-style.

By the eighties, the rest of the world began to recognize that something rather remarkable was taking place in Silicon Valley. The great consumer electronics revolution of the decade before had first opened their eyes to the Valley and now came a growing realization that this little entrepreneurial dynamo might represent both America's hope and its future. Their curiosity was further piqued when journalists and sociologists and politicians traveled to the Valley and returned with stories of hot tubs and T-shirted tycoons and instant millionaires and solemnly intoned, like the journalists who had visited Lenin's new Soviet Union, that they had seen the future and that it worked—and was a lot of fun besides.

Now, forty years after Hewlett and Packard worked in the garage, thirty years after Shockley came back to California, and more than a decade after the death of the legendary Fairchild, the world had heard of Silicon Valley. When a local artist went back to the Pratt Institute in Brooklyn in the mid-seventies, and was asked where she lived, her reply of "Sunnyvale" drew blank stares. A retirement village near Palm Springs perhaps? So she took to saying "San Francisco." When she returned on a visit in 1981 and was asked where she was from, she again hesitatingly attempted "Sunnyvale" again. This time she was met with arched eyebrows. "Oh," the New Yorkers said, *"Silicon Valley."*

The 1980s have been a banner decade in the dissemination of the Silicon Valley myth. That year Steve Jobs of Apple appeared on the cover of *Time* as part of a story on Valley entrepreneurship. Pac-Man also made a huge splash, as Atari became one of the colloquialisms of the era. In his State of the Union address, President Ronald Reagan mentioned the role of the electronics industry—notably the Valley—in maintaining America's competitive edge against foreign economic threats. Silicon Valley, which had once chafed at not being recognized for its importance, now found itself the center of world attention—to its chagrin. Now, every bad quarterly earnings, every inadequate product, every scandal became front page news. The leading local paper, the San Jose *Mercury-News,* which had all but ignored the Valley until the end of the seventies, now seemed devoted to the topic, with expanded business sections and computer sections and banner headlines every time there was an important merger or retirement or product introduction. In return, the paper grew so rich on the Valley's classified ads that it became one of the most profitable papers in America and the diamond in the Knight-Ridder diadem.

A corpulent Sunday *Mercury-News* was only one sign of the enormous success of Silicon Valley. There was also the respect given to the Valley's leaders whenever they went East to talk to the Wall Street boys or to Congress, or the attention given to every utterance of one of the Valley's congressmen, Ed Zschau, founder and former president of Systems Industries. It was apparent too in the enormous influence David Packard had among the world's leaders at the annual Bohemian Club outings, on the Trilateral Commission, in Ronald Reagan's kitchen cabinet, and during the visit by the Queen of England. The success of Silicon Valley was also apparent in the many electronics trade shows, like the Western Computer Conference, the SemiCon shows, the Consumer Electronics Show (which drew everyone from computer companies to porn film distributors) and Comdex, the computer distributors show. Each, filled with Valley companies, their counterparts and descendants from around the country, the trade press that lived off of them and the network cameramen looking for the latest hot products, drew as many as eighty thousand people wherever they were held, each visitor struggling for a glimpse of the future.

Most of all, the power and vitality of Silicon Valley was apparent in its effect on the daily life of the average person. That a Zimbabwe farmer might have a digital watch on his wrist, a Peruvian Indian might play a video game in the local town hall, or a Sri Lankian learn mathematics on a personal computer was a measure of the pervasiveness of the Electronics Revolution. That each of these devices contained circuits equivalent to million-dollar, warehouse-sized computers two decades before was indicative of the tremendous power of Moore's Law and the ability of Silicon Valley firms to drive technology and price along its curves.

Thus, in the 1980s, Silicon Valley itself came to have a meaning in the world's languages, a jargon term encompassing all the features of the Valley Myth, combined with a yearning either to be there or to re-create it back at home. It was no surprise that the Valley was visited by representatives of most of the states and of other countries, like Ireland, provinces like Bavaria and cities like Vancouver, all attempting to understand the Valley's secrets, to coax Valley companies away and above all to bring a little of Silicon Valley's prosperity and optimism home with them.

As always, when the rest of the world has discovered the latest gold rush, it is already showing hints that its days might be numbered. The Gold Rush of 1849, the Comstock and the Klondike had all ended because they had depleted their source of riches. Some said the same was becoming true of Silicon Valley. Here the resources weren't mineral but sociocultural: Silicon Valley endured because it created new companies; and it did this through a very precise combination of educational facilities, investment capital, a support network of suppliers, consultants and customers, a pleasant environment and an ample pool of talented people. These were all there when Fairchild was in its glory days, and even more so during the systems boom of the seventies. But by the eighties, the Valley seemed to be drowning in its own success.

The signs were everywhere: the horrendous traffic on each major east–west arterial, the urban crowding of restaurants and theaters and shopping centers and every other gathering place, the endless and increasingly frightening stories of chemical leaks and toxic waste pollution, the increasing threats of unionization, the growing battle among companies for a piece of the smaller and smaller labor pool and home prices run up so high the only people who could still afford to buy in the Valley were people who already lived here and had made a killing selling their previous home.

Says Roy Brandt, former vice-president of personnel at National Semiconductor:

> I used to come down here and see the prune orchards in Santa Clara and wander through them. When I first came in 1969 it was a wonderful life-style. You could buy a house at a relatively inexpensive price and your heating bill was a fraction of that in New England. You could buy fresh vegetables off the back of trucks.
>
> And it was like that well into the seventies. Then I went away [to Motorola] for a few years and when I returned I couldn't believe it. The quiet dead-end street that I had lived on now was plowed through right to Fairchild and there were suddenly a dozen tilt-ups where there had been one before. And now the highways were just wall-to-wall cars and people.
>
> The housing thing was a shock, too. I came from a fabulous 3,800-square-foot home in Paradise Valley, Arizona, sitting on two acres with a pool. And when I moved back out to Silicon Valley in 1978 I made the mistake of describing the general characteristics of my Arizona house to my real estate agent— only to find out that to duplicate that house here would cost me half a million dollars. Today that house would be well over a million dollars. And that was when interest rates were 8 percent, so you can imagine what it was like to people who came a few years after.

The result was the steady flow of workers out of the Valley. The bigger Valley firms moved their manufacturing operations out the Valley, placing them in little Silicon Valleys and Silicon Gulches around the world. This exodus was led, of all companies, by Hewlett-Packard, the firm that had started it all. By 1977, its president, John Young, had realized that Silicon Valley could no longer support expansion in manufacturing. He predicted that the Valley would by the end of the century become a "white-collar ghetto" composed of the executive offices and research laboratories of established firms (as well as a few prototype manufacturing lines) and then a panoply of start-up firms. The middle, the industrial side, of Silicon Valley would disappear, moved to Phoenix or Portland or Boise.

By the eighties, the most successful Silicon Valley companies had reached the status of true multinational corporations, with manufacturing and sales operations scattered throughout the world. They quickly encountered problems they had never dreamed of, like export licensing laws, terrorism, bribery, cultural and language barriers, dictatorial regimes, revolutions and war. They also ran into local mores so odd that they simply had no idea of how to deal with them, like Malaysian witch doctors dancing in the aisles between printed-circuit-board assembly lines to ward off evil spirits.

It wasn't that different at home. The sustained industry boom from 1977 to 1981 placed enormous employment pressures on Silicon Valley firms to keep their lines running at top speed. The result was a sudden influx into the local labor market of people who had never before been targeted by the industry: Boat People, social undesirables, ex-cons. In the words of Roy Brandt, "All you had to do to get a job was to be able to breathe on a mirror and leave an image."

The result, he says, "was an influx of thousands of people who couldn't speak English." And they quickly became the core labor of a number of companies, bringing their unassimilated social structures with them. For example, National Semiconductor had to deal with late-night Filipino gang wars in the back of one of its Valley plants between contingents of San Francisco and San Jose gangs.

The companies also found themselves employing junkies and thieves and people so antisocial that they wrecked whatever harmony there might have been on the polyglot assembly floor.

A greater threat to the Valley companies was unionization. During the seventies, this had not been much of a threat, first because of the general ineptitude of the local union organizers and then because the sustained boom kept workers not only happy but so mobile that a quorum could never be reached for a union vote.

But booms don't last. Recessions are also fairly safe times for companies fearing the threat of unions, because employees, worried about job security and a shortage of alternatives, are rarely interested in making waves. It's during the periods of transition, going in and out of a downturn, that there is the greatest threat. Then, employees either facing layoffs or frustrated that they aren't sharing in the company's success grow bitter, then alienated, then confrontational.

This might have occurred in 1974–75, when the semiconductor was slashing employment with cruel disregard for the lives of its workers. What little union leadership there was in the Valley had scant understanding of the natural Sun Belt resistance to unions and even less about high technology. Luckily, the semiconductor industry, as it watched laid-off employees leave the industry forever, learned its lesson about being so cavalier about its labor pool. By the time the next recession was rolling around in 1980, Jerry Sanders was swearing that AMD would never fire another soul, and all the semiconductor houses took extended holidays, reduced work weeks and held temporary shutdowns rather than lose the employees it now realized were very important people. Most showed the same prudence during the 1985 downturn. Monolithic Memories, for example, shut down the entire company for more than a week. (The one surprise was Intel, which, apparently secure in its reputation, fired nine hundred people.)

Unfortunately, the systems houses did not learn by example but had to be taught their own painful lesson.

As the 1982 recessionary layoffs began there was still resistance among Valley workers to the idea of unions. In this they were correct: unions would mean the death of Silicon Valley, because for an entrepreneurial environment to work it must be a meritocracy, an anathema to seniority-oriented unions. Such an environment needs a mobile workforce that can quickly jump from a waning to a waxing industry and is willing to sacrifice short-term time and salary in the hope of enormous long-term gain. Unions, by their nature, demand workforce stability and established wages and hours.

That's only one side of the scale. On the other is how the workforce is treated. If it is protected and talked with and feels part of the organization, as it does, say, at Intel, HP or Rolm, then no problem. But if the workforce is mistreated, distrusted and, worst of all, feels forgotten by management, then the future of Silicon Valley be damned, those people need the protection of a union.

In 1983, Atari with its layoffs and lack of employee communication achieved new lows in alienation and found itself facing the first major Silicon Valley union vote. If ever there were high-tech workers deserving of a union, it was the Atari employees. Still, they turned it down. Apparently it was not yet time.

But one day it may be, and union experts can already predict the scenario. First, the combination of an economic downturn (to create a stable workforce) and a local company treating its people badly will result in a shocking union victory. The union will then negotiate with the company not for increased benefits or an improved work environment, but for the most visible of all commodities: higher hourly wages. In exchange for equality or even reductions in every other benefit, the union will land the highest hourly wage in the Valley. And it will use that wage as a selling point to all the other workers in the Valley—and company after company will fall to unionization. At that point, Silicon Valley will die.

Still, that day may never occur. If the semiconductor industry is any indication, perhaps the systems industry will have learned from the Atari disaster and treat its employees with the respect they deserve. Most firms already operate in that manner.

As the decade progressed, there was a feeling among some that Silicon Valley had bypassed its Baroque era and evolved directly into the decadence of its Rococo period, at least on the Valley's industrial side. Culturally the place was still in the 1950s, still suburbia, with few artistic institutions and even those underused and undersupported.

It was in the business sector where growing evidence seemed to indicate that perhaps the entrepreneurial incubator was now turning into an unsupervised daycare center. As the papers carried stories of the latest capers by Soviet spies and chip thieves and IBM stings to nail crooked Japanese businessmen, it was hard not to see omens of a pending decline. It seemed that perhaps the rules of the Silicon Valley game had now become sufficiently standardized that they could be subverted by con men, media stars, snake oil salesmen and even children. Valley veterans remembered the prediction made years before by some high-tech Cassandra that when the electronic era was over, when the profits and losses from the thousands of companies, large and small, were added up, the bottom line would be written in *red*.

Around the time Atari began its layoffs, an eighteen-year-old student at Fremont High School in Sunnyvale was facing a possible jail sentence for what school officials claimed was an act of vindictive vandalism on the school's computer system. The young man, Robert Nelson, Jr., a computer prodigy, claimed it was an accident that had led to the erasure of part of the school's records.

Young Nelson was a true child of Silicon Valley. His father was a computer engineer at nearby National Semiconductor. Divorced, Robert Sr. lived in a modest home on the poorer side of Bayshore in Sunnyvale with his two sons and five computers. The youngest son, Robert Jr., though measured a genius, was never a good student. Only science interested him, and when personal computers came around about the time he was in junior high school, the boy knew what he wanted to do for the rest of his life.

In high school, Robert Jr. found himself in the midst of others who shared his point of view, and they spent most of their free time in the school's computer lab. The rest of the time, young Robert was like a fish out of water—shy, withdrawn, barely communicating, and increasingly convinced that others didn't give him the respect he felt his talents deserved.

By the time he was a senior, Robert Jr.'s talents were considerable. He was even hired by a Utah company that made electronic equipment for the blind. But at school, Robert's relationships with authorities deteriorated.

The problems began in December 1982 when Robert found out how to crack the security system on Fremont High's computer files, a challenge he took up, he said, because parents were secretive on the subject. His timing couldn't have been worse, because about that time obscene messages began turning up on the computer. Young Robert admitted later that though he didn't do it he knew who did.

When Robert told his father what was going on at school, the elder Nelson, fearing administrative reprisals against his son, suggested that the youth not inform his teachers directly but leave clues in the computer files hinting that the code could be broken. The reason for this odd suggestion by Robert Sr. is not clear, and in late December Robert Jr. was caught.

"Their reaction was completely different than I expected," said Robert Jr. "They started accusing me of things but wouldn't tell me what. They started treating me like a misfit, a juvenile." He was given the worst punishment possible for a boy of his type: he was barred from the computer room for six weeks. "I got depressed and didn't feel like going to classes. Someone in the school turned them all against me. I was only trying to help."

When he finally returned to the computer lab, Robert Jr. found himself under close surveillance. On the second day he was caught breaking a rule and was expelled from the class, but still allowed to use the lab.

Two days later, Robert was back in the lab, again illegally working on the school's secret computer program. He claims that he had discovered a faulty section of the program and was in the midst of replacing it with one he had written himself when the accident occurred. Whatever the reason, half the program flew off into electronic oblivion and young Robert found himself charged with vandalism and facing a fine and maximum sentence of six months in jail.

For the senior Nelson, this represented a clear-cut case of incompetent instructors trying to hamper the development of a young man more talented than they. "As far as I'm concerned, computer literacy is on trial here," he said. ". . . Teachers have always had to face students who are more proficient than they are, but this may be the first time in history that they've had students who know an order of magnitude more *than they ever will. It's got them intimidated."

The complaint to police, filed by Fremont High, claimed that young Nelson, a brilliant but arrogant teenager, had vandalized the computer out of revenge for his suspension. They added that he was a lonely youth without friends who struck back at his peers and his teachers by misusing his talents. The school also noted that outside of computers, Nelson had become a straight-F student, only earning a D the previous semester in mythology becaue he had devised a "minotaur in the labrynth" video game for the final project.

In July 1983, after Robert missed his high school graduation, a judge dismissed the case. In the end, the lack of a high school diploma did not seem to faze Robert Jr. He already knew Silicon Valley was less interested in degrees than in technical acumen. Even before his school mates had put on their caps and gowns, Robert Jr. had started his own business doing custom programming for a major computer chip company.

It was stories like this, and the growing consensus that Silicon Valley had lost some of its innocence and perhaps some of its vitality, that became the subject of speeches and articles by Valley folk and outsiders during the 1980s. Some noted the Atari union vote as a sign of bad things to come, others the exodus of talent from the Valley. Conservationists pointed at the toxic waste problem, feminists noted that in this male-only bastion, only 110 of the Valley's more than 3,000 companies had women in positions of vice-president or higher. Moralists were shocked at the Valley's degradations, while artists dismissed the place as the dullest, least enlightened and most boring spot on the planet. *Inc.* magazine ran an insightful if one-sided piece in September 1982 entitled

"Storm Clouds over Silicon Valley," which included mention of the growing crime rate, the skyrocketing cost of living and the deteriorating environment, and added: "It is difficult to say just when the unquestioning optimism and enthusiasm ended, when people began to suspect that the growth had been too fast, that technological wonders and millionaires in shirt-sleeves weren't going to solve the Valley's problems, and, in fact, created some of them . . ."

Others weren't so jaundiced. When the economy boomed again in 1983 and more new companies than ever popped up like crocuses hidden beneath the snow awaiting the first hint of economic warmth, it was hard to play Cassandra and predict the imminent fall of Silicon Valley. Sure, Atari was fallen and Trilogy was in trouble and Osborne was just a ghost, but among the new companies springing up, how many new comets were there to fly across the sky in a flaming path?

Regis McKenna, public relations man turned visionary, saw the ebb and flow of companies as part of an ongoing upward growth by the Valley, not a sign of its decline. Silicon Valley, he said, "will go through its period of creative destruction, and we have seen some of this already with the passing from preeminence of firms like Philco, Raytheon and Fairchild." Nevertheless, he said, "the return on investment and the venture network will continue to stimulate new happenings in Silicon Valley for some time . . . companies will expand from Silicon Valley to other areas, primarily in the Sun Belt, and, as they expand, pieces of the culture and the network go with them."

Silicon Valley, McKenna added, will remain a viable economic entity because it still "is an archetypical phenomenon, its culture is infectious, and we are educating the rest of the world on how to survive the twenty-first century."

At about the time McKenna was saying this, a Silicon Valley entrepreneur was arrested for hiring contract killers to murder his estranged wife. The police claimed the executive did this because he feared his wife would get his stock.

At the geographical center of Silicon Valley, in a no-man's land between Sunnyvale and Cupertino, two large freeways (280 and 85) meet in a confusing jumble of ramps and overpasses. This intersection is less than a mile in one direction from Apple Computer, in another from De Anza Junior College, in another from Fremont High and the once-graffitied wall on Fremont Avenue and in another from the house Bob Noyce lived in when he first came to Silicon Valley.

It may be the most desolate spot in the Valley. The only activity is the thousands of passing cars daily, the only apparent life the endless artificial-looking acres of deep green iceplant. Yet, beginning in mid-1982 and intermittently ever since, a golden eagle could be seen perched on one of the light poles atop one of the overpasses. He wasn't a great-looking eagle—in fact, was a little the worse for wear—but he was big and heroic nevertheless. And he seemed to symbolize two things, one actual and the other metaphorical.

In one sense, the arrival of this eagle was proof that the Valley was growing older, maturing. What had been the Valley of Heart's Delight had been bulldozed and paved out of existence for decades; now time and nature, like sprouts through cracks in sidewalks, were beginning to reassert themselves. Late at night raccoons could be seen coming out of drains in Sunnyvale and opossums lumbered past modern Monte Vista High School in Cupertino. In the once stark housing developments, the tall trees grown up over the years now sported squirrels and the once-silent mornings were filled with the sounds of songbirds. Now the eagle had returned after a forty-year absence.

The works of humanity also were beginning to show the effects of time. Brilliantly bright residential streets were now tree-lined, modernistic stores looked dated, once new concrete tilt-ups turned a dark gray and were adorned with ivy. Mayfield Mall, one of the Valley's first shopping malls, went out of business, and, to close a circle, was sold to Hewlett-Packard as a sales office.

Of course the Valley was still growing, expanding outward around the base of the bay and south into the farmlands of Gilroy and Morgan Hill. In the center of the Valley, where new space was almost gone, companies did the next best thing: they began to build vertically. Towns like Sunnyvale and Cupertino, which never had a building taller than a four-story firemen's practice tower, found themselves on the brink of becoming true metropolitan centers like San Jose and San Francisco. Both figuratively and literally, Silicon Valley was growing up. It even made plans to build a $40-million museum to celebrate itself.

The golden eagle symbolized something else as well. In his aggressive, solitary existence, he captured the spirit of the Valley's entrepreneurs, and of the society they had created. All of them, Hewlett and Packard, the Varian brothers, Shockley, Noyce, Bushnell, Wozniak and Jobs, had been lonely hunters perched over a blasted landscape looking to make their way. The Valley they and hundreds of other less well known entrepreneurs like them had built was a manifestation of their world view: stark, driven, obsessive, brilliant and intensely alive. It was a wonder to behold, a treasure to be cherished, a machine that made some men wealthy and created, out of nothing, productive careers for millions of the rest.

But in the end, and behind all of the stories and anecdotes and glitter, it was still the lonely, empty and sometimes violent world of the golden eagle on the overpass.

When I was a teenager, I used to drive from my home in Sunnyvale to Cupertino up Stevens Creek Road and then up a side road that led to the old oriental tower of the Maryknoll Missionaries Seminary and retirement home. There was a hill on that road, topped by a water tower where I used to park my dune buggy late at night. It was the perfect place to neck with a date or drink and listen to music with my buddies, because that hill was the first of a series of increasingly tall hills that rose up from the flat alluvial plain of the valley floor into the Santa Cruz Mountains. For that reason it had a magnificent sweeping view, stretching from Gilroy at the extreme south end of the Valley, up Bayshore Freeway through the middle cities of Santa Clara, Sunnyvale and Mountain View. The cars on Freeway 280 roared by right below us.

If we got out and stood in the right spot, we could look north to the Hoover Tower at Stanford University near Palo Alto, then north to the cities of the peninsula and, on the right night, in the right weather, and with a little bit of imagination, we could see the lights of San Francisco and the Bay Bridge.

Far off to the east, we could see the lights of the East Bay: Oakland, Hayward, Milpitas—and in between, the immense, bottomless black gulf of the San Francisco Bay, a yawning empty space in the midst of a galaxy of streetlights.

When I first began parking on that hill in the late sixties, the bay wasn't the only pitch-dark region before me. Throughout Santa Clara Valley, between and around the islands of city lights, there were numerous black lakes and ponds—which by day became farms and orchards and vacant fields.

As the years passed these ink pools began to dry up and disappear, their receding banks crowded with new dots of lights. Each month we could chart the change; an orchard in Sunnyvale gone, replaced by the lights of a parking lot; a field in Cupertino disappeared, replaced by the regularly arrayed streetlights of a housing development; a farm in Santa Clara vanished under the brilliant lights of an office building.

Every month and every year the Valley grew brighter, the dark areas fewer and smaller. Where once the darkness had predominated, seeming to threaten the fragile little pockets of light, now the reverse was true, the few pockets of cool black left were rapidly being burned away by the inexorable advance of the millions of hot little pinpricks.

Toward the end, all the black pools were gone, and the Valley had become a brilliant galaxy of lights.

And then the lights began to creep up the mountainsides . . .

One night, after years of being away, I drove out to the hill and found its sides scraped away and festooned with stakes and streamers. Within days foundations were laid and a couple of months later the hill was covered with half-million-dollar custom homes.

Now this view of the Valley, with its brilliant new seemingly endless plain of light, would be the private property of a select group of Silicon Valley tycoons who had made it—the Big Score.

INDEX

Crime (criminal underground), 237–47,
  398–99, 409
  See also Stealing
Crockett, Dave, 46
Crosby, Bing, 64
Cunningham, James, 248
Cvietusa, Don, 290–91, 364

Dalmo Victor Co., 62
Dataquest Corp., 219, 323
Decathlon Club, 331
Defense Department, U.S., 156, 163
De Forest, Lee, 14–15, 19, 192, 324
Descartes, René, 258
Difference Engine, 194
Digital logic chips (circuits), 132–33, 199,
  209, 214
Diodes, 192
Discrete devices, 209
Disks, for information storage, 215
Disney, Walt, Studios, 32, 357
Divorce, 395–96
Dobkin, Robert, 131, 133, 134
Dolby, Ray, 65
Dolby Noise Reduction Circuit, 65
Douglas Aircraft Co., 171–72
Drinking, 97, 99
Drori, Zeev, 156–57
Drugs, 5–6, 398, 399, 404–10
Dummer, G. W. A., 205
Dvorak, John, 304
Dyno Electronics, 241

Eagle Computer, 321
Earthquakes, 13
Eccles, W. H., 193
Edison, Thomas, 12, 15, 192
E.D.V. Elektronik, 241, 242
8008 microprocessor, 142, 144, 146
Eldred, Ken, 295–96
Electromechanical relays, 195–96
Electromechanical systems, 258
Electronic Arrays, 162
Electronics industry, 214–18
  entrepreneurs in. *See* Entrepreneurs
  jargon of, 190
  understanding of, 189–91
  See also Semiconductor industry

Electronics revolution, 191
  life cycle of, 16–18
Elwell, Cy, 13–15
Emert, Win, 400, 403
Employees
  shortage of (late 1970s), 262
  See also under individual companies
ENIAC computer, 196, 198
Entrepreneurs, 261–62, 274–80, 288–89,
  291, 324–25
  wealth of, 322–25
  See also Venture capital industry
EPROMs, 241–43, 346
Esparza, Marijane, 406
Espionage, industrial, 3–4
  See also Intelligence agents, foreign;
  Trade secrets, theft of
Esquire (magazine), 73
Evans, Robert, 313–14
Exxon Corp., 307

Faggin, Federico, 142, 143
Fairburn, Hamilton, 411
Fairchild, Sherman, 87–88
Fairchild Camera and Instrument Corp.,
  70, 85, 89, 93, 110, 115, 116, 155
  early history of, 87–88
Fairchild Semiconductor, 73, 85–113,
  182, 411–12
  buy-out at (1960), 93
  competitive pressure and, 99–100
  Corrigan as president of, 126, 154–56
  Cox, Marshall at, 94–97
  decline and fall of, 104–13, 153–56
  departure of employees from, 93–94,
    102–3, 105–13, 125
  eccentricities of employees of, 98–99
  Hogan as president of, 110–12, 124–27,
    153–54, 179–81
  Hogan as vice-chairman of, 126, 154
  IBM and, 90
  integrated circuits and, 91–93
  manufacturing problems at, 104–5
  marketing department at, 100, 103–4
  as mythical company, 85–86
  Noyce at, 80–82, 100–2, 104, 106–8,
    124, 172, 174
  Noyce's resignation from, 110, 138–39